DIPLOMACY SHOT DOWN

DIPLOMACY SHOT DOWN

The U-2 Crisis and Eisenhower's Aborted Mission to Moscow, 1959–1960

E. BRUCE GEELHOED

University of Oklahoma Press : Norman

This book is published through the generosity of Edith Kinney Gaylord.

Library of Congress Cataloging-in-Publication Data

Names: Geelhoed, E. Bruce, 1948– author.
Title: Diplomacy Shot Down : The U-2 Crisis and Eisenhower's Aborted Mission to Moscow, 1959–1960 / E. Bruce Geelhoed.
Other titles: U-2 crisis and Eisenhower's aborted mission to Moscow, 1959–1960
Description: Norman : University of Oklahoma Press, [2020] | Includes bibliographical references and index. | Summary: "Explores how Dwight D. Eisenhower's long-anticipated visit with Nikita S. Khrushchev in 1960 became a casualty of the U-2 crisis and how his failure to visit the Soviet Union had a negative impact on Soviet-American relations during the Cold War."—Provided by publisher.
Identifiers: LCCN 2019045360 | ISBN 978-0-8061-6485-4 (hardcover)
ISBN 978-0-8061-8642-9 (paper)
Subjects: LCSH: Eisenhower, Dwight D. (Dwight David), 1890–1969. | Khrushchev, Nikita Sergeevich, 1894–1971. | United States—Foreign relations—1953–1961. | Cold war—Diplomatic history. | United States—Foreign relations—Soviet Union. | Soviet Union—Foreign relations—United States. | National security—United States—History—20th century. | Aerial reconnaissance, American—History—20th century. | U-2 (Reconnaissance aircraft) | Nuclear weapons—Government policy—United States—History—20th century.
Classification: LCC E835 .G395 2020 | DDC 327.7304709/045—dc23
LC record available at https://lccn.loc.gov/2019045360

The paper in this book meets the guidelines for permanence and durability of the Committee on Production Guidelines for Book Longevity of the Council on Library Resources, Inc. ∞

Copyright © 2020 by the University of Oklahoma Press, Norman, Publishing Division of the University. Paperback published 2022. Manufactured in the U.S.A.

All rights reserved. No part of this publication may be reproduced, stored in a retrieval system, or transmitted, in any form or by any means, electronic, mechanical, photocopying, recording, or otherwise—except as permitted under Section 107 or 108 of the United States Copyright Act—without the prior written permission of the University of Oklahoma Press. To request permission to reproduce selections from this book, write to Permissions, University of Oklahoma Press, 2800 Venture Drive, Norman OK 73069, or email rights.oupress@ou.edu.

*To Deborah Geelhoed,
my wife and partner*

Contents

Preface / ix

Introduction: Far Eastern Trip (Withdrawn) / 1
1. The Man of the Hour, August 11–15, 1945 / 11
2. The Two Invitations, July–August 1959 / 26
3. Eisenhower's Peace Offensive, September–December 1959 / 48
4. Preparations, January–May 1960 / 68
5. The Missile Gap and the FY 1961 Defense Budget, January–May 1960 / 109
6. The Crash, the Crisis, and the Collapse, May 1–24, 1960 / 143
7. Eisenhower in the Soviet Union: Moscow, Leningrad, and Kiev, June 10–14, 1960 / 181
8. Eisenhower in the Soviet Union: Moscow and Irkutsk, June 15–19, 1960 / 218

Conclusion: "The Stupid U-2 Mess" / 242

Notes / 261
Bibliography / 301
Index / 309

Preface

This book covers the ten-month period from July 1959 to May 1960 when President Dwight D. Eisenhower aggressively sought to "thaw" the tensions of the Cold War before he left office in January 1961. The story begins with Eisenhower's surprising announcement in early August 1959 that he and Nikita S. Khrushchev, the premier of the Soviet Union, had agreed to exchange visits to each other's countries as a first step in reducing some of the ill will that then existed between the United States and the Soviet Union. The story ends with the U-2 crisis of May 1960, when the Soviet Union shot down an American reconnaissance aircraft piloted by Francis Gary Powers. The chain of events that followed the capture of Powers by the Soviets led to the collapse of the long-anticipated Four Power summit conference in Paris in May and Khrushchev's withdrawal of his invitation to Eisenhower to visit the Soviet Union in June.

I argue that the great tragedy of the U-2 crisis, and the prolonging of the Cold War that resulted, was *not* the collapse of the Paris summit but, instead, the withdrawal of Ike's invitation to visit the Soviet Union. The major item for discussion at the summit by the four national leaders—Eisenhower, Khrushchev, British prime minister Harold Macmillan, and French president Charles de Gaulle—was a prospective agreement to limit the testing of nuclear weapons. Historians disagree as to whether the Four Power summit would have resulted in the agreement to limit nuclear tests. However, as an icebreaker in the tensions of the Cold War, Eisenhower's upcoming visit to the Soviet Union in June 1960 had tremendous potential not only for an improvement in

Preface

American-Soviet relations but also as a positive example of diplomacy for Eisenhower's successor. After visiting the United States in September 1959, Khrushchev was excited to welcome Eisenhower to the Soviet Union and had made extensive preparations throughout his country for Ike's arrival. In addition, Eisenhower was personally popular in the Soviet Union, and he knew that, after the overwhelmingly positive reception he had received from the Russian people when he visited the Soviet Union in August 1945, a reservoir of goodwill would await him when he made his second trip to the country. Unfortunately, Ike never made that second visit and he lost the opportunity to capitalize on that unique opportunity of extending a hand of friendship to the Soviet people.

This book deals primarily with three American leaders: President Dwight D. Eisenhower; Thomas S. Gates, his third secretary of defense; and James C. Hagerty, his press secretary. With eighteen months left in his presidency, Eisenhower was searching for a legacy, one that involved the removal of the deadly animosity that had prevailed between the United States and the Soviet Union since 1946. To accomplish this goal, Ike wanted to achieve a breakthrough in the Cold War and he was willing to engage the Soviet leadership, personally, in that effort.

At the same time Eisenhower was pursuing his legacy, Thomas Gates was looking for a graceful way to exit Washington. After six years at the Navy Department, Gates wanted to return to private life and resume his business career in Philadelphia. He fully intended to resign his position as secretary of the navy in the spring of 1959 and then rejoin his partners at the investment banking firm of Drexel and Company. However, a totally unexpected set of circumstances intervened in the spring of 1959 and led to Gates's appointment as deputy secretary of defense in June and then secretary of defense in December. By the time Gates left Washington in January 1961, he had compiled the second-longest tenure, behind only James H. Douglas, secretary of the air force and deputy secretary of defense, of any of Eisenhower's senior leaders at the Pentagon.

Thomas Gates's elevation to the upper echelons of the Pentagon's leadership occurred shortly after the death of Secretary of State John Foster Dulles in May 1959. The death of Foster Dulles led to a change in the composition of the men who advised Eisenhower on national security policy. While Dulles had jealously protected his role as Eisenhower's primary adviser in this area, his death left a vacuum that was quickly filled by several men in the State Department, in the Pentagon, and on the White House staff. These individuals included Christian A. Herter, Dulles's successor as secretary of state; C. Douglas Dillon, the under secretary of state; and Robert D. Murphy, the under secretary of state for political affairs. Gates and James Douglas, the deputy secretary of defense, soon joined Herter, Dillon, and Murphy in this realm, making the formulation of national security policy a much broader enterprise than it had been in the previous six years of the administration. On the White House staff, Eisenhower came to place an increasing reliance on Gordon Gray, the national security adviser; Andrew J. Goodpaster, his trusted staff secretary; and James C. Hagerty. All of the individuals just mentioned were intimately involved not only in providing critical advice to Eisenhower but also in direct, almost daily, interactions with each other.

Thomas Gates was not a member of Eisenhower's inner circle, at least in personal terms. But he was a trusted adviser to Ike on defense policy, and it became his responsibility to shepherd the administration's fiscal-year 1961 (FY 1961) defense budget through a Congress controlled by the political opposition during the politically charged environment of a presidential election year. Passage of the administration's defense budget, Eisenhower and Gates hoped, would also take the steam out of the noisy, nagging political issue of the "missile gap" that had plagued the administration since 1958. Gates succeeded in this objective, but not without some false starts and mistakes along the way. Although a relative latecomer to decision-making on national security, Gates still managed to establish an effective rapport with Eisenhower and was included in the group that accompanied Eisenhower to the Paris summit.

For James Hagerty, the U-2 crisis and the missile gap controversy were only the latest in a number of highly charged political situations that he had dealt with since becoming Eisenhower's press secretary in 1953. A lifelong journalist and newspaperman, Hagerty entered the service of Dwight D. Eisenhower during the presidential campaign of 1952 when he signed on to handle Ike's relations with the press. Once elected, Eisenhower named Hagerty to the position of press secretary and gave him wide discretion in discharging the responsibilities of that office.

Between 1953 and 1960, Hagerty essentially performed two major responsibilities for Eisenhower: managing the press operation and serving as a shrewd behind-the-scenes political adviser and tactician. As a consequence of handling those two duties, Hagerty saw his own power and influence grow with the councils of the administration.[1]

In handling the White House press operation, Hagerty provided the definition for the modern office of the press secretary. As the administration's chief spokesperson, Hagerty organized the White House press office smoothly and efficiently. As a former newspaper reporter, he understood the need for press access to the president and he ensured that reporters received prompt statements and presidential speeches to use for their stories. He also began the practice of scheduling regular news conferences with the president, unless Eisenhower was out of Washington. For the first time, Hagerty allowed the members of the White House press corps to quote Eisenhower directly without obtaining prior permission. Most important, in 1955, Hagerty permitted the president's news conferences to be carried via newsreel and television.

Throughout Ike's presidency, Hagerty was a shrewd political adviser, and occasionally a canny tactician for the president. For example, Hagerty became the administration's voice when Eisenhower encountered serious health setbacks, first in 1955 with a heart attack, then in 1956 with his lengthy hospitalization following surgery for ileitis, and then a slight stroke in 1957. Hagerty also became Eisenhower's informal liaison to the Senate during the administration's conflicts with Senator Joseph McCarthy in 1953 and 1954.

During the last two years of Eisenhower's presidency, Hagerty became a vocal advocate within the administration for an aggressive effort by Eisenhower to erase the unfortunate popular perception that, due either to ill health, age, or simply boredom, he had become physically and emotionally disengaged from the rigors of the presidency. As historian William I. Hitchcock has noted, after the Republican Party's disastrous showing in 1958's off-year congressional elections, Hagerty proposed that Ike regain political momentum through a vigorous series of travels to Europe, Asia, and Latin America as an American goodwill ambassador for peace, and thereby counteract the charges from his critics in Congress and the press that he had become a golf-playing, do-nothing president. Hagerty included a possible visit to the Soviet Union in this proposal.

Eisenhower and his key advisers were sensitive to the charges by the political opposition that he was physically and emotionally detached from the presidency, especially since these accusations were largely

Preface

untrue. As Thomas Gates recalled, "By late 1959, [Eisenhower] had sufficiently recovered from his illnesses . . . to keep a very active pace. I never saw him slacken his pace; Eisenhower thrived on work. He liked the presidency and felt comfortable in it."[2]

Once Eisenhower announced the exchange of visits with Nikita Khrushchev on August 3, 1959, he eventually gave Hagerty the twin responsibilities of organizing the arrangements for press coverage of his visit and, more important, nailing down the particulars of his itinerary and the places he was to visit within the Soviet Union. For the second responsibility, Hagerty worked closely with Hans N. Tuch, the American embassy's press and cultural attaché, during Hagerty's advance visit to the Soviet Union on April 6–10, 1960, in preparation for Eisenhower's scheduled visit in June.

By early May 1960, both Thomas Gates and James Hagerty had done their jobs, at least as far as Eisenhower's impending visit to the Soviet Union was concerned. Partially due to Gates's strenuous efforts, a Democratic-controlled Congress was about to pass the administration's defense budget with only minor adjustments, and thereby deal a serious blow to those politicians who were attempting to exploit the issue of the missile gap. For his part, Hagerty had visited the Soviet Union and laid the groundwork for Ike's visit. The momentum appeared to be clearly on the administration's side as it awaited Eisenhower's historic trip to Russia.

The structure of this book differs from a traditional work of history. The introduction and the first six chapters essentially deal with the unfolding, and eventual failure, of Eisenhower's carefully prepared strategy to thaw the Cold War. The last two chapters include the texts of the remarks and speeches Eisenhower would have given had he made his visit to the Soviet Union in June 1960. I also provide some editorial commentary about those various speeches. These materials present the reader with a glimpse of what Eisenhower would have spoken to the Soviet leadership and to the Russian people as a guest in their country. These speeches have not been published until now. I then include a conclusion that attempts to provide a perspective on these extraordinary events in 1959 and 1960.

Every historian owes numerous debts of gratitude to the various people who have provided the assistance necessary to complete a book. First, I began this project in 1981, more than three decades ago, when I served as

Preface

the research assistant to Thomas S. Gates, working under the supervision of the Faculty of Arts and Sciences at the University of Pennsylvania. I wish to acknowledge the support of the Dean's Office of the Faculty of Arts and Sciences, as well as the assistance of the archivists at the Van Pelt Library of the University of Pennsylvania. In particular, these archivists were able to help me work with the Thomas S. Gates Papers that are part of its collections. I also wish to thank the INA Foundation and the Smithkline Beckman Foundation for their funding support through the University of Pennsylvania for the early stages of this project.

Second, I wish to acknowledge my gratitude to the staff of the Dwight D. Eisenhower Library for their assistance over the years. I especially wish to thank Kevin Bailey, archivist, and Mary Burtzloff, director of audiovisual archives, for their patience and cooperation. I am also grateful to several other photo-archivists who have helped me identify illustrations for this book. These individuals include Maryrose Grossman at the John F. Kennedy Presidential Library and Museum, Ryan Pettigrew at the Richard Nixon Presidential Library, and Elizabeth Druga at the Gerald R. Ford Presidential Library.

Third, I wish to thank several of my colleagues in the Department of History and in the Honors College at Ball State University for their assistance and support. At various times, I received research assignments that enabled me to continue my work on Dwight D. Eisenhower and Thomas S. Gates. C. Warren Vander Hill, provost and professor of history emeritus, has been my mentor for close to five decades and I will never be able to repay Warren for his wise counsel. Elaine Nelson and Lisa Johnson of Ball State's Department of Interlibrary Loan tirelessly worked to find for me the important materials that were available from that source. A particular thanks to Elaine and Lisa. Also, Ally Witte expertly prepared the book's index.

Fourth, this is the second book project that I have done with the University of Oklahoma Press. I wish to thank Adam Kane, editor-in-chief, Steven Baker, managing editor, Charles Rankin, former editor-in-chief, and especially Tim Bryant, an expert copyeditor. Their assistance and helpfulness have been especially valuable.

Finally, I am especially grateful to my family, including Deborah Geelhoed, my loving wife of forty-eight years, to whom this book is

Preface

dedicated, and our two sons, Marc and Steven. For them, my work on this project has meant many different moves, from living in Philadelphia, Washington, D.C., and even Oxford, U.K., as well as numerous trips to the Eisenhower Library in Abilene, Kansas. My family has endured all of these disruptions with patience and good humor.

Any errors of fact or interpretation are mine.

Muncie, Indiana
January 2019

Introduction
Far Eastern Trip (Withdrawn)

President Dwight D. Eisenhower expected to visit the Soviet Union between June 10 and 19, 1960. He had visited the Soviet Union once before, in August 1945, shortly before the end of World War II, at the personal invitation of Joseph Stalin.[1] Now, in 1960, Eisenhower planned to make another trip to the Soviet Union, this time as the invited guest of Soviet Premier Nikita S. Khrushchev, the victor in the power struggle in the Kremlin to succeed Stalin after his death in March 1953.

On August 3, 1959, Eisenhower announced at a news conference that he and Khrushchev had scheduled an exchange of visits to each other's countries at a date and time to be announced later. It was a package arrangement. Khrushchev visited the United States between September 15 and 27, 1959, as Eisenhower's guest. Eisenhower's visit to the Soviet Union was to occur sometime later, as Khrushchev's guest, with the two leaders eventually agreeing that Ike's trip to the Soviet Union was to occur in mid-June 1960.

These two visits, the first by Khrushchev to the United States and the second by Eisenhower to the Soviet Union, represented an attempt by both leaders to remove some of the tension that existed in the relations between the two countries.[2] Both visits essentially began as goodwill gestures by the two leaders, the chance to give both Eisenhower and Khrushchev an opportunity to meet people in each other's countries and, more important, to learn about the culture and traditions of the other. To almost no one's surprise, the visits inevitably took on different characteristics and purposes, given the vast chasm of disagreement that existed at the time between the United States and the Soviet Union. The two sides were at loggerheads on the issues of divided Berlin, divided Germany, and the dangerous escalation of the nuclear arms race. When Khrushchev visited the United States, he and Eisenhower engaged in some extremely difficult negotiations over the future status of Allied access rights to West Berlin. However, Khrushchev and Eisenhower also agreed to participate in a Four Power summit conference in 1960, along with British prime minister Harold Macmillan and French president Charles de Gaulle, at a site to be determined later. The objectives of the conference would be to discuss the issue of Berlin and a possible agreement leading to a suspension of nuclear weapons tests. After the conference, Eisenhower was scheduled to visit the Soviet Union.[3] In both the United States and Europe, diplomatic observers were hopeful that the forthcoming summit meeting might produce some tangible progress toward a nuclear test ban and that Eisenhower and Khrushchev might discuss the matter further when Eisenhower visited the Soviet Union.[4]

For Eisenhower, this second trip to the Soviet Union promised to be the culmination of his presidency, perhaps even of his entire professional career. Since 1941, Eisenhower had been involved in matters of war and peace almost continuously and at the highest levels: first, as supreme Allied commander in World War II, then as the first commander of the military forces of the North Atlantic Treaty Organization (NATO) in the early 1950s, and finally as president of the United States since 1953. In terms of continuous service to the United States, Eisenhower had compiled a record not seen since the days of George Washington, who was, interestingly, Eisenhower's hero.[5] Eisenhower viewed this trip to the Soviet Union as a return to a country he had visited in 1945, and according to journalist Harrison Salisbury, the "crowning achievement" of his administration.[6]

Eisenhower's second visit to the Soviet Union had the potential to change the direction of the Cold War, for at least two reasons. First, Eisenhower himself, by the sheer magnetism of his personality, was a crowd pleaser par excellence. As historian William I. Hitchcock has written, the decade of the 1950s in the United States was certainly the Age of Eisenhower, but in other respects Ike was the world's first citizen, the man who had beat Adolf Hitler, settled the Korean War, and kept the peace during the dangerous early years of the Cold War.[7] After announcing on August 3 the upcoming exchange of visits with Khrushchev, Eisenhower traveled to Europe to consult with the three other Western leaders: Macmillan, de Gaulle, and Konrad Adenauer, the chancellor of the Federal Republic of Germany (West Germany). In each of the three capitals—London, Paris, and Bonn—more than a million people crowded the streets to glimpse the American president as he rode by in his motorcade. Then, later in 1959, prodded by his press secretary, James Hagerty, Eisenhower embarked on an eleven-nation goodwill tour throughout Europe, the Middle East, and Asia. The crowds that greeted him were massive: several hundred thousand people in Rome, 700,000 in Ankara, more than 1,000,000 in Karachi; more than 1,000,000 in Delhi; another 750,000 in Tehran, another 750,000 in Athens, 1,500,000 in Madrid, and finally, 500,000 in Casablanca.[8] No other American political leader up to that point in history had received more adulation from people in the United States and throughout the world than Dwight D. Eisenhower.

The Eisenhower persona had its unique brand of charisma. Thomas Gates, Eisenhower's third secretary of defense, was in the delegation that accompanied him to London, Paris, and Bonn. Gates was astonished at the reception that Eisenhower received. "No one could draw a crowd like Eisenhower," Gates observed.[9]

Moreover, Eisenhower inwardly understood and appreciated that his personal magnetism could strengthen his position as a goodwill ambassador when he visited the Soviet Union. Early in 1960, the political leadership of the Soviet Union, and Khrushchev in particular, began making elaborate preparations for Ike's visit to their country. Like Eisenhower, Khrushchev was attempting to pursue a relaxation of tensions, and he was prepared to give the president a lavish reception. As Monte Reel has written, Khrushchev was the first "partner for peace" the United States had encountered in the Cold War, a reformer who had denounced the Stalinist era, freed thousands of political prisoners, and was attempting to make Soviet society more open.[10] Many of the Soviet people, for their part, may also have remembered Eisenhower's visit to the Soviet Union in 1945 and were likewise looking forward to giving him the warmest of welcomes, especially considering that World War II was still a recent memory for much of the Soviet population. "People in the Soviet Union

Introduction

liked Eisenhower," Sergei Khrushchev, the son of Nikita Khrushchev and later a senior fellow at the Watson Institute for International and Public Affairs at Brown University, said. "Eisenhower was the Soviet hero . . . because he had decided not to take Berlin. He was a general *and* an honest politician" (emphasis added).[11] As a person well known to the Russian people, respected and even admired by them, and more immune to the effects of Soviet propaganda than any other U.S. politician, Eisenhower was the ideal American leader to seek a détente with the Soviet Union.

Eisenhower also saw great potential in a prospective visit to the Soviet Union. Consider the opinion of Milton S. Eisenhower, Ike's younger brother, who accompanied Vice President Richard M. Nixon on his visit to the Soviet Union in July 1959. "Dwight Eisenhower wanted very much to visit the Soviet Union," Milton Eisenhower recalled. "If I may say, that when I remember the kind of reception that I got, merely as a brother, I don't know what would have happened if he had traveled all over [the] country. I think it would have been a great moment."[12]

Second, members of the national and international press corps were prepared to descend upon Moscow and the Soviet Union and provide extensive, and sometimes live, coverage of Eisenhower's visit. More than four hundred reporters and commentators from the world's major newspapers and radio and television networks were assigned to cover the Eisenhower visit. Recognizing Ike's visit as potentially the most important event of the postwar era to that point, the assembled personnel from the world's news organizations were prepared to provide unprecedented coverage in case it led to a positive breakthrough in relations between the United States and the Soviet Union. If the crowds in the Soviet Union turned out in the numbers that greeted Eisenhower in the other capitals he had visited, the television cameras would be there to broadcast these receptions back to the United States and to Western Europe.

In recognition of the visit's importance, the news organizations assigned their key reporters and commentators to cover it. Many of the individuals who later achieved prominence in the American media and became instantly recognizable to American readers and viewers during the 1960s and 1970s were sent to cover Eisenhower's prospective visit. A partial listing of these individuals includes Marvin Arrowsmith and John Scali of the Associated Press, there to join their colleagues

Introduction

Preston Grover, Stanley Johnson, and A. I. Goldberg, who were already assigned to Moscow; Merriman Smith from United Press International, who joined Henry Shapiro; Harrison Salisbury and James Reston of the *New York Times,* who joined Max Frankel and Osgood Caruthers; Peter Lisagor of the *Chicago Tribune*; Robert Donovan and Marguerite Higgins of the *New York Herald Tribune*; Chalmers Roberts of the *Washington Post*; Charles Mohr from *Time*; Charles Roberts from *Newsweek*; John Daly from ABC News; Walter Cronkite, Robert Pierpoint, Daniel Schorr, and Don Hewitt from CBS News, who were to join Marvin Kalb; and David Brinkley, Ray Scherer, and John Chancellor from NBC News.

The international press was also well represented in terms of assigning key individuals to the visit. From Great Britain, the *Sunday Times* sent Henry Brandon, the *Telegraph* sent Ian Ball, and the British Broadcasting Corporation sent Douglas Stuart. In addition, the major newspapers in Australia, Denmark, France, West Germany, and Japan also sent reporters to cover the visit.[13] To summarize, the American and international media were prepared to cover the Eisenhower visit to Russia as an unprecedented event.

Third, Eisenhower was to be given the opportunity to speak directly to the Russian people through three televised broadcasts: first when he visited Leningrad, second when he visited Kiev in the Ukraine, and the third when he visited Moscow. Vice President Richard Nixon had spoken directly to the Russia people via a radio and television broadcast on his visit to the Soviet Union in July 1959. While it was impossible to gauge the impact of Nixon's speech on the people of the Soviet Union, it was nevertheless an opportunity for an American leader to open a crack, however small, in the tightly closed society of the Soviet Union as well as an opportunity to speak directly to the Soviet people about the goals of the United States in the present international environment.[14]

The audience for Eisenhower's broadcasts was certain to number in the millions, perhaps tens of millions, of viewers and listeners. The prospect of Eisenhower extending the hand of friendship to the Soviet people, while also not neglecting to mention the areas where the United States and the Soviet Union disagreed, was potentially great. With the exception of Franklin D. Roosevelt's visit to Yalta in Crimea for his wartime conference with Stalin and British prime minister Winston Churchill in

Introduction

February 1945, no American president had visited the Soviet Union and spoken directly to its people. Eisenhower was now going to be granted that opportunity. No wonder that feelings of optimism and expectation were widespread in the United States and the Soviet Union.

The record of history, unfortunately, shows that Dwight D. Eisenhower never visited the Soviet Union in June 1960, and that he and Nikita Khrushchev never successfully negotiated a nuclear test-ban agreement. Eisenhower's failure to visit the Soviet Union occurred as the result of a colossal failure of an American U-2 aerial surveillance mission, piloted by Francis Gary Powers, on May 1, 1960.

The U-2 program, directed by the CIA, had been in operation since the mid-50s, and overflights of the Soviet Union started in 1956. Eisenhower had asserted that the flights would be detected sooner or later. However, under extreme pressure from Allen Dulles, the director of the Central Intelligence Agency, and Richard Bissell, the deputy director of the CIA, Eisenhower agreed to one final U-2 flight between April 25 and May 1, even though the Four Power summit conference, scheduled to take place in Paris, was less than a month away. When Powers failed to reach his destination of Bodo, Norway, on May 1, the administration reacted with a cover story that he was flying a plane involved in weather research. Dulles and Bissell had assured Eisenhower and his closest national security advisers that, in the event of an accident to the U-2, no pilot would survive and the administration, attempting to explain the loss of the aircraft, operated on this basis.[15] The enormous falsity of the cover story became obvious on May 5 when Khrushchev revealed that the Soviets had parts of the destroyed aircraft and, even worse from the American perspective, on May 7 when Khrushchev announced that Powers had survived the crash and was in Soviet custody. Before long, the Soviets announced that they intended to put Powers on trial for espionage.

To clarify this confusing and embarrassing situation, Eisenhower held a press conference on May 11 in which he accepted responsibility for ordering the U-2 flights, justifying them on the basis of the extensive network of espionage that the Soviets operated in the United States and the closed nature of the Soviet society that made it difficult to ascertain the capabilities and intentions of the Soviet regime. "No one wants another Pearl Harbor," Eisenhower forcefully stated.[16] He also indicated, however,

Introduction

that he intended to travel to Paris, and he expressed the view that the U-2 incident should not affect the business of the summit conference.

When the leaders of the United States, the Soviet Union, Great Britain, and France convened in Paris on May 16, it quickly became clear that Khrushchev had other plans for the summit because of the U-2 incident. Eisenhower's statement at the press conference on May 11, accepting responsibility for the overflights, had essentially only increased Khrushchev's vulnerability within the Soviet hierarchy. On May 16, in an aggressive and hostile opening statement, Khrushchev made what amounted to a series of nonnegotiable demands of Eisenhower, stating that in order for the conference to continue, Eisenhower must terminate the U-2 flights; punish those responsible for them, which presumably meant firing Allen Dulles, a longtime nemesis of the Kremlin; and publicly apologize to Khrushchev for the "hostile act" of violating Soviet airspace. In response, Eisenhower replied that the flights had been discontinued, but he refused to punish anyone in the administration for the U-2 program, nor apologize to Khrushchev and the Soviet Union for the aerial surveillance program. Khrushchev then abruptly left the conference room and refused to return until Eisenhower met his demands. Eisenhower refused to accommodate Khrushchev, and the summit conference ended before it had barely begun.[17]

The main item on the agenda for the Paris summit was to be the negotiation of a nuclear test-ban agreement between the Soviet Union and the three western nations. At the conference, however, the subject of a test-ban agreement never made it to the discussion stage. Khrushchev raged against the U-2 flights; Eisenhower sought to justify the American position on aerial surveillance; and Prime Minister Macmillan and President de Gaulle attempted to persuade Khrushchev to set aside the matter of the U-2 episode, make it a subject for future negotiations between the United States and the Soviet Union, and then proceed to discuss nuclear test bans. Khrushchev refused, and then, worse, postponed (which was tantamount to withdrawing) Eisenhower's invitation to visit the Soviet Union, then scheduled for a month away. All four leaders left the conference empty-handed. The U-2 crisis had delivered a crushing blow to Eisenhower's objective of thawing the tensions of the Cold War.[18]

When Eisenhower returned to the United States, he received a hero's welcome for not yielding to Khrushchev's demands and acting with

Introduction

dignity when confronted by Khrushchev's intemperate and even rhetorically abusive behavior. But Ike knew that the damage was irreversible as long as he remained in the White House. As historian Robert A. Divine has written, "During his last few months in office, [Eisenhower] was unable to regain the momentum he had been trying to create toward easing Cold War tensions. Instead, he found himself the prisoner of events," as Khrushchev began to test the American position in Cuba, the Congo, and in Indochina.[19]

In conclusion, historians always struggle when they attempt to assess the impact and significance of events that never occurred. Such exercises, of necessity, must include a certain amount of speculation and conjecture. One may assume this to be the case with Khrushchev's postponement/withdrawal of the invitation to Eisenhower to visit the Soviet Union in June 1960 as well as the effect that particular trip may have had on Soviet-American relations. We are, however, able to see how diplomats, both in the United States and in the Soviet Union, made assiduous, extensive preparations for the visit and how Eisenhower's journey might have unfolded. At the Dwight D. Eisenhower Library in Abilene, Kansas, researchers may read the materials in Eisenhower's presidential papers, specifically in the Ann Whitman File, International Series, as well as in the papers of James Hagerty, Eisenhower's press secretary and trusted adviser, that reveal the planning for the visit and how Eisenhower was to spend his time in the Soviet Union. We also know what Ike, most likely, would have said in his formal, prepared remarks to the Soviet leadership and to the Soviet people.[20]

The file in the Ann Whitman International Series is ominously entitled "Far Eastern Trip (withdrawn)," indicating that Eisenhower never made this second visit to the Soviet Union. With the failure to make the trip, Ike missed his final opportunity to thaw the Cold War and, as he later ruefully told his science adviser, George B. Kistiakowsky, that his efforts may well have succeeded, except "for the stupid U-2 mess."[21] From these papers, it is possible to show what Eisenhower, most likely, would have said and done in the Soviet Union from an official perspective. What is not possible to ascertain, of course, is how the Soviet people would have responded to Eisenhower, nor as to whether he and Khrushchev would have completed a nuclear test-ban agreement. What can be concluded, however, is that the potential did exist, in a best-case scenario, for an improvement in the overall climate of the international situation had Eisenhower visited the Soviet Union in June 1960. That such an improvement was never allowed to occur was, of course, the greatest disappointment, tragedy even, of Eisenhower's presidency.

For that reason, sometimes an event that did *not* happen can have as great, or perhaps an even greater effect on history than an event that actually happened. Because of the cancellation of Eisenhower's visit to the Soviet Union, one might argue, both countries lost a multitude of opportunities for improving their relationship and taking steps toward a more open international environment. First, the cancellation of Ike's visit prevented an opportunity for closer, person-to-person contacts between Americans and Russians, and a chance to view each other, and each other's societies, in a different light. Second, the cancellation meant that Eisenhower and Khrushchev were unable to test out their personal strategies of how an improved relationship between heads of state might become a useful diplomatic device in the Cold War. As historian David Reynolds has written, "Summitry is really a recent invention—made possible by air travel, made necessary by weapons of mass destruction and made into household news by the mass media of newsreels and television."[22] Eisenhower's outreach to Khrushchev in 1959 and 1960 essentially met Reynolds's criteria for effective summitry, but the cancellation of his visit made it impossible for him to realize his long-sought objective of improving relations with the Soviet Union before leaving office in 1961.

Third, in the realm of unintended consequences, the cancellation of Eisenhower's visit resulted in the failure of the American and western news media to visit the Soviet Union and broadcast the historic events that would have transpired. These broadcasts would have opened up the Soviet Union to audiences around the world. Had Ike visited the Soviet Union, the broadcasts of his travels and meetings would have given millions of people their first glimpse into modern life in this hitherto-closed society. One can speculate, once again, that the effect of this international glimpse into the Soviet Union by the Western media might have resulted in increased travel and contacts between peoples of other nations (Americans to be sure, but others as well) and the Soviet Union as the world digested the impact of the meetings between Eisenhower and Khrushchev.

Instead, the collapse of the Paris summit and the cancellation of Ike's visit to the Soviet Union led to another prolonged period of mistrust and

Introduction

recrimination, and ultimately to more military spending and an intensification of the Cold War.[23] The U-2 crisis and its aftermath were the great unforced errors of the Eisenhower presidency. In the final analysis, Eisenhower was unable to reconcile his desire to "melt some of the ice" of the Cold War with his policy imperative of insuring, to the maximum extent possible, that the United States was not vulnerable to a surprise attack, with nuclear weapons, by its primary adversary.

To understand the full scope and magnitude of Soviet-American relations in 1959 and 1960, however, it is necessary to go back to August 1945, when Dwight D. Eisenhower made his first and only visit to the Soviet Union. It was that experience in 1945, one might argue, that gave Ike the tempting notion in 1959 that another visit to the Soviet Union might help to change the direction of the Cold War and improve the prospects for world peace.

Chapter 1

The Man of the Hour, August 11–15, 1945

On August 11, 1945, General Dwight D. Eisenhower, the supreme Allied commander of the Supreme Headquarters Allied Expeditionary Forces in Europe, left Berlin in the company of Marshall Georgi Zhukov, the commander of the Red Army during World War II, for a flight to Moscow. A closely guarded secret, Eisenhower's visit to the Soviet Union occurred during a momentous week in world history. Three months earlier, on May 6, 1945, Eisenhower accepted the surrender of German forces and on May 8, Germany surrendered to Russian forces in Berlin. World War II in Europe had officially ended. On August 6 and 9, the United States attacked the Japanese cities of Hiroshima and Nagasaki with atomic weapons, attacks that killed more than 300,000 Japanese people and demolished two of Japan's major cities. The Soviet Union, pledged to enter the war against Japan ninety days after the surrender of Germany, was already pressing its attacks against Japanese forces in Manchuria. As Eisenhower's C-54 transport aircraft, named *Sunflower II*, touched down in Moscow, the surrender of Japan and the end of World War II in the Pacific appeared to be imminent, perhaps within two or three days.[1]

Few Americans have seen their personal and professional fortunes improve so dramatically and so rapidly as did Dwight D. Eisenhower between 1941 and 1945. After graduating from West Point in 1915, Eisenhower carried out a number of assignments in the army during the years of World War I and in the 1920s and 1930s. He had remained stateside during World War I, however, and his career prospects appeared to suffer as a result of his failure to obtain command and combat experience during the Great War.[2]

Still, Eisenhower developed a reputation as a capable and imaginative officer. When the United States entered World War II in 1941, Army Chief of Staff General George C. Marshall summoned Eisenhower to Washington from his post at San Antonio, Texas, and placed him in the Pacific and Far Eastern Department of the War Plans Division. Ike attacked his new duties with the diligence and imagination that he had previously displayed. In June 1942, Marshall was so impressed with Eisenhower that he selected him to command the combined British and American forces in the European Theater of Operations, choosing Ike for this coveted post ahead of 366 senior officers.[3] For Eisenhower, the sudden rise to command authority was exhilarating, especially after more than twenty years as a "lifer" in a peacetime army. "I'm going to command the whole shebang!," he triumphantly told his wife, Mamie.[4]

The stage was thus set for the great triumphs of the Allied armies under Eisenhower's command during World War II. As supreme Allied commander, Eisenhower oversaw the defeat of Axis forces in North Africa and Italy during 1943. In 1944, he commanded Operation Overlord and directed the Allied offensives in the west that finally resulted in Germany's surrender. Victory in Europe catapulted Eisenhower to unprecedented fame and popularity. In 1942, he had left the United States as a relatively little-known soldier, but he returned to America in 1945 as the man who beat Adolf Hitler.[5]

For his part, Marshall Georgi Zhukov could lay more than an equal claim with Eisenhower for recognition as an instrument of the military defeat of Hitler's *Wehrmacht*. Zhukov grew up in an impoverished family in Kaluga, southwest of Russia. After spending time as a cobbler's apprentice, Zhukov fought for the Russian army in World War I and joined the Communist Party after the Bolshevik Revolution in 1917. He fought in the Russian Civil War on the side of the Bolsheviks and remained in the Red Army afterwards. During the 1930s, he managed to advance in his career, at virtually the same time that Joseph Stalin, the Soviet premier, was violently purging the upper ranks of the Soviet military. Stalin first called upon Zhukov in 1939 to defeat an invasion of Manchuria by Japanese forces at the battle of Nomonhan. When the forces of Nazi Germany attacked the Soviet Union in June 1941, Stalin sent Zhukov first to Leningrad to organize its defense and then summoned him to Moscow and placed him in command of the Red Army's defense of Moscow against the advancing forces of the *Wehrmacht*.

After helping to save Moscow, Zhukov was transferred to Stalingrad to assist in the eventual defeat of German forces in that region in 1943. From there, Zhukov was assigned to command the Red Army's forces that were attempting to open a path into the besieged city of Leningrad in 1944. After that assignment, Zhukov took command of the Red Army as it fought against the Nazis into Poland and ultimately into Germany. The Russian people correctly believed that Zhukov was their man who beat Hitler. Other military observers shared that view. As military historian Alistair Horne has written, Zhukov was "recognized as the most successful commander" in World War II.[6]

In June 1945, the Allies established the Allied Control Council, also known as the Four Powers (the United States, the Soviet Union, the United Kingdom, and France). The council was charged with the occupation of defeated Germany. Eisenhower was placed in control of the American zone of German occupation and Zhukov of the Russian zone. At that time, Eisenhower, then 55, and Zhukov, then 48, met and immediately formed a close working relationship as well as a personal friendship. As journalist Harrison Salisbury, who reported for United Press International in Russia during World War II, recalled, "The two men (Eisenhower and Zhukov) had met in Berlin, and they were really very similar personalities and they just took an instant liking to each other."[7]

Not everything went smoothly between Eisenhower and Zhukov during this period, of course. Numerous instances of tensions occurred between the American and Soviet authorities as they discharged their new responsibilities. Eisenhower also became frustrated by Zhukov's reluctance to exercise independent leadership, since Zhukov appeared to refer just about every major decision to Andrei Vishinsky, his political representative, before taking any final action. "If I sent such small details to Washington for decision I would be fired and my government would get someone who would handle such things himself," Ike told Zhukov on one occasion.[8]

Regardless, Eisenhower and Zhukov often compared and contrasted the tactics of their respective armies during World War II and, perhaps more important, worked out an agreement whereby American troops evacuated the Russian zone while forces from Great Britain and the United States went to Berlin for the postwar occupation of that city.[9] Eisenhower frequently mentioned the need for the United States and the Soviet Union to cooperate peacefully as they faced the uncertain circumstances of the postwar world.

Once *Sunflower II* landed in Moscow, a reporter for the *New York Times* explained, "Wearing battle dress and his Kansas grin, General Eisenhower plunged affably into the swarm of receptionists—General Alexei Antonov, chief of the General Staff of the Red Army; Air Marshal F. Y. Falaleyeff; W. Averell Harriman, the United States ambassador; Sir Archibald Clark Kerr, the British ambassador; Foo Ping-sheung, the Chinese ambassador; General Georges Catroux, the French ambassador; Edwin W. Pauley, head of the United States Reparation Commission; and [more] military and naval bigwigs than a fairly competent group of reporters was able to assemble, identify and classify in one working day."[10]

Dwight Eisenhower's visit to the Soviet Union in August had been in the diplomatic works for some time. In fact, Joseph Stalin had invited Eisenhower to attend the Soviet Union's victory parade in Moscow on June 24, but Ike was unable to attend because he was scheduled to return to the United States at that time to participate in the celebrations that marked the end of the war in Europe. With the four wartime allies—the United States, Great Britain, France, and the Soviet Union—now involved in the postwar occupation of Germany, however, Stalin renewed the invitation for another visit, this time to coincide with the Soviet Union's National Sports Parade on August 12. One might speculate that Stalin and the leadership of the Soviet Union, given Franklin D. Roosevelt's sudden passing in April and the tension that developed between President Harry S. Truman and Stalin at the Potsdam Conference in July, may have viewed Eisenhower as the next American president in the postwar period and, for that reason, it made sense for them to get to know him better.

Both President Truman and Ambassador Harriman urged Ike to accept Stalin's invitation. Harriman also proposed that Eisenhower and Zhukov exchange visits to their respective countries, with Ike coming to Moscow in August and Zhukov visiting the United States in October.[11] In terms of promoting closer relations between the United States and the Soviet Union, the somewhat unexpected bond of friendship that had developed between Eisenhower and Zhukov was potentially one device that both sides intended to use in their attempts to find common ground with the other. Emphasizing Zhukov's importance, Stalin had designated him as Eisenhower's official host for his visit to Russia.[12]

Accompanying Eisenhower on his visit were Brigadier General Lucius Clay, Brigadier General Thomas Jefferson "T. J." Davis, Master Sergeant Leonard Dry, and then-Lieutenant John S. D. Eisenhower, Eisenhower's son. Clay had been assigned to Germany in April 1945 to assist with the occupation and later was to play the key role in the airlift that broke the Soviet blockade of Berlin in 1948–1949. Davis was a longtime staff officer and one of Eisenhower's most trusted advisers. Dry was Ike's chauffeur. Lieutenant Eisenhower came along to provide staff assistance to his father. Despite the special pleadings of many members of his staff in Frankfurt who wanted to visit Russia, Eisenhower purposely kept the size of the entourage quite small, "because of the limited accommodations in Moscow."[13]

After leaving the airport, Eisenhower and his party rode to Spaso House, the home of the American ambassador, where they were the guests of Harriman and his daughter Kathleen. Later that day, Eisenhower went to the Soviet military headquarters for a meeting with General Alexei Antonov, who explained the Russian plan for defeating Japanese forces in Manchuria. Antonov expressed confidence that the Russians intended to play a major role in the defeat of Japan, just as they had in the defeat of Germany. Antonov and Eisenhower conferred until late in the evening on August 11.[14]

Despite the outward display of cordiality between Eisenhower and the Russians, the Americans soon learned about Soviet displeasure with one particular American action. During his meeting with Antonov, Eisenhower presented the Soviet leader with the Order of Chief Commander of the Legion of Merit, the highest decoration he could award to a foreigner. The problem was that the Americans had already presented several British officers with the Distinguished Service Medal, which to Americans is a higher award than the Legion of Merit. As Major General John R. Deane, the chief of the U.S. Military Mission in Russia, later recounted in his memoir, *The Strange Alliance*, "The Russians set much store on decorations in general and had presented Eisenhower with the

'Order of Victory,' their super-super award. The Russians were upset that Zhukov, [General Ivan] Koniev, [General Konstantin] Rokossovsky and Antonov were awarded something that was not considered by Americans to be the best they had in the bag."[15]

The Soviets responded immediately to this apparent show of disrespect by the Americans. The next morning, August 12, Soviet newspapers made scant mention of Ike's presence in Moscow. Was Eisenhower going to receive the diplomatic cold shoulder from Stalin and the other members of the Soviet hierarchy? Their behavior at the National Sports Parade that day would go a long way toward answering that question.

Stalin, Eisenhower, and the National Sports Parade

Russia's National Sports Parade began at noon on Sunday, August 12, in Moscow's Red Square. It was the first such event that Russia had held since it was attacked by Germany in 1941. The question for the Americans was how the Russian people were to treat Eisenhower, given that the official line of the Communist Party appeared to be that Ike was not entitled to any special attention. The crowd of people attending the parade was estimated to be around 50,000, with 40,000 being athletes and another 5,000 to 10,000 being those who had received invitations.

As the time for the beginning of the parade grew near, Eisenhower, Harriman, and Deane rode by car to Red Square. Eisenhower left the car about three blocks from the square and started on a short walk to his place of observation along the parade route. Almost immediately, the Russian crowd recognized Eisenhower and people broke into long, prolonged cheers for their American visitor. The cheering followed Eisenhower for the entire distance to Red Square, a display of "spontaneous and unrestrained admiration," to quote John Deane.[16] In recounting this enthusiastic outburst of affection for Ike by the Russian people, Deane later wrote that "It takes some sort of spontaneous combustion to highlight the differences between the party line and the will of the people [in the Soviet Union], and it is only occasionally that one is aware that differences do exist."[17]

At noon, Stalin appeared with the members of the Soviet Politburo and strode to the top of the platform above Lenin's Tomb. Then came a surprise: after the crowd acclaimed Stalin and the Party leadership, Antonov approached Eisenhower and asked him if he wanted to accept Stalin's invitation to observe the parade with him on the platform. Eisenhower initially hesitated since American protocol required that Harriman, as the representative of President Truman, should receive such an invitation before Eisenhower.[18] Antonov then proposed an alternative: did Eisenhower wish to invite "two of his associates" to accompany him to the reviewing platform? Eisenhower then asked Harriman and Deane to join him atop Lenin's Tomb to observe the parade.[19] It was the first occasion in which Stalin had afforded an opportunity for a non-Russian to stand in the exalted space where the deceased Lenin was laid.

For the next five hours, Eisenhower, Harriman, and Deane observed the parade along with Stalin and the Soviet hierarchy. The experience was certainly a test of physical stamina, for the spectators as well as the athletes. As Eisenhower later described the event in his wartime memoir, *Crusade in Europe*, "We stood for five hours on the tomb where the show went on. None of us had ever witnessed anything remotely similar. The groups of performers were dressed in the colorful costumes of their respective countries and at times thousands of individuals participated in unison."[20]

Eisenhower may have been impressed by the spectacle of the National Sports Parade, but Harriman and Deane most assuredly were not. For Deane, "fully conscious of the honor [to stand atop Lenin's Tomb] even though I attained it by sliding in on Eisenhower's coattails," the entire event was "most colorful but also extremely boring."[21] Harriman and Deane also thought that the Soviets had essentially manufactured an event for the benefit of a privileged few in the Party leadership. While the parade included more than 40,000 athletes, there were only 5,000 or so invited guests for the event. Vyacheslav Molotov, the Soviet foreign minister, was in Stalin's delegation to observe the parade, and he asked Ambassador Harriman whether Americans held similar sporting events. In response, Harriman told Molotov that, in the United States, "sports spectacles were rather different with only a handful of players and tens of thousands of spectators."[22]

Nevertheless, the occasion of the National Sports Parade provided Eisenhower with the unique opportunity to meet Stalin, and through an interpreter, to engage him in conversation. According to some reports, Stalin impressed Eisenhower as a "benign and fatherly" person, words not usually used to describe the Soviet leader.[23] Through an interpreter, "we conversed intermittently during the entire period of the show," Ike recalled, noting that Stalin was especially interested in how America's achievements in science, industry, and education had given the American people their enviable standard of living. Stalin expressed a desire to raise the living standards of the Soviet people because World War II had devastated so much of the Soviet economy, especially in industry and in agriculture. "We know that we are behind [the United States] in these things and we know that you can help us," he said.[24]

Eisenhower understood the veracity of Stalin's comments. On the plane ride from Berlin to Moscow, he had observed, from the air, the devastation that the conflict against Germany had ravaged on the Russian countryside. A recurring point in the conversation that day between Eisenhower and Stalin was the need for the United States and the Soviet Union to cooperate in peacetime as they had during the war against Germany and then in the war against Japan.

Later, on August 12, Eisenhower and Zhukov attended a soccer match in Moscow's main stadium. With a crowd estimated at 70,000 to 80,000 gathered in the stadium, the word quickly got out that Eisenhower was present. Before the match began, Eisenhower met Zhukov in a reception room off the main state box at the top and center of the stands. Once the two men appeared in the box, the entire crowd stood and cheered. The ovation was deafening.

When the match ended and Eisenhower and Zhukov stood to leave, the cheering from the crowd resumed once again. The ovation grew louder and louder in volume. As Brooks Atkinson reported the scene for the *New York Times,* "Being unable to say anything in Russian, General Eisenhower put his arm around Marshall Zhukov as a gesture of goodwill."[25] Ike's demonstration of friendship with Zhukov further energized the crowd into another prolonged outburst of cheering and applause. Describing the scene, Averall Harriman later wrote, "Both men (Eisenhower and Zhukov) got to their feet and the cheers in the stadium surpassed anything I had ever heard. I had never seen such enthusiasm anywhere. It was clear to me that next to Roosevelt himself, Eisenhower had become the human symbol of cooperation between the two countries."[26] Likewise, John Deane recorded that the enthusiastic outburst of affection for Eisenhower "was a sincere demonstration by a representative cross section of the Russian people of their affection for the American people as embodied in Eisenhower [that] was heart-warming and reassuring to us Americans who were there."[27]

Sightseeing in Russia

Zhukov had informed Eisenhower that no place in the Soviet Union was off-limits to him. On August 13, Eisenhower and his party chose to visit the Moscow subway, an art gallery, and the Sturmovik airplane factory. Ike expressed a special admiration for St. Basil's Cathedral in Red Square, a church with "a singularly impressive medieval" beauty. He also visited the Kremlin, taking with him members of Deane's military mission and staff from the American embassy. Eisenhower personally met the members of Deane's staff, "a memorable day in their otherwise drab existence," Deane recorded. Eisenhower took close to sixty people with him on the visit to the Kremlin, an unprecedented opportunity for Americans to see "the accumulated treasures of the czars, including jewelry, costumes, flags and decorations organized in a magnificent display."[28]

During the evening of August 13, Stalin hosted Eisenhower, the members of his delegation, and the staff of the American embassy at a magnificent dinner in the Kremlin that lasted well into the late evening. To no one's surprise, the evening's dinner featured endless toasts to Soviet-American cooperation in the postwar period.

On August 14, Eisenhower and his party visited several of Russia's collective and state farms outside of Moscow. Knowledgeable about farming from his boyhood experiences growing up in Kansas, Eisenhower conversed intelligently about agriculture with the Soviet farmers. Once again in the company of Zhukov, Eisenhower made another positive impression upon the Russian people.[29]

When they left the farms, Eisenhower and Zhukov returned to Moscow in the same vehicle. Eisenhower's destination was Spaso House and, upon arrival, Ike invited Zhukov to join him for lunch. Ike's invitation placed Zhukov in an awkward position, since Soviet officials were not allowed to visit the homes of foreigners without permission from higher authority in the Soviet hierarchy. Within the diplomatic world, of course, these invitations were not made on the spur of the moment, as Eisenhower had just done. Zhukov was in a bind: he did not want to appear rude to Ike and there wasn't time to contact the hierarchy for permission. So, as John Deane recalled, "In he came."[30] Deane later told Ike that he had "never achieved a greater victory and hoped that he appreciated it."[31]

Eisenhower also met with representatives of the Soviet Union's press corps on August 14. "I see nothing in the future that would prevent Russia and the United States from being the closest possible friends," he told the reporters. "If we are really going to be friends, we really must understand each other."[32] Ike also touched on several other important topics. For one, he extolled the virtue of a free press, as practiced in the United States. "One thing we must all keep in mind," he said. "In our country, under the principles governing our affairs, there is no censorship of the press. Occasionally some portion of that press gives me the devil . . . [but] I, like every other soldier of America, will die for the freedom of the press, even for the freedom of newspapers that call me everything that is a good deal less than being a gentleman."[33] He also expressed his admiration for the contribution of Russian factory workers to the defeat of the Axis. "When the full history of the war is written," Eisenhower stated, "the Russian factory worker will be recognized as a hero. Today I particularly took pleasure in seeing some American machine tools in a Russian factory. It shows the people of America wished to help the people working here."[34]

On the evening of August 14, Ambassador Harriman held a magnificent dinner for Eisenhower, his party, and guests from the Soviet Ministry of Foreign Affairs (MFA) and the armed services. Rumors were everywhere that a Japanese surrender to the Allies was imminent. In the middle of the dinner, Harriman received an urgent message to report to the MFA. In Harriman's absence, Eisenhower became the substitute for the evening's program. When Harriman returned, he brought news of the Japanese surrender, news that set off a celebration that extended well into the rest of the evening.

Despite the momentous news, Eisenhower was quick to observe the reaction of Marshall Semyon Budyonny, a member of the Soviet Union's military hierarchy, and a man who was close to Stalin. Eisenhower asked Budyonny if he was pleased that the war with Japan was over. "Oh yes," Budyonny said, now considerably inebriated from the evening's festivities, "but we should have kept going until we killed a lot more of those insolent Japanese."[35] In fact, the Soviets were contemplating a campaign of big-time payback against the weakened Japanese enemy. Still bitter over their defeat by Japan in 1904–1905 and the territorial losses they suffered, as well as the humiliations inflicted by the Japanese since that time, the Soviets were already attacking Japanese forces in Manchuria in preparation for dividing the spoils of the War in the Pacific.[36] Eisenhower was not impressed with Budyonny's response, knowing that the Soviet Marshall was apparently willing to sacrifice more Russian lives in his pursuit of retribution against Japan.

The Visit to Leningrad

Before Eisenhower left the Soviet Union, he expressed the desire to visit Leningrad and pay tribute to the defenders of the city that had withstood the siege of the Germans during the bitter days of World War II. In fact, as historian Anna Reid has written, the German blockade of Leningrad during World War II was the deadliest siege of a city in human history. Between September 1941 and January 1944, 750,000 Russians starved to death. Russian casualties at Leningrad were thirty-five times greater than British casualties suffered during the Blitz and four times greater than the bombings of Hiroshima and Nagasaki. [37] Furthermore, American journalist Harrison Salisbury has estimated that the combined total of fatalities caused by starvation and military combat at Leningrad ranged from 1,300,000 to 1,500,000.[38]

On August 15, after a scant two or three hours of sleep the night before, Eisenhower, Zhukov, and their delegations arrived in Leningrad. The Russian leadership in the city rolled out the red carpet for Ike and his party. At a luncheon held by the mayor of Leningrad that included the civil and military leaders of the region, the group was entertained by dancers as well as vocal and instrumental musicians. Eisenhower told the mayor how impressed he was with the talent of the Russian dancers and musicians. "Any Russian would cheerfully go hungry all week if by doing so he could, on Sunday, visit an art gallery, a football game, or the ballet," the mayor replied.[39]

At the luncheon in Leningrad, another surprise occurred. When the time came for toasts, Zhukov asked Lieutenant John Eisenhower to offer a toast. Anticipating just such a moment, John Eisenhower was prepared and he rose to his feet and offered "a toast to the common soldier of the Great Red Army." The guests at the luncheon, including Marshal Zhukov, responded to the toast enthusiastically, certainly a relief for John Eisenhower.[40]

Dwight D. Eisenhower, Georgi Zhukov, and the American and Soviet delegations left Leningrad and flew back to Berlin after concluding their visit. On the return flight, the weather deteriorated and the Americans and the Russians experienced a rather rough journey. Nevertheless, Eisenhower and Zhukov spent the time talking about their respective military campaigns against the Germans and the differences in their tactics for fighting the Nazis. By the time the two groups landed in Germany, it was clear that Eisenhower and Zhukov had added to the depth of their friendship.

Meanings

Dwight D. Eisenhower's trip to Moscow in August 1945 was a tentative step forward in promoting closer Soviet-American relations in the immediate postwar period. Both Stalin and Zhukov spoke admiringly of Eisenhower to Ambassador Harriman after Ike's departure. "General Eisenhower is a very great man," Stalin said, "not only because of his military accomplishments but also because of his human, friendly, kind, and frank nature. He is not a *gruby* [coarse individual] like most military [leaders]."[41] For his part, Zhukov also appreciated Ike's authenticity and overall decency. "I liked his simplicity, informality, and sense of humor," Zhukov later said. "It seemed to me that he understood the great sacrifices of the Soviet people."[42] As far as other Soviet military leaders were concerned, Eisenhower was the one American commander who possessed the leadership skills and organizational ability that were necessary to command troops on the Eastern front.[43]

Eisenhower's perceptions of the Soviet hierarchy, in contrast, were not necessarily insightful. After his encounter with Stalin at the National Sports Parade, Eisenhower expressed the view to Ambassador Harriman that Soviet-American relations, in the longer term, would be harmonious because he expected Zhukov, at some point, to succeed Stalin at the top of the government of the Soviet Union. "Once Zhukov was in charge," Ike said, "the United States would have no difficulties with the Soviet Union."[44]

As matters turned out, Eisenhower's perception of the Soviet Union's leadership environment in the postwar period was erroneous. "What Eisenhower failed to realize was that the first and most important thing which Stalin had to do once the war ended was to reassert the full authority, his full personal authority and party authority, over these generals who might become Bonapartes," Harrison Salisbury explained.[45] Harriman and Deane also subscribed to Salisbury's views. In their view, the Soviet hierarchy feared the prospect of "Bonapartism," of placing a military man at the head of the Communist Party. At one point during World War II, Stalin had even told Harry Hopkins, Roosevelt's emissary, that "Napoleon had run away with the French Revolution."[46]

Stalin may have had good reason for apprehension about the very popular Zhukov, who was the one commander in the Red Army whose exploits in World War II provided him with a public stature that rivaled that of the Soviet dictator. And, in fact, Zhukov went into eclipse in the Soviet leadership shortly after Eisenhower's visit, especially once relations between the two countries began to worsen in the fall of 1945. More seriously, the Soviet leadership canceled Zhukov's return visit to the United States in October. Years later, Eisenhower grudgingly conceded to Harriman that his assessment of Zhukov's influence had been correct.[47]

Regardless of the future problems between the two countries that had yet to manifest themselves, in August 1945, each side sensed a genuine desire for peace on the part of the other. As John Deane wrote, "During Eisenhower's visit, we encountered huge masses of people and small groups of people. We could almost physically feel the attitudes of kindliness with which they regarded us."[48] In Harriman's view, "The Eisenhower visit was a genuine outpouring of long-suppressed feeling by the Russian people" for friendship with the United States.[49]

Eisenhower undoubtedly returned to Germany mindful of two lessons he had learned while in Russia. First, he had witnessed, at first hand, the devastation that World War II had wreaked upon the Soviet homeland. "When we flew into Russia in 1945," Eisenhower later wrote, "I did not see a house standing between the western borders of the country and the area around Moscow."[50] He had spoken with Russian people who had lost family members and loved ones in the struggle against

Germany. He sensed that the Russian people desperately wanted a return to peace, and especially peace with the United States.

Second, Ike had experienced direct interactions with Stalin, Zhukov, Antonov, and the members of the Soviet hierarchy as well as with ordinary Russians in the streets and on the farms. He even met Nikita S. Khrushchev, then the leader of Ukraine and a member of the Politburo. Admittedly, the contact between Ike and Khrushchev in 1945 was perfunctory, a nod by each man in the other's direction atop Lenin's Tomb on August 12 and a brief introduction by Stalin of one to the other at the main dinner on August 13. As Sergei Khrushchev recalled, the conversation at the dinner between Eisenhower and Khrushchev was brief and hardly noteworthy. Stalin simply introduced the two men informally: "Khrushchev, this is Eisenhower; Eisenhower, this is Khrushchev," as Sergei Khrushchev recalled.[51]

To a degree matched at the time only by such individuals as Harriman and Deane, Eisenhower had demonstrated the ability to communicate effectively with the Russians, both the masses of the Soviet people and the leadership. For them, Dwight D. Eisenhower was the man of the hour.

Importantly, the meetings with Stalin, in particular, stayed in Eisenhower's memory. In March 1953, early in his first term as president and shortly after Stalin's death, Eisenhower spoke with Emmett John Hughes, his principal speechwriter, about his conversation with Stalin atop Lenin's Tomb in August 1945. "I remember that in one four-hour session I had with Stalin, damn near all he talked about was the essential things his people needed—homes and food and technical help," Eisenhower recalled. "When he talked about seven people to a room in Moscow, he seemed to me just as anxious as you or I would be looking at an American slum problem."[52]

Likewise, Eisenhower was permanently affected by his experience in the Soviet Union and his observation of the extreme suffering of the Russian people during World War II. In his own mind, Eisenhower was able to draw a distinction between the character of the Russian people, the sacrifices of the Red Army during the war, and the totalitarian nature of the Soviet political and economic system. As Andrew Goodpaster, his closest adviser in the White House, once explained, Eisenhower "never tried to whip up hatred toward the Soviets. He felt they had a mistaken system and a system that did not respond to the needs for the people of the world, but he did not try to fan any kind of emotion."[53]

Nevertheless, the outward displays of cordiality did not prevent some ominous impressions of the Soviet Union that the Americans experienced, impressions that visibly illustrated the difference between the two societies. For example, upon arriving at the airport in Moscow on August 11, John Eisenhower witnessed Russian troops "in formation and [their] goosestepping made me feel vaguely uncomfortable."[54] Similarly, John Eisenhower also wrote that the National Sports Parade, despite being an impressive spectacle, "reminded me of pictures that I had seen of prewar Nazi Germany."[55] Stalin's cult of personality, evidenced by the pictures and banners of the Soviet leader throughout Red Square, was enough to give the Americans some pause about the future direction of the Soviet state.

Finally, Dwight Eisenhower's visit to the Soviet Union in August 1945 was an unqualified personal success for him, a notable event in the middle of the brief postwar "honeymoon" between the United States and the Soviet Union, in John Eisenhower's description.[56] The experience provided Ike with some assurance that, should he ever again be required to negotiate directly with the leaders of the Soviet Union, he could approach such discussions with the confidence borne of his first visit to Russia. The honeymoon was about to end, however, as relations between the United States and the Soviet Union quickly deteriorated during the early years of the Cold War.

Chapter 2

The Two Invitations, July–August 1959

On August 3, 1959, President Dwight D. Eisenhower strode into a press conference in the Executive Office Building across the street from the White House. James Hagerty, Eisenhower's loyal and trusted press secretary, who had been with the administration from its outset in 1953, accompanied the president to the press conference. Before Ike began to address the reporters, Hagerty took his customary seat behind Eisenhower, to the president's left. By this point in Ike's presidency, Hagerty had emerged as one of his closest advisers. Described by Emmett John Hughes, Eisenhower's primary speechwriter, as "quick and shrewd [and] a master technician of press relations," Hagerty was completely loyal to Eisenhower and Ike returned Hagerty's loyalty by giving him almost complete control of his relations with the press. Throughout his presidency, Eisenhower had followed a practice, instituted by Hagerty, of holding regularly scheduled news conferences with the White House press corps, and Hagerty was the behind-the-scenes mastermind of those events. Since 1955, upon Hagerty's initiative, these news conferences were televised and, as Eisenhower's political opponents soon came to realize, the events became potent political weapons that Ike used to maintain his popularity with the American people.[1] The press conference on August 3 was not regularly scheduled, though, as Eisenhower had specifically requested this particular meeting.

Eisenhower had big news to share with the reporters. "I asked this morning for this special press conference on the subject of the impending exchange of visits between Mr. [Nikita] Khrushchev and myself," Ike said. "Now, while in Europe this has been one of the worst-kept secrets of a long time, still I think that there may be enough special interest in the matter as to justify you people taking your time to come here this morning."[2]

Special interest indeed: Eisenhower was about to announce that he and Nikita S. Khrushchev, the premier of the Soviet Union, were to visit each other's countries over the course of the next several months. As Ike explained in his initial comments to the reporters, "Some time back, I suggested to the State Department that I believed in the effort to melt a little bit of the ice that seems to freeze our relationship with the Soviets, that such a visit as I proposed would be useful. We studied this thing, and in early July, I initiated the correspondence that finally brought about an agreement. Some of the details, exact details, are yet to be agreed between the diplomatic agencies of our separate, several governments."[3] The reporters understood immediately what Eisenhower was doing: he was acting boldly, almost unilaterally, to take some steps to thaw the icy environment of the Cold War.

Next, the president read a prepared statement that outlined the terms of the agreement for the exchange of visits, a statement that Ike indicated was identical to the one then being issued in Moscow. As he stated,

> The President of the United States has invited Mr. Nikita Khrushchev, Chairman of the Council of Ministers of the U.S.S.R., to pay an official visit to the United States. Mr. Khrushchev has accepted with pleasure.
>
> The President has accepted with pleasure Mr. Khrushchev's invitation to pay an official visit to the U.S.S.R. later this fall.
>
> Mr. Khrushchev will visit Washington for 2 or 3 days and will also spend 10 days or so traveling in the United States. He will have informal talks with the President, which will afford an opportunity for an exchange of views about problems of mutual interest.
>
> On his tour of the United States, Mr. Khrushchev will be able, at first hand, to see the country, its people, and to acquaint himself with their life.
>
> President Eisenhower will visit Moscow and will also spend some days travelling in the Soviet Union. This will provide further opportunity for informal talks and exchange of views about problems

of mutual interest with the Chairman of the Council of Ministers of the U.S.S.R. On his tour of the Soviet Union, President Eisenhower will likewise be able at first hand to see the country, its people, and to acquaint himself with their life.

Both Governments express the hope that the forthcoming visits will help create better understanding between the U.S. and the U.S.S.R. and will promote the cause of peace.[4]

Eisenhower then briefly followed up on the statement by explaining that no connection existed between the two visits, or his visit to the Soviet Union, and the discussion then extant in diplomatic circles about a possible summit meeting between the leaders of the United States, the Soviet Union, Great Britain, and France. Eisenhower explained to the assembled reporters that his proposed visit to the Soviet Union "has no direct connection with any later possible summit meeting. . . . So, I want to make it clear that this is a personal visit for the purposes that I have outlined and are given in this statement, but with the hope that it will do something to promote understanding and possibly progress toward peace in the world."[5]

In the question period that followed Eisenhower's prepared statement, the reporters of the White House press corps asked Eisenhower to expand on the details of his opening remarks. Robert J. Donovan, White House correspondent for the *New York Herald Tribune*, asked whether "Mr. Khrushchev will come directly to Washington first, or will he go to New York and then here, or how?" The Soviet Union was then sponsoring a national exhibition in New York and rumors had circulated in the press that Khrushchev might use the occasion of the Soviet Exhibition to visit the United States and then meet with the president while he was still in the country. Eisenhower's response to Donovan was vague: he simply replied, "I can't tell you a thing about details. I can't give you the exact dates, the exact times, the exact schedules, or exactly how he will come here."[6]

Chalmers M. Roberts of the *Washington Post* asked Eisenhower if he intended to accompany Khrushchev while he was in the United States or whether Khrushchev planned to accompany Eisenhower while he was in the Soviet Union. Eisenhower replied that it would not be "feasible for me to go all the way through the United States with him. But certainly, there might be some visiting around. I don't know, the details are just something I just don't know anything about yet." Roberts followed up:

"But you do expect to get to Russia before the winter closes in there?" The comment brought about laughter in the room.[7] Ike replied, "Well, there, I don't know. I would say, the fall doesn't end until December 22nd, so if I stick with my schedule, it will have to be before that, but that's about all I can say."[8]

Notwithstanding the uncertainty of Eisenhower's responses to the questions of the reporters, two facts were not in dispute. First, Nikita Khrushchev was about to become the first leader of the Soviet Union to make an official visit to the United States.[9] Second, after an interval of fourteen years, Dwight D. Eisenhower was about to make his second visit to the Soviet Union. On this occasion, however, he was not visiting as the supreme commander of the Allied expeditionary forces, but as the president of the United States.

A Different International Scene

By August 1959, Dwight D. Eisenhower had reckoned with the reality that the circumstances of the Cold War had dictated the pace of his presidency between 1953 and 1959. First came the war in Korea, a conflict that Eisenhower managed to bring to a conclusion in 1953. Then, for the rest of the 1950s, the Soviet Union maintained its stranglehold on its satellite nations in eastern Europe. Germany and its former capital city of Berlin remained divided and militarily occupied by Soviet and Western forces. The Middle East erupted in violence in 1956 with the Suez crisis and in 1958 with the disturbance in Lebanon. The United States and the People's Republic of China came dangerously close to military confrontations in 1955 and 1958.

Amidst all of these crises was the terrifying nuclear arms race that intensified throughout the 1950s. Both the United States and the Soviet Union were spending enormous, hitherto unheard-of sums of money in peacetime for defense in an attempt to strengthen their strategic arsenals. By 1959, the military power of the United States and the ability to project it, both in the conventional and strategic realms, exceeded that of the Soviet Union. Nevertheless, the numerical advantage in manpower that the Soviet Union maintained in eastern Europe continued to be an obstacle to a relaxation in tensions between the great powers.

Still, both sides had undertaken efforts to minimize some of the rancor that characterized the international scene in the 1950s. In July 1955, for example, the leaders of the United States, the Soviet Union, Great Britain, and France met at Geneva, Switzerland, for the first meeting of heads of state since the end of World War II. At this meeting, Eisenhower presented his now-famous Open Skies proposal, whereby each country was to agree to permit aerial inspections of the other's defense installations. The information obtained from such aerial surveillance would enable each side to assess the military capability of the other and thereby rule out the possibility of a surprise attack, or of an attempt to gain a military advantage over the other. The Russians turned down Eisenhower's proposal, dismissing Open Skies as a "propaganda stunt" unworthy of serious consideration. At a purely social event during the conference, Nikita Khrushchev approached Eisenhower and vigorously exclaimed, "Nyet, nyet, nyet!" to describe his reaction to Open Skies.[10]

Other reasons existed for Khrushchev's opposition, of course. As Sergei Khrushchev told the author in April 2011, his father did not agree to Open Skies because then the Americans would "know that we're not as strong as we say; they must not know how really we are weak."[11]

Khrushchev may have also traced his sensitivity to aerial surveillance of the Soviet Union to his experiences in World War II when the German *Luftwaffe* conducted repeated overflights of Soviet territory prior to the launch of Operation Barbarossa (the German invasion of the Soviet Union), in June 1941. As David M. Glantz and Jonathan M. House have written, "German high-altitude reconnaissance aircraft flew over Soviet territory on more than 300 occasions (prior to the German attack), prompting repeated diplomatic protests but little defensive action."[12] Those overflights provided the German high command with critical information about the full range of Soviet military preparations and capabilities on its western border.[13] Khrushchev must have realized that neither in the Politburo nor in the Red Army did any support exist for Eisenhower's Open Skies proposal. For the members of the Soviet leadership, most of whom experienced World War II, aerial surveillance constituted the first step in a devastating first strike.

Thus, despite the so-called "Spirit of Geneva" that emerged from the Geneva conference, relations between the United States and the Soviet Union did not improve appreciably. Regardless, as historian George

Feifer has written, even though Eisenhower and Khrushchev accomplished "little of substance . . . their hours together in Geneva, *actually talking,* [emphasis Feifer's] was itself an achievement. Many on both sides considered it dangerous and possibly traitorous for their leader to expose himself to the other's deviousness."[14]

Both sides took a more positive, tangible step toward improving their relations early in 1958, however. On January 27, 1958, the United States and the Soviet Union agreed to the terms of the Lacy-Zaroubin Agreement, an "Agreement Between the United States of America and the Union of Soviet Socialist Republics on Exchanges in the Cultural, Technical and Educational Fields." This agreement, named after its two principal negotiators, Ambassador-at-Large William S. B. Lacy for the United States and Ambassador G. N. Zaroubin for the Soviet Union, has received little attention from scholars, which is unfortunate because the agreement almost immediately affected Soviet-American relations. And, it must be added, the agreement was vintage Eisenhower in concept and scope: let the politicians get out of the way and allow normal, ordinary citizens from each country to interact with each other. Improved relations at the political level will follow as a natural consequence.

Essentially, the Lacy-Zaroubin Agreement called for citizen exchanges of Russians and Americans in the broad field of cultural affairs. In specific terms, the agreement included exchanges in the areas of radio and television broadcasts; industry, agriculture, and medicine; visits by cultural, civic, youth, and student groups; visits by members of delegations from the Supreme Soviet of the Soviet Union and the United States Congress; theatrical and musical groups; university educators; athletic teams; as well as the development of tourism; exchanges of exhibits and publications; and establishment of direct air flights between the two countries.[15]

The Lacy-Zaroubin agreement even specified certain particular events that were scheduled to occur in 1958 and 1959. For example, in the realm of music and dance, the Soviet Union's Ministry of Culture extended an invitation to the Philadelphia Orchestra, and its musical director Eugene Ormandy, to visit the Soviet Union in the spring of 1958, with the Russian ballet troupe of the Bolshoi Theatre scheduled to visit the United States in 1959. Other celebrities, including Bob Hope, Elizabeth Taylor, and Lana Turner, as well as the Harlem Globetrotters basketball team and the Holiday on Ice figure skaters, also visited the Soviet Union in the spring of 1958. Then, in April 1958, the American pianist Van Cliburn won the first Tchaikovsky International Piano Competition in Moscow. Although not a part of the American-Soviet exchange program, Cliburn nevertheless thrilled Soviet audiences with his piano artistry and soon developed a huge following in Russia.[16] In the realm of athletics, the Lacy-Zaroubin agreement outlined the terms for a major competition in track and field between teams from the two countries to begin in the summer of 1958 and to alternate between the venues of the respective countries in subsequent years.

More important to the area of great power diplomacy, the Lacy-Zaroubin agreement established the arrangements for the display of national exhibits "as an effective means of developing mutual understanding between the peoples of the Soviet Union and the United States." In 1958, both countries sponsored exhibits in the country of the other on the topic of the peaceful uses of atomic energy. In 1959, the Soviets opened the Soviet National Exhibition in New York and the United States opened the American National Exhibition in Moscow.[17] As Jenny Thompson and Sherry Thompson, daughters of Llewellyn E. Thompson, the American ambassador to the Soviet Union at the time, wrote in *The Kremlinologist*, the biography of their father, "It is hard to measure, but also hard to overestimate, the importance of cultural exchanges. [Ambassador] Thompson saw with patience and exposure to each other as people, there could then come accommodation."[18]

To accommodate what became a steady stream of American visitors to the Soviet Union as a result of the Lacy-Zaroubin agreement, the State Department appointed Hans N. (Tom) Tuch, a career Foreign Service officer, as the first press and cultural attaché at its American embassy in Moscow.[19] Hans Tuch, therefore, became the first American diplomat to oversee the deployment of cultural affairs as a tool to improve relations with the Soviet Union. As it turned out, Tuch received the assignment to make the preparations for Vice President Richard M. Nixon's trip to Moscow in July 1959. Working with Herbert Klein, Nixon's press secretary, Tuch dealt with the vice president's entourage as well as the more than 120 members of the American press corps that made the trip to Moscow. In the spirit of the Lacy-Zaroubin agreement, Nixon escorted Khrushchev through the American Exhibition, where the two men subsequently engaged in their now-famous "kitchen debate," an encounter that improved Nixon's standing considerably in the presidential preference polls back in the United States. Interestingly, Nixon remembered Hans Tuch's exhaustive efforts on his behalf and he later sent Tuch a certificate identifying him as a member of Nixon's "Kitchen Cabinet." Tuch kept the certificate as a permanent, prized possession.[20]

For people who were watching and listening, Nixon's visit to the Soviet Union in July 1959 carried hints about a possible visit by Eisenhower to the Soviet Union before he left office in 1961. On July 25, 1959, Nixon read a message of greetings from Eisenhower to the Soviet people about the opening of the American exhibit. The message from Ike linked his visit to the Soviet Union in 1945 to the prospect of another future visit. As Eisenhower's statement read, "The fact that the Soviet and American peoples were comrades-in-arms during the great war concluded fourteen years ago remains fresh in my memory. . . . At the end of that war, in August of 1945, I had the privilege of visiting the Soviet Union itself. On that visit, I was struck by the devotion and dedication of the people of the Soviet Union to the defense of Mother Russia. . . . Nothing that has happened during the interval has dimmed my admiration for the great people of the Soviet Union. . . . I wish that I could have been here to open this Exhibition in person. *It has long been my hope to return to the Soviet Union to see not only my wartime friends but also the great progress you have made in rebuilding your ruined cities and factories. Perhaps the time may come when this desire will be realized"* (emphasis mine).[21]

The Problem of Berlin

Dwight Eisenhower's efforts to improve relations with the Soviet Union, as demonstrated by his announcement of the exchange of visits at the press conference on August 3, 1959, occurred during a year that had not gone particularly well for him up to that point. On November 10, 1958, Khrushchev gave a speech in Moscow in which he demanded the termination of the four-power occupation status of Berlin and declared his intention to hand over control of access to West Berlin to the communist regime in East Germany.[22] On November 27, 1958, he sent a diplomatic note to the United States, Great Britain, and France, demanding that West Berlin (the Allied sector of Berlin) be turned into a neutral city with its access controlled by the East Germans. In effect, Khrushchev delivered an ultimatum: the West had six months to reach an agreement on Berlin or the Soviet Union would sign a separate treaty with East Germany and give the East Germans control of access routes to Berlin. On January 10, 1959, he presented the Western powers with a draft peace treaty that conformed to his views of the new structure of Berlin and East Germany.[23] Khrushchev's ultimatum raised fears in the West about the prospect of another emergency period in Berlin reminiscent of the Soviet blockade and the resulting Allied airlift of 1948–1949.

Khrushchev's threatening behavior tended to obscure the weakness of East Germany at that time. Since World War II, West Germany had grown stronger economically and politically and had developed into the economic powerhouse of western Europe. After the Soviet Union's unsuccessful blockade of Berlin in 1948, and then the numerous protests in Germany, Hungary, and Poland in the mid-1950s against Communist regimes in those countries, thousands of East Germans, especially in the skilled professions, used Berlin as their "escape hatch" to flee into West Berlin and then into West Germany. By 1956, the Soviet authorities had estimated that more than a million East Germans had fled the communist rule since 1948.[24]

Moreover, the Western powers refused to recognize East Germany diplomatically, a further humiliation in the eyes of the Soviet Union. In 1957 the British had agreed to the deployment of American medium-range ballistic missiles in their country, an action that further strengthened the military aspects of the NATO alliance. By 1958–1959, the Western position in Europe was growing stronger, not weaker, and a source of serious concern to the Kremlin.

Still, Khrushchev's motivations in fomenting a new crisis on Berlin remain unclear. Was he attempting to isolate West Germany? Was he attempting to use the Berlin issue to force the Western powers to recognize East Germany and thereby strengthen the Soviet hold on central Europe? Was he trying to split the NATO allies by playing to some possible differences on the status of Berlin? Was Khrushchev attempting to force the West into a summit meeting in which the Soviet premier would be seen as an equal of Eisenhower? Whatever his motivation, as long as Khrushchev kept the ultimatum in effect, the tensions remained. Within the inner councils of Eisenhower's diplomatic and military advisers, May 27, 1959, the expiration of Khrushchev's six-month deadline, became known as "K-Day."[25]

In early February, Ike received some unexpected, and not entirely appreciated, help in the response of the Western alliance to Khrushchev's ultimatum. The help came from Harold Macmillan, Britain's prime minister, who revealed on February 2, 1959, that he had accepted an invitation from Khrushchev to visit the Soviet Union in late February and early March.[26] For his part, Macmillan had become deeply worried about the Berlin problem, even to the point of seeing the situation as perilously analogous to 1914, when events spun out of control and all of Europe plunged into World War I. The Great War was a conflict in which Macmillan himself sustained injuries that physically plagued him for the rest of his life.

Of all the western leaders—Macmillan, de Gaulle, and Adenauer—Eisenhower enjoyed the closest rapport with Macmillan. The two men had met in 1943 in Algiers when Prime Minister Winston Churchill appointed him Minister Resident to Eisenhower's combined military staff in the North African campaign. Macmillan and Eisenhower established a close personal and working relationship during World War II and then, when Macmillan became Britain's prime minister in the aftermath of the Suez Crisis in late 1956, they both worked assiduously to repair the strained relationship between the United States and Britain. The basis of their relationship became one of sharing their personal views through a frequent correspondence, advance consultation on major issues of policy, and cooperation on defense programs.[27] Their efforts largely succeeded to the extent that, by 1959, British-American relations were on a stronger footing than at any time in the postwar period.

Despite the largely satisfactory relationship between Eisenhower and Macmillan, however, the Americans and the British differed on one major aspect of diplomacy. The difference concerned the advisability of direct negotiations between the heads of state. In the tradition of Winston Churchill, Macmillan became an advocate for summitry. "What I envision," Macmillan later explained in *Pointing the Way*, the last volume of his published memoirs, "is a series of meetings, each one leading on to the next. Even if a summit meeting was not going to make any progress at all."[28]

Eisenhower and particularly Secretary of State John Foster Dulles did not share Macmillan's enthusiasm for summitry. Dulles was especially opposed to this type of diplomacy, fearing that the Soviets might attempt to turn the results of any summit meeting into communist propaganda victories. In accurately describing Dulles's resistance to direct negotiations with the Soviets, historian Henry Kissinger wrote, "John Foster Dulles perceived the East-West conflict as a moral issue and sought to avoid negotiations on almost any subject until a basic transformation of the Soviet system had occurred."[29]

Not that Macmillan did not try to change the attitude of the Americans, particularly Eisenhower's, about the potential value of summitry. For example, in the spring of 1958, Macmillan accepted an invitation to deliver a commencement address from the trustees of DePauw University, in Greencastle, Indiana. The invitation from DePauw came in recognition that Macmillan's grandfather, Dr. Joshua Belles, was an alumnus of the school. Like Winston Churchill, whose mother was Jennie Jerome and came from a New York socialite family, Harold Macmillan also had an American mother, Helen Tarleton (Nellie) Belles Macmillan and the Belles family lived in Spencer, Indiana, not far from Greencastle. Nellie Macmillan had married Harold Macmillan's father, Maurice Macmillan, after meeting him in Paris, where she was studying music and art following the death of her first husband, John Hill. Harold Macmillan treasured his combined British-American ancestry and learned much from his mother about the isolationist impulses in American foreign policy.[30]

Macmillan's itinerary called for him to give the commencement address at DePauw on June 8, 1958, and then travel on to Washington, D.C., for meetings with Eisenhower and members of Congress. Knowing that Macmillan intended to visit the United States in June, Eisenhower sent Macmillan a letter on April 3, 1958, inviting him to join him to give the commencement address at Johns Hopkins University in Baltimore where Ike's brother, Dr. Milton S. Eisenhower, was the president. Macmillan responded to Ike with a letter on April 10, accepting the invitation.[31] So, on June 10, Eisenhower and Macmillan flew by helicopter to the campus of Johns Hopkins University, where both men delivered short speeches to the graduates. Obviously aware that the event was going to be covered by the national press, Macmillan took the occasion to press his argument for summitry, probably to Eisenhower's irritation. "Naturally, I do not believe that at a Summit, or at any other meeting," Macmillan said, "five or six men can in four days bridge the immense chasm between the two concepts. But, if conditions are favourable, and the will is there, they might make first a little progress here, and then a little there, and so bring us out of a condition of stalemate into a condition of negotiation."[32] Despite Macmillan's plea for an embrace of summitry, the American position on the subject remained unchanged.

Nevertheless, Macmillan pressed ahead, relying on Sir Patrick Reilly, the British ambassador to the Soviet Union, to get his invitation from Khrushchev. Reilly worked in great secrecy and, despite some tortuous negotiations with the Russians, managed to acquire an invitation for Macmillan. This diplomatic initiative was a solo effort on Macmillan's part. Few British know of his efforts in this respect and both Eisenhower and Foster Dulles, then seriously ill, learned of Macmillan's plans only days before the invitation was received.[33]

Eisenhower and Dulles concluded that Macmillan was engaged in some diplomatic grandstanding, primarily for domestic political purposes. "Macmillan faces a [general] election, probably in the fall, and wants to be the hero who finds a way out of the Cold War dilemma," Dulles told Eisenhower, an observation that contained a good deal of truth.[34] Likewise, Eisenhower was hardly pleased with Macmillan's venture into personal diplomacy with Khrushchev, especially since Macmillan had previously championed the importance of advance consultation between him and Eisenhower. A few weeks later, Ike confessed to some befuddlement about Macmillan's intentions. "There is something behind all this, even more than Macmillan's political ambitions and the forthcoming general election," Ike told Christian Herter, the under secretary of state. He confessed to being unable to "put a finger on" the motivation for Macmillan's behavior. To protect himself, Eisenhower bluntly told Harold Caccia, the British ambassador to the United States, that the prime minister "can call there [the Soviet Union] . . . but he can't speak for us."[35]

Macmillan departed London for Moscow on February 21 and, upon arrival, became the first British prime minister since Winston Churchill to visit the Soviet Union. As Macmillan described it, his purpose for the visit was not to negotiate but rather "to ascertain Russia's real intentions and establish better understanding. It was a reconnaissance rather than a negotiation."[36] But Macmillan did negotiate with the Russians. After a week of travel, dinners with Khrushchev, and endurance of a certain amount of rhetorical abuse from the Russians, Macmillan achieved a modest breakthrough. On February 28, Macmillan and his party arrived in Leningrad, where they were met by Anastas Mikoyan, one of the Soviet Union's deputy premiers, and Andrei Gromyko, the Soviet Union's foreign minister. Mikoyan and Gromyko informed Macmillan that the Russians wished to discuss the Berlin matter at a future meeting of the foreign ministers of the United States, the Soviet Union, Great Britain, and France. The Russians, therefore, were willing to drop the deadline for the ultimatum, although the ultimatum itself still remained in effect.

On March 2, Macmillan sent Eisenhower a cable, noting with considerable satisfaction the change in the Soviet position. Sometime later, Macmillan told Ike that Khrushchev's attitude toward the Berlin issue was one of accommodating the status quo while searching for a diplomatic solution, at least for the moment. "Where the tree has fallen, let it lie," Khrushchev reportedly told the prime minister.[37] On March 3, Macmillan returned to London and the British press generally applauded his efforts in Moscow.

So, in this first bilateral meeting of any western leader with Khrushchev, what did Macmillan accomplish? First, he succeeded in interpreting Khrushchev's behavior and motivations to Eisenhower and the other Allied heads of state. As historian Kitty Newman has written, "[The visit] provided Western leaders with a vital new understanding of Khrushchev's personality and his objectives."[38] In Macmillan's estimation, Khrushchev embodied many of the characteristics that the prime minister discerned in the Russian people: "clever, naïve, inexperienced, suspicious of everyone else and yet cynical themselves."[39]

Second, Macmillan deserved a considerable amount of credit for defusing some of the tensions over the Berlin issue during his meetings with Khrushchev and the Soviet leadership. As diplomatic historian Townsend Hoopes later wrote, "Macmillan revealed Khrushchev's firm desire not to provoke a military confrontation with the West over Berlin." Despite the frustrations of dealing with the unpredictable Khrushchev and his inscrutable associates, Macmillan managed to insist on future negotiations with the Soviets to resolve the Berlin dispute, first at the level of the foreign ministers, and eventually with a summit. As a result, Hoopes contended that "much of the intense anxiety was taken out of the 'deadline' crisis."[40]

To the extent that imperatives of domestic politics drove Macmillan's risky attempt at a diplomatic breakthrough in Moscow, he deftly managed to conceal them. Andrew J. Goodpaster, Eisenhower's staff secretary and probably his closest adviser on national security, looked with admiration at how Macmillan arranged the political benefits from the trip. Goodpaster summed up Macmillan's performance in two words: "Pretty shrewd."[41]

The success of Macmillan's visit to the Soviet Union, and his exercise of personal diplomacy with Khrushchev, had another unexpected consequence. It opened the door to direct negotiations between Khrushchev and Eisenhower, although such negotiations appeared highly unlikely early in 1959. Both leaders came to desire such a meeting in fairly short order, although the extent of their desires remained well hidden until the summer. By that time, Eisenhower was prepared to take some major risks for peace that he had hitherto, perhaps boxed in by Dulles's resistance, been unwilling to make. After Dulles's death on May 24, the record shows that Eisenhower became more assertive, personally, with the Soviet Union.

Melting the Ice

Henry Kissinger has written that Eisenhower "embodied that strange phenomenon in American politics by which presidents who appear to be most guileless often turn out to be the most complex."[42] To illustrate Kissinger's point, it is helpful to examine Eisenhower's response to a question posed to him by Fletcher Knebel of Cowles Newspapers at his press conference on August 3. Knebel asked Ike whether "it was just two items of correspondence, you invited him and he accepted, or was there more than that?" when it came to the issuance of the invitation to Khrushchev. To the laughter of the reporters, Eisenhower replied that "I'd say it is a little bit more complicated than that."[43] Indeed, it *was* more complicated than that and one might even argue that it was Khrushchev, instead of Eisenhower, who initially proposed the two visits when, in early July, he told several American governors who were visiting the Soviet Union that he thought an exchange of visits between himself and Eisenhower would be beneficial.

Eisenhower, for his part, was quick to pick up on the significance of these remarks by the Soviet leader. On July 10, in a meeting with Christian Herter, who had become secretary of state after the death of John Foster Dulles, Douglas Dillon, now the undersecretary of state, and Andrew Goodpaster, Ike stated that he wanted to talk personally with Khrushchev and was willing to use the opening of the Soviet Exhibition in New York as a suitable occasion for a meeting. The suggestion called for Khrushchev to open the exhibition, give a speech before the United Nations, and then remain in the United States for talks with Eisenhower. In return, Eisenhower was to visit the Soviet Union after he left India as part of his international goodwill trip in October. The invitation to Khrushchev was conditional on some progress at a future meeting of the foreign ministers, meaning that the United States would expect some concessions from the Soviets at the level of the foreign ministers, perhaps such as a willingness to agree on an agenda for the possible summit meeting.[44]

Rumors about this type of understanding between the Soviets and the Americans were circulating rapidly in the White House press corps. In fact, at the press conference on August 3, Felix Belair of the *New York Times* asked Eisenhower for confirmation of that particular understanding. As Belair asked, "The impression has somehow been received, Mr. President, that in considering a possible visit by Mr. Khrushchev to the United States, that before you would issue an invitation to him, there would have be some evidence of give [at the meetings of the foreign ministers.] I mean in the sense of give and take on the part of Mr. Khrushchev, on Western principles. May we take it that there has been some such indication?"[45]

Eisenhower answered Belair's question by, in effect, not answering the question. "No, I don't think you can say that, Mr. Belair. This is what I have said: the holding of a summit meeting and negotiation, that that would be, to my mind, absolutely impractical and as the State Department says, counterproductive unless we could count on some positive results."[46]

To make his invitation to Khrushchev, Eisenhower turned to Robert D. Murphy, then the deputy undersecretary of state for political affairs. At this point, it is worth mentioning that Eisenhower had turned to Murphy on numerous occasions to handle delicate diplomatic assignments for him. These occasions occurred as early as 1943, when Murphy served as President Franklin D. Roosevelt's representative to Ike's staff during the North African campaign. Murphy was later Eisenhower's representative at the establishment of the Allied Control Council in Germany and at the Potsdam Conference in July 1945. During Eisenhower's presidency, Ike dispatched Murphy to the Middle East in 1956 during the Suez crisis and to Lebanon in 1958 during that crisis as the person to convey the interests of the United States to leaders of the countries involved in those disputes.[47] To observers of American diplomacy, it probably came as no surprise that Eisenhower turned to Murphy, once again, as his troubleshooter in July 1959.

Murphy accordingly met with Frol Kozlov, deputy premier of the Soviet Union, on July 12 at the Soviet Exhibition in New York. Kozlov's presence in New York to open the exhibition was part of some deft bilateral diplomacy whereby Vice President Nixon opened the American exhibit in Moscow and Kozlov opened the Soviet Exhibition in New York, in the same month. "The visits of Nixon and Kozlov," according to Harrison Salisbury, "were exchanges at a slightly lesser level. The Nixon-Kozlov trips were a package arrangement and they went very, very well. It was in the course of the Nixon trip to Moscow that the United States agreed to issue an invitation to Khrushchev to visit the United States, with of course the implicit understanding that Eisenhower would pay a return trip to the Russia."[48]

Murphy gave Kozlov the letter with the offer to Khrushchev of a visit to the United States, but without mentioning the precondition of progress at the level of the foreign ministers.[49] Then, in the words of Andrew Goodpaster, "The Russians snapped it up just like that!"[50] On July 22, Khrushchev indicated his acceptance of Eisenhower's offer to visit the United States for a ten-day period, a longer visit than Eisenhower had anticipated. The fact that Khrushchev was coming to the United States without making any prior concessions on Berlin irritated the president but, as he later said, he "would have to pay the penalty" and follow through on the invitation.[51]

The matter of the issuance of these two invitations, one for Khrushchev to visit the United States and the other for Eisenhower to visit the Soviet Union, has become the subject of considerable disagreement among biographers of both Eisenhower and Khrushchev. Many of Eisenhower's biographers, including Herbert S. Parmet, Stephen E. Ambrose, and Jean

Edward Smith, have accepted the explanation advanced by Ike himself, and later reinforced by John Eisenhower, that Murphy simply failed to understand his instructions and did not establish the link between progress at the meeting of the foreign ministers and the issuance of the invitation. Aleksandr Fursenko and Timothy Naftali, two of Khrushchev's biographers, have likewise accepted this explanation.[52] Further, Andrew Goodpaster, probably the closest man to Eisenhower during that point in his presidency, expressed to the author, on two separate occasions, his firm insistence that "the State Department [meaning Murphy] dropped the ball on that one."[53] Also, in what has been described as a contentious meeting that involved Eisenhower, Murphy, Goodpaster, and Douglas Dillon, Murphy accepted the blame for the mistake, thereby receiving Ike's sharp criticism, even as these individuals went about discussing the preparations for Khrushchev's visit to the United States.[54]

Other historians and journalists who have written about this episode have drawn considerably different conclusions. For example, Campbell Craig in his book *Destroying the Village: Eisenhower and Thermonuclear War* argued that Eisenhower swung around to Macmillan's point of view on dealing with Khrushchev—a view that such issues as the Berlin situation and the escalating arms race needed to be handled through a summit meeting and direct negotiations between the heads of state of the United States, the Soviet Union, Great Britain, and France.[55] In March 1959, when Macmillan visited the United States after his meetings with Khrushchev in Russia, Ike expressed the view that he would not participate in a summit, "come hell or high water," as long as Khrushchev's ultimatum remained in effect, equating such a meeting under those conditions as akin to appeasement.[56] But, by the summer of 1959, and especially following the death of John Foster Dulles in May, Eisenhower had decided to venture into personal diplomacy as a tactic for improving relations with the Russians. In Craig's view, Eisenhower's demonstration of frustration with Murphy was an act, or as journalist Evan Thomas has written, a "charade," designed to conceal his satisfaction with the outcome of Murphy's interactions with Kozlov while also disguising the fact that he had backed down on his previous preconditions for such a meeting.[57] The fact that Ike had backed down from his previous position might explain why he talked around the question asked by Felix Belair on August 3.

Other observers, such as Khrushchev's biographer William Taubman and Jim Newton, another of Eisenhower's biographers, have supported the views of Craig and Thomas. As Taubman wrote, the story "of [Murphy's] snafu is hard to believe; indeed some historians do not believe it." Newton has written that Eisenhower, far from being disappointed with Murphy after learning of Khrushchev's acceptance of the invitation, was actually pleased. Newton quotes the reaction of Ann Whitman, Eisenhower's trusted secretary, who noted that Ike "was happy as a lad" when he learned that Khrushchev was coming to the United States.[58]

Given such disagreements over Eisenhower's strategy and tactics with the invitation to Khrushchev, it is instructive to note Murphy's recollection of the episode. In his memoir, *Diplomat among Warriors,* Murphy explained the motivation for the invitation as a tactic divorced from the tensions created by Khrushchev's ultimatum over Berlin. As Murphy wrote, "A few months before I retired from the Foreign Service, it occurred to some of my State Department colleagues and me that a substantial impact might be made on the thinking of the Soviet masses if President Eisenhower could tour the length and breadth of the Soviet Union, appearing at all kinds of public gatherings, giving interviews to the Communist press, [and] making radio and television speeches."[59] In Murphy's thinking, therefore, the key to obtaining a visit by Eisenhower to the Soviet Union was the extension of a visit by Eisenhower to Khrushchev to visit the United States. It is important to remember that Murphy had been with Eisenhower in Germany in 1945 and recalled the remarkable impact that Eisenhower had made on the Soviet people during his visit to Russia. Again, as Murphy wrote, "the name of Eisenhower had special significance for the Russian people, who associated it with American support of the Red Army and victory in World War II. Other than Roosevelt, no American name meant so much to so many Russians, and during Eisenhower's visit to Moscow in 1945, the people generously displayed their friendly sentiments."[60]

In pursuit of a far different objective than Eisenhower had in mind, therefore, in his encounter with Kozlov in New York, Murphy extended the invitation to Khrushchev, with the only qualifier being that Eisenhower would be extended an invitation to visit the Soviet Union. Significantly, in his memoir, Murphy makes no mention of any failure on his part to understand Eisenhower's instructions, nor of Eisenhower's expression of any dissatisfaction to him about his handling of the interaction with Kozlov. Murphy does credit himself, however, "with having as much to do with initiating Khrushchev's visit to the United States as anybody and I prepared the recommendation to the White House urging it."[61]

The question persists as to the intention of Eisenhower with the two invitations, and the intention of Murphy with them, since their respective accounts of the episode differ so markedly. Eisenhower was using the language of "melting some of the ice" in Soviet-American relations, searching for an accommodation with the Soviets leading to a possible détente. Murphy, on the other hand, appeared to be thinking of using Eisenhower's tremendous popularity, perhaps as evidenced by his reception by the Soviet people in 1945, as a means of advancing American interests, and even strengthening the American position (and possibly weakening the Soviet position?) vis-à-vis the Soviet Union in the Cold War. Also, the exchange of visits in 1959–1960 was faintly reminiscent of Harriman's proposal for an exchange of visits by Eisenhower and Zhukov to their respective countries in 1945. Was Murphy mindful of that overture in 1945 when he advocated the visits in 1959? Either way, one is left with the question: was Eisenhower "happy as a lad" because he now realized that Khrushchev would be coming to the United States, or that he was going to the Soviet Union?

The Outline of a Strategy

As matters stood in late summer, 1959, the outline of Eisenhower's strategy to thaw the Cold War was coming into sharper focus. The strategy consisted of four central elements: a visit by Nikita Khrushchev to the United States in September, a Four Power summit in 1960 at a date to be established, a visit by Eisenhower to the Soviet Union, and passage of the FY1961 defense budget. To make the strategy effective, Eisenhower faced two challenges. First, he needed to consult extensively with Harold Macmillan, Charles de Gaulle, and Konrad Adenauer about the timing and agenda of the summit conference and the development of a coordinated approach to Allied policy regarding the Soviet Union, especially on the issues of Berlin and divided Germany.

The Two Invitations

The second challenge was more complicated, in many respects, than the consultations with the Western allies. In October 1957, the Soviet Union had successfully launched *Sputnik,* the first satellite to orbit the earth. The success of *Sputnik* led to a near-hysterical reaction within the United States that the Soviet Union was about to overtake the United States in terms of its military capability. Eisenhower made two television addresses, one on November 7 and another on November 13, to reassure the country, and more specifically, to address the administration's critics in Congress, that the president was pursuing an effective military program.

Despite Eisenhower's assurances, fears of Russian military advances persisted in the United States during the post-*Sputnik* period. "One of Dad's errors was misunderstanding the impact of Sputnik," John Eisenhower remembered. "He expected people to be more mature than they were [and] he didn't like to have to say the same thing more than once."[62] Misplaced though they may have been, these fears led to the creation of a serious political issue, the so-called "missile gap," by the end of 1958. The missile gap and the assertion that the Soviet Union was about to overtake the United States, if it hadn't already done so, in the production and deployment of intercontinental ballistic missiles armed with nuclear warheads, was a potent political issue with a number of constituencies that were committed to its propagation. Journalists and opinion-makers, defense contractors, some active and retired military officers, presidential aspirants in both of the major political parties, and even some academics, all contributed to the persistence of the missile gap as a political issue.[63]

As the missile gap continued to attract public attention, the administration found itself increasingly on the defensive as the presidential election of 1960 approached. Within the heat of an election year, the administration needed to obtain congressional passage of its FY 1961 defense budget, as close as possible to its budgetary limits, and navigate its military program through a Congress controlled by its political opposition in the Democratic Party.

Passage of the defense budget, therefore, was essential to Eisenhower's initiative to promote détente with the Soviet Union. If the nation's defenses were not secure, so the argument went, how could Eisenhower expect to enter into agreements with the Soviet Union that might potentially jeopardize its military position relative to its primary adversary?

45

Still, Eisenhower was hopeful that his plans would succeed. When Harold Macmillan visited Washington in March 1960, Ike took him to the Civil War battlefield at Gettysburg, where the two men talked about what they perceived to be some promising changes in the international environment, including the prospect for more diplomatic interaction with the Soviet Union and, thanks to the Lacy-Zaroubin agreement, more cultural exchanges between east and west. As historian Peter G. Boyle has written, "Eisenhower looked forward to his visit to the Soviet Union. . . . [with] his itinerary of visits to the Kremlin in Moscow, the Hermitage in St. Petersburg [then Leningrad], Kiev, and finally a return to Moscow, where he was to be given an honorary degree at Moscow State University."[64]

If Eisenhower's peace initiative were to succeed, what positive results could he expect? First, there would be a relaxation of tensions between the two superpowers and their respective allies. Second, there could be a mechanism established for frequent and regularly scheduled summit meetings to discuss the obstacles that remained in the path of improved relations between the respective countries. The era of confrontation might give way to an era of negotiation, at least in the near term.[65] Third, Ike hoped that negotiations with the Soviet Union would yield some progress on slowing down the nuclear arms race and decreasing the enormous sums that the United States continued to spend on defense. The prospect of runaway defense spending was the one concern on Eisenhower's mind as he approached the end of his presidency. "God help the nation when it has a President who doesn't know as much about the military as I do," Eisenhower told Andrew Goodpaster on one occasion.[66] Could the national economy continue to absorb these unprecedented military expenditures without putting the country permanently on a wartime footing? Fourth, could improved Soviet-American relations open more than a crack into the hyper-secretive, closed nature of Soviet society and especially the motivations behind the decision-making of its leadership? In 1955, Khrushchev had wagged his finger menacingly at Eisenhower, saying "Nyet, nyet, nyet!" when Ike proposed Open Skies, an indication that the Soviets had no intention of allowing any country to look into the inner workings of the Soviet state. As Andrew Goodpaster later wrote, "The Communists, as Eisenhower often said, regarded secrecy as one of the primary elements of their military and political strength—that is, secrecy along with deception and misinformation."[67] Ike hoped that his venture into personal diplomacy would result in a better American understanding of Soviet intentions and capabilities.

And finally, the success of Ike's peace initiative would set the course for a successful presidential campaign for Richard Nixon as his successor. Despite Eisenhower's personal reservations about Nixon's leadership potential for the presidency, the vice president was still vastly preferable, in Ike's mind, to any of the Democratic Party's presidential aspirants, men such as John F. Kennedy, Lyndon B. Johnson, and Stuart Symington, all of whom were attempting to extract maximum political benefit from the issue of the missile gap. From that perspective, the Old Soldier was again prepared to make the most determined effort for peace of his presidency.

Chapter 3

Eisenhower's Peace Offensive, September–December 1959

Following the announcement on August 3, 1959, of the forthcoming exchange of visits—Premier Nikita Khrushchev to the United States and President Dwight D. Eisenhower to the Soviet Union—the Eisenhower administration began preparing to unfold Eisenhower's strategy to thaw the tensions of the Cold War. The strategy had a number of moving parts. First, Eisenhower intended to meet with his European allies—Harold Macmillan, Charles de Gaulle, and Konrad Adenauer—to discuss the Khrushchev initiative. Second, Ike needed to prepare for Khrushchev's visit to the United States, scheduled for mid to late September. Third, assuming a successful visit by Khrushchev, Eisenhower, Macmillan, de Gaulle, and Adenauer planned to meet once again to set the date and agree upon an agenda for the Four Power summit conference with the Soviet Union, anticipated in the spring of 1960.

The regimen that Eisenhower had set for himself was potentially physically exhausting, as well as prone to unforeseen diplomatic mishaps, but the president was determined to press ahead with his attempt to promote a more peaceful world. Given his normal preferences, Eisenhower most likely wished to avoid personal diplomacy, and this was personal diplomacy on a scale not witnessed since the years of Franklin D. Roosevelt during World War II. As Eisenhower later wrote in *Waging Peace*,

Ahead lay months, I knew, of strenuous work with our Western Allies, as well as with Khrushchev,—and some time later possibly a summit meeting. In many ways, especially from the viewpoint of precedent, I regretted that normal diplomatic channels, even including formal meetings among foreign ministers, were being markedly ignored. Prospects for even the slightest prospects in easing world tensions now seemed to lay, for the time being at least, in direct contacts between the heads of government.[1]

"The crowds went on and on"

On August 26, 1959, Eisenhower left Washington for West Germany and consultations with Konrad Adenauer. It was Eisenhower's first flight aboard the "new" Air Force One, a Boeing 707 jetliner. As historian Stephen Ambrose has written, Ike "was hooked" by the "exhilarating experience" of high-speed jet travel, "the silent, effortless acceleration of the new presidential aircraft."[2]

After conferring with Adenauer, Eisenhower flew to Great Britain to meet with Macmillan, and also to participate indirectly in the prime minister's political preparations in advance of a British general election. As John Foster Dulles had predicted back in February, Macmillan planned to call for a general election in September, and he was determined to make the best use of his time, politically, with Eisenhower.

Eisenhower and his party arrived at London's International Airport at Heathrow at 6:45 P.M. on August 27. Given the time of arrival, Macmillan expected only a modest turnout of well-wishers along the route to central London. He was wrong. As Macmillan recounted in his memoir, *Riding the Storm:*

> We drove together in an open car. The distance is seventeen miles. It took us nearly two hours. There was a wonderful turnout all along the route. It was a re-markable demonstration of confidence and goodwill. It was also impressive from another point-of-view. The car moved at a snail's pace. All of the roads and streets were crowded and there was no security of any kind. Most of the time

the President stood up and waved to the people, and some of the time, I stood up also and waved by his side.[3]

The Americans who were traveling with Eisenhower were likewise overwhelmed by the British response. On the ride from Heathrow to London, Andrew Goodpaster traveled in a car with Tim Bligh, an officer in the Royal Navy (who later became a personal friend). Both men were awestruck by the reception given to the president. "The crowds went on and on," Goodpaster remembered. "There was a tremendous outpouring of affection for Eisenhower, who was always a hero in Britain. But it also symbolized that the British knew that the United States was with them."[4]

Eisenhower's itinerary also included a short visit to Balmoral Castle, where he and the other Americans were guests of Queen Elizabeth II and the members of Britain's royal family. Eisenhower also traveled to Chequers, the country estate of the prime minister, to discuss Khrushchev's forthcoming visit to the United States as well as the status of the disarmament negotiations then going on between the United States and the Soviet Union.[5]

The purely political part of the visit was a joint appearance by Eisenhower and Macmillan on British television on August 31. The setting for the broadcast was the living quarters of 10 Downing Street, then undergoing renovation. It was to be a casual, extemporaneous conversation between two old friends who simply chatted about the nature of their friendship, the positive relationship between the United States and Great Britain, and the success of their talks over the previous two days.

Actually, the idea for the broadcast came during a conversation between Harold Evans, Macmillan's press secretary, and James Hagerty. Both men believed that a televised appearance by Eisenhower, in an informal setting, was the best method of publicizing his appearance throughout Great Britain. Evans also believed that Macmillan could put his skills as a conversationalist and host to great effect in a relaxed setting.[6]

But the televised broadcast was anything but extemporaneous and spontaneous. Macmillan left nothing to chance when it involved the political impact of a conversation with the leader of the Free World. First, Macmillan used the Conservative Party's paid political broadcast for his half-hour with Eisenhower. As Alexander Macmillan (Lord Stockton), a grandson of the prime minister, later told the author, Macmillan "wanted to have absolute control over the broadcast." He chose not to use the "free time" offered by the British Broadcasting Corporation for the event because he "wanted no interference" from BBC producers, directors, or reporters. Macmillan completely controlled the broadcast, including the selection of Norman Collins as the director of the program. As Alexander Macmillan recalled, "Collins was an independent film producer who actually taught my grandfather how to operate on television." In the view of Collins, the broadcast needed to come across as two leaders talking to people in their living rooms. "Ike knew what was going on and I think he felt he was being manipulated quite a long way," Alexander Macmillan remembered.[7]

Stylistic considerations aside, the broadcast was also far removed from the casual, intimate conversation that the British viewers saw on their television sets. The program was carefully scripted and, fortunately, the historical record has been preserved of this broadcast. In Eisenhower's presidential papers is the actual script for the program, including Eisenhower's handwritten notes for the event, down to Ike's final comments, "God Bless Your Gracious Queen."[8]

Intentionally, the television program touched on no controversial topics, although at one point, Macmillan pressed Eisenhower, ever so slightly, on the subject of a summit meeting involving the various heads of state. "I have always wanted a summit and I believe that your initiative [with Khrushchev] will put us into position to get it under the best conditions," Macmillan said.[9] Eisenhower demurred on Macmillan's suggestion for a summit, but he did use the occasion to state his views that the wishes of ordinary people for peace were greater than those of the national leaders. "I like to believe that people, in the long run, are going to do more to promote peace than our governments," Eisenhower told Macmillan. "Indeed I think that people want peace so much that one of these days governments had better get out of the way and let them have it."[10]

Following the broadcast, Macmillan's political opponents in the Labour Party sharply criticized him for "exploiting" Eisenhower's visit and for injecting the American president into the forthcoming general election campaign. "Blatant electioneering!" charged James Griffith, the deputy leader of the Labour Party, describing Macmillan's behavior with Eisenhower.[11] (To be fair, Secretary of State Herter met with several members of Britain's Labour Party while the Americans were in

Chapter 3

Britain.) Macmillan denied the accusations of his opponents, of course, but on September 7, after Ike had left Britain, Macmillan asked Queen Elizabeth II for a dissolution of Parliament, the first step in the start of a general election campaign, and the general election was called for October 8. Macmillan and the Tories won a surprisingly strong victory in the election, winning 365 seats in the House of Commons to Labour's 258. On October 9, Eisenhower sent a cable of congratulations to Macmillan. "I have just heard the results of yesterday's elections," Ike wrote. "I want to tell you how much I look forward to the continuation of that spirit of close friendship and cooperation which has made our association so rewarding in the past."[12]

So the question needs to be asked: did Eisenhower intentionally meddle in the British General Election in 1959? Technically, he did not, since Macmillan did not call for the election until after Eisenhower had left Great Britain and the formal political campaign was not officially underway. But most political observers in Britain believed that an election campaign was in the offing, and in the British tradition, the major political parties were making their preparations in recognition of that possibility. Macmillan's courtship of Eisenhower was politically masterful, especially since it showed that both men were on first-name terms with each other.

But Macmillan's continuation as prime minister also served Eisenhower's purposes, and his willingness to appear on television with the prime minister proved the point. British-American cooperation was essential, at the time, to American foreign policy in Europe, especially with regard to NATO. For Eisenhower's peace offensive to work in the fall of 1959, he needed British support, the type of support that he knew would come from his relationship with Macmillan.

On September 7, Dwight D. Eisenhower returned to the United States after his visits to Bonn, Paris, and London. By any measure, the consultations with Macmillan, Adenauer, and de Gaulle were productive and reassuring, at least to the extent that Eisenhower managed to convince the other three leaders that the United States did not intend to make any agreements with the Soviets behind their backs. Moreover, the receptions given to Eisenhower in Bonn, Paris, and London were massive and overwhelming. Thomas Gates, recently appointed and confirmed as the deputy secretary of defense, was in the party that accompanied

Eisenhower and he too was astonished at the receptions that Eisenhower received. "The trip from the airport in Bonn to the city should have taken about 20 minutes," Gates remembered. "It took the better part of two hours." But the reception that Ike received in West Germany was, in fact, smaller than the one he received in Paris. "The turnout [in France] was by far the greatest that it had been in all of Europe," Gates recalled. On Eisenhower's ride from Orly Airport to central Paris, de Gaulle estimated that one million Parisians turned out to welcome the President.[13]

Following Eisenhower's visit to London, John Hay Whitney, the American ambassador to Great Britain, sent a cable to Secretary Herter that described Eisenhower's presence in London. "Personal impact of President was enormous," Whitney wrote. "President was acclaimed in manner exceeding that accorded any other foreign leader in peace-time years. Normally undemonstrative British people turned out in force to greet President everywhere along the way. He left them with image of vigorous, active, and healthy President sincerely dedicated to search for peace and willing to lead his country along untried but promising paths in the quest."[14] In September 1959, the image was clear in the United States, Western Europe, and probably throughout the world: Dwight D. Eisenhower remained the man of the hour.

The Cold War Roadshow: Khrushchev in the United States

Nikita Khrushchev visited the United States on September 15–27, 1959, accompanied by his wife, Nina Petrovna, his children, and an entourage that included fifty-four people. Considering the enormous importance attached to this visit, it was impressive that Khrushchev traveled to the United States so soon after Eisenhower announced the agreement for the exchanges on August 3. Prior to Khrushchev's arrival in the United States, however, James Hagerty learned that representatives from the Soviet embassy were nervous about certain aspects of the visit. At 11 A.M. on September 14, Hagerty met with M. A. Kharlamov, press officer of the Soviet Ministry of Foreign Affairs, and Georgi Bolshakov, the Soviet Union's press liaison with the administration. Kharlamov and Bolshakov had two questions for Hagerty. First, the two Soviets questioned whether the presence of five reporters from the Free Chinese News Agency (from the Republic of China on Taiwan) might potentially "embarrass" Khrushchev were they allowed to question him at the premier's various events. Hagerty informed Kharlamov and Bolshakov that the five Chinese reporters were "accredited correspondents in the United States and [were] free to cover any news development."

The second question, somewhat similar in nature, involved Leon Volkov, who was *Newsweek* magazine's specialist on Soviet affairs. Volkov had defected from the Soviet Union in 1945 as a pilot in the Soviet air force and, since the late 1940s, had been a reporter and columnist for *Newsweek*. Volkov's reporting obviously was not considered favorably by the Kremlin. Hagerty gave the same reply to Kharlamov and Bolshakov regarding Volkov's status as he did about the Chinese reporters. In each case, he asked the Soviets if they wished to lodge a protest. None was forthcoming.

Kharlamov and Bolshakov then made another request of Hagerty. They asked if the Chinese reporters and Volkov could not "be permitted to get up in the front ranks of photographers," thereby making it more unlikely that they could ask questions of Khrushchev. Hagerty told Kharlamov that these individuals "would be treated equally with all other correspondents and that I could not make any such guarantee." By this point, it was obvious to Kharlamov and Bolshakov that their intervention with Hagerty was destined for failure. Hagerty was not through having fun with the Soviets, however. He told both officials that "when the President went to Moscow there would be news representatives of Red China covering the President and that we would have no objection since undoubtedly those Red China correspondents are accredited to cover the news in Moscow." Hagerty's comment brought a laugh, as well as a shrug of the shoulders, from Kharlamov, who added that he simply wished to call these matters to the attention of the press secretary.[15]

Journalist Peter Carlson has provided a fascinating account of Khrushchev's visit in his book, *K Blows Top*. Carlson's book also formed the basis for a compelling and entertaining documentary produced by the Public Broadcasting Service (PBS) entitled *Cold War Roadshow*.[16] Both Carlson's book and the *Cold War Roadshow* showed how the Soviet leader's presence in the United States grabbed the attention of the country. The itinerary for Khrushchev's visit called for two days of talks with Eisenhower in Washington, followed by a cross-country tour of the United States with stops in New York, Los Angeles, and San Francisco, as well as a visit to a farming community in Iowa, and then concluding with two more days of talks with Eisenhower in Washington. Eisenhower's purpose for the Khrushchev visit was clear: "I want him to see a happy people," Ike said. "I want him to see a free people, doing exactly as they choose within the limits that they must not transgress the rights of others."[17]

Once on tour, so to speak, Khrushchev reveled in the strenuous schedule that had been set out for him. Eisenhower had designated Henry Cabot Lodge, then serving as the American ambassador to the United Nations, to act as Khrushchev's official host. An astute politician, Lodge established an effective rapport with Khrushchev and the Soviet delegation, even though the tour experienced its share of tense moments. For one, out in California, Khrushchev thought that he and his family, plus his entourage, were going to be allowed to visit Disneyland, only to be informed by Lodge that security concerns prevented such a visit. Then, Norris Poulson, the mayor of Los Angeles, made a tastelessly provocative anti-Soviet speech at a luncheon given for Khrushchev.[18]

Khrushchev responded angrily to Poulson's remarks. "If you want the arms race, very well, we accept that challenge," the Soviet leader responded. "As for the output of rockets—well, they are on the assembly line."[19] After the luncheon, when queried by his son Sergei about the veracity of his "assembly line" remark, Khrushchev admitted that he had been bluffing. "It's not important how many missiles you have," Khrushchev said, "Americans just have to *believe* we have them."[20]

A more pleasant encounter occurred in California when Khrushchev visited one of the factories of IBM, the leading manufacturer of computer technology in the United States. The idea for the visit originated with Thomas J. Watson, Jr., the chief executive officer of IBM, who regarded such an event as "a surefire way to make IBM stand out."[21] Business considerations aside, he was familiar with the Soviet Union in a way that few Americans were at the time. Watson had served in the Army Air Corps during World War II and one of his assignments involved the shipment of American aircraft to Russia. He had spent several months in 1942 in Moscow. Later, in the spring of 1959, Watson visited Russia on business and walked the streets of Moscow for the first time since the war.

Chapter 3

Once Watson decided to invite Khrushchev to visit one of IBM's manufacturing facilities, he contacted the State Department, where officials expressed no opposition to such a visit but were pessimistic that Khrushchev would accept. Undeterred, Watson sent an invitation directly by telegram to Khrushchev. Watson learned nothing further about the matter until he received an urgent telephone call at his office in Armonk, New York, from Gav Cullen, the manager of IBM's plant in San Jose, California. Cullen informed Watson that two senior Soviet military officers wanted to inspect the plant in anticipation of Khrushchev's visit. Khrushchev was coming to IBM, for sure, as Watson learned from Cullen.

Watson prepared extensively for Khrushchev's visit. He quickly learned that Khrushchev was an unpopular figure within the ranks of some of IBM's employees. Following the Russian (and Khrushchev's) suppression of the anti-Soviet revolt in Hungary in 1956, and the subsequent migration of tens of thousands of Hungarian refugees to the United States and the countries of western Europe following the crackdown, IBM had, in Watson's words, "led American industry" in hiring Hungarian refugees. Antipathy toward the Soviet Union, and of Khrushchev personally, the so-called Butcher of Budapest, ran especially strong among this group of IBM's employees.[22] Watson wanted no embarrassing incidents, either for the United States or for IBM, when Khrushchev came to visit the plant in San Jose. Acting on advice from the State Department, Watson issued the following statement to the employees in San Jose: "My invitation to Premier Khrushchev is not an endorsement of his regime. I think the interests of the United States will be advanced by his visit. Anybody who objects to his visit can have two days off with pay."[23] Watson later estimated that approximately twenty employees of IBM chose to take his offer and absent themselves during Khrushchev's visit. The rest of the employees were on hand to give the Soviet Premier a proper welcome.

Khrushchev arrived at IBM's facility in San Jose shortly before lunch on September 21, 1959. Earlier that day, he had met with members of the longshoremen's union in San Francisco, who had not given him "so much as a Ritz cracker to eat."[24] Known for his legendary appetite for good food, Khrushchev was famished when he arrived at the IBM plant and, fortunately, Watson had scheduled lunch before giving the Soviet leader a tour of the factory. Despite Watson's instructions to his caterer to serve only an "average meal" for Khrushchev and the IBM employees, the caterer prepared a sumptuous meal consisting of "beautiful California salads [and] an array of cold meats that would have graced the Waldorf."[25] Khrushchev treated himself to bountiful helpings of fried chicken, potatoes, fruit salad, onion soup, orange juice, and iced tea.

Then he toured the IBM factory. Pausing to speak individually with numerous IBM employees, he also witnessed a demonstration of IBM's newest computer, entitled the RAMAC. Even this demonstration, however, had overtones of the Cold War. Watson had selected Eddie Corwin (formerly Eddie Sochaczewski), a Polish immigrant who had served in the Polish cavalry during World War II, been captured by the Nazis, and then endured six years as a prisoner-of-war, to make the presentation. Given twenty minutes to make his presentation to Khrushchev, Corwin planned to use the last five minutes of his time to ask Khrushchev about the status of Polish exiles in the Soviet Union. Watson bluntly informed Corwin that such questions were out of order, since Khrushchev was a guest of IBM. Corwin grudgingly gave Watson his "word of honor" that he would not pursue the subject and the demonstration proceeded in that fashion.[26] But, judging from Khrushchev's response to the day's program at IBM, what attracted the premier the most was the efficiency of the IBM cafeteria, not the efficiency of IBM's production lines.

"We, too, have lots of telephones"

Once Nikita Khrushchev returned to Washington, he and Eisenhower began their final negotiations prior to the Soviet leader's departure. These talks provided the last opportunity for the president to "get inside Khrushchev's head," in the words of Andrew Goodpaster, and make some progress that hitherto had eluded the diplomats in both countries.[27] What quickly became evident in the interactions between Khrushchev and the Americans, however, was the Soviet leader's extreme sensitivity to any implication that his country was not the equal of the United States. Three examples occurred that revealed the nature of Khrushchev's sensitivity.

First, one of the enduring memories of the Khrushchev visit were the rides that he took in Eisenhower's presidential helicopter. The impetus for these travels came from Eisenhower's desire to give Khrushchev an aerial view of the nation's capital and see the bustling commerce of the local traffic as well as the expanse of homes in the city and in the suburbs. So despite some initial misgivings from Khrushchev's security detail about flying in an American helicopter, Khrushchev agreed to accompany Eisenhower in flights over the city, as well as to and from Camp David, the presidential retreat in Maryland, where the negotiations between the two men were scheduled. General Vernon Walters, Eisenhower's translator, recalled one testy exchange between the two men on one helicopter flight during the Washington rush hour. From the air, Khrushchev looked out of the helicopter and saw the enormous volume of cars on the roads, as well as the multitude of private homes in the various neighborhoods. "What a waste! What a waste!" he said to Eisenhower. "What waste?" Eisenhower asked. "All of those people riding to and from work—they should be riding buses and saving gasoline," Khrushchev contended. And, according to the Soviet leader, "All these people living in private homes when they should be living in apartment houses and saving land for agricultural production."

By this point, Ike had had enough: "Agricultural production? Don't talk to me about agricultural production. . . . We've both got an agricultural problem. Yours is shortages and ours is the surpluses for which we pay a billion dollars [in] storage a year. You know, our people want to drive their own cars; and our people want to live in individual homes; and in our system we try and give people what they want rather than tell them what's good for them." Khrushchev stood his ground: "Well, my people don't want private automobiles," he said, to which Eisenhower replied, "If you really believe that, I don't know how long you'll occupy your job."[28]

The second example concerned the presidential helicopter itself. It quickly became evident to the Americans that Khrushchev admired the helicopter and gladly accepted one as a gift from Eisenhower before he returned to the Soviet Union. Back in the Soviet Union, however, Khrushchev insisted that the military build him a helicopter like Eisenhower's, instead of the "great big lumbering machines," to quote Harrison Salisbury, that Khrushchev was forced to use. To Khrushchev, the presidential helicopter was a symbol of a "very advanced state and he was always saying that Russia had to be more advanced than the United States." So, to the exasperation and even anger of the Soviet military, the

Russian military spent a year designing and constructing a helicopter for Khrushchev that resembled Eisenhower's chopper.[29]

A third example involved an incident that occurred during one of the luncheons at Camp David for the two delegations. John N. (Jack) Irwin, the assistant secretary of defense for international security affairs, was present at this particular luncheon and recalled the following episode. "Eisenhower, at [the] luncheon was just making conversation [with Khrushchev] and I think a phone call had just come," Irwin remembered. Eisenhower excused himself from the table and went into another room to take the call. "After the President came back from the phone call, he said [to Khrushchev], 'Do you have the same nuisances with telephones that we do? It seems to me that we're always having to answer telephones. It's a real problem.'" Khrushchev, completely misunderstanding the nature of Eisenhower's comment, was immediately offended by Ike's question about "having telephones." "Clearly out of a sense of insecurity," Irwin recalled, Khrushchev shot back, "We too have lots of telephones," as though the United States was not the only country with an advanced system of telephones.[30]

When Eisenhower and Khrushchev met at Camp David, central to the discussion was the status of Berlin—and Khrushchev's lingering ultimatum. But Khrushchev, anxious for a summit meeting with Eisenhower and the other Western leaders, was hardly as dogmatic and inflexible on the issue as he had been even six months previously. As Goodpaster later wrote, Khrushchev maintained that "it was not really an ultimatum," but rather a method for the Soviets and the East Germans to prevent the migration of "well trained educated people" out of the Communist bloc into the safety of West Germany. But to Eisenhower, the migration of people who were fleeing Communist rule was Khrushchev's problem, not his. Ike said that he would resign the presidency before he would accept any time limit on American withdrawal from Berlin.[31] Finally, Khrushchev agreed to drop the ultimatum on Berlin, essentially as the price he was willing to pay for Eisenhower's agreement to participate in a summit with the other heads of state.

So, in important respects, the talks between Eisenhower and Khrushchev at Camp David and in Washington revealed Khrushchev's willingness to remove the dispute over Berlin as an obstacle to further negotiations. Also, in what seemed at the time to be a relatively minor decision, both leaders agreed to postpone Ike's visit to the Soviet Union until after the summit conference ended in the spring of 1960.[32] It was obvious that Khrushchev, having received what he perceived to be a warm welcome from Eisenhower in the United States, was obviously welcoming the prospect of a visit by the president to the Soviet Union. Eisenhower had taken Khrushchev to his farm at Gettysburg and introduced him to his son, John, John's wife, Barbara, and their four children, David, Barbara Ann, Susan, and Mary Jean. Khrushchev relished his encounter with the entire Eisenhower family and, upon departing the United States, told the president to have his grandchildren accompany him when he came to the Soviet Union in 1960. "I'll bring the whole family," Eisenhower said. "You'll have more Eisenhowers there than you [will] know what to do with."[33]

As Khrushchev's plane left Washington for the flight back to Moscow, Eisenhower realized that he had completed the first element in the strategy: a successful visit by Khrushchev to the United States and the removal of the ultimatum over Berlin. Back in Moscow, Khrushchev announced to the crowd upon his landing at Vnukovo Airport, "I have gained the impression that [Eisenhower] sincerely wants to see the end of the Cold War. I am confident that we can do a great deal for peace." And then, reminiscent of Ike's visit to the Soviet Union in 1945, Khrushchev exclaimed, "Long live Soviet-American friendship."[34]

Project Lida Rose

Khrushchev's successful visit to the United States provided some definite momentum to the scheduling of the summit meeting of heads of state in 1960. Eisenhower followed up with a letter to Khrushchev on November 2, 1959, informing him that he planned to meet with Harold Macmillan, Charles de Gaulle, and Konrad Adenauer in Paris on December 19 to begin discussions about the date and the agenda for the meeting.[35] Then, on November 28, 1959, Eisenhower sent another letter to Khrushchev, this time exploring the subject of his return visit to the Soviet Union. "I am anxious to begin to think in more concrete terms about the date and arrangements for my return of your visit to the United States," Ike wrote. "I have reviewed my schedule and, having in mind your suggestion with respect to the timing of my visit, i.e., May or June, I would now plan to leave this country on the night of June 9 to stay a week to ten days in your country."[36] Continuing in the letter, Eisenhower informed Khrushchev that he had received an invitation to visit Japan for two days following his trip to the Soviet Union. Eisenhower wished to leave for Japan "direct from the Soviet Union and then return to the United States via the Pacific." By taking such a route, Ike then would be able to "visit some of the points of interest in the central and eastern parts of your country" before leaving for Japan.[37]

Ike's suggestion to Khrushchev that he depart the Soviet Union through an eastern route raised some red flags in the leadership of the Red Army. Fearful that Air Force One would be equipped with aerial surveillance technology (which it was) that could photograph Soviet military installations (which it could), the Soviet military preferred that Eisenhower travel across the Soviet Union in Russian planes, and then switch planes to Air Force One from a far eastern location. Such a stipulation was unacceptable to the Americans, of course, for obvious security reasons.

Nevertheless, Khrushchev was willing to accommodate Ike's wishes. Eisenhower wrote to Khrushchev on December 3, 1959, to allay the premier's concerns. "I am grateful for your consideration of my suggestion that I might, on my visit to Russia, go out through Siberia," Eisenhower said. "There is no hurry about the matter, and I shall await your further decision. I do want to assure you personally that I had no military consideration of any kind in mind, but made the suggestion simply as what seemed to be the best way to get more easily to Tokyo."[38]

Despite Eisenhower's disavowal of "any military consideration" in his request, that disavowal did not extend to Allen Dulles, who saw the potential for converting Air Force One into a reconnaissance aircraft. Along with the Soviet Union's tight secrecy, Dulles was increasingly concerned about the extensive network of espionage that the Soviets built and maintained not only in the United States but also among the Western allies. During the 1950s, 360 people had been convicted of espionage for the Soviet Union in the United States, Finland, France, the Netherlands, Japan, Norway, Sweden, Canada, Turkey, the United Kingdom, and West Germany.[39]

The extent of Soviet espionage was vexing to Eisenhower, also. "We would have to expose all our intelligence sources and methods in order to obtain a conviction [for espionage]," Eisenhower told the National Security Council in May 1960. "Even if convicted, a spy could probably be sentenced to only six years and be replaced by six more spies. In this situation about all the FBI can do is keep spies under surveillance."[40] The open nature of American society provided countless opportunities for Soviet agents to discover the details of much of America's national security apparatus.

Dulles was convinced that one technique the Soviets employed was to turn the aircraft used by emissaries of Soviet bloc countries and Soviet officials posted to the United Nations into reconnaissance aircraft with aerial photographic capabilities built into their structures. In fact, at the time of the U-2 crisis (see chapter six, below) in May 1960, the FBI had discovered an attaché with the Czech embassy taking photographs of American military installations from flights on commercial planes. Dulles also believed that the TU-144 airplane used by Khrushchev to fly to the United States had a similar capability.[41] It was a de facto low-budget and low-tech method of espionage, but its effectiveness was potentially very great.

Given such suspicions, Allen Dulles proposed to retrofit Eisenhower's Air Force One into a similar aircraft. The name given to this exercise was Project Lida Rose, named after a song from the popular musical *The Music Man* that was then playing in the United States. The CIA took control of Eisenhower's presidential airplane and moved it to a secret hangar at Andrews Air Force Base. Under the tightest security and at a cost estimated at $1,000,000, the CIA's mechanics and technicians installed high-resolution cameras and electronic control mechanisms in the belly of Air Force One's fuselage.[42]

In its test flights, the retrofitted Air Force One flew at 30,000 feet and took photographs that were so precise that the CIA's photo-interpreters could read the numbers on license plates on automobiles moving across the highways.[43] In their recounting of Project Lida Rose, Jerald F. Ter Horst and Ralph Albertazzie leave open the question of whether Eisenhower knew about Project Lida Rose, thereby giving himself a measure of "deniability" if word about the secret project ever came to light.[44] However, had Eisenhower's trip to the Soviet Union not been canceled, it's clear that that Air Force One would have brought back valuable strategic information obtained through this unique and innovative project.

The Western Summit and the King of Nepal

Between December 19 and 21, 1959, Eisenhower, Macmillan, de Gaulle, and Adenauer met in Paris to discuss the upcoming arrangement for the summit meeting of the heads of state of the United States, the Soviet Union, Great Britain, and France. This conference involving the four leaders has occasionally been referred to as the "Western Summit" and, considering the important subjects that were discussed at the conference, has received surprisingly little attention from scholars. The first meeting of the four leaders took place on Saturday, December 19. After de Gaulle made the welcoming statements, Macmillan took the initiative in outlining the business of the conference: the date of the summit meeting, the place of the meeting, the composition of the note inviting Khrushchev to attend the meeting, and the matter of setting an agenda for the meeting.

When the subject turned to disarmament as a possible item on the agenda, Eisenhower made a statement that was bound to startle his colleagues. Ike explained that he had changed his thinking about disarmament in recent months. At the time, when the United States had a monopoly on nuclear weapons, discussions about disarmament had focused on the destruction of nuclear stockpiles. But now, Eisenhower argued, the emphasis should be on inspection and control of the testing of nuclear weapons, rather than the abolition of these weapons. The summit meeting might provide an opportunity to take a step in that direction.[45]

The four leaders then turned to a discussion of the time and place for the meeting, a conversation that must have seemed exasperating to the participants. First, as to place, Macmillan initially proposed Paris as a site. President de Gaulle then inquired as to the best time for the meeting. Adenauer then suggested Geneva as a possible location, a logical suggestion in view of the fact that Switzerland was a neutral country and since Geneva was the site of summit conference in 1955, "the facilities were available there."[46]

Macmillan again joined the discussion, mentioning the possibility of a series of summits to be held on a fairly regular basis, "rotating between the capitals: Paris, Washington, and London" and, perhaps later, even Moscow. Perhaps to Macmillan's surprise, Eisenhower replied "that this could be so."[47] Macmillan opposed the choice of Geneva as the site for a summit, since negotiations there had never been successful and it would be good to break "the curse on Geneva, where nothing ever seemed to go right."[48] Charles de Gaulle agreed; the city was too crowded and Khrushchev could hardly be expected to like Geneva (even though the Soviets had come to Geneva without complaint in 1955) with its Calvinist history.[49] Paris was the final choice.

Even before this rather roundabout discussion on the choice of location for the summit, the four leaders had another tedious conversation. The notes of Amory Houghton, the American ambassador to France, who was attending the meeting, provide a record of the conversation:

> Discussion timing conference then ensued. After some discussion de Gaulle indicated that he would like to come to the US prior to the summit meeting. April 19–23 were indicated as possible dates for de Gaulle to visit US. President said he would attempt to have the King of Nepal's visit [moved] up to April 22–24. Summit conference would then be held April 27–May 1. Macmillan said he could even continue on May 2 but repeat not beyond as he had Commonwealth Prime Ministers meeting May 3–14. All parties agreed there would be fixed termination date for conference. De Gaulle said he would have liked to have summit conference in May, while Macmillan would have preferred mid-April. Note: on the May 2 issue, Eisenhower explained that this 'would be moving the King of Nepal and he had already been moved several times.' Subject to checking there was general agreement on April 27–May 1 and it was also agreed that there would be a western summit April 26.[50]

Reflecting on the discussion, in retrospect, it is intriguing to note the importance that Eisenhower attached to keeping his date for meeting with the King of Nepal, Mahendra Bir Bikram Shah Dev, especially considering the stakes involved in the forthcoming summit meeting. During the discussion, Ike mentioned that Nepal "was a country on the verge of being gobbled up" in border disputes with both China and with India, and the United States was "anxious to reassure Nepal [of American support]."[51] Eisenhower had become aware of Nepal's anxieties during his recent visit to India and had not been able to visit Nepal but had sent a message to the king, opening up the possibility of his coming to the United States.[52] Macmillan supported Eisenhower on the subject of his contacts with the King of Nepal, stating that he "shared the United States' view about the importance of Nepal and that the King of Nepal was himself coming on a state visit to the United Kingdom later in the year."[53] Nevertheless, Eisenhower's commitment to his meeting with the King of Nepal essentially ruled out the possibility of holding the summit in late April, a circumstance that was later to have fateful consequences.

Another problem quickly presented itself with the proposed date of April 27–May 1. The four leaders had overlooked May 1 as May Day in the Soviet Union and that Khrushchev certainly expected to spend the national holiday in Moscow. To accommodate Khrushchev, therefore, the date of the summit conference was moved ahead to May 16.[54] Once the four leaders moved to a date in mid-May, they dropped the suggestion of holding a Western summit before the meeting in Paris.

The agenda for the summit conference was left somewhat vague in the discussions between Eisenhower, Macmillan, de Gaulle, and Adenauer. Eisenhower initially proposed to limit the agenda to "disarmament and related questions." Both de Gaulle and Adenauer wanted to include the status of divided Germany, but Eisenhower and Macmillan did not support this suggestion.[55] Regarding Germany, Eisenhower expressed a preference to study the "situation to see what could be done if the Soviets attempted to starve out Berlin while technically respecting our right of access to our garrisons there."[56] Sensing what he perceived to be a lack of resolve on the part of the other leaders, Adenauer emotionally argued that Berlin was "a symbol and yielding there would [bring] fatal results for the West."[57] Seeing the difficulties inherent in the German situation, though, the four leaders finally decided to limit their discussions at the summit to the issue of disarmament.

On December 29, 1959, Eisenhower wrote to Khrushchev, noting his satisfaction with Khrushchev's agreement to attend the summit conference and suggesting the date of May 16, 1960 for the beginning of the conference in Paris. Khrushchev responded to Eisenhower on the following day, December 30, 1959, stating that the date was acceptable to him.[58] With the agreement for the conference now in hand, another step forward had been taken toward the achievement of the second element of Eisenhower's strategy, a successful summit conference with Khrushchev.

On January 12, 1960, Eisenhower wrote to Khrushchev again, suggesting the dates for his visit to the Soviet Union. Ike proposed to visit

Chapter 3

Russia from June 10 to 14, 1960, arriving in Moscow on June 9 and departing for Japan on June 14. He thanked Khrushchev for arranging for his departure from the Soviet Union from Irkutsk in Siberia, using Air Force One. Clearly, Khrushchev was willing to make concessions in an effort to make Ike's visit successful.[59]

Next, Eisenhower sent Khrushchev another letter on January 21, 1960, in which he outlined the places that he wished to visit while in the Soviet Union. "I should particularly like to see, in addition to Moscow, Kiev, and in the Lake Baikal region, Irkutsk. Of course, if time would permit I would also like very much to go back briefly to Leningrad, but would omit that visit if in your judgment some other area would be better."[60] In this letter, Eisenhower also confirmed that Khrushchev agreed that he could use Air Force One for his flights across the Soviet Union. "This [request to use Air Force One] must have presented some problems for you, and I am grateful for your efforts to accommodate my request," Ike wrote.[61]

"But what could happen?"

At the end of 1959, the diplomatic environment between the Western allies and the Soviet Union had changed remarkably. The year had begun with considerable anxiety about the ultimatum Nikita Khrushchev had set down about the status of East Berlin. Direct communication between the leaders of the Western Allies and the Soviet Union was virtually nonexistent. By December, the international climate had shifted noticeably. Earlier in the year, Macmillan and Khrushchev had engaged in direct negotiations in Moscow during Macmillan's visit in February and March. Eisenhower had engaged in direct talks with Khrushchev during the Soviet leader's visit to the United States in September. Under pressure from Eisenhower, Khrushchev had withdrawn the ultimatum over Berlin and Eisenhower had expressed his willingness to participate in a forthcoming summit conference with the Soviet Union in the spring of 1960.

Other significant, but less noticeable, gestures had also taken place. For example, Eisenhower and Khrushchev exchanged gifts as an outgrowth of their meetings in Washington. While visiting Eisenhower's farm at Gettysburg, Pennsylvania, Khrushchev complimented Eisenhower on his impressive herd of Black Angus cattle, saying that he wished to improve the industry of cattle breeding in the Soviet Union. Eisenhower responded by generously agreeing to send Khrushchev one of the heifers from his Black Angus herd. Later, Admiral Lewis Strauss, the chairman of the Atomic Energy Commission, also agreed to send Khrushchev a young bull and another heifer from his herd of Black Angus as a further gesture of friendship.[62]

In response, once he returned to the Soviet Union, Khrushchev arranged to send Ike a gift of shrubs and seedlings native to the Soviet Union. Eisenhower accepted Khrushchev's gift as "an enduring souvenir of your visit [to the United States] and our talks."[63] Khrushchev also sent Eisenhower some gifts of Russian toys to be used as Christmas presents for the Eisenhower grandchildren. Ike promised Khrushchev that the gifts "will make for a Happy Christmas but, in accordance with tradition, these presents will remain a secret until discovered by them on Christmas morning."[64]

Despite the positive talks in Moscow and Washington, however, as well as the gestures of goodwill between the various leaders, the fact remained that no diplomatic breakthroughs, either on the status of divided Germany or on disarmament, had yet occurred. Presumably, the forthcoming summit and perhaps future negotiations between the heads of state on those topics would yield progress leading to a more peaceful world. Yet, the early stages of what Eisenhower's advisers had hopefully described as The Great Thaw had started to take shape. Eisenhower's spirits were rejuvenated by the prospect of positive changes in the international environment.[65] Khrushchev was of a similar mind, as Sergei Khrushchev has recounted. "Father thought that the world situation encouraged hope for a successful summit—if nothing went wrong, naturally," he wrote. "But what could happen?"[66] At the beginning of 1960, the strategy of personal diplomacy appeared to be opening doors toward a more optimistic future.

Chapter 4

Preparations, January–May 1960

Preparations for President Dwight D. Eisenhower's visit to the Soviet Union began early in the spring of 1960. The preparations were extremely complex but essentially dealt with communications between the State Department and the American embassy in Moscow about the itinerary for Eisenhower's visit, and between James Hagerty, Eisenhower's press secretary, and the embassy about arrangements for members of the American and international press who were to cover the visit. Hans Tuch, as the embassy's press and cultural attaché, drew the responsibility for working with Hagerty and the White House Press Office while Secretary of State Christian Herter and Undersecretary of State Douglas Dillon, communicating with Llewellyn Thompson, the American ambassador to the Soviet Union, handled the details of the president's itinerary and his various engagements.

At the beginning of 1960, the omens were promising for a productive visit by Eisenhower to the Soviet Union in June, given the exchange of gifts between Eisenhower and Khrushchev at Christmas and their subsequent correspondence regarding the plans for the forthcoming trip. Then, between February 7 and 9, 1960, Henry Cabot Lodge, the United States ambassador to the United Nations, visited the Soviet Union in a nonofficial capacity as a tourist. Notwithstanding this status, Lodge held a series of lengthy conversations with Khrushchev and the two men discussed the forthcoming summit conference in Paris as well as Eisenhower's visit. Even given Lodge's status as a tourist, Khrushchev reminded the American ambassador that a "politician was always a politician and always available to talk politics." Khrushchev treated Lodge, his American host on his previous visit to the United States, with "great cordiality" and told him that Eisenhower would be free to travel anywhere in the Soviet Union, including to military bases. Eisenhower was also free to travel to Siberia "if he wished to."[1]

On the subject of the summit conference, Khrushchev made an interesting observation. Sounding somewhat like Harold Macmillan, Khrushchev expressed the opinion that the Paris summit might be the first in a "series" of summits in which meetings of this type could be conducted on a regular basis. In that respect, these meetings would be expected to involve Eisenhower's successor, whoever that might turn out to be.

Another morale booster occurred on February 18, 1960, when Mikhail Menshikov, the Soviet ambassador to the United States, brought a delegation of Soviet visitors, led by Dimitri Polyansky, a member of the Presidium of the Soviet government's Central Committee, to the White House for a conversation with the president. Accompanying Polyansky were nine other Soviet officials. The delegation was on a three-week tour of various places in the United States, giving special attention to farms, factories, schools, and leaders of state governments in eight states, among them Illinois, Colorado, North Dakota, and Florida.

At the beginning of the meeting, Polyansky presented Eisenhower with a medal of the Soviet icebreaker *Lenin,* with a space ship on the back of the medal. In presenting the medal to Eisenhower, Polyansky said that it "was made of amber and symbolized the breaking-up of the ice of the cold war."[2] Eisenhower responded to Polyansky by saying that "breaking up the ice of the cold war would certainly be a great relief to him."[3] The conversation moved amicably on to other subjects, including the exchange of Christmas gifts between Eisenhower and Khrushchev. Polyansky then said that he wished to convey the warm regards of Premier Khrushchev to Eisenhower and his family. "Chairman Khrushchev frequently speaks of his friendship with the President and its importance to Soviet-American relations," Polyansky observed. "The President would be received as a most welcome guest on his forthcoming trip to the USSR."[4] The meeting ended with Polyansky's comment to Eisenhower that the Americans whom he had met impressed him as "talented, hardworking [people] who wanted peace." For his part, Eisenhower spoke positively of the benefits of exchanges between Soviet and American citizens. "People like to meet people," Ike said, "and want to find a common language." He asked Polyansky to convey his "warm greetings" to Khrushchev and his family.[5]

The Environment in Moscow

The staff of the American embassy in Moscow was small and, given the realities of the Cold War, the Americans worked in a mostly hostile environment. As a reporter for *Time* magazine wrote in 1962, "The grimy, grey ten-story U.S. Embassy is always under siege. From nearby apartments all visitors are watched. The embassy staff is permanent prey for Soviet plainclothesmen (even children are sometimes shadowed by police), and telephone 'bugs' in offices and homes are taken for granted. Though social contacts with Russian officials have become easier . . . the tiny (about 200) U.S. diplomatic colony still lives and works in oppressive isolation."[6]

Hans Tuch and his family personally experienced this oppressive isolation. "It was very restricted," Tuch recalled. "We were very circumscribed. We were never left alone without the KGB 'goons,' as we called them, following us and being with us every moment of the day and night when we went out. Even when you went to the theater or to the opera, the ballet, they would always be with you."[7]

Even so, diplomatic service in Moscow at the height of the Cold War had its compensations as far as the staff of the American embassy was concerned. "It was an ideal American embassy," Hans Tuch recalled. "You had no hierarchy, you had no protocol. It was a small embassy. I counted—we had 14 substantive officers in the embassy, other than the military. There were 14 substantive officers, there were 16 military officers, and there were about ten administrative types in the embassy, and that was it. . . . We were all working stiffs. . . . [It] was a very tight, very small, very collegial type of embassy in those days."[8]

The American ambassador to the Soviet Union was Llewellyn (Tommy) Thompson, a veteran diplomat who entered the United States Foreign Service in 1928 after graduating with a degree in economics from the University of Colorado. He served in Russia during World War II as the second secretary in the embassy. During his first posting to the Soviet Union, Thompson became fluent in Russian. Appointed ambassador in 1957, by 1960 Thompson had become highly respected for his knowledge of the Soviet Union and especially for the personal rapport he had established with Nikita Khrushchev. Thompson's many admirers often referred to his "unruffled diplomatic style," a quality that was later to be tested in 1960. Under Thompson's low-key leadership style, the American embassy functioned "smoothly with no great drama," according to one diplomat assigned to Moscow at the time. "Everyone knew what they had to do," the diplomat recalled. Thompson "relied on . . . people doing their job."[9]

Thompson was also renowned as a "skillful poker player, routinely winning $300–400/session when playing some of the American correspondents [who were] stationed in Russia at the time."[10] Thompson continued the custom of Sunday night poker games at Spaso House, the ambassador's residence in Moscow. The poker games had begun when Charles "Chip" Bohlen was the American ambassador and, as Bohlen's successor, Thompson invited sixteen players, drawn from the diplomatic community in Moscow, journalists, and officials at the American embassy, to the weekly contests. One diplomat who played poker both during Bohlen's tenure and Thompson's remembered that the experience was different after Thompson arrived in Moscow. "Bohlen played poker to have fun," the diplomat recalled. "Thompson wanted to win."[11]

For both the staff of the American embassy and officials in the Soviet Union's Ministry of Foreign Affairs (MFA), Tommy Thompson was the indispensable American in Moscow. As Vladimir Toumanoff, a political officer in the American embassy, once described the ambassador, "Thompson had established a truly almost unbelievable degree of confidence and trust with this extraordinary personality called Khrushchev." In Toumanoff's opinion, Khrushchev only trusted two people in the Soviet Union: his wife, Nina Petrovna, and Tommy Thompson. "With Thompson, [Khrushchev] knew he would not be deceived, not be lied to, and that he would get accurate, thoughtful information and opinion—that Thompson genuinely represented the United States government, the President, and that he had the President's confidence and was the epitome of what an Ambassador should be."[12]

Chapter 4

In March, Thompson was brought into the preparations for Eisenhower's visit when Secretary of State Christian Herter cabled him on March 14, asking for Thompson's "urgent advice" on Eisenhower's proposed itinerary and the content of the numerous speeches and remarks that Eisenhower was expected to make during the various events that would be scheduled for him in Russia. Thompson responded immediately, cabling back to Herter on March 15. Acknowledging that the "general line of [the] President's speech will of course be affected by [the] outcome of [the] Summit Conference," Thompson suggested that Eisenhower's comments should reflect "our understanding of 'peaceful coexistence' and 'Cold War' with particular emphasis on our concept of one world with diverse individual national cultures and political and social systems in contrast to Soviet concepts of two hostile camps of which one must in the end prevail."[13]

Continuing along that theme, Thompson explained to Herter that Eisenhower's remarks could also focus on the idea that "few bilateral problems between Soviet Union exist and that our difficulties arise out of problems involving other countries (i.e. Germany) and out of conflict between our respective systems and beliefs."[14] The ambassador also stressed that Eisenhower could refer to the progress made by the two leaders when Khrushchev visited the United States in 1959. In addition, Thompson stated that Eisenhower could argue that these problems "can and must be overcome" as both leaders moved further along in their common desire for peace.[15]

In contrast, the ambassador also pointed out areas that Eisenhower needed to avoid in his public comments, including matters that included "concrete references to Soviet internal system which might imply we seek overthrow [of the] present regime and that he should also avoid remarks which might tend to weaken Khrushchev's personal position in [the] Soviet regime."[16] Thompson did believe, however, that Eisenhower could use the occasion to point out how American democracy functioned and how the Soviet people often received a "distorted image" of the American system. Concluding his cable, Thompson explained that "There are many pitfalls to be avoided and should any advance drafts of President's remarks become available I should welcome opportunity to submit comments."[17]

Preparations

The Emergence of James Hagerty

While Thompson and the staff of the American embassy wrestled with the details of Eisenhower's itinerary and the content of his remarks in Russia, James Hagerty was dealing with the arrangements for the American and international press coverage of the presidential visit. He soon discovered that he faced a staggering task, given the sheer number of the reporters who would be assigned to cover Eisenhower's visit. In March, therefore, Hagerty reached out to the press for any suggestions about how to handle their coverage of the visit. Not surprisingly, suggestions from the press were not long in coming.

On March 30, Hagerty received a letter from Elmer W. Lower, the manager of special events for the National Broadcasting Company (NBC) about its concerns. "Dear Jim," Lower wrote, "Ray Scherer has told me that you would welcome any questions we have concerning coverage of President Eisenhower's trip to Russia in June. I have attached a rather long list." Long it was, with ten separate questions for radio coverage of the visit, nine questions for news film for television, and six questions for live television. Uppermost in Lower's mind was the matter of any possible censorship by the Soviets of Eisenhower's remarks as well as the technical capacities of Soviet broadcasting and its ability to coordinate with American facilities.[18]

Other reporters also wrote to Hagerty, giving their assessment of the problems that they encountered when they covered Vice President Richard Nixon's visit to the Soviet Union in July 1959. On April 4, for example, Robert Pierpoint of Columbia Broadcasting System (CBS) News wrote to Hagerty, listing a number of his concerns. "We are planning extensive coverage with many people going over in advance," Pierpoint wrote. "Our biggest worry is transportation and communication with these people inside Russia. Most of them will be leapfrogging ahead of the President to set up camera coverage, arrange shipping problems, plan spot sound reportages, etc. They will need all the cooperation you might be able to squeeze from the Russian government."[19]

Hagerty also received another lengthy letter on April 4 from John Scali, a reporter for the Associated Press (AP), outlining the numerous problems that the press corps encountered during the Nixon visit. "As per your suggestions," Scali wrote to Hagerty, "here is a brief rundown on some of the problems that came up in Russia while covering Vice President Nixon. I will try to limit this to the practical, off-beat problems, completely confident that you have foreseen and will handle the others."[20]

In his letter to Hagerty, Scali focused on four major problem areas that the press encountered during the Nixon visit: making collect telephone calls, sending cable copy, staffing of phones and cable points, and special desks for reporters in hotel lobbies. Taken together, these problem areas visibly demonstrated the acute shortage of communications technology that existed in the Soviet Union by contrast with the technology that the reporters were accustomed to in the United States.

First, on the matter of making collect telephone calls, Scali wrote that "Sometimes the [Soviet] operators would allow you to make collect telephone calls to London, Paris, and other Western points so you could dictate your stories [and] sometimes they would NOT."[21] This practice handicapped the reporters considerably because sometimes the Russian operators demanded that the press pay in cash, in advance, before the calls were placed. Scali estimated that 98 percent of all wire copy went via phone lines. The uncertainty about whether the operators would place these calls meant that the reporters needed to carry "big wads of cash" and, as Scali explained, "how many rubles can you carry?" Scali told Hagerty to insist from the Soviets that "any reporter assigned to cover the president could make collect calls to his office merely by informing the operator of his wishes."

Second, the reporters wanted to charge the expenses for their cable copy directly to the account of their newspaper(s), or in the case of a news service such as the AP or United Press International (UPI). Instead the Russians insisted that each reporter bring the cable copy directly to the filing desk in the lobby of the Ukraine Hotel for transmissions from Moscow. The Russians also insisted on cash payment for the cable copy before it could be transmitted. As Scali reported, "If you sought to charge [the expense] to an account such as the AP's, [the Soviet officials] would act bewildered." This laborious process inevitably led to delay in the filing of stories and the Soviet officials would not inform the reporters whether their stories had been sent. Questions of Soviet censorship also entered into the picture, leading to mistrust, confusion, and frustration all around. Scali urged Hagerty to insist that the cable copy of reporters be transmitted using the account of the publishing organizations and that the reporters be notified promptly of any delay in the transmission of their stories.[22]

Third, Scali noted the problem of inadequate staffing by the Soviets of telephones and cable points. This particular problem created consternation for the American reporters who were along to cover Nixon. As Scali explained: "In some places the Soviets only had two people dealing with some 100 reporters clamoring for telephones and shoving copy at them. Cable filing points were usually in the lobby of hotels. Reporters would queue up in lines which move[d] agonizingly slow. In Leningrad, for example, the same girl had to clear outgoing telephone calls, accept the money for them in advance, accept and count wordage for each dispatch. I will never forget Al Otten (*Wall Street Journal*) standing before that gal for 90 minutes while she laboriously counted each word of his dispatch. As soon as the phone would ring, she would answer it, talk in Russian for about five minutes and then resume counting from the beginning again—vuhn, two, trees (sic) . . . while Otten screamed."[23]

Scali's solution to this problem: he urged Hagerty to insist that the Soviets have at least six officials at each filing station, and cable point, who were authorized to accept copy; *all* (Scali's emphasis) of the officials to be fluent in English, and the Soviet foreign ministry or press office designated a person at each filing station to handle unexpected difficulties.[24]

Fourth, Scali told Hagerty to urge the Soviets to appoint administrative staff who could "expedite turning in and getting your passport back, getting room assignments, changing money, and solving other problems." The reporters covering Nixon found themselves folded into the schedules for other guests of the Soviet Union, including 1200 visitors from Ukraine, for example, whose presence slowed down the normal routine of press coverage of the Nixon visit. As Scali recorded, on one occasion, "It took two hours and 40 minutes to pay the plane fare for flying around inside Russia." Qualified administrative staff were essential, in Scali's estimation, to streamline the procedures that the working press followed as they reported on Eisenhower's travels. After presenting a thorough discussion of the problems that the press encountered, and the recommended solutions, Scali closed his letter to Hagerty, writing "Best regards (and Good luck.)"[25]

Chapter 4

Setting Up Ike's Itinerary

Ambassador Thompson and the staff of the American embassy also became involved with officials of the Soviet Union's Ministry of Foreign Affairs in the plans for Eisenhower's visit. On March 22, Thompson was summoned to the MFA by Vasily Kuznetsov, the deputy foreign minister. Also present at the meeting was Anatoly Dobrynin, the chief of the United States section in the MFA, who was assigned to be the liaison between the MFA and the American embassy. The purpose of the meeting was to discuss the proposed itinerary for Eisenhower's visit in June. Thompson and Kuznetsov also discussed the desirability of scheduling an itinerary for an advance party to visit the Soviet Union several weeks prior to Eisenhower's arrival. The advance party was to be led by James Hagerty and Thomas Stephens, Eisenhower's appointments secretary.

The discussions between Thompson and Kuznetsov, not surprisingly, also focused on the matter of whether American aircraft, other than Ike's Air Force One, would be permitted to enter Soviet air space or whether aircraft, other an Air Force One, would have to fly to a destination outside the Soviet Union, and then passengers would enter the Soviet Union on Soviet aircraft. The Russians were obviously highly sensitive, for good reason, about American aircraft being equipped to take aerial photographs of any military or industrial facilities. Thompson indicated as much in his cable to Washington describing the meeting: "I suspect reason is that they intend taking certain security precautions such as camouflaging military installations which they do wish [to] be obliged," he wrote.[26]

Kuznetsov then gave Thompson the first draft of Eisenhower's proposed itinerary. The itinerary itself was revised numerous times before it finally became satisfactory, both to the White House and the Soviets, but the essential chronology for the visit remained the same as the one presented to Thompson on March 22. For the record, this is how the itinerary initially appeared when presented by Kuznetsov to Thompson:

Friday, June 10:   Arrival in Moscow at the beginning of afternoon; ceremonies at airport; arrival at residence [in the Kremlin]; official visits to K. Ye. Voroshilov and N.S. Khrushchev.[27]
Evening: official dinner

Preparations

Saturday, June 11:	Morning: meet with N.S. Khrushchev;
	Afternoon: Private luncheon (at exhibit); 1500: visit exhibition of national economy of USSR; 1700: reception at American Embassy
	Evening: Attend ballet "Swan Lake" or "Stone Flower"
Sunday, June 12:	Morning: Attend church, drive through city
	Afternoon: luncheon at [Khrushchev's] dacha
	Evening: Free
Monday, June 13	1000—Departure from Moscow, 1100—arrival Leningrad
	Afternoon: Private luncheon, sightseeing of city, including Hermitage [28]
	Evening: Official dinner and speech
Tuesday, June 14	1000 Departure from Leningrad
	1130 Arrival Kiev
	Afternoon—Private luncheon; visit to collective farm or state farm
	Evening—Official dinner and speech
Wednesday, June 15	1000 Departure from Kiev
	1100 Arrival Moscow
	Afternoon: Free
	Evening: President's dinner at American Embassy for Soviet officials
Thursday, June 16	Morning: Meeting with N.S. Khrushchev
	Afternoon: Moscow University; visit scientific institution or industrial enterprise
	Evening: Soviet official reception
	2000—Speech to Soviet audience, transmitted by television and radio
Friday, June 17	1100 Departure from Moscow
	2140 Arrival Irkutsk; Travel to Lake Baikal, private supper; overnight stay at Lake Baikal
Saturday, June 18	Morning: Sail on Lake Baikal;
	Afternoon: Private luncheon; arrival in Irkutsk
	Evening: official dinner and speech

Chapter 4

Sunday, June 19   0900 Departure from Irkutsk;
Midday: Luncheon on plane;
1415 Arrival in Khabarovsk;
1515 Departure from Khabarovsk
1720 Arrival Tokyo[29]

On March 23, the following day, Secretary Herter cabled to Ambassador Thompson that the itinerary submitted the previous day should not be considered the final word on the subject but that the embassy staff could use the document as the basis for "informal" discussions with officials at the MFA about the details of Eisenhower's schedule such as any "sightseeing" that he might want to do in Moscow, Leningrad, or Lake Baikal.

Therefore, Herter instructed Thompson to "take into account" the following points when working on any revisions in Eisenhower's itinerary. First, Eisenhower wanted, "if at all possible" to have an hour of rest before lunch each day. A rest break after lunch would be granted "only in case of necessity."[30]

Second, Mamie Eisenhower intended to accompany the President on the trip to Moscow but, as Herter wrote, "First Lady plans [to] remain in Moscow during President's trip to Leningrad and Kiev and will move to Spaso [House] from Kremlin on June 13. She customarily attends only official dinners and receptions."[31]

That Mamie Eisenhower intended to accompany the President to Russia was an important signal, by itself, of the importance that Ike attached to the visit. The first lady hated to fly, perhaps because of the discomfort caused by Miniere's disease, an ailment that led to dizziness and often caused her to walk unsteadily.[32] During the numerous travels that Eisenhower made in the last half of 1959, Mamie remained in Washington. Once having made the long journey by air to Moscow, Mamie had no desire to travel by air to Leningrad and Kiev. The trip was going to be a tremendous physical challenge for her as, after leaving Russia, Ike still planned to travel to Japan and other destinations in Asia before returning to the United States via a very long flight across the Pacific Ocean.

Also on March 23, Thompson sent another cable to Herter with a more detailed outline of the events on Eisenhower's itinerary. The detail that Thompson outlined in the cable was a powerful indicator of the momentum that was building for Dwight D. Eisenhower's second visit to Russia.[33]

The Travels of the Advance Party

Before Eisenhower visited the Soviet Union, the administration arranged for an advance party to travel to Russia to meet with Soviet officials to discuss the arrangements for the visit. As mentioned previously, the advance party was led by James Hagerty and Thomas Stephens, Eisenhower's appointments secretary. Ambassador Thompson and the staff of the American embassy acted as the hosts for the advance party. The Hagerty-Stephens party was scheduled to visit the Soviet Union on April 6–10 and the group planned to cover the various places scheduled for Eisenhower's planned itinerary in June. On March 14, Secretary Herter sent Thompson a cable that identified the size of the advance party and instructions as to how accommodate the group while in the Soviet Union. The advance party consisted of thirteen White House staff, seven State Department staff, and Colonel William Draper, the pilot of Air Force One. The flight of the advance party was significant in that the flight intentionally followed the same route intended for Eisenhower on his flight to Russia in June.[34] On March 17, Thompson cabled to Herter, outlining the expectations for the advance party.[35]

The itinerary for the advance party was exhausting, perhaps needlessly so. The group left Washington at 8 A.M. on Tuesday, April 5, and arrived in Copenhagen, Denmark, at 9:45 P.M. The next day, Wednesday, April 6, the group left Copenhagen at 11 A.M. and flew directly to Moscow, arriving at 3:00 P.M. On Thursday, April 7, the group remained in Moscow for meetings with Soviet officials and members of the American press stationed in Russia. On Friday, April 8, the itinerary called for the group to fly to Leningrad, where they spent the day. On Saturday, April 9, the group left Leningrad for Kiev, where they likewise spent the day. On Sunday, April 10, the group left Kiev for Moscow, where they remained through Monday, April 11. Then they departed Moscow at noon on Tuesday, April 12, and they flew to Copenhagen, then on to Iceland, and then on to Anchorage, Alaska. The flight to Anchorage was necessary because the advance party intended to fly on to Japan and the Soviet authorities were unwilling to permit the Americans to fly easterly across Siberia, for security reasons. By not permitting the advance party to fly east to Japan, across the USSR, the Soviets significantly added to the length of the journey.

On Wednesday, April 13, the advance party left Anchorage at noon, crossed the International Date Line, and arrived in Tokyo at 2:30 P.M. on Thursday, April 14. They remained in Tokyo for the next three days, April 15, 16, and 17. On Monday, April 18, they flew from Japan to Honolulu, where they remained for one day. Finally, after a time change, the group left Hawaii for California and then flew on from there to Washington, arriving at 11 P.M.[36]

The Hagerty-Stephens party had important business to accomplish in Moscow, obviously. James Hagerty, in particular, wanted to meet with as many American correspondents as possible to discuss the arrangements for covering the Eisenhower visit and avoid some of the problems that had occurred during the Nixon visit. In a cable to Thompson on March 21, Secretary Herter suggested that the embassy should arrange for Hagerty to meet with members of the American press before he met with Soviet press personnel. This suggestion does not appear to have been followed since the advance party spent the afternoon of April 6 at the American embassy and the morning of April 7 with Soviet officials, Hagerty and Stephens, and Ambassador Thompson discussing the arrangements for their visit. Hagerty spent the afternoon with press officials from the MFA.[37]

For the remainder of the advance party's visit, Hans Tuch accompanied the group to its various destinations. The key meeting of the visit occurred on Monday, April 11, and involved Thompson, Hagerty, Tuch, and V. I. Avilov, the deputy chief of the press section of the MFA. The meeting chiefly concerned the arrangements both for American reporters living in Moscow and those who would be with the traveling press party. Avilov agreed to supply Hagerty and the staff of the American embassy with an *aide memoire* that outlined the various accommodations that the Soviet authorities would provide to the press that was covering Eisenhower's visit. Tuch followed up with Avilov on April 18, after the departure of the advance party, based on a prior telephone conversation with him about the facilities that would be made available to the

American reporters. Chief among Tuch's concerns was the availability of a "number of local telephone lines to enable correspondents to phone into the Press Center stories about the President's activities."[38]

Satisfied that the plans were moving forward in good order, Tuch sent a letter to Hagerty (now back in the United States) on April 19, enclosing a copy of his letter to Avilov and outlining some of the issues involved. He informed Hagerty that later in the week he would send him a list of the permanently accredited American correspondents in Moscow as well as those American correspondents who were posted by their American newspapers in other European locations.[39] Tuch informed Hagerty that he had asked Avilov about the status of the *aide memoire* that set out the terms and conditions that the Russians expected to follow. As Tuch recalled, he "got the usual Soviet reply, 'It is being prepared.'"[40]

Eisenhower Bearing Gifts

No aspect of Dwight D. Eisenhower's visit to the Soviet Union dramatized its importance more than the sheer volume of newspaper reporters, radio and television correspondents, and various technicians who were scheduled to go to Russia on the trip. Hagerty and Tuch essentially worked out a system with the Soviets whereby there would be facilities for four hundred correspondents in Moscow and three hundred correspondents to accompany the Eisenhower group outside of Moscow.[41] By May 7, 1960, the lists of those accompanying the presidential party were finalized. Those traveling to Russia, and then on to Japan, were divided into four lists, according to the following categories:

List 1: News media personnel travelling on the round-the-world press plane accompanying the presidential party for the entire trip. This list number[ed] 90 individuals.

List 2: News media personnel, mainly Americans, wishing to enter the Soviet Union prior to President Eisenhower's arrival in Moscow.

List 3: Technicians from American radio, television, and photographic services who desire to enter the Soviet Union and travel in advance to the Soviet Union to prepare the necessary coverage of the president in those cities.

Chapter 4

List 4: 125 news personnel who will be travelling as per agreement with Soviet authorities, on Soviet press planes within the Soviet Union.[42]

Preparations for Eisenhower's trip to the Soviet Union also included an extensive list of gifts that Eisenhower was to present to the family of Nikita Khrushchev. These gifts were outlined in a letter that Eisenhower received from Douglas Dillon, who was acting as secretary of state while Secretary Herter was traveling to Paris for the summit conference. The gifts were divided into those for Khrushchev, those for members of Khrushchev's family, and those for high-ranking Soviet officials. The gifts reflected American culture and history. As Dillon wrote to Ike, "I strongly believe that [the gifts] will contribute significantly to increase the impact of your visit. In a country such as the USSR where such gifts are customary, the presentation of a personal memento from you or on your behalf will have particular meaning."[43]

The list of presents ran to a seven-page document. The list, moreover, reflected the somewhat complicated nature of Nikita Khrushchev's family history. Khrushchev married for the first time in 1914, to Yefrosinya Ivanovna Pisoreva. Khrushchev's marriage to Yefrosinya produced two children: Julia and Leonid, who was a pilot in the Soviet Air Force and was killed in combat during World War II. Prior to his death, Leonid married Luyubov Illiarovna, and the couple had a daughter, Julia. In 1919, Yefrosinya Khrushchev died from typhus. In 1924 Khrushchev met and married Nina Petrovna Kukharchuk. Although they did not register their marriage until 1965, the couple lived together as husband and wife until 1971, when Khrushchev died.[44] Khrushchev and Nina Petrovna had three children: Rada, Sergei, and Yelena.

Khrushchev himself was to receive a motorboat and a set of 2500 slides of the Art of the United States. The motorboat, in particular, was impressive, being a new craft that was water-jet propelled instead of propeller-driven. Nina Petrovna was to receive a set of luggage. Sergei Khrushchev was to receive a slide projector since he was "an avid camera fan [and the] projector will handle [the] slides being given Khrushchev."[45]

There were also gifts for Khrushchev's three daughters: Rada (Mrs. Aleksei Adzubei), Julia, and Yelena. Rada and her husband had accompanied her parents during their visit to the United States in September

1959 and had "indicated a great interest in America and American literature." She was to receive a *Guide to the Study of the United States,* a book published by the Library of Congress, as well as a travelling cosmetic case. Julia, Khrushchev's daughter from his marriage to Yefrosinya Pisoreva, was an interior designer in the Soviet Union, and was to receive the *Complete Book of Interior Decorating,* by Mary Derieux, and a traveling cosmetic case. Yelena Khrushchev, then a 21-year-old student at Moscow University, was to receive a summer handbag and, like her sisters, a traveling cosmetic case.[46]

The American embassy in Moscow also suggested gifts for Khrushchev's grandchildren. Rada and Aleksei Adsubei had three children: Nikita, age seven; Aleksei, age five; and Ivan, age one. The embassy recommended that Nikita receive a Flexible Flyer sled (certainly a coveted possession!) and a construction kit for a model boat or train. The embassy recommended a "moulded plastic horse and large-size blocks" for Aleksei and "stuffed toys" for Ivan.[47] Sergei Khrushchev was the father of Nikita, eight months old at the time, and the embassy also recommended a gift of stuffed toys for him.

To show the degree of attention that the embassy was giving to the matter of gifts for Khrushchev's family, it recommended a gift for Julia, the child of Leonid, Khrushchev's son from his first marriage to Yefrosinya Ivanovna Pisoreva. Julia was the daughter of Leonid and his wife, Lyubov Illiarovna, and was close to her grandfather. As a student, she accompanied her grandfather on his tour of Southeast Asia in February 1960.[48]

The list of gifts also included those for high-ranking officials of the Soviet government, including Kliment Voroshilov and Leonid Brezhnev, members of the Soviet Presidium; Andrei Gromyko, the Soviet foreign minister; Vasily Kuznetsov, the deputy foreign minister; and Anatole Dobrynin, head of the American section of the MFA.[49]

There were also gifts indicated for the people who Eisenhower would meet at his various stops on the itinerary. Especially interesting was the fact that Eisenhower's group was permitted to bring Bibles (both the King James Version and the Revised Standard Version), as well as hymnals in American editions as presents for the leaders of the Baptist Church in Moscow, where the president was scheduled to attend worship services on the morning of Sunday, June 12. The embassy staff noted that the hymnals would be useful for the Americans since, "in contrast to the [Russian] Orthodox church, there is a good deal of congregational singing in the Russian Baptist Church."[50]

A Dacha, a Highway, and a Golf Course

While James Hagerty, the leadership of the State Department, the MFA, and the staff of the American embassy were working on the final arrangements for Eisenhower's visit, Nikita Khrushchev was involved in his own preparations. Cities and towns across the Soviet Union were cleaning themselves up and making ready for Ike. As Aleksandr Fursenko and Timothy Naftali have written, "Leningrad was sporting new colors in May 1960. There were greens and newly painted yellows on some buildings and along the main railway and new fences sprouting. Russia's second city was undergoing a facelift in preparation for a special American visitor, a man whose military exploits had earned him a place in Soviet hearts."[51]

The popular expectations for Eisenhower's visit were evident to the Soviet watchers in the American embassy, too. As Vladimir Toumanoff recalled, "The prospect of a visit by Ike, the wartime hero and ally, the epitome of U.S.-Soviet cooperation in an agonizing, mortal struggle, was such a relief from the prevailing fear of war that the Soviet population simply stampeded out of control in their enthusiasm and eagerness to show their gratitude, love for Ike, and yearning for peace with America."[52]

Khrushchev spent a considerable amount of time speaking with his son, Sergei, about the arrangements for Ike's visit. Where should the face-to-face talks between the two leaders take place, in trying to emulate a Camp David–type of experience for Eisenhower? Should the talks be held at Gorky II, Khrushchev's dacha outside of Moscow, or at the Novo-Ogaryonovo guesthouse, the place where Richard Nixon had stayed the previous summer? Khrushchev decided on the guesthouse; the dacha at Gorky II had only one bathroom and toilet for use by the guests. As Sergei Khrushchev wrote, "By American standards, only people who lived in the slums lived in such conditions."[53]

Khrushchev obviously wanted the visit to make a positive impression on Eisenhower, even to the extent of changing his views on the addition

Preparations

of government buildings in the Soviet Union. As recorded by Sergei Khrushchev, "Father acquiesced without argument to the building of special villas in various parts of the country to receive his high-ranking guest," Khrushchev wrote. "One was located on the picturesque site of the celebrated Lake Baikal, in Siberia."[54]

Thus was constructed outside of Irkutsk what became known as the Eisenhower Dacha, a Soviet version of Camp David. Irkutsk was the last stop on Eisenhower's visit, and the Eisenhower dacha was, in the words of journalist Harrison Salisbury, "a great gesture of Russian extravagance." The villa was built on an enormous bluff overlooking Lake Baikal, one of the most scenic beautiful places in the world."[55] Khrushchev also had a hard-surface road built to travel to the dacha from the area surrounding Lake Baikal. The local population came to refer to this hard road as the Eisenhower Highway.[56]

Khrushchev also took notice of Eisenhower's long-standing affection for the sport of golf, but finding a golf course in the Soviet Union was virtually impossible. As Harrison Salisbury once observed, "Golf was never popular in Imperial Russia. There was only one golf course at that time which was in St. Petersburg (later Leningrad, of course), for the foreign colony there, on the outskirts of St. Petersburg and, curiously enough, that golf course was maintained all during the revolutionary period, up till World War II. Then it was destroyed in the fighting around Leningrad and they abandoned it. So there was no golf course in Russia."[57]

Relative to Salisbury's point, Ambassador Tommy Thompson had encouraged Khrushchev to build a golf course in the Soviet Union for use by the diplomatic community, since "diplomats like to play golf." Thompson also explained to Khrushchev that the presence of a golf course might pay off for the Soviets in terms of some additional prestige for the nature of their society. Khrushchev listened to Thompson, but there is no evidence that he viewed golf as anything more than a decadent Western pastime until the time of Eisenhower's impending visit.[58]

Thus did Khrushchev decide to have a golf course built for Ike and even, so the story went, took some lessons on how to play golf himself so that he could enjoy a round with Eisenhower. In his oral history, Salisbury mentioned that he believed that Khrushchev had ordered the construction of a golf course in the Crimea to be used during the

Eisenhower visit. Salisbury acknowledged, however, that he could not confirm the story and a golf course in the Crimea does seem odd since Eisenhower's itinerary did not include any time scheduled for travel in that part of the Soviet Union.[59]

For an alternative view, however, we may take the account by Hans Tuch, who told the author that he was once asked by a Soviet diplomat (unnamed) in the Ministry of Foreign Affairs if the library at the American embassy had any books on the design and construction of golf courses. "Of course not," Tuch told the Soviet official, but he added that he would ask for a book on that subject to be sent from the United States to the American embassy and he would see to it that the Soviet official received the book once it arrived. "I never put two-and-two together," Tuch later recalled, not mindful that the Soviets intended to build a golf course specifically for Ike's visit. Years later, Tuch made a visit to Siberia and while riding on the train into Irkutsk he looked out the window and noticed a four-hole golf course, then in disrepair and overgrown with grasses and weeds. If the course had ever been in use, it gave no such indication. But Tuch correctly surmised that that this was the golf course that Eisenhower would have been able to use in his stopover on the way to Japan. Thus, in addition to building a magnificent dacha for Eisenhower, and a hard road leading to it, the Soviets also intended to build a golf course (The Eisenhower Links?) to include in the complex on Lake Baikal. Everything considered—the highway, the dacha, and the golf course—it was not so much to believe that it was not merely the Eisenhower Dacha but instead the Eisenhower Resort.[60]

Finally, in addition to the physical arrangements for Eisenhower's visit, changes were occurring in the relationship between American diplomats in Moscow and their interactions with the Russian people, as well as in their interactions with Soviet diplomats in the days and weeks leading up to the Eisenhower visit. Vladimir I. Toumanoff noticed the change in attitudes in Moscow following the visit by Richard Nixon to the Soviet Union in July 1959, and following Khrushchev's visit to the United States in September 1959. After these events, as well as the effects of the Lacy-Zaroubin agreement, according to Toumanoff, " 'Peace and Friendship' and 'The Spirit of Camp David' became the new, overwhelming Soviet propaganda slogans. . . . The bars against contact between Soviet citizens and foreigners, particularly Americans, suddenly came tumbling down. They didn't vanish by explicit direction from Moscow. They vanished more by the radical change in the atmospherics, the suddenly favorable propaganda treatment of the United States."[61]

In this new environment, Toumanoff noticed some important departures from past behavior by Soviet citizens. First, there was a noticeable absence of hostility toward the United States and Americans. Again, as Toumanoff recalled, "In my travels and in Moscow, I met many Russians and other Soviet citizens . . . [I]n all these random contacts not once did I encounter anger, antagonism, or hostility toward the U.S." In fact, as was often explained to him, the Soviet government was the source of the effort to disparage the United States and Toumanoff's acquaintances resented this pressure. "We know they [the Soviet authorities] lie to us," the Russians told Toumanoff. "Maybe your President Eisenhower will come here on his visit. If he does we will give him a welcome such as no Soviet leader has ever had."[62]

Second, this enthusiasm for Eisenhower and his visit must have worried the hard-line elements in the Soviet hierarchy, elements that were highly suspicious of Khrushchev's attempt at rapprochement with the United States. Soviet citizens were being told that it was now safe, and in some respects were encouraged to have contacts with Americans. If the widespread, enthusiastic reception for Ike got "out of control," as Toumanoff reasoned, might it "accelerate and grow to torch [the hard-liners], the Party, and the nation?"[63]

By the end of April and the beginning of May, the diplomatic preparations were well in hand for Dwight D. Eisenhower's visit to the Soviet Union. But 1960 was a presidential election year in the United States and, back in Washington, Eisenhower needed to confront a different set of political circumstances. On the defensive since 1958 over the issue of the "missile gap," Eisenhower and Thomas Gates, his recently appointed secretary of defense, needed to gain the passage of the administration's defense budget for fiscal year 1961 in an increasingly hostile political climate. Passage of the FY 1961 defense budget was vital if Eisenhower expected to engage in meaningful negotiations on the issue of disarmament when he met Khrushchev in Paris for the summit conference in May and later when he visited the Soviet Union in June. Moreover, the administration's political opposition in the Democratic Party controlled both houses of Congress. The stage was thus set for a contentious round of political combat about the future of America's national defense policy and its impact on the broader international situation. As the events of the winter and spring of 1960 were about to prove, the administration found it much easier to work with the Soviets in Moscow on the details of Eisenhower's visit than with its critics in Washington on the issue of the missile gap.

President Dwight D. Eisenhower addresses the White House press corps at a news conference on August 3, 1959. At this conference, Eisenhower announced that he and Soviet premier Nikita Khrushchev had agreed to an exchange of visits to each other's countries. James C. Hagerty, Eisenhower's press secretary, is seated to his left. Photo 77-1-394, Dwight D. Eisenhower Library

On Vice President Richard Nixon's visit to the Soviet Union in July 1959, Premier Khrushchev took him for a boat ride down the Moscow River. Bathers were permitted to approach the boat and shake hands with Nixon. Knowing of Khrushchev's love for watercraft, the Eisenhower administration intended to give the Soviet leader a new-model boat as a present when Eisenhower visited the Soviet Union in June 1960. Once Khrushchev withdrew Eisenhower's invitation, however, the boat was returned to the United States. To Nixon's left is Dr. Milton S. Eisenhower, Ike's younger brother and the president of Johns Hopkins University at the time. Milton Eisenhower was part of the delegation that accompanied Nixon to the Soviet Union. Richard Nixon Presidential Library.

Hans N. (Tom) Tuch (far left), the press and cultural attaché at the American Embassy in Moscow, translated for Premier Khrushchev, center, during the visit to Moscow of Vice President Richard Nixon (far right), in 1959. To the left of Nixon is Milton Eisenhower. Tuch was also involved in the details of managing Nixon's visit. He later worked with press secretary James Hagerty on the planning for Eisenhower's proposed visit to the Soviet Union in June 1960. Richard Nixon Presidential Library.

On August 26, 1959, President Eisenhower visited the Federal Republic of Germany, arriving in Bonn in a motorcade with West German chancellor Konrad Adenauer. The enthusiasm for Ike by the West German people was overwhelming, as the photo shows. Photo 65-154, Dwight D. Eisenhower Library.

President Eisenhower visited London during August 27–31, 1959, for talks with British prime minister Harold Macmillan. Ike also appeared on British television with Macmillan, thus greatly enhancing the prospects of the Conservative Party in the soon-to-be-announced British general election. Photo-65-466, Dwight D. Eisenhower Library.

President Eisenhower visited France on September 1–4, 1959. Ike was greeted by French president Charles de Gaulle at Orly Airport, and they traveled by motorcade to central Paris, cheered by a crowd of nearly one million Parisians. Photo 64-117, Dwight D. Eisenhower Library.

Enormous crowds gathered to cheer President Eisenhower and French president Charles de Gaulle when they appeared in public during Eisenhower's visit to France in September 1959. Photo 64-373-5, Dwight D. Eisenhower Library.

During President Eisenhower's visit to France, Parisians thronged to the central part of Paris to welcome the American president. As Thomas S. Gates, Eisenhower's secretary of defense, once observed, "No one could draw a crowd like Eisenhower." Photo 64-373-14, Dwight D. Eisenhower Library.

President Eisenhower and Soviet premier Nikita Khrushchev arrive at Camp David for their talks in September 1959. An unidentified American official greets Khrushchev as he exits the automobile. At Camp David, Eisenhower and Khrushchev agreed to postpone Eisenhower's visit to the Soviet Union to the spring of 1960. Photo: 73-757-7, Dwight D. Eisenhower Library.

The four leaders of the Western alliance gathered in Paris for the Western summit in December 1959. Left to right, Prime Minister Harold Macmillan, President Dwight D. Eisenhower, President Charles de Gaulle, Chancellor Konrad Adenauer. Photo 73-803-360, Dwight D. Eisenhower Library.

Left to right, Macmillan, de Gaulle, Adenauer, and Eisenhower met at the Western summit in Paris in December 1959, to discuss, among other subjects, the location and scheduling of the Four Power summit between the United States, the Soviet Union, Great Britain, and France in the spring of 1960. Photo 73-803-362, Dwight D. Eisenhower Library.

President Eisenhower and James Hagerty, Ike's press secretary. In 1959–1960, Hagerty's role as a political adviser to Eisenhower expanded beyond his official duties as press secretary. He also played a leading role in the planning for Eisenhower's proposed visit to the Soviet Union in the spring of 1960. Photo: 72-920-2, Dwight D. Eisenhower Library.

President Eisenhower and Llewellyn E. Thompson, Jr., the American ambassador to the Soviet Union. "Tommy" Thompson was to serve as Eisenhower's host when he visited the Soviet Union in the spring of 1960. Photo: 72-2269-3, Dwight D. Eisenhower Library.

Thomas S. Gates, secretary of defense, 1959–1961. It was Gates's responsibility to shepherd the administration's defense budget for FY 1961 through a Congress controlled by the political opposition in the Democratic Party. Photo 74-271, Dwight D. Eisenhower Library.

Left to right, General Nathan Twining, Congressman Gerald R. Ford (R-Michigan), and Secretary of Defense Thomas S. Gates confer before the opening of hearings in the House of Representatives on the administration's defense budget in 1960. Gates and Ford had known each other since World War II, when both men were officers aboard the USS *Monterey*. Gerald R. Ford Presidential Library.

Francis Gary Powers (far left), shown in 1954–1955 with other pilots in the U.S. Air Force's 508th Strategic Fighter Wing. Powers was the pilot shot down in his U-2 airplane over the Soviet Union on May 1, 1960. National Museum of the U.S. Air Force.

Clarence "Kelly" Johnson, the chief executive of the Lockheed Corporation, was the driving force behind the design, manufacture, and testing of the U-2 surveillance aircraft. In this photo, one of the U-2s manufactured by Lockheed is in the background. Office of Public Information, Lockheed Company-California via the National Museum of the US Air Force.

On January 27, 1961, the recently released RB-47 pilots met their wives at Andrews Air Force Base upon their safe return to the United States. Nikita Khrushchev later told President John F. Kennedy, at their meeting in Vienna in June 1961, that he had helped Kennedy defeat Richard Nixon in the 1960 presidential election by postponing the release of the pilots until after the election. Left to right, Gail Olmstead, Captain Freeman Bruce Olmstead, Captain John McKone, Connie McKone. Photo AR 62990-A, Abbie Rowe. White House Photographs. John F. Kennedy Presidential Library and Museum, Boston.

On January 27, 1961, President John F. Kennedy welcomed Captain Freeman Bruce Olmstead, Captain John McKone, and their wives, Gail and Connie, to the White House following the safe return of the airmen to the United States. Photo: AR 6299-G, Abbie Rowe, White House Photographs, John F. Kennedy Presidential Library and Museum, Boston.

President Richard M. Nixon and First Lady Pat Nixon attended worship services at the All-Union Council of Evangelical Christian Baptists during their visit to Moscow in May 1972. In this photo, President and Mrs. Nixon stand at the entrance to the church, which was also the one that was on President Eisenhower's itinerary for his visit to the Soviet Union in 1960. Nixon was the first American president to visit the Soviet Union since the end of World War II, a distinction that Eisenhower had sought for himself in 1959–1960. Richard Nixon Presidential Library.

Chapter 5

The Missile Gap and the FY 1961 Defense Budget, January–May 1960

As events in 1960 moved closer to the Four Power summit in Paris in May and President Eisenhower's trip to the Soviet Union in June, the timing never appeared better for a productive dialogue between the United States and the Soviet Union. For the United States, moreover, the balance of forces relative to its military strength vis-à-vis that of the Soviet Union was strongly in its favor. While the Soviet Union continued to hold a numerical advantage in manpower, with the Red Army still occupying East Germany and parts of eastern Europe, the United States was vastly superior in virtually every other measure of strategic power. Due to agreements reached with Great Britain in the 1950s, the United States had established bases for long-range bombers and intermediate range ballistic missiles in Britain.[1] America's Atlas program for land-based intercontinental ballistic missiles (ICBMs) was undergoing rapid development and was scheduled for deployment before Eisenhower left office in 1961. More significantly, the United States was closing in on the successful completion of its subsurface ballistic system with the deployment of the Polaris nuclear-powered submarine program scheduled for late 1960. What became known as the strategic triad—the capability to deliver nuclear weapons from land-based ICBMs, long-range bombers, and submarines—was virtually complete by the end of Eisenhower's last year in office.

The growth of American military power during the years of the Eisenhower administration was unprecedented. Robert B. Anderson, who served as secretary of the navy, deputy secretary of defense, and secretary of the treasury, witnessed this unparalleled growth of American military strength in the 1950s. "We were going through as striking a period as ever existed in American military history as far as capability was concerned," Anderson told the author. "When we came into office, we had not a single active jet squadron; everything was experimental. Then the first atomic submarine was begun and finished. We had an atomic bomb but no H bomb. I acted as the agent for the president on the construction of the hydrogen bomb. The period from 1953 to 1961 was the most revolutionary in American history [in terms of military technology]. When we left office, we knew that we had, for the first time in history, the capability to destroy nations completely. The basic raw power existed."[2]

While Eisenhower and his advisers on national security policy had enormous confidence in American military strength and its capacity to deter any significant Soviet threat, that confidence was not shared by the political opposition in the Democratic Party, particularly those individuals with presidential aspirations, as well as some prominent members of the press, some outspoken military leaders, a few ambitious Republican politicians, well-known defense contractors, some researchers at think tanks, and several academics. In the post-*Sputnik* environment, many voices expressed the alarmist viewpoint that an overly cost-conscious Eisenhower administration had permitted a dangerous missile gap to develop between the United States and the Soviet Union. The missile gap controversy, like the "bomber gap" controversy of 1956, was for the most part "nothing more than imaginative creations of irresponsibility," in the words of defense analyst Dino Brugioni, or as Eisenhower himself said, "a useful piece of political demagoguery in 1960."[3] The persistence of the missile gap issue, however, continued to plague the administration politically during the early months of 1960.

The Specter of Surprise Attack

In reality, Eisenhower's main concern was not with comparisons of American military strength and that of the Soviet Union. Instead, his focus was on two other matters: the capability of the Soviets to launch a surprise missile attack on the cities of the United States and the pervasive secrecy that the Soviets attached to their military intentions and capabilities. Eisenhower often spoke with great emphasis on these two subjects. "Actually the only thing we fear is an atomic attack delivered by air on our cities," Eisenhower once told William Bragg Ewald, a member of the White House staff in the 1950s and later one of his biographers.[4] Andrew Goodpaster also spoke about how Eisenhower expressed his views on those subjects. "The Japanese attack on Pearl Harbor in December 1941 was one example of a surprise attack," according to Goodpaster. But the Korean War also broke out in a surprise attack by North Korea on South Korea in June 1950. "When combined with our own experience at Pearl Harbor a decade before," Goodpaster recalled, and "with the concern that a determined opponent could attack using newer, much more powerful and destructive weapons, the fears of a surprise attack on the United States became a constant concern to President Eisenhower once he took office in January of 1953, as I am sure that it was with his predecessors."[5]

The other important problem was the matter of secrecy. "The Communists, as Eisenhower often said," Goodpaster again noted, "recognized secrecy as one of the primary elements of their military and political strength—that is, secrecy along with deception and misinformation."[6] The twin fears about a possible surprise attack and the pervasive secrecy of Soviet society made it essential for the administration to develop a system of intelligence that made it possible to assess, as close to humanly possible, the dimensions of the Soviet strategic arsenal.[7]

As mentioned previously, in 1955 Ike attempted to penetrate the secrecy of the Soviet Union at the summit in Geneva by presenting what has become known as his famous Open Skies proposal, whereby both the United States and the Soviet Union would provide blueprints and charts of their airfields and then allow aerial reconnaissance of those installations. The leaders of Great Britain and France who attended the conference greeted the Open Skies proposal favorably, but Nikita Khrushchev vigorously opposed the entire concept.[8]

In Goodpaster's view, even before Eisenhower made his Open Skies proposal, the administration had already begun the search for a program to satisfy Eisenhower's view that "intelligence was of vital importance to the national security and to the conduct of political and military affairs."[9] Prior to his meeting with Khrushchev at Geneva, Eisenhower had enlisted the American scientific community in a dramatic effort to improve the country's intelligence capability. In 1954, Eisenhower named James R. Killian, the president of the Massachusetts Institute of Technology, to recruit what became known as the Technological Capabilities Panel, a group of leading scientists and physicists who were charged with integrating the latest scientific advances into the national intelligence program.[10]

Enter the U-2

One scientist who Killian recruited was Edwin Land, the founder and president of the Polaroid Corporation, who took an immediate interest in a design for a high-altitude surveillance aircraft developed in California by Clarence "Kelly" Johnson, president of the Lockheed Corporation. This high-altitude aircraft had the potential to penetrate Soviet airspace and, using film developed by Polaroid, obtain valuable photographic images of Soviet military installations. This top-secret program, under the overall direction of the CIA and not the military services, led to the development of the U-2, an aircraft able to fly at heights up to 70,000 feet. Richard Bissell, the deputy director of the CIA, was placed in overall charge of the U-2 program, ranging from the construction of the aircraft at Lockheed's so-called "Skunk Works" in California to the identification of targets for flights over the Soviet Union, the selection of pilots to fly the U-2, and their scheduling. In Land's view, the U-2 was the perfect marriage of espionage and high-tech innovation, a conceptual breakthrough that changed the entire nature of how intelligence was gathered and utilized in the Cold War.[11]

On July 4, 1956, the U-2 made its first flight over the Soviet Union, taking off from a base in Wiesbaden, West Germany, and flying a course that took the pilot over Moscow and Leningrad. The CIA wished to see the status of a naval shipyard and an airfield for heavy bombers in the area around Leningrad.[12] On July 5, Richard Bissell received a cable that the flight had concluded successfully. As Bissell recalled, "[The] photographs were remarkable. We obtained perfectly beautiful high altitude photographs of Leningrad and Moscow in which one could literally count the number of automobiles in the streets."[13] Also on July 5, Bissell informed Allen Dulles, the director of the CIA, who then went to the White House to give Eisenhower the good news. "The U-2 was built to fly over Russia," Thomas Gates, Eisenhower's third secretary of defense, who took office in late 1959, recalled.[14] The administration had the aircraft that could supply it with information about the extent of Soviet military capability.

When the U-2 program was in its infancy, the Eisenhower administration attempted to enlist the British as partners in the enterprise. The joint project, known as AQUATONE, began in 1956 when Anthony Eden was Britain's prime minister and the United States stationed three U-2 aircraft at Lakenheath air base in Britain. From Lakenheath, U-2 pilots flew several flights over eastern Europe but not over the Soviet Union. The British role in the U-2 project ended abruptly, but only temporarily, in 1956. The unfortunate incident that led to the initial cancellation involved a courtesy call that a Soviet naval vessel made at the British seaport of Portsmouth. Once the ship was in port, British intelligence units sent a Royal Navy frogman underneath the ship to examine its signaling gear. Three days later, the British discovered the frogman's dead body lying in the Portsmouth harbor. The Eden government concluded that the risk was too great to allow the Americans to undertake an espionage program on British soil, and the United States began a search for another base for the U-2s.[15]

In 1957, Harold Macmillan succeeded Eden as Britain's prime minister and he quickly expressed an interest in a renewal of the British role in AQUATONE. Eisenhower and Macmillan discussed the U-2 program, and Britain's participation in it, at their bilateral meeting in Bermuda in March 1957. On March 22, Macmillan sent Eisenhower a note that officially expressed his interest in renewing the British role in U-2 flights.[16]

Eisenhower wasted no time in accepting Macmillan's offer. On March 23, he wrote to Macmillan, "[We] are pleased that you found your way clear to allow United Kingdom bases to be used for AQUATONE, if it should at some time become necessary."[17] After Eisenhower and Macmillan reached their agreement in 1957, the United States began to train pilots in Britain's Royal Air Force and soon the British became involved in the operational details of the U-2 program, flying from bases in the United Kingdom, Turkey, and Pakistan.[18]

Between 1956 and 1960, the U-2 proved its value as the key factor in obtaining intelligence about the status of the Soviet Union's military preparedness. The flights provided valuable photographic information on what the Soviet military was doing, or in the words of Andrew Goodpaster, *not* doing.[19] As a result, Eisenhower possessed the ability to design an American defense program with hard evidence of the opponent's military capability. He did not need to embark on crash programs to correct strategic deficiencies, or to spend more on defense, which even then was taking more than 50 percent of the federal budget.

The Political Atmosphere of the Post-*Sputnik* Era

As valuable as the U-2 program was from the perspective of policy and planning, the unprecedented secrecy surrounding it made it almost useless from a political standpoint. Since the administration could not reveal the U-2's value publicly, it unfortunately left itself open to criticism from its opponents that its policies were not adequately defending the country. Thomas Gates once stated this dilemma succinctly. According to Gates, in an oft-quoted comment, "We were flying the U-2, and we had the dope [intelligence, that is], but we could not say we were flying the U-2 and nobody knew about the U-2. It was the best-kept secret in the history of the country, from its inception to its manufacturing under Kelly Johnson out there [in California] in a shed at Lockheed. It was an unbelievable thing, that U-2."[20]

Given such restrictions, the administration's critics had ample latitude in which to make their charges. Then, late in 1959 and early in 1960, Nikita Khrushchev, without intention and perhaps to his surprise, handed the administration's critics some ammunition for their attacks. In November 1959, Khrushchev maintained that "Now we have such a stock of rockets, such an amount of atomic and hydrogen weapons, that if they attack us, we could wipe our potential enemies off the face of the earth." Russian factories were capable of producing "250 ballistic missiles with nuclear warheads" annually.[21] Then, on January 14, 1960, Khrushchev delivered a widely reported speech in Moscow in which he again praised the Soviet effort in the production of ICBMs. First pointing out that he intended to reduce the Red Army by one-third, from 3,623,000 men to 2,423,000 within the next two years, Khrushchev went on to say that this reduction was possible due to the rapid growth of the Soviet Union's strategic arsenal. According to Khrushchev, the Soviets had "a formidable stockpile" of nuclear weapons, "well-concealed rocket bases," and "a lead of several years in rocket development and production." More ominous was Khrushchev's claim that the Soviets had a "fantastic new weapon" in production.[22]

Then, on January 18, 1960, the Russians successfully test-fired a "dummy" rocket 7,800 miles from a point in Soviet Central Asia to a point in the Pacific south of Hawaii. The successful launch of the rocket/missile, landing less than two miles from its intended target, as well as Khrushchev's speech of January 14, emboldened the administration's critics. Even Secretary of Defense Gates was forced to concede that the launch "was damn good," if it landed that close to its intended target.[23] In the aftermath of the test, the Soviets stated that the rocket was intended for future space exploration, instead of for military purposes, but the administration's critics were not convinced. Was this rocket launched on January 18 evidence of the fantastic new weapon that Khrushchev had mentioned on January 14?

In retrospect, we now know that Khrushchev's speech was designed to reduce, not provoke, tensions with the United States. By indicating his intention to reduce the size of the Red Army by one-third over the next two years, Khrushchev was attempting to lessen, not increase, the pressure on the Berlin issue in the months leading up to the summit conference in May. After meeting with Eisenhower in Washington, and then seeing the enormous prosperity of the United States, Khrushchev had returned to the Soviet Union convinced that the government needed to reduce military spending if it hoped to improve the living standards of the Soviet people. In a conversation with Ambassador Tommy Thompson on January 18, Khrushchev said that the reduction in the Red Army would enable him to withdraw "many soldiers" from East Germany and Hungary "where local forces were adequate." In the discussions with Thompson, Khrushchev bemoaned the fact that there was such "a great expense [in] keeping Soviet troops outside [the] Soviet Union."[24] As Khrushchev was learning the hard way, maintaining the Soviet military presence in eastern Europe was a costly enterprise.

Khrushchev's boasting about the impressive record of Soviet rocket and missile production was essentially a bluff. Khrushchev admitted the bluffing in early February 1960 during a conversation with Henry Cabot Lodge, then touring the Soviet Union in advance of Eisenhower's scheduled visit in June. (See chapter four, above.) Lodge indicated to Khrushchev that it appeared the Soviet Union was well ahead of the United States in terms of rocket production. "No, we're not," Khrushchev replied, "not really." Almost certainly, Khrushchev hoped that Lodge would convey that information to Eisenhower when he returned to the United States, but that conversation appears to have never taken place.[25]

Bluff or not, Khrushchev's strident remarks fed the anxiety in the United States about what people perceived as a growing Soviet missile capability. The previous year, in January 1959, Secretary of Defense Neil McElroy, in testimony before Congress, gave remarks that his critics later interpreted to mean that the Soviet Union might achieve a three-to-one advantage in ICBM production over the United States by the early 1960s. McElroy had inadvertently fallen into a semantic trap. He had merely expressed a view as to the volume of production that the Soviets *could* achieve but not whether any intelligence indicated that the Soviets intended, or had the capability, to achieve such an ambitious objective. It didn't matter that U-2 flights had uncovered no ICBM installations in the Soviet Union. The public didn't know that, and what they remembered was McElroy's remark about a three-to-one advantage for the Soviet Union as well as Khrushchev's speeches, which seemed to reinforce a possible Soviet strategic advantage.[26]

Unfortunately, both for Khrushchev and Eisenhower, the American intelligence establishment tended to focus more on the Soviet leader's statements about rocket production and, especially, concealment of rocket installations, than on his promises to reduce the size of the Red Army. As Jenny and Sherry Thompson have written, their father reported back to Washington that Khrushchev's speech of January 14 was a positive step toward improving his chances for a productive dialogue with Eisenhower in Paris, despite the fact the Soviet military vigorously opposed the planned reductions in the size of the Red Army.[27]

Ever since the launch of *Sputnik*, the American intelligence establishment, even in possession of U-2 photography, had tended to overestimate the size of the Soviet Union's strategic arsenal. As matters stood in January 1960, the administration's National Intelligence Estimate essentially split the difference between the "exaggerated predictions of the U.S. Air Force and the smaller projections of the U.S. Army" when it came to interpreting U-2 photographic images.[28] According to Thomas Gates, the "Air Force [photo-interpreters] saw a missile in every barn," "the Army [photo-interpreters] saw nothing" and "the Joint Chiefs of Staff and the Navy" were "sort of in the middle." In Gates's estimation, this was also true of Allen Dulles's position, although Gates believed that Dulles was not assertive enough in resisting the overestimates of Soviet missile capability.[29] As a result, the administration found itself in the uncomfortable position of having to concede that, beginning as early as 1961, the Soviet Union was on a pace to surpass the United States in the production of ICBMs.

Khrushchev's comments about Soviet rocket production also emboldened those, both in the military services and elsewhere, who advocated significant increases in overall military spending. Interservice rivalry had become a tribal ritual of the Pentagon in the 1950s, and vocal elements in the military departments, especially in the air force, were quick to latch on to overestimates of Soviet military prowess as a reason to lobby more vigorously for increased spending for their particular service, especially in the final year of the Eisenhower administration. Having lost the battle with Eisenhower for massive increases in defense spending, especially in manpower, during the 1950s, the armed services were gearing up for a battle over substantial increases in military spending once Ike's successor took office in 1961.

Thomas Gates and the FY 1961 Defense Budget

For the Eisenhower administration, the best course of action in dealing with the political issue of the missile gap was to secure the passage of its FY 1961 defense budget. Obtaining the bipartisan passage of the defense budget, in a Congress controlled by the Democratic Party, promised to be the most effective means of providing for the security of the country, defusing the partisan criticism surrounding the missile gap, and perhaps most important, putting Eisenhower in a strong position domestically when he began negotiations with Khrushchev in May. Passage of the defense budget within the administration's proposed spending limits was essential to Eisenhower's goal of obtaining an agreement on testing limitations and thereby achieving, as he said to Charles de Gaulle in March, his "splendid exit" from the presidency.[30]

To guide the administration's defense budget through Congress, Eisenhower turned to Thomas Gates, who he appointed secretary of

Chapter 5

defense on December 1, 1959, and who was subsequently confirmed by the Senate on January 28, 1960.[31] A veteran of combat as a naval intelligence officer during World War II, Gates had pursued a prosperous career as an investment banker in Philadelphia with the firm of Drexel and Company before coming to the Navy Department as undersecretary of the navy in September 1953. Initially, Gates intended to serve in the Navy Department for two years before returning to private life, but he ultimately agreed to serve the full length of Eisenhower's first term. Then he accepted Eisenhower's appointment as secretary of the navy in 1957 but once again wished to limit his service to two years, intending to resign in the spring of 1959. Early in 1959, therefore, he submitted his resignation to Eisenhower and began making plans to return to Philadelphia.

Other events then intervened. First, William B. Franke, Gates's choice as his successor as secretary of the navy, became ill with hepatitis and Gates agreed to remain in the post (even though he had technically resigned) until Franke recovered his health. As Gates later recalled the circumstances, "Eisenhower accepted my resignation and gave me a nice medal and his citation, and I was engaging myself in a series of farewell parties. Then my successor Bill Franke got hepatitis. I said [to Franke], 'Well, I've been here for six years and there's no reason for you to think of taking this job over if you're not well. You'd better go back up to Vermont and get yourself well, because this isn't any job [that you can do] unless you can go 24 hours a day [for] every day of the week. It doesn't make any difference to me whether I stay for another month or two, I've been here a long while anyway, so I'll stick around until you get well.'"[32]

Eventually, Franke recovered sufficiently to take over from Gates early in June 1959. But in the meantime, another event intervened when Donald A. Quarles, the deputy secretary of defense, died suddenly on Friday, May 8. Secretary of Defense McElroy recommended to Eisenhower that Gates succeed Quarles. On Saturday, May 9, Ike asked Gates to come to the White House and discuss an appointment as the successor to Quarles. As Gates recalled the conversation, "I told him, 'Mr. President, you forget. I'm no longer here; I've resigned. My plans are to do something else.'" Ike replied that "we've got to change all that" and as Gates recalled, "Eisenhower could lean pretty hard. I asked him if I could have until Monday [to consider the appointment]. Anne [Gates's wife] and I commissioned the *Sequoia* [the yacht that belonged to the secretary of the navy] and went down to Quantico [the Marine Base at Quantico, Virginia], and sat around and talked to some Marines. No one tried to talk me out of *not* taking the job but once we got back, I still didn't have my mind made up. When I left the house on Monday, Anne asked me—'What are you going to tell him and I said 'I'll be damned if I know.' Once at the White House, I told Ike that I'd do it. It plays hob with my personal plans but I guess it is my duty." Gates also later explained that the entire experience confirmed the often-repeated maxim that "you don't say 'no' to the president."[33]

When Gates informed Eisenhower on May 11, 1959, that he would take the position as DEPSECDEF, he was mindful that he was most likely committing himself to staying at the Pentagon until the end of Eisenhower's presidency. Asked by reporters for his reasons in accepting the position, Gates said that "I couldn't think of any reason not to do it, except I didn't want to, and that wasn't good enough."[34] Many years later, Gates also commented that "Eisenhower was a very difficult man to say 'no' to."[35]

Margaret (Peggy) Stroud, who served as Gates's secretary throughout his years at the Pentagon, confirmed that Gates faced a difficult decision in May 1959. "Mr. Gates resisted the DEPSECDEF job about as hard as anyone can but finally figured that it was a job that needed doing so he'd do it," Stroud said. "Loyalty to Mr. Gates was primary: loyalty to the President, and loyalty to the Navy."[36] Stroud also expressed another sentiment, one that Gates later disputed (although not with Stroud): "It seemed to me that he must have been told that he would soon become SECDEF," she added. "McElroy was not the strongest SECDEF, in my opinion. I felt that [Gates] would be it."[37]

Neither at the time nor later, however, did Gates maintain that he received any such indication from Eisenhower that he would become SECDEF. He naturally assumed that, given the death of Donald Quarles, McElroy would also stay at the Pentagon for the remainder of Eisenhower's presidency. But McElroy fully intended to resign as SECDEF once he had finished his two-year commitment, and he informed Eisenhower on September 16, 1959, about his plans to leave the administration. He also recommended that Gates succeed him as SECDEF. The exact date of McElroy's departure was kept confidential between the two men, however, and Eisenhower never gave Gates any indication that he would be succeeding McElroy.[38]

According to Gates's recollection, he learned about McElroy's departure over the weekend of November 22–23, 1959, when he visited Eisenhower in Augusta, Georgia, where Ike was enjoying some rounds of golf at the Augusta National Golf Club. As Gates remembered, he had left Washington on the morning of November 22 to fly to Augusta and take up some defense matters with the president. He was in the locker room at Augusta National when Ike told him, "I guess McElroy is really going to leave so you're going to have to take his place. I told the President that I wasn't expecting to be SECDEF but that I would do the best that I could in the job. Ike then said, 'Well, this late in the game, how am I going to get anybody else?' Eisenhower always appealed to your sense of duty and responsibility. Nor was there any question in his mind that I would do anything but accept."[39]

These circumstances regarding the appointment as SECDEF are important in revealing the nature of the relationship between Eisenhower and Gates. As Gates recalled, his relationship with the president was "business, strictly business." He certainly was not an intimate of Eisenhower, either socially or personally. "Eisenhower was a difficult man to get to know in human terms; he dealt with people at arm's length," Gates once observed. "There were only a few people—Milton Eisenhower, Pete Jones, Slats Slater, Bob Woodruff, Bill Robinson, and Al Gruenther—who were really close to him personally. For me, it was always 'Mr. President' when it came to Eisenhower, even when we visited him in California after he left office."[40]

Intentions versus Capabilities

Regardless of the circumstances, Thomas Gates took office on December 2, 1959 (on an interim basis), just before the 1960 presidential campaign began to occupy the nation's attention. The degree to which the missile gap controversy had come to occupy the official thinking in Washington became evident on January 13, 1960, when Eisenhower held a press conference and, on the same day, Gates began his initial testimony to Congress on the administration's FY 1961 defense budget. At his news conference, Eisenhower faced questioning from reporter Sarah McClendon as to whether the administration was treating defense policy on a partisan basis.

In response, Eisenhower stated that "I don't take it very kindly—the implied accusation that I am dealing with the whole matter of defense on a partisan basis . . . I've spent my entire life in this, and I know more about it than almost anybody, I think, that is in the country because I have given my life to it, and on a basis of doing what is best for the Government and for the country. I believe that the matter of defense has been handled well and efficiently in the proposal that will be before the Congress within a matter of a day or so; and I think that those people that are trying to make defense a partisan issue are doing a disservice to the United States."[41]

Later in the news conference, Eisenhower received a question from Edward T. Folliard of the *Washington Post*, whose question essentially treated the missile gap as an acknowledged fact. Folliard asked the president that, assuming the United States might be "second best in the missile field," would he be weakened in his negotiating position with Khrushchev at the upcoming summit conference. Eisenhower responded, "Well, let's put it this way: such an argument . . . presupposed that I come to any conversation in the feeling of inferiority: that I am a little bit frightened. I assure you I am not. I believe in the United States power, and I believe it is there not to be used but to make certain that the other fellow doesn't use his. I am not in the slightest degree disturbed by such a possibility as you speak of."[42]

Eisenhower's optimistic assessment of American power was merely a prelude to a chorus of criticism that lasted for at least another month. Gates experienced a taste of the criticism himself when he got off to a poor start with his testimony before the House Subcommittee on Defense Appropriations on January 13. The defense budget that he proposed came in at $40.577 billion, including military construction, an enormous figure in the administration's total budget request of $79.5 billion. The defense request called for $9.546 billion for the army; $12.013 billion for the navy; $17.737 billion for the air force, and $1.8 billion for the office of the secretary of defense and other activities. In terms of retaliatory power, the budget included extensive funding for the Atlas and Titan ICBM programs, the Polaris submarine program, manned bombers, carrier aircraft, intermediate-range ballistic missiles, and tactical aircraft.[43]

Anticipating questioning from the subcommittee about the relative capability of the United States versus the Soviet Union in missile capability, Gates stated the following: "Just matching our competitor, missile for missile, is not the answer. The simple piling up of ever larger numbers of a single weapon, without regard to their ability to survive a surprise attack or to perform effectively under a wide range of conditions, would not only be enormously costly but would not assure our security."[44]

Not surprisingly, the attention of the subcommittee turned quickly to the subject of Soviet missile capability. George Mahon, the well-respected and longtime chairman of the subcommittee, engaged Gates in the following exchange:

> MAHON: [You] argue that the opponent must not only be able to launch a massive attack on this country but he must be able to launch an attack on specific military targets if he is hoping to destroy our retaliatory power?
> GATES: That is correct, Mr. Mahon. If he fails to destroy our retaliatory power in his first blow, of course, he commits suicide.
> MAHON: He commits suicide. So he has a different problem from us?
> GATES: That is correct.[45]

Gates also received some support in the hearing from Congressman Gerald R. Ford (R-Michigan), his former fellow officer aboard the USS *Monterrey* in World War II and the ranking Republican on the subcommittee. At the outset of his questioning, Ford asked that a resumé of Gates's career in the navy during World War II as well as his experience at the Pentagon during the 1950s be entered into the record. Throughout his testimony, Gates had been emphasizing that the deterrent capability of the United States was sufficient to protect the country from a surprise missile attack, regardless of whatever advantage the Soviets might have, or not have, in missile technology. To illustrate, Ford and Gates engaged in the following exchange:

> FORD: On page 4 of your statement, Mr. Secretary, there is this sentence:
>
>> It is the conclusion of those who have analyzed this matter that even a surprise attack by all the missiles the Soviets could muster would not destroy enough of our retaliatory forces to enable him to make a rational decision to attack.
>
> Is there any significance you use only the word "missiles?"

GATES: The airplanes that he has we probably would be able to get warning, identify, and intercept. The real element of surprise would have to involve his missiles against which—*if he has any yet* [author's emphasis]—we do not yet have adequate warning. I think a true surprise attack would have to be a missile attack.

We have a warning capability against attack with the DEW [Distant Early Warning] line and other systems. I would assume, if he was going to attack, he would attack with airplanes as well as missiles.[46]

Gates's initial testimony before the House Subcommittee on Defense Appropriations would most likely have gone smoothly and positively for the administration, except for a brief passage in his opening statement to the subcommittee. In that statement, Gates alluded to the fact that American intelligence estimates regarding Soviet missile strength were based on "intentions" and not "capability." As the statement read, "Heretofore, we have given you intelligence figures that dealt with the theoretical Soviet capability. This is the first time that we have had an intelligence estimate that says, 'This is what the Soviet Union will do.'"[47]

The passage about intentions and capability enabled the administration's critics to claim that Eisenhower and Gates were using conjecture, instead of reliability, as a means of predicting the Soviet Union's future military behavior. With Khrushchev already claiming that the Soviets had an enormous stockpile of nuclear weapons, how could the administration, in good conscience, formulate a defense program that was not based on Soviet capability?

On January 21, Gates held a press conference at the Pentagon, where he attempted to clarify the meaning of his earlier remarks to the appropriations subcommittee. He largely did not succeed, however, primarily due to some probing but not necessarily hostile questioning from John Norris, who covered the Pentagon for the *Washington Post*. As Norris asked, "Mr. Secretary, disregarding any present day problems, as an old intelligence officer [referring to Gates's assignments in the navy during World War II], do you agree with basing your plans on estimates of intentions of an enemy rather than capabilities?"

Gates tried to work out of the semantic trap that he had created for himself, telling Norris, "I believe in basing it on the best intelligence that we can get, and these are the estimates that I am using." Norris continued, "Isn't that something that has never been done in the past, basing intelligence on intentions rather than capabilities? Isn't that something that intelligence officers don't like to do?" Once again, Gates tried to slip sideways. "No, I don't think so," he said. "I think they are based on the most accurate information they can get and this is the most accurate information the Department of Defense can get."[48]

Most of the reporters who covered the Department of Defense were aware that the Pentagon got significant amounts of intelligence about Soviet military strength from two large radar installations, one located in Turkey and the other in the Aleutian Islands. These installations were able to "see" 1000 miles into the Soviet Union and to observe missile launches, their trajectories, and the accuracy of their impacts.[49] But Gates was not using the intelligence obtained from these sources as his determining factor; he was using the U-2 data. The U-2 photography had given the United States more precise information about the Soviet Union's military capability, which the administration was using to formulate its defense program, but Gates was obviously not at liberty to disclose the means by which the administration acquired the information for these more precise estimates.

Gates was having a tough time. One cartoonist satirized him with a depiction of him gazing into a crystal ball as a way of determining defense policy. Richard Russell, Lyndon B. Johnson, and Stuart Symington all criticized the tenor of Gates's comments. Symington's criticism was the most scathing, charging Eisenhower with "juggling the intelligence books" in order to accommodate his overall spending plans.[50]

Gates recognized that the administration, in general, and the Department of Defense in particular, were in a tough political fight in Congress, one that unfortunately promised to focus on the ratio of ICBMs that the Soviet Union possessed, or would possess, compared with that of the United States. On January 16, therefore, Gates communicated some firm guidance to the civilian and military leadership in the Pentagon about the proper response to Congressional inquiries about such ratios. His guidance went as follows:

"Questions are going to be raised by various committees in Congress concerning the relative numbers of ICBMs in US and USSR forces. The answers in cross examination to all such questions should be along the following lines: 'The only figures which we pay any attention to are contained in the National Intelligence Estimate. These estimates are not made by any individual, but represent the best intelligence point of view that can be obtained by the persons responsible for the writing of the National Intelligence Estimate under the direction of the director of the Central Intelligence Agency. The Central Intelligence Agency advises the National Security Council and the President. Authority to release information contained in the National Intelligence Estimate can only be obtained from the President or in a classified briefing by the Director of the Central Intelligence Agency upon approval of the President.' . . . I have personally advised the Chairman of the Department of Defense Subcommittee (George Mahon, D-Texas) of the House Committee on Appropriations of this position. It is expected that all members of this Department will be guided in their dealings with the Congress and the public by the Defense position outlined herein." Also included in the guidance was a firm warning: "It is possible that some numerical ratio of numerical strengths may leak out through some thoughtless action on the part of some individual. Such action on the part of any member of this Department would be most serious and would lead to appropriate disciplinary action." As Gates was soon to discover, however, obtaining adherence to this guidance proved to be a difficult task.[51]

Tommy Power and Joe Alsop

More problems quickly presented themselves. On January 19, in a speech to the Economic Club of New York, and then again on January 28 in a speech to the American Legion, General Thomas Power, USAF, the commander of the Strategic Air Command (SAC), gave two speeches in which he advocated a 24-hour airborne alert for the American manned bomber fleet to prevent it from being wiped out in a surprise missile attack by the Soviet Union, as well as an expansion of the Air Force's B-70 strategic bomber program, then in its experimental stage. Of the two speeches, Power's speech on January 19 had the greatest impact whereby he laid out the nightmarish scenario that "only 300 ballistic missiles could virtually wipe out [America's] entire nuclear retaliatory capability in thirty minutes."[52] Interestingly, in both speeches, Power was not necessarily calling for an expansion of the American ICBM capability. Nevertheless, the "missile gap" critics jumped on Power's remarks as another example of the insufficiency of the American defense effort.

The fact that the administration's critics quickly embraced Power's views did not negate the fact that his remarks were hypothetical and unrealistic given the state of readiness of American forces at the time. As Gates later argued persuasively to congressional committees and in his news conferences and other public statements, Power's argument was faulty in the extreme. First of all, it assumed, erroneously, that the Soviets had acquired the missile capability that Power stated. It also assumed that bases of the Strategic Air Command would all be unprotected at the exact moment when the Soviets chose to strike and that the Soviet attack would be undetected prior to launch *and* that their missiles would have 100 percent accuracy. More importantly, Power's speeches failed to include the attack potential of the Polaris submarines, which were becoming a far more lethal weapon than manned bombers. Even given the virtual impossibility of a Soviet missile attack on the SAC bases, the Polaris submarines would be able to survive the attack and respond with a counterstrike that would decimate the Soviet Union.[53]

Years later, Gates spoke about his displeasure with General Power. "I think Tommy Power was really acting in terms of prejudice a bit, toward the air force struggle for power, [and the] struggle for a larger increase in the defense budget," Gates told the author. "He gave the so-called missile gap issue a big boost."[54] "In fact, Power kicked the missile gap argument off. Tommy Power was a problem child for [me]. . . . Tommy Power was a damn good officer, hell of a commander of SAC. . . . But he was a difficult fellow because he made too many speeches, and his speeches got me in trouble."[55]

When it rains, it pours. At the same time as the speeches given by General Power, the syndicated columnist Joseph Alsop began a six-part series in which he aggressively promoted the missile gap as a virtual foregone conclusion. In fact, Alsop's criticism of the Eisenhower administration's defense policy had begun as early as August 1, 1958, when he argued in a column published in the *New York Herald Tribune* that the Soviet Union would overtake the United States in missile production over a three-year period beginning in 1961. Alsop contended that the Soviets would have 100 ICBMs by 1961, 500 by 1962, and 1500 by 1963. By contrast, the United States would have no ICBMs in 1959, 30 by 1960, and 70 by 1961. Shortly after Alsop's article appeared, Senator John F. Kennedy (D-Massachusetts) charged the administration with allowing a "missile lag" to occur.[56] Alsop had succeeded in the initial creation of a major political issue.

Journalist Evan Thomas has provided an explanation for the hawkish views that Alsop expressed in his columns. According to Thomas, at the outset of the Eisenhower administration, Alsop sought to cultivate a relationship with Robert Cutler, Eisenhower's first national security adviser, and thereby use off-the-record conversations with Cutler as the basis for some of his columns. Alsop and Cutler had been classmates at Harvard, as well as members of Harvard's Porcellian Club, and Alsop apparently hoped that an "old school" type of appeal to Cutler would win him over as an inside source. Cutler refused Alsop's overture, however, leaving the journalist to search for sources within the Democratic Party, chiefly senators Lyndon Johnson and Stuart Symington, as well as sources within the military and in the CIA, including Allen Dulles and Richard Bissell.[57]

Beginning on January 25, therefore, one week after General Power's speech to the Economic Club of New York, Alsop began his six-part series of columns devoted exclusively to the missile gap controversy. Interestingly, while generally writing in a strong, critical tone of the administration, Alsop withheld serious criticism of Thomas Gates personally. In his January 25 column, for example, he referred to Gates as "the able, new secretary of defense." On January 26, he wrote that since the "survival [of the United States] quite literally depends on Secretary Gates being right [in his views about intentions and capabilities] it is important to know whether his confidence in the estimates is well founded. . . . Hence the published facts are dead against Secretary Gates."[58]

The four remaining articles in Alsop's series were equally alarmist in tone. On January 27, Alsop wrote that the "Eisenhower Administration is gambling the national future on the assumption that the Soviets cannot possibly have a number of operational ICBMs equivalent to 10 months capacity at our own Atlas missile plant." On January 28, he wrote that "Pearl Harbor was the result of the last time the American government based its defense posture on what it believed a hostile power would probably do and not on what the hostile power was capable of doing." On January 28, January 29, and January 30, Alsop used the term "Russian roulette" to describe the administration's approach to its missile program vis-à-vis that of the Soviet Union.[59]

Eisenhower was furious over the Alsop columns, at one time describing the columnist as "absolutely the lowest form of animal life on earth."[60] Likewise, Gates thought that Alsop was sensationalizing the missile gap controversy for his own purposes and his columns tended to reinforce public support for the views of the air force and, more specifically, those of General Power.[61]

Alsop's columns also had their effect in Moscow. As Aleksander Fursenko and Timothy Naftali wrote, "From Khrushchev's perspective the most unnerving development in the missile gap debate that he saw played out in U.S. newspapers was the start of a highly influential series of articles by Joseph Alsop that seemed to wrap all the prevailing missile gap lore with a bow."[62] Given Power's speeches, Alsop's articles, and the political rhetoric of the Democratic Party's presidential aspirants, the administration found itself unquestionably on the defensive at the end of January.

Thus, at the beginning of February, Thomas Gates was beleaguered and feeling the strain. On February 2, he and James Douglas, the DEPSECDEF, went to the White House for a meeting with Eisenhower and Andrew Goodpaster to discuss the status of the defense budget in Congress. He acknowledged that the program was in some disarray on Capitol Hill. Gates had spent a good part of January testifying before congressional committees about the defense budget, first to the House Appropriations Committee on January 13–15, then to the Senate Armed Services Committee on January 19, the House Armed Services Committee on January 21–22, and finally to the Senate Appropriations Committee on February 1. He discovered that Power's speeches had an impact on numerous congressmen and senators who were referring to them in their questioning.[63] Also, General Nathan Twining, the chairman of the Joint Chiefs of Staff, Allen Dulles, and Gates had all given different estimates of Soviet missile capability in their testimonies. Most disconcerting to Gates, however, was the testimony of Dulles to the Senate Preparedness Subcommittee on January 29 when the CIA director had provided "figures to the Congress that Defense had never seen prior to that time, and that had previously not been disclosed to Congress."[64]

Eisenhower was reassuring, telling Gates "to keep his sense of humor" because he "knew more about the subject" than did his critics. Ike was displeased with Dulles, though, stating "with some vehemence" that Dulles should not give "detailed figures to Congressional group[s] whose only purpose seems to be to misuse them and misinterpret their meaning."[65]

Gates also raised the point that he was having "a good deal of trouble" with the congressional committees because of McElroy's "three to one" comment in 1959. "With all the activity going on it is hard to avoid a few mistakes," he admitted. Eisenhower then told Gates, in effect, to relax and go about doing his job. Ike told the SECDEF that his record was fine and that he should "keep up the good work."[66]

The Administration Strikes Back

Despite the early setbacks, the Eisenhower administration believed in the validity of its defense program and refused to surrender the field to its critics. Eisenhower spoke forcefully against the missile gap–related criticisms and in support of Gates at two news conferences, one on January 26 and the other on February 3. On January 26, asked by Chalmers M. Roberts of the *Washington Post* about Gates's references to intentions and capabilities, Eisenhower responded, "Now, I think that we should never talk about an argument between intention and capability. Both of these are, of course, necessary when you are making an intelligence estimate. Let me point this out: we've got all of the power that would be necessary to destroy a good many countries. We have no intention of using it and the whole world knows it. . . . I think that Mr. Gates will find ways of clarifying exactly what he meant; because, in my opinion, he is a very splendid civil servant."[67]

The missile gap was once again front and center in the minds of the White House press corps when Eisenhower held another news conference on February 3. In the second question of the conference, Merriman Smith of UPI referred to comments, recently made by the administration's critics, that "we are well behind the Russians in military development, with little or no prospect of catching up," and asked

Ike for his views on such comments. "I am always a little bit amazed about this business of catching up," Eisenhower stated. *"What you want is enough, a thing that is adequate.* [Emphasis mine.] A deterrent has no added power once it has become completely adequate for compelling the respect of any potential opponent for your deterrent and, therefore, to make him act prudently."[68] Eisenhower then pointed out that almost $7 billion was being budgeted in the FY 1961 defense budget for "missiles of all kinds," adding "This, it seems to me, is getting close to the point where money itself will [not] bring you any speed, any quicker development."[69]

The next questioner was Rowland Evans of the *New York Herald Tribune*, who asked Eisenhower for his views about General Power's call for a 24-hour airborne alert. "Too many of these generals have all sorts of ideas," Ike responded forcefully. "But I do point this out: I have got the Secretary of Defense, whom I trust, and who I know is honest in his study, analysis, and conclusions. That is Secretary Gates."[70]

After his difficult encounters with the House Subcommittee on Defense Appropriations on January 13 and then with reporters at his press conference on January 21, Gates also began to find his feet and set out to refute the criticism of Joe Alsop and Tommy Power. On January 28, he participated in a televised interview with Senator Prescott Bush (R-Connecticut) and was asked to comment about the missile gap issue. The exchange went as follows:

> BUSH: Now, we hear talk in the newspapers and in politics, about the so-called "missile gap"—the fact that the Russians are going to have a missile advantage over us in due course, and very soon. The question I want to ask you is to comment about the missile gap, and are we likely to be vulnerable to attack in the early '60s because of the missile gap?
>
> GATES: We believe that according to our best estimates, the Soviet Union will have moderately more numbers of missiles in production and in operation around 1962, after which the numbers will close. However, the intercontinental missile is only one way of doing this terrible business; meanwhile, we are expanding our own missile program, putting missiles on our bomber force, and bringing into operation Polaris submarines which we believe will offset

any so-called missile gap, at least from the point of view of the validity of our deterrent.[71]

On February 1, Gates testified before the Senate Subcommittee on Defense Appropriations and appeared for the first time before Senator Symington, who was emerging as the Democratic Party's spokesman on defense. Before the hearings, James (Don) Hittle, Gates's military assistant in charge of congressional relations, was apprehensive. "Stuff was just raining down on Tom Gates," Hittle recalled, anticipating another difficult encounter with a congressional committee.[72] Hittle didn't have long to wait, as Symington and Gates began a round of verbal sparring:

> SYMINGTON: You mentioned your position on some of these matters was also the position of scientific and military experts. You would call Gen. Power an expert in the field of strategic airpower, would you not?
>
> GATES: I would call him one of our experts; yes, sir.
>
> SYMINGTON: If General Power is correct [about the need for a 24-hour airborne alert], and he is a man who has spent much time in the field, it would take 150 ICBMs plus the 150 IRBMs we know they already have to destroy our deterrent capacity, would it not, as he puts it?
>
> GATES: If SAC sat on their hands and did nothing, and if General Power's comments are correctly quoted. . . . So, without admitting that his statistics on the mathematical probability are necessarily correct, I would like to point out that he gave this speech for the purpose of obtaining an airborne alert, part of which we have bought in the programs that we are presenting to the committee.[73]

Gates endured a lengthy session of rhetorical combat with Symington, with the senator wanting a greater effort devoted to defense while the secretary supported the adequacy of the administration's program. Interestingly, the battle lines for the missile gap controversy were being drawn along the lines of General Power's advocacy of an airborne alert, not for more spending on missile development. Still, the issue remained. At news conferences on February 11 and February 17, Eisenhower pointed out how he believed that his prior experience in the military, as well as being the commander-in-chief, influenced his decisions. Merriman Smith of UPI once again raised the subject on February 11:

> SMITH: Mr. President, every day the public is being subjected to a new chapter in the controversy over the missile gap between this country and Russia. Now, this argument, as you are well aware, is being waged in public by men who are supposed to be experts in the defense requirements of the country. Is there anything you can say to us today to explain this controversy to the public; and, in this connection, sir, are you thinking of a nationwide speech on the subject?
>
> EISENHOWER: I want to point out again—possibly I don't need to—that I have been in the military service a long time. I am obviously running for nothing. I want only my country to be strong, to be safe, and to have a feeling of confidence among its people so they can go about their business.[74]

Then, on February 17, Eisenhower responded forcefully to a question from Charles Shutt of *Telenews* as to whether the administration's economic policies were shortchanging the defense effort. Shutt asked, "Mr. President, two of the many charges that your defense critics have made against you and your administration are that the administration has been complacent in advising the country of the danger we face in world affairs. The other is that the economy may stand in the way of developing some weapon or a series of weapons we may need. Sir, do you believe the administration has misled the people in any way, or that any money has been withheld from any weapon we might need?"

Eisenhower rejected such criticism, regardless of the source. As he said, "If anybody—anybody—believes that I have deliberately misled the American people, I'd like to tell him to his face what I think about him. This is a charge that I think is despicable. I get tired of saying that defense is to be made an excuse for wasting dollars. I don't believe that we should pay one cent for defense more than we have to."[75]

Eisenhower's concerns about the numerous charges and counter-charges about the adequacy of the administration's defense program led him to take the unusual step of including a section about defense in the nationwide speech that he gave to the country on February 21 before his tour of South America. The speech was not a major address solely on the issue of defense, a possibility that Merriman Smith had raised in the news conference on February 11, but rather part of a much longer speech dealing with hemispheric relations. For Ike, however, the section in the speech that dealt with defense had a number of purposes: first, to assure the country that America's military program was safeguarding the country; second, to show how America's retaliatory power, or its deterrent, made the whole notion of a missile gap untrue; and third, to show that American military strength relative to the Soviet Union was actually increasing. "We have created a great deterrent strength," Eisenhower said, "so powerful as to command and justify the respect of knowledgeable and unbiased observers here and abroad." The deterrent included a manned bomber force; "hundreds of Air Force bombers deployed the world over"; aircraft carriers and tactical aircraft armed with missiles "steadily augmenting the armament of all ground and other military units"; longer-range ballistic missiles, such as "our ATLAS missile, already amazingly accurate [and] operational last year"; "missiles of intermediate range in forward military bases"; and, finally, Polaris, "an almost invulnerable weapon [that] will soon be at sea."[76] Eisenhower concluded his remarks by saying, "Today in the presence of continuous threat, all of us can stand resolute and unafraid—confident in America's might as an anchor of free world stability."[77]

Eisenhower's speech on February 21 represented a turning point in the administration's fortunes relative to its critics. From that point forward, it went on the offensive in defending its program in Congress, with the press, and to the country, rather than merely react, as had been the case in January, to the views of its critics.

Thomas Gates had largely finished his congressional testimony on the FY 1961 defense budget by the end of February. What still awaited him, however, was testimony before the Preparedness Investigating Subcommittee of the Senate Armed Services Committee. Lyndon B. Johnson, the senate majority leader, was also the chairman of the subcommittee. For Gates, the previous three months had been harrowing, to say the least. Most mornings, he was arising at 4:30 A.M. to review briefing information on the status of the defense budget in Congress. On days when he testified before congressional committees, he returned to the Pentagon later in the day to tackle the day's business that had piled up in his absence. Moreover, the political environment was such that Gates himself had become a target of the political opposition owing to his support of the defense budget. "LBJ was under pressure from Symington," Don Hittle recalled. "There was definitely a 'Let's Get Gates' attitude" in some corners of Capitol Hill.[78]

Despite the political maneuvering, however, Gates had managed to establish a working relationship with Lyndon Johnson that, ironically, had occurred as a result of a tangle he had with Johnson about one year earlier. At the end of 1958, while Gates was secretary of the navy, he had initiated a round of cost cutting at thirty-two naval installations across the United States. One of the operations designated for cost reduction was the closing of the overhaul and repair department at the Corpus Christi Naval Air Station (NAS) in Corpus Christi, Texas. The navy's proposed closing of this department at Corpus Christi NAS meant the termination of 3,005 civilian employees in Johnson's home state of Texas. Moreover, Gates had taken this action without consulting Johnson in advance, certainly a political mistake on his part.

In response to Gates's decision, Johnson assigned Kenneth Belieu, the chief investigator of the preparedness subcommittee, to review the navy's action and then issue a report to the subcommittee. Not surprisingly, Belieu's final report concluded that the navy's decision was "ill-planned and hastily arrived at."[79] Johnson obviously wished to have Gates reverse his decision and retain the civilian jobs at the Corpus Christi NAS. On January 21, 1959, Johnson summoned Gates to a meeting in his office in the Senate. Also attending the meeting were Belieu, Sam Rayburn (D-Texas, who was the Speaker of the House of Representatives), and George Mahon. Accompanying Gates to the meeting was Captain Noel Gayler, his chief naval aide.

As Gayler recalled the meeting, "Ken Belieu had gone down to Texas and came back with an excellent lawyer's brief, concluding that the closing was not a money-saving proposition and would be wasteful. The Belieu pitch lasted quite a while and after which, LBJ said, 'Now, Mr. Secretary, in the light of all this information, don't you think that you should reconsider your decision? And Tom Gates said 'No.'"[80] An awkward silence ensued until Gates informed Johnson that he would allow Johnson to review the staff study by the navy department's Bureau of Aeronautics that formed the basis for his decision. Gates and Gayler then left Johnson's office and returned to their car for the ride back to the Pentagon. Again, Gayler recalled the conversation. "In the car [Gates] said, 'Noel, if I'd retreated one inch, they'd have cut out my liver.'"[81]

Not surprisingly, relations between Gates and Johnson remained frosty for a long while until Gates became the SECDEF. Then Gates credited an intervention by Robert Anderson, then secretary of the treasury, with Johnson to "normalize" relations between the two men. A native Texan, Anderson was a friend both of Johnson and of Sam Rayburn and managed to smooth out the misunderstandings that had remained after the episode involving Corpus Christi. Gates later recalled Anderson's role in the situation. LBJ was "a rough fella," Gates recalled. "Finally, Bob Anderson helped us patch things up. He told Johnson that I was [reasonable] and that he could work with me. After Johnson and I patched things up, he invited me over to visit him about three times a week. So I'd go over to his big suite of rooms in the Senate; pictures of him were all over the walls. Then around 5:30, he'd get up and say, 'Let's go see the Speaker.' Then we'd go and see [Sam] Rayburn. Other than Bob Anderson, I think I was the only member of the Eisenhower Administration to get in that room, which included Rayburn, LBJ, and John McCormack [D-Massachusetts, the house majority leader]. Once I got in that room, I quit worrying because [after that] I was always part of the club. I knew that however much they might beat me to death politically, they wouldn't hurt me much because I told them what they wanted to know about defense. Johnson and I got along well after that."[82]

Still, Gates anticipated rough treatment from the preparedness subcommittee when he was called to testify on March 16, if for no other reason than that it meant another skirmish with Senator Symington. Eisenhower must have sensed the apprehension on Gates's part and invited him to the White House in the early evening of March 15 for an exercise in morale-building. Once again, as Gates recalled, "Eisenhower sent for me one evening and asked me if I'd come up and have a Scotch with him, and I did. He said, 'How are you making out? I know you're having a tough time. 'I said, 'Yes.' He said, 'I'm trying to help you in my press conferences.' I said, 'I know you have and thank you.' He said, 'Are you almost through?' I said, 'Well, I've only got one to go, but that's the roughest of all. That's the Lyndon Johnson preparedness committee, tomorrow morning.' He said: 'That shouldn't be too bad.' I said 'Yes, it will. What's more that's under oath. That's an investigation. 'He said, 'You tell them that you won't take their damn oath. You took an oath of office, the same as I did. Just stand up there and tell 'em you won't take their oath.' I said, 'Well, some nights it's easy to be President. I think I'll have another Scotch.' But that [conversation] cheered me up. . . . Eisenhower always had a sense of helping his troops when they needed help, but leaving them to run their own jobs. I knew that I had the president's support and there wasn't much that the committee could do to me."[83]

Eisenhower's gesture of support energized Gates and made him considerably more relaxed as he awaited the preparedness hearings scheduled for March 16. Arriving at the Senate prior to the start of the hearings, though, Gates encountered a problem. His prepared statement had not been delivered and that was a serious error. Tremendous difficulties awaited any Cabinet officer who testified before a congressional committee without a prepared statement to give to the members. Don Hittle called Gates from the Pentagon. "Stall!" Hittle said, while he and his staff furiously tried to get the copy machine in the Office of the Secretary of Defense (OSD) to function properly. So Gates started a conversation with Senator Leverett Saltonstall (R-Massachusetts), the ranking Republican on the subcommittee, and they spoke to Johnson while the OSD staff hastily rode over to the Capitol with copies of the statement. Johnson also approached Gates before the hearing began and told him, "This isn't going to be too bad."[84] Literally at almost the last minute before the hearings were called to order, Don Hittle's assistant rushed in with five copies of the statement and Gates "marched into the hearing with aplomb."[85]

The chief counsel for the subcommittee was Edwin Weisl, an attorney from New York, and he did most of the initial questioning of Gates. Not surprisingly, Weisl focused on the numerical advantage in ballistic missiles that the Soviets allegedly were soon to enjoy over the United States. Gates held his ground, telling Weisl that "numbers are misleading because you have to reconcile the other factors that go into numbers and we are talking about only one weapons system, not other weapons systems."[86] Weisl also explored the question of whether the Russians might attempt a surprise attack on the United States, especially in view of General Power's previous statements. On that point, Weisl and Gates exchanged the following remarks:

WEISL: What assurance have you that the Russians won't make a surprise attack, similar to the attack by the Japanese on Pearl Harbor?

GATES: We do not believe the Soviet Union is interested in committing suicide.

WEISL: Are you trying to read his mind?

GATES: No, sir, I am not trying to read his mind. I am saying he is perfectly capable of seeing what we have in being that will destroy him if he initiates that surprise attack.

WEISL: You heard the testimony of General Power, that if . . . the Soviets had a certain number of ICBMs, they might be able to destroy completely our retaliatory striking force.

GATES: Yes.

WEISL: If we had no warning system and no airborne alert of adequate proportions.

GATES: This was a hypothetical, mathematical analysis made with no timetable, no estimate of our condition of readiness and I referred to it, I believe, as being somewhat unrealistic.

WEISL: Do you disagree with General Power?

GATES: Yes, sir.[87]

After Weisl finished, Senator Symington resumed the questioning of Gates. Much of Symington's questioning was given over to an exploration of the ratios in the defense capabilities between the United States and the Soviet Union. It quickly became clear, however, that both Symington and Johnson wanted only modest increases in defense spending as it related to missiles. In his questioning, Symington was the first to raise the subject in general terms, while Johnson more specifically focused on increased funding for the ATLAS and POLARIS programs. Johnson and Gates engaged in the following exchange:

JOHNSON: Mr. Gates, I am going to leave very shortly, and before doing so I want to thank you again for being with us this morning. I want to take this opportunity of emphasizing what I believe you already know, and that these committees before whom you are appearing today recognize you as a very sincere, dedicated, devoted, and patriotic public servant. We know your responsibilities are heavy and far flung. So are ours in the Congress, because of the unquestionability of our Nation's ability to defend itself against threat rests not only our American heritage, but the peace of the world. It is in that spirit that I tried to conduct these hearings. I have a few questions that I think you can answer briefly and I would like to have them in the record.

First, are you contemplating any operational facilities to the POLARIS and ICBM programs over those contained in the original submitted fiscal year 1961 budget?

GATES: I am using your word, "contemplating," Mr. Chairman. I am. We are reviewing other possibilities, and will continue to review them, in the case of POLARIS, contingent on other tests.

JOHNSON: Now, what would you do if we were to grant the Air Force's original request for 17 ATLAS squadrons rather than the 14 approved? In other words, suppose after we have heard the Central Intelligence Agency's estimates and we have heard from the Army, the Navy, the Air Forces, and other experts, such as the Chairman of the Joint Chiefs of Staff and former members of the Joint Chiefs, we conclude it is necessary to appropriate funds for X squadrons. You may be called upon to make a recommendation to impound those funds. You realize that this is a pretty serious responsibility you would be taking if, in effect, you veto the action of both branches of Congress.

GATES: I certainly do, Mr. Chairman.

JOHNSON: Have you ever made such a recommendation?

GATES: No, I never have, Mr. Chairman.

JOHNSON: You would stop, look, and listen before you did so, wouldn't you?

GATES: Yes, sir.[88]

Thus, the preparedness hearings ended with the clear marker that the Democratic Congress expected the administration to ask for additional defense spending, especially in the strategic area, but the good news was that the Congress was willing to allow the administration to, in a sense, fill in the details. So the next step was up to Eisenhower and to Gates to come up with some acceleration in the Pentagon's existing defense requests. To his credit, LBJ had managed to convey the sense of the Congress, or at least of the Senate, without any further inflammation of the missile gap issue.

The Missile Gap and the FY 1961 Defense Budget

Budget Revisions

With the sense of Congress in mind, Gates returned to the Pentagon and began meeting with the members of the Joint Chiefs of Staff to "contemplate" a modest increase to the missile effort. Actually, Gates had been in these discussions, as Johnson noted, with his associates prior to the hearings on March 16. Eventually, his suggested revisions included an expansion of POLARIS, an expansion of the Ballistic Missile Early Warning System, and increases in the number of missiles in each ICBM squadron. Still, even with the suggested changes, the revised total amount of funding that the administration was requesting from Congress was slightly lower than the original budget submission. Gates discussed these suggestions with Eisenhower on March 18 and, after extensive discussion within the Pentagon, obtained Eisenhower's agreement on April 6.[89]

On the same day, Gates once again appeared before the House Subcommittee on Defense Appropriations to discuss the revisions. Congressman George Mahon generally supported the revisions although he, like Johnson, expressed concerns about the sufficiency of the new program. Nevertheless, the revisions encountered no serious opposition when presented to the House.[90]

By this time, it was clear to most political observers in Washington that much of the heat had dissipated from the earlier hypercharged atmosphere in Congress about defense spending, as well as in the press. In fact, when Eisenhower held a news conference on March 30, he received virtually no questions from the reporters about the controversy over missile strength. The conference on March 30, in fact, was given over mostly to Eisenhower's just-concluded talks with British Prime Minister Harold Macmillan on the subject of disarmament, the first time in 1960 that the White House press corps had not asked Ike to comment specifically on the missile gap.[91] As a political issue, the missile gap was losing much of its momentum and appeared to be of considerably less importance as the presidential campaign approached.

But with the FY 1961 defense budget well along the way to eventual passage, Thomas Gates wanted to emphasize the worthiness of the administration's defense program. He chose his address to the annual meeting of the Associated Press in New York on April 25 to make that statement. In the speech, Gates laid out the achievements of the defense program, focusing on its deterrent capability, since Eisenhower took office in 1953. He also criticized the views of those who contended that the administration had failed to develop a defense program that protected the country. Gates's speech to the Associated Press was the most forceful address that he had given as SECDEF. An excerpt of that speech reads as follows:

> I came to the Pentagon in September of 1953. In the short span of one man's service, let us look at what has happened.
>
> In 1953 no ship afloat was powered by atomic energy. Today we have nine nuclear submarines already in commission and 23 under construction or conversion. Under construction is a nuclear-powered [aircraft] carrier, a nuclear-powered cruiser and a nuclear-powered frigate. The *Nautilus* has cruised under the North Pole, followed by the *Skate*; the *Seawolf* has stayed underwater for an unprecedented 60 days. The nuclear-power submarine has revolutionized sea warfare and rightly caught the imagination of the world.
>
> In 1953 the POLARIS system was merely a dream. This year it becomes a reality, as two of these submarines, each capable of firing 16 atomic tipped missiles while submerged, join our active defense forces.
>
> In 1953 an airplane which was expected for the first time to operate at speeds greater than the speed of sound was in the very early design stage. Today, MACH 2 aircraft are part of our regular forces, and a MACH 3 plane is in our active research and development program.
>
> In 1953 we were devoting our full energies to the development of air-breathing missiles such as the SNARK and the NAVAHO. The ballistic missile–ATLAS—was a concept only. It was surrounded by doubters; its proponents asserted it could be operational by 1965. Today the first ATLAS are in position on the Pacific Coast, with an astonishing record of successful test firings, and a proved accuracy that has far exceeded the hopes of even a year ago. Meanwhile the early air-breathing missiles have been developed, been produced, become operational, and then been superseded in the swift program of technology.
>
> In 1953, the Intermediate Range Ballistic Missiles, JUPITER and THOR, were not even contemplated. Today the THOR is

The Missile Gap and the FY 1961 Defense Budget

in the hands of our Allies in the United Kingdom, and it was a JUPITER booster which in 1958 launched this nation's first satellite into space.

These changes have occurred in less than seven years—the time that used to be regarded as par for the course in the development of a fighter aircraft.

Meanwhile, with the impressive record in research and engineering, our forces in being have demonstrated their ability to react quickly and effectively to situations that have arisen—such as those at Lebanon and Quemoy. We have been a strong force in keeping the peace.

Who says this is a backward, second-second class military record? I say it is superb.[92]

On April 29, the House Appropriations Committee passed the FY 1961 defense budget. The full House of Representatives approved the budget on May 5, slightly less than two weeks before the start of the summit conference in Paris. The Senate bill added additional funding so that the final defense budget that Eisenhower approved resulted in total spending of $40.991 billion, or almost $600 million more than the administration originally requested.[93]

But once the House passed the defense budget, the administration had gained the upper hand on the defense issue, at least for the moment. Even though the final defense budget did not reach final congressional approval until July 7, Eisenhower still had the ability to go to Paris without leaving behind a trail of partisan rancor over the issue of military spending.[94] Likewise, Thomas Gates had done his job, moving the administration's defense program through a Congress controlled by the Democratic opposition and in a white-hot presidential election year. His political skills in forming a rapport with Lyndon Johnson, Sam Rayburn, and George Mahon, as well as with Republican leaders like Leverett Saltonstall and Prescott Bush in the Senate and Jerry Ford in the House, played significant roles in his ability to get the administration's program enacted. "With Eisenhower as president, and Johnson and Rayburn in the Congress, you always knew that on defense and foreign policy you'd win, though for political purposes they might give you hell," Gates once told Eisenhower biographer William Bragg Ewald.[95]

Chapter 5

The passage of the FY 1961 defense budget was mostly a victory for Eisenhower, who tenaciously defended the administration's program against its vigorous critics, men such as Stuart Symington in the Senate, Joseph Alsop in the press, and even active military officers like Tommy Power. In this effort, Ike never flagged—not in his news conferences, in his public speeches, his conferences with members of the Joint Chiefs of Staff, or in bolstering the faltering morale of administration front-liners like Gates. Occasionally, Ike's personal side shone through, as on April 6, 1960, when he sent the following letter to Gates:

Dear Tom,

If possible, on Sunday, [April 10, Gates's birthday], I suggest you read no newspapers, or listen to no television pundits—especially those that relate to the state of our military defenses. Otherwise, I don't see how you possibly can have the enjoyable birthday anniversary that you most certainly deserve.

Pay no attention to the slings and arrows and know that you have my warm felicitations and, as always, my best wishes.

With personal regard, and Happy Birthday,
As ever,
DE
P.S. And do try to get some rest![96]

The task of having to defend his defense budget must have been extremely distasteful for Eisenhower, especially since his critics were challenging him on his strong point, defense policy and national security, where his achievements and credentials were unparalleled in the United States of the 1950s. As Monte Reel has written, "If his critics believed the heaviest burden Eisenhower shouldered was his golf bag, they were underestimating him. Particularly in matters of national security, Eisenhower was an informed leader."[97] By the end of April 1960, Eisenhower had achieved two of his objectives: a successful visit by Nikita Khrushchev to the United States and the passage of the administration's defense budget. What remained next was the summit in May followed by his visit to the Soviet Union in June.

Chapter 6

The Crash, the Crisis, and the Collapse, May 1–24, 1960

At his press conference on April 27, 1960, President Dwight D. Eisenhower received a question from Robert Pierpoint of CBS News about his expectations for the upcoming Four Power summit in Paris, scheduled to begin on May 16. Given the list of problems at the time, especially the issues of disarmament and the future status of Berlin, Pierpoint asked Eisenhower about his "hopes for the Summit conference."[1] "I think that the most we can hope for, at this time," Ike replied, "is [some] ease of tension, some evidence that we are coming closer together—sufficiently so that people have a right to feel a little bit more confident in the world in which they are living and in its stability."[2]

Despite this expression of low-balled, diminished expectations, Eisenhower was cautiously optimistic about the upcoming summit. Even if no substantive agreements were reached at Paris, the process of deliberation between the four leaders held out the prospect for a noticeable improvement in the international situation.

Less than one week later, Eisenhower's hopes for a successful summit meeting with Nikita Khrushchev came crashing to earth as, on May 1, the Soviets brought down an American U-2 aircraft, piloted by Francis Gary Powers, on a surveillance flight over the Soviet Union. Powers miraculously survived the crash, but was apprehended by Soviet authorities, and subsequently tried and convicted for espionage. Khrushchev used the crash of the U-2, the capture of Powers, and eventually Eisenhower's acceptance of responsibility for the overflight as the rationale for, first,

Chapter 6

walking out on the summit meeting and, second, postponing and, in effect, canceling, Eisenhower's visit to the Soviet Union scheduled for June. The tensions of the Cold War quickly returned as the United States and the Soviet Union embarked on a renewed period of recrimination and animosity.[3]

A number of factors influenced the decision by the Eisenhower administration to schedule such a risky act of espionage so close to the summit meeting in Paris. Near the top of the list was the pressure that Allen Dulles, the director of the CIA, and Richard Bissell, the deputy director, applied to Eisenhower for one additional flight prior to the summit. Dulles and Bissell feared that any agreement reached in Paris might lead to a suspension of the U-2 program, and the U-2 flights were, until new satellite technology became operational, the primary means of acquiring intelligence about the Soviet Union's military programs. But second, Eisenhower also acknowledged the wisdom of having the latest information that was available about the Soviet Union's military programs when he went to Paris, especially since the administration was still under partisan political attack over the issue of the missile gap.[4]

Once the Soviets managed to bring down the U-2 and capture Powers, however, the Eisenhower administration in general, and the president specifically, reacted with an uncharacteristic measure of hesitation and even confusion. First, the administration essentially lied about the fate of the U-2 and its pilot when it went missing on May 1 and in the next few days that followed. On May 5, when Khrushchev revealed in Moscow that the Soviets had brought down the aircraft and collected some of its wreckage, the administration temporized once again until on May 7, when Khrushchev showed that the Soviets held Powers, "quite alive and kicking." The administration had hoped to protect Eisenhower from taking responsibility for the overflights, but it quickly became clear that such a strategy was virtually impossible in the light of Khrushchev's revelations. Eisenhower admitted as much on May 9 at a meeting of the National Security Council by saying that the U-2 activity "had been going on for years; consequently, it was inevitable that it would be revealed sooner or later." Finally, on May 11, Eisenhower asserted himself, taking responsibility for the U-2 program and the flight by Powers, justifying it on the basis of the closed Soviet society and its "fetish of secrecy and concealment."[5]

But the administration's tentative responses to Khrushchev's statements, surprisingly, created greater problems for the Soviet leader than for Eisenhower. Under pressure from hard-line elements within the Soviet hierarchy for his overtures to Eisenhower in 1959 and early 1960, as well as for his announced reductions in the manpower levels of the Red Army, Khrushchev hoped for a rapprochement with Ike that the president's admission of acceptance for the U-2 flights made impossible. As C. Douglas Dillon, the undersecretary of state at the time, told the author, the U-2 crisis "made it impossible to have the summit. . . . Khrushchev had lost face; how could he sit down with someone who had been flying planes over Moscow?"[6]

Given his predicament, Khrushchev nevertheless went to considerable lengths to save the situation, even pleading with Ambassador Tommy Thompson at a diplomatic reception in Moscow on May 9, "This U-2 thing has put me in a terrible spot," Khrushchev told Thompson. "You have to get me off it."[7] But the efforts on both sides to cast aside their discord ultimately failed. Charles E. "Chip" Bohlen, Thompson's predecessor as the American ambassador to the Soviet Union, and at the time an adviser on Soviet affairs to Secretary of State Herter, once put it succinctly: "The downing of the plane *and* [emphasis mine] the capture of the pilot made the problem insoluble."[8]

The Crash

The aerial surveillance mission that Francis Gary Powers undertook on May 1, 1960, had its roots in three events that occurred in 1959 and 1960: photos obtained by American intelligence officers who accompanied Vice President Richard Nixon's flight over Sverdlovsk when Nixon visited the Soviet Union in July 1959; Nikita Khrushchev's speech in Moscow on January 14, 1960; and the meeting of the President's Foreign Intelligence Advisory Board (PFIAB) on February 2, 1960.

First, Jenny Thompson and Sherry Thompson revealed in their book, *The Kremlinologist,* that when Richard Nixon visited the Soviet Union in July 1959, his delegation included several American intelligence officers who were assigned to gather information about the Russian ICBM program. After Nixon met with Khrushchev in Moscow, he and his delegation left the Soviet capital to visit Leningrad, Novosibirsk, and Sverdlovsk. While flying over Sverdlovsk, sometimes regarded as "Russia's Pittsburgh," for its industrial capacity, the intelligence officers engaged in what might be called "low-tech" aerial surveillance by photographing suspected missile sites. The photographs were later turned over to Richard Bissell and the CIA. Bissell then used the photographs of the Sverdlovsk region to convince Eisenhower to send the U-2 piloted by Francis Gary Powers over this part of the Soviet Union.[9]

Second, as discussed previously (see chapter five, above), Khrushchev's speech on January 14, 1960, designed to allay suspicions about the Soviet Union's military intentions in eastern Europe, had almost the opposite effect. By using such language as a "stock of rockets" and "well-concealed rocket bases," Khrushchev only raised apprehensions, especially at the CIA, where a consequence of the speech was the renewal of pressure on Eisenhower for more overflights before any more "concealment" could occur.

Third, on February 2, Eisenhower met with the PFIAB and it was clear that the group wanted to recommend a much more aggressive series of overflights. General James Doolittle, one of the board's leading members, argued that the military capability of the Soviet Union was expanding and more overflights were necessary to monitor any more advances in the Soviet Union's military technology. But Eisenhower was skeptical about the necessity for more overflights; he had not seen any such advances beyond those which Khrushchev had discussed with him at Camp David. Moreover, in a poignant and even prophetic remark, Eisenhower said that "he has one tremendous asset in a summit meeting, as regarded [the] effect in the free world. That is his reputation for honesty. If one of these aircraft were lost when we are engaged in apparently sincere deliberations, it would be put on display in Moscow and ruin the President's effectiveness."[10]

Despite Eisenhower's reservations, he nevertheless authorized a resumption of the U-2 overflights. As John Eisenhower recalled, against Ike's caution "were arrayed the technical and policy judgments of Bissell, Dulles, Goodpaster, Twining, and [Eisenhower] gave way" owing to his trust in these advisers.[11] There was another dimension to the U-2 program, as well. In 1959 and 1960, British Prime Minister Harold Macmillan authorized U-2s flown by RAF pilots to engage in reconnaissance flights over the Soviet Union. In fact, on February 5, 1960, virtually the same time as the PFIAB meeting, British Flight Lieutenant John MacArthur left Peshawar, Pakistan, for a U-2 mission over several suspected Soviet missile sites. MacArthur found no evidence of any ICBM construction, but he did photograph a facility for making a new medium-range bomber.[12] MacArthur's flight occurred just prior to Ambassador Henry Cabot Lodge's visit to Moscow on February 7–9, 1960. Lodge may or may not have been aware of MacArthur's recent overflight when he spoke with Khrushchev. According to Lodge, Khrushchev treated him with the "utmost" cordiality, not reflecting any tension over yet another penetration of Soviet airspace by a U-2.[13]

It stands to reason that the Soviets tracked MacArthur's flight just as they had the previous U-2 flights flown by American pilots. Whether they knew that MacArthur was British is unclear. However, on March 5, Khrushchev delivered a brief speech in Moscow in which he urged restraint by the nations that were involved in the upcoming summit conference. He had just returned to the Soviet Union after a twenty-four-day tour of India, Burma, Indonesia, and Afghanistan. In his speech, Khrushchev encouraged all countries not to take any actions that "could complicate matters" before the summit conference. "The Soviet Union goes to these talks full of readiness, together with other countries, to ease international tension and to bring about a settlement of outstanding questions," he said. "We on our side have done and will do everything to create a favorable atmosphere for the forthcoming talks. . . . The thing now is that no country should by one action or another complicate matters."[14] The question remains: was Khrushchev using this speech to warn the Americans (and perhaps the British, as well) not to make any more U-2 flights before the summit and thereby "complicate matters"?

Nevertheless, the CIA proceeded with scheduling the next U-2 flight by an American pilot. On April 7, Bissell asked Eisenhower for permission to fly the U-2 on April 9. Called Operation Square Deal and piloted by Bob Ericson, the flight focused on an area near the city of Plesetsk in northern Russia where the Soviets were thought to be working on an ICBM installation. Soviet radar tracked the flight and the Russians did not file a diplomatic protest, an odd development since previous overflights had resulted in such protests. The flight revealed no new missile construction, however.[15]

Chapter 6

Ericson's flight over the Soviet Union angered Khrushchev, the Soviet military, and the hard-liners in the Kremlin who opposed Khrushchev's attempt to improve relations with the United States. Moreover, the Soviet air defenses performed miserably in their attempts to intercept Ericson as he flew over several key military installations, at Sary Shagan, Semipalatinsk, Dolon, and Tyuratam. As historian Curtis Peebles has written, the Soviet air defenses had ample opportunities to fire air-to-air and surface-to-air (SAM) missiles at Ericson but failed to coordinate their ground control and communications systems. Ericson exited Soviet airspace, into Iran, without being fired on, and with his photographs. Khrushchev established a commission to investigate the failures of the April 9 effort and, as a result of the commission's investigation, reprimanded "a number of generals and senior officers."[16] These reprimands from Khrushchev sent out a clear message to the Soviet air defenses: as Jenny Thompson and Sherry Thompson wrote, bring down the next American (or British) U-2 or plan to "move permanently to Siberia."[17]

Dulles and Bissell continued to press Eisenhower for one more overflight prior to the opening of the summit conference on May 16. At this point, and considering the events that were to follow, some speculation is appropriate. At the Western Summit in December 1959, Eisenhower, Macmillan, de Gaulle, and Adenauer searched for a date for the Four Power summit conference. Originally, the four leaders proposed a summit conference in Paris for the third or fourth week in April but, for a number of reasons—Eisenhower's previously postponed meeting with the King of Nepal, Macmillan's meetings with the Commonwealth ministers, de Gaulle's desire for a visit to Washington before the summit conference—the "early" summit date was set aside in favor of a "later" summit date after May 1, the Soviet Union's national holiday. More than likely, Khrushchev would have accepted any date conveniently scheduled before or after May 1. It is highly possible that, if the Western leaders had agreed on the earlier date, such as the one proposed for April 22–26, Operation Square Deal would have been the last U-2 flight before the summit conference. Under those circumstances, Eisenhower may not have been willing to authorize any more overflights after April 9.

Moreover, the U-2 flight on April 9 provoked considerable internal outrage at the United States within the councils of the Kremlin. "When will they poke their noses in again?" Khrushchev asked after Ericson's flight. Khrushchev was perplexed: why would the American government risk an international incident so close to the summit? Had Eisenhower authorized the flight or was it the work of the hated Allen Dulles and the CIA? (Both, as it turned out.) Khrushchev saw no point in filing another note of diplomatic protest since it would be only another admission of Russian weakness. Was the United States, Khrushchev wondered, trying to expose Soviet weakness on the eve of the summit?[18]

What's more, Operation Square Deal took place at exactly the same time that James Hagerty and his advance party were touring the Soviet Union in preparation for Eisenhower's visit in June. On April 9, when Ericson was overflying the Soviet Union, Hagerty and selected members of his party were leaving Leningrad en route to Kiev.[19] For Khrushchev, it must have appeared that the Americans were sending mixed signals: conducting hostile aerial espionage, on the one hand, while members of the administration were engaged in friendly talks with Soviet officials on the other.

After Operation Square Deal, Dulles and Bissell met with Eisenhower to request another flight before May 16. The rationale for the flight was to observe any possible construction of an ICBM site near Plesetsk as well as the possibility of construction of an ICBM base near Sverdlovsk in the central part of the country. Eisenhower relented: he approved one more flight. On April 25, Andrew Goodpaster informed Bissell that, "After checking with the President, I informed Mr. Bissell that one additional operation may be undertaken, provided it is carried out prior to May 1. No operation is to be carried out after May 1."[20]

The name given to the mission was Operation Grand Slam. The pilot selected for the mission was Francis Gary Powers, the most experienced of the U-2 pilots and a veteran of the program since 1956. The flight path called for Powers to depart from a base in Peshawar, Pakistan, and fly completely across the Soviet Union, obtaining aerial photography of virtually every known military asset of the Russians, but specifically those around Sverdlovsk and Plesetsk.[21] Given its proximity to the start of the summit conference, as well as the imminent deployment of satellites with a reconnaissance capability, Operation Grand Slam may well have been the last of the U-2 flights over the Soviet Union. As matters turned out, of course, it *was* the last of such flights during the Eisenhower administration. For this mission, the code name for Powers was Puppy 68.[22]

Chapter 6

Then came the problems. The weather and cloud cover over the Soviet Union failed to cooperate. On April 25, such weather conditions over the Soviet Union made the flight impossible. On April 28, the weather cooperated but Powers had not taken his preflight physical examination. On April 29, the weather turned bad once again; snowfall at Sverdlovsk ruled out the possibility of flying that day. On April 30, too much cloud cover again prevailed over the Soviet Union.

These postponements created problems for the selection of the aircraft. To maintain secrecy, the U-2 selected for the flight was ferried, under cover of darkness, between the base at Incirlik, Turkey, and the base at Peshawar each night on April 27 and April 28. As a result, the aircraft needed to be pulled out and given scheduled maintenance by April 30.[23] The U-2 that Powers used for the flight, therefore, was not the one originally assigned, and the one that the pilot preferred. Instead, Powers was flying a U-2, number 360, that had "a reputation for cranky performance" in the words of historian John Prados.[24] In 1959, this particular aircraft had almost been destroyed during a "crashed" emergency landing in Japan. Powers called the plane "a dog. Something was always going wrong with it."[25]

On May 1, 1960, Francis Gary Powers took off from his base in Peshawar, Pakistan, and entered Soviet airspace at 5:36 A.M. After traveling more than 1,300 miles, number 360's autopilot malfunctioned. Flying over Sverdlovsk, Powers felt a dull "thump," followed by a violent convulsion, which caused him to lose control of the aircraft. Shrapnel from a Soviet SAM missile launched from a battery near Sverdlovsk had penetrated the outer skin of the U-2 and shredded its fuel system. Powers and the U-2 plunged to the earth, with fragments of the damaged plane falling everywhere.

Powers managed to escape from his doomed aircraft, opened his parachute, and descended to the earth, where he awaited certain capture by the Soviet authorities. As he fell toward the ground, Powers thought that "the landscape below looked like parts of Virginia. As if wishing I could make it so."[26] Once on the ground, he was quickly apprehended and then taken into custody by two police. In his possession, he had a poison needle that could be used to commit suicide. He did not use it. In the minds of at least some individuals in the administration, Powers should have used the needle if he faced capture by the Soviets. Thomas Gates, however, never blamed Powers for his refusal to take his life. Years later, Gates recalled, "I don't know what [Powers's] instructions were, but I'm sure that nobody would give instructions to a person to kill himself.... I hope they wouldn't anyway." Then Gates observed, sarcastically, that "There [were] some brave heroes after this happened that said of course [Powers] should have killed himself but I don't know, when you face that kind of a moment of truth, I don't know how you answer that kind of a question unless you face it personally. I'm sure he was not ordered to kill himself." Was Gates critical of Powers's behavior at the time? "No, not at all."[27]

What had gone wrong? How had the Soviets managed to shoot down this particular U-2, after having failed to bring down Ericson and his U-2 just three weeks earlier? Two versions, one belonging to Richard Bissell and the other to Sergei Khrushchev, of the fate of Powers's doomed flight bear some examination. According to Bissell, "our luck just plain ran out." While Powers was flying near the Sverdlovsk region, the Soviets fired three SAM missiles at his plane. One missile missed completely; a second struck and destroyed a Soviet MiG aircraft that was trying to intercept Powers; and the third missile detonated close enough to Powers "to damage the outer layer of the aircraft."[28] After losing control of the plane, Powers eventually managed to struggle free but was unable to press the destruct mechanism of the plane. The Soviets, thereby, were able to capture the pilot as well as the wreckage of the U-2, including the rolls of film that had been taken during the flight.

In an interview with the author more than a decade before the publication of Bissell's memoir in 1995, C. Douglas Dillon agreed with Bissell's analysis, contending that the Soviets shot down the U-2 with a SAM, "from a battery which we knew the Russians were installing but which we didn't think was operational. We could see the Russian interceptors going up to 40,000 feet and then fire their rounds at the plane and missing."[29]

Sergei Khrushchev's account of the Powers episode is considerably more detailed and differs significantly from that of Bissell. According to Sergei Khrushchev, the Soviets learned of the penetration of their airspace by the "intruder" early in the morning of May 1. News of this latest overflight left Nikita Khrushchev in a foul mood, especially since he had a full day's worth of activities planned for May Day. Charles Bohlen later recalled that flying over the Soviet Union on May Day was like "Spitting in a Bolshevik's eye." Soviet missile forces were available, but their status was uncertain due to the holiday. As the leaders of the Soviet air forces watched the path of Powers's flight from their command center in Moscow, it appeared that the "intruder" knew the path to take in order to evade the missile batteries on the ground below. Then, inexplicably, Powers changed the path of his aircraft and came back into the range of the Soviet SAMs. The Soviets gave the order to fire the missiles: only one was launched and it appeared that the "intruder" was about to escape.[30]

Then, at 8:53 A.M., a flash appeared in the sky, followed seconds later by the "faint sound of an explosion." On the ground, the Soviet air force officers initially thought that the "intruder" was performing a maneuver designed to evade his attackers. Then, a second battery fired three missiles at Powers, whose plane was not eluding its attackers, but was disintegrating and falling to the ground. At this point, it is helpful to point out the extreme vulnerability of the U-2 to attack by a SAM. Robert Rhodamer, a veteran of numerous U-2 flights, wrote that "the vulnerable aspect of the U-2 at that high altitude was that all you had to do was disturb the atmosphere in front of the airplane and that would make the engines flame out [because] the air flow was so low."[31] It is entirely possible, therefore, that even without the near-miss explosion of the Soviet SAM, the flights of the missiles themselves might have been sufficient to cause the U-2 to self-destruct.

Of those missiles fired at Powers by the second Soviet battery, the first missile shot had exploded behind the U-2, causing the damage described by Bissell and Dillon. Then, in the second round of missiles, two missed but one hit the falling aircraft, by then only 18,000 feet above the ground. One of the missiles struck and destroyed a MiG aircraft sent to intercept Powers, however. The fact that the Russian air force also lost a pilot, Sergei Safronov, in their attempt to shoot down Powers remained a closely guarded secret in the Soviet Union for decades.[32]

On the ground, Powers was apprehended by several Russian citizens who drove over to him from a nearby collective farm. They helped Powers to his feet and cut off the shroud lines to his parachute. They asked him how he felt and what his identity was. Powers responded unintelligibly. "Are you Bulgarian?, Bulgarian?" they asked. Powers nodded, to the negative. Then, one Russian wrote "U.S.A." on one of the car's dirty windows, and Powers nodded affirmatively. His captors took him to the nearby state farm in Sverdlovsk, where he was released to the KGB, soon destined to begin a two-year incarceration.[33]

At the same time in Moscow, Khrushchev and the members of the Soviet hierarchy watched the May Day parade from their viewing stand atop Lenin's Tomb. It was from that location that Khrushchev received the news of Powers's capture. Members of the staff of the American embassy were also watching the May Day parade from rooms at the Hotel Nacional overlooking Red Square. They quickly realized that something unusual was happening, judging from the huddle that was occurring among the Soviet leadership atop Lenin's Tomb. As Hans Tuch recalled, "We were watching the May Day parade from the Hotel Nacional when a military officer [Marshal Sergei Bryuzov, the commander of Soviet air defense] came up to Khrushchev and gave him the news. Everyone left the reviewing stand all at once."[34]

When Powers failed to reach his destination at Bodo, Norway, feelings of concern spread in Washington. Was Powers alive or dead? If he was alive, where was he? Had the plane been destroyed or did the Soviets have any of its wreckage? Even if the Russians had Powers and the aircraft, would they admit it? As Douglas Dillon recalled, "We had been following the plane by radar. We knew where it was, and knew that it had gone down. It just started to circle and lose altitude, and finally disappeared. So we didn't know what to do."[35] The disappearance of Powers and the U-2 was hardly good news, but the administration was not inclined to draw any hasty conclusions at that point. The presumption, of course, was that Powers could not survive a crash and that a cover story could be released to the press stating that "a weather research plane" had been lost in a mission over Turkey.[36] On May 2, Goodpaster conferred with John Eisenhower about the missing U-2. As John Eisenhower recalled, "General Goodpaster told me about the plane going down.... Our only reaction was just feeling sorry for the pilot and that was about all there was to it because we were assured [by the CIA] that nobody would ever be taken alive."[37]

The decision to release a cover story that was demonstrably false was but the first in a series of unforced errors that later resulted in the failure of the summit conference and the cancellation of Eisenhower's visit to the Soviet Union. As Alexandr Fursenko and Timothy Naftali have written, in the event of a downed U-2, Eisenhower was presented with two courses of action from the outset of the U-2 program in 1956: admit the existence of an espionage program based on aerial surveillance as a cold, hard necessity of the Cold War or concoct a demonstrably false cover story. The first alternative had its defenders, most notably two prominent scientists, Edwin Land of the Polaroid Corporation and James Killian, Eisenhower's science adviser. In their estimation, the necessities of the Cold War required the United States to maintain a strong intelligence capability, especially in view of the concern about a surprise attack by an enemy with nuclear weapons. In the event of a failed U-2 mission, the United States should use that argument as the basis for its actions. Richard Bissell, on the other hand, advocated the route of the cover story and Eisenhower supported the second approach, assuming that no pilot could survive the crash of a U-2, despite the fact that several U-2 pilots *had* survived crashes in training exercises over the desert in Arizona. On May 3, knowing that an American U-2 had been lost over the Soviet Union, the administration released its cover story about the lost weather research plane to the press under the provenance of the National Aeronautics and Space Administration (NASA). Hardly a murmur of interest appeared on May 3 and May 4 to challenge this rather unique story.[38]

May 5–9, 1960

At 4 A.M. on May 5, Secretary of Defense Thomas Gates unexpectedly woke to a telephone call informing him that the Joint Chiefs of Staff had put into operation a civil defense exercise at High Point, North Carolina, a place known as "The Rock," which required the evacuation from Washington of the president and his chief advisers. Gates dressed hastily and then was driven by his wife, Anne, to a helicopter pad in northwest Washington about ten minutes from his home, where he awaited evacuation to High Point.[39]

Arriving at the pad, Gates greeted Allen Dulles, his companion for the flight. Once airborne, Dulles reached inside his coat pocket and pulled out a single sheet of paper. "Here, Tom," Dulles said, staring straight ahead, "Read this."[40] From Dulles's message, Gates learned that Khrushchev claimed to have the wreckage of the U-2 and intended to reveal this startling information in a speech before the Supreme Soviet in Moscow. The falsity of the cover story was about to become known internationally. A major international incident was in the process of unfolding.

On May 5, Khrushchev gave his speech to the Supreme Soviet, and the dispatch that Allen Dulles showed Tom Gates was a clear reflection of that speech. Seated in the audience for the speech were American Ambassador Tommy Thompson and Vladimir Toumanoff, a political attaché in the American embassy. As Toumanoff remembered the scene, Khrushchev gave a very long speech but saved the news about the downing of the U-2 for the climax. Interrupted by wild applause, Khrushchev went on and on, blaming American "perfidy" and its "appalling, nefarious" behavior. In his harsh denunciation of the United States, Khrushchev kept his eyes fixed on Thompson, who showed no response to these remarks. Thompson was a "masterful poker player," according to Toumanoff, and his unflappability served him well on this occasion. After Khrushchev finished the speech, Thompson and Toumanoff returned to the American embassy, where Thompson immediately prepared a telegram to be sent to the State Department. To the members of the embassy's staff, Thompson appeared visibly upset about not being informed about the U-2 flights.[41]

A further analysis of Khrushchev's speech on May 5 was revealing as much for what he left unsaid as for what he said. He did not mention Powers, nor did he suggest that the Soviets had acquired anything of value from the wreckage. Perhaps just as important, Khrushchev made no attempt to link Eisenhower with the overflight, instead blaming "militarists in the Pentagon or the CIA."[42]

Back at "The Rock" in North Carolina, it was not clear to Eisenhower and his advisers what the exact situation was in Moscow, since Khrushchev had not mentioned anything about the status of the pilot. Therefore, after a brief meeting of the National Security Council, Eisenhower met with Allen Dulles; Douglas Dillon, representing Secretary of State Herter, who was flying back from Turkey after a meeting of the North Atlantic Council in Istanbul; Gordon Gray, national security advisor; Andrew Goodpaster; and Thomas Gates to discuss the U-2 situation. Eisenhower left the discussion shortly afterward and the consensus of those who remained was that, despite Khrushchev's speech, the administration intended to hold to the cover story and that the State Department, but not NASA, would make any necessary public statements. Goodpaster was designated to convey that information to James Hagerty, who was to handle the inevitable press inquiries. Back in Washington, however, Hagerty apparently told Goodpaster that the administration needed to follow the cover story, and refer inquiries to NASA.[43] Given that understanding, the president should not accept any responsibility for the U-2 program, in general, or for this particular flight.

At the meeting between Dulles, Dillon, Gray, and Goodpaster, Gates was the only one who disagreed with the recommendation that the president should not admit responsibility for the doomed mission. Gates held out the prospect that Powers was not dead, a suspicion that conditioned his approach to the matter of Eisenhower's responses to the Soviet charges and his unwillingness to assume that Powers was not alive until he learned conclusively to the contrary.[44] For that reason, Gates pressed the argument that both the president and the administration should admit the overflights and not involve the prestige of the presidency in an "international lie."[45] A strong case existed for the overflights from the standpoint of national security, given the widespread presence of Soviet espionage in the United States and the closed nature of Soviet society. In Gates's estimation, while the acceptance of responsibility might be embarrassing to the administration, it would be far more damaging to American prestige and the president's reputation if Eisenhower became trapped in his own falsehood.

Gates was also concerned that, if Eisenhower failed to accept responsibility for the overflight, his political critics would charge him with neglecting his responsibilities. "I thought that we were in such a serious condition that either the president had to assume responsibility for [the flight]," Gates later told the author, "or he'd be accused of not minding his job, and of playing golf all the time. He was quite sensitive to [that criticism] and I thought it would be a tragedy if [the situation] took that twist."[46] So, in Gates's view, Eisenhower should take responsibility for the flights, announce their suspension, and then deal with whatever consequences might result.

No sooner had Eisenhower and his advisers returned to Washington, however, than a cable marked "most urgent" came to the State Department from Tommy Thompson in Moscow. At a reception in Moscow at the Ethiopian embassy, Thompson overheard a comment by Yakov Malik, the Soviet Union's deputy foreign minister, that the Soviet government had not yet decided how it was going to bring the U-2 flight before the United Nations "because they were still questioning the pilot who had parachuted to safety."[47] He reported the possibility that Powers might be alive and subject to Soviet interrogation. In Washington, however, Thompson's cable arrived too late for the administration to start thinking about changing its strategy and moving away from the cover story.[48]

On the same evening, May 5, Press Day in the Soviet Union, Hans Tuch attended a reception sponsored by the Union of Soviet Journalists. When Tuch arrived at the reception, several Soviet journalists approached him and expressed their criticism of the American overflight of their country. Tuch, of course, knew nothing about the U-2 program. As he later recounted the episode, "I said, 'Well you know, something to the effect that it's an unfriendly act to shoot down the plane of a nation you are supposedly having a good relationship with." Then one of the Soviet journalists told Tuch, "The plane was flying over Sverdlovsk. . . . We had to shoot it down." Tuch asked where the shootdown occurred, but the journalist backed off and the other onlookers quickly dispersed. Tuch left the reception, returned to Spaso House, and told Thompson about his encounter at the reception. Thompson told Tuch to return to the embassy, prepare a telegram for the State Department, and send it. "In his laconic way," Tuch said, Thompson said that "they'll want to hear it as soon as possible." Tuch sent the message to Washington that evening, but mysteriously the cable was not stamped as received by the State Department until the following day.[49]

Back in Washington, the discussion that occurred at the meeting at The Rock on May 5 involving Gates, Dillon, Goodpaster, Gray, and Allen Dulles stands out as one of the more serious mistakes made by the administration during the U-2 crisis. In this instance, it was more an example of who was *not* at the meeting, than of who attended. Four individuals who might have been able to offer different perspectives on the administration's response to Khrushchev, and who were not present, included Secretary of State Herter, then flying back from Europe; General Nathan Twining, chairman of the Joint Chiefs of Staff, who had missed his connection for the flight to High Point; Vice President Richard Nixon, who was not in Washington at the time; and James Hagerty,

Chapter 6

the press secretary. The contributions of these individuals may have been pivotal to the outcome of the crisis: Herter because it was his State Department that bore the responsibility of being the public voice of the administration; Twining because it was his responsibility to address any military implications of the Soviet capture of an American pilot and reconnaissance aircraft; and Nixon to address the political implications of the U-2 crisis in a presidential election year. In Hagerty's case, he was not a member of the National Security Council and so was not included in the group that went to the Rock. Nevertheless, had Hagerty been present, he would have known about the change in instructions regarding information about the dissemination of news about the loss of the U-2. Lacking the contributions of these individuals, the administration stumbled ahead into the trap that Khrushchev was setting for it.

On May 6, after the administration had released another version of the cover story, Khrushchev demonstrated more gamesmanship by showing a photo of the wreckage of the plane, except that it was not the wreckage of Powers's U-2. As Sergei Khrushchev wrote, his father was biding his time, waiting for the proper time to embarrass the Americans. "Let them [the Americans] worry about it," he said. "Let's see what the State Department dreams up. When they've become completely enmeshed in lies, we'll show them the living pilot. But in the meantime—not a word."[50]

Then, on May 7, Khrushchev spoke once again to the Supreme Soviet. In this speech, he showed photographs of the real wreckage of the U-2 and of Powers, who was "quite alive and kicking." Eisenhower heard the news about Powers when he was playing golf at the Gettysburg Country Club with his friend George Allen. As Clint Hill, the Secret Service agent who was protecting Ike recalled, "Eisenhower flew into a state of rage [upon hearing that Powers was alive]. Curse words spewed from mouth, his neck veins bulged, and he was clutching his golf club so hard that I thought he was going to break it in half."[51] Eisenhower had clearly found the news of Powers's survival "unbelievable." Dulles and Bissell had assured him that no pilot could survive an attack on a U-2 and that had proven to be false. Thomas Gates also was astonished that Powers had survived. "I don't think anybody ever suspected we'd have both a possibly live airplane and a wholly live pilot," Gates remembered years later. "That was a coincidence. I think that nobody ever conceived that Powers could live through being shot down."[52]

The Crash, the Crisis, and the Collapse

By this point, officials at the State Department, including Secretary Herter, who, after he returned to Washington, tried to keep up with the moment-by-moment unfolding of the U-2 crisis, continued their attempt to keep Eisenhower from direct acknowledgment of the Powers flight, ultimately settling on the explanation that Eisenhower had not authorized the flights.[53] Since Khrushchev had attempted to lay the blame for the flight, both on May 5 and on May 7, on unnamed "Pentagon militarists," Gates was furious at the State Department's refusal to specify the authorization of the flights. Despite Gates's protests, Herter held firm to the position that Eisenhower needed to be protected.[54] But Gates continued to press his case that Eisenhower needed to accept responsibility for the flight. In a meeting with Herter and Allen Dulles on May 9, Gates analyzed the situation from his perspective. The Soviet Union, was a "closed" country, Gates argued, that had rejected the Open Skies initiative in 1955, then "talked of [peaceful] coexistence" while continuing to build their "military potential." Given those factors, the United States "would have been negligent in protecting U.S. and Free World security" without the U-2 flights. Moreover, the "President [had] approved [this] policy," just "not each detail."[55]

In London, Harold Macmillan was undergoing his own private anguish, beginning on May 7, when he learned of Khrushchev's speech that acknowledged the capture of Powers. Admittedly, he had known about the loss of the U-2 as early as May 5, but he had hoped that the incident would have no serious repercussions, certainly none serious enough to jeopardize the summit conference in Paris, now only about one week away. Nevertheless, he had his anxious moments. "The Americans have created a great folly," he wrote in his diary. "One of their machines have been shot down by a rocket it is said, a few hundred miles from Moscow. The Russians have got the machine, the cameras, and the pilot."[56]

Macmillan's first concern at this point was to attempt to salvage the summit, but also to keep from having to disclose any British involvement in the U-2 program.[57] Communicating through Robert Murphy, Macmillan suggested that the Americans try to change the subject, simply by refusing to discuss intelligence matters, as was the customary response in diplomatic circles. However, the American response to the loss of the U-2 had been changing almost daily, Macmillan was pessimistic that the Americans could work their way out of what was becoming an exceptionally embarrassing situation.[58]

Chapter 6

Khrushchev was also behaving mysteriously. In public, he lashed out at the Americans for the overflights and threatened retaliation against Pakistan, Norway, and Turkey, countries that were providing bases for the U-2 flights. Privately, he was reserved, at least in word if not in action. On May 9, at a reception at the Czech embassy, Khrushchev sought out Tommy Thompson, asking him to help resolve the difficulties with the Americans. More important, several Soviet marshals came up to Thompson and pleaded. "We want to smooth this over. We don't want war with the United States."

Khrushchev also raised another matter with Thompson. "One thing that bothered him," Khrushchev told the ambassador, was that "Soviet public opinion" was such that there could be "resentment" expressed toward Eisenhower during his visit and he "did not want any such thing to happen." Thompson indicated to Khrushchev that "the opposite was true" and, in his cable back to Washington, expressed the view that Khrushchev was fearful that Ike may have been well received in the Soviet Union, despite the U-2 situation, thereby creating an embarrassing situation for him and the Soviet leadership, not for Ike.[59] This conversation between Khrushchev and Thompson on May 9 may have been the first indication that the Soviet leader was looking for a way to keep Ike out of the Soviet Union.

Khrushchev also sought Macmillan's help, writing to him on May 8. While complaining about the overflights, Khrushchev still kept open the prospect of the summit conference. It was Khrushchev's first attempt to enlist Macmillan as an intermediary. Macmillan wrote a conciliatory reply to Khrushchev and concluded it in a hopeful tone: "I look forward very much to renewing on 16 May the friendly acquaintance and intimate discussions which commenced during my visit to your country last spring."[60]

Macmillan hoped the Eisenhower administration would let the matter rest until the four leaders met in Paris on May 16 and refrain from any additional substantive public comment. But, as Sergei Khrushchev has pointed out, "both sides misjudged the situation."[61] Khrushchev's persistent refusal to blame Eisenhower, and his attempts to absolve Ike of responsibility, indicated a willingness to keep the door open for continuing the dialogue with the president that had been established at Camp David. However, once the Soviets had conclusive proof of the

American U-2 surveillance program, and more important, had demonstrated the ability to shoot down a spy plane, Eisenhower could not indefinitely refuse to accept responsibility for the flights. He needed to refute Khrushchev's allegations that "militarists in the Pentagon and the CIA" controlled national security policy without presidential oversight. Ike refused to admit that he was not in control of his administration and also refused to find a convenient scapegoat for the failure of the flight. The path of avoiding responsibility that Khrushchev had outlined for Eisenhower, perhaps out of a desire to preserve a now-strained relationship, was simply unacceptable.

May 11: "No one wants another Pearl Harbor"

At 10:29 A.M. on May 11, Eisenhower held a news conference to clarify the administration's position on the U-2 crisis. He had finally decided to intervene and take control of the situation. Ike began the news conference with the comment that "I have made notes from which I want to talk to you about this U-2 incident" and indicated that he would deal with four topics: the need for intelligence gathering, the nature of intelligence gathering, how intelligence gathering should be viewed, and finally, why the U-2 incident should not distract the major powers from working to resolve "the real issues of the day."[62] Regarding the first point, the need for intelligence gathering, Eisenhower used language that every adult American understood: "No one wants another Pearl Harbor. This means that we must have knowledge of military forces and preparations around the world, especially those capable of massive surprise attacks."[63] He then referred to how "secrecy in the Soviet Union" and its "fetish of secrecy and concealment" was responsible for much of the international tension then existing in the world, especially in view of every country's desire to prevent a surprise attack on its cities. Then, Eisenhower accepted responsibility for the overflights, stating that "ever since the beginning of my administration I have issued directions to gather, in every feasible way, the information required to protect the United States and the free world against surprise attack and to enable them to make effective preparations for defense."[64] In essence, Eisenhower had taken the course of action that Thomas Gates had recommended at The Rock on

Chapter 6

May 5: Eisenhower should accept responsibility for the U-2 program as a "distasteful but vital necessity" in the modern world.[65]

Referring to the second and third topics, Eisenhower stated that "Open societies, in the day of present weapons," are the only answer. He referred back to his Open Skies proposal of 1955 and how the adoption of that program "would assure that no surprise attack was being prepared against anyone." Continuing, he stated that he intended to make another proposal for Open Skies at the summit meeting in Paris, "as a means of ending concealment and suspicion."[66]

Eisenhower concluded his remarks in a hopeful vein, saying that the U-2 incident should not "distract" the leaders of the United States, the Soviet Union, Great Britain, and France, from attempting to resolve the "real issues": the search for a solution to the status of Berlin and of a divided Germany, arms control, and the whole range of east-west relations. "This is what we mean when we speak of working for peace," Ike said.[67] Eisenhower's remarks indicated that he intended to attend the summit conference and negotiate with Khrushchev. He also intended to make his visit to the Soviet Union in June. In response to a question from Lawrence H. Burd of the *Chicago Tribune* as to whether the U-2 incident might jeopardize the visit, Eisenhower responded, "You can never tell from one day to the other what is happening in the world, it seems . . . but I expect to go [to Russia]; put it that way."[68]

Eisenhower's press conference on May 11 left no doubt as to his acceptance of responsibility for the U-2 program in general and of the flight by Francis Gary Powers specifically. His acceptance of responsibility was controversial, to say the least. Many individuals, such as Harold Macmillan, thought the proper course of action was that governments customarily refuse to discuss intelligence matters, and such an approach may have been open had not the Soviets captured Powers. In fact, as Douglas Dillon once observed, "We felt very strongly in the Department of State, and were backed up by Allen Dulles in the Central Intelligence Agency, that the President should not take responsibility for this course of action, that that would cause international troubles, and that this was not the way foreign policy was conducted. Allen Dulles offered and insisted that he take full responsibility for it, and if necessary that he be replaced, so that [the] policy of the United States would not be upset and could go on—that this was something he had done on his own. . . . We hoped that [Dulles's offer to resign] might not be necessary, but we thought it was entirely unnecessary for the President to be personally involved."[69]

The problem, of course, with any presidential denial of responsibility for the overflight on May 1 was the Soviet Union's capture of Powers. In the words of James Hagerty, the government had "strap[ped] an American made plane to [his] back" and Ike could not deny responsibility for that fact.[70] Hagerty had come around to the position that Eisenhower needed to accept responsibility for the U-2 flight or, as Douglas Dillon recalled, "it would look like the president didn't know what was going on in the government. There had been a lot of [political] attacks about that time saying he didn't know what was going on but, of course, that was wrong, because he did know and did get involved."[71]

Eisenhower saw the matter in a slightly different light. As he later told an interviewer, he did not "want to be in the position of going out and negotiating with Khrushchev and having to make the lame excuse, 'Well, these things [U-2 flights] were done but I didn't know anything about them.' Why, from there on he'd have said, 'Well, I don't think you run your own government."[72] The unfortunate result of his acceptance of responsibility, however, was to jeopardize the upcoming summit meeting and, just as importantly, his planned trip to the Soviet Union.

No one in the American government could be certain of Khrushchev's response to Eisenhower's acceptance of responsibility. But Khrushchev had entered a precarious moment himself. As Max Frankel, the Moscow correspondent for the *New York Times*, later wrote, "Imagine Khrushchev's horror in early May . . . when his own anti-aircraft rockets forced him to confess that his missile bases were not at all concealed. If the U-2s continued to count his missiles, his generals would demand an alarming increase in their number, eating up all the savings he had gained from reducing his army. 'Say it isn't so,' he kept begging Ike."[73]

But Eisenhower refused to say it wasn't so. Douglas Dillon believed that Eisenhower's primary motive, perhaps not the only one, in accepting responsibility for the U-2 flights was his adherence to his own personal code of integrity, that he had authorized the flight and "that it was unfair to put the blame on Allen Dulles, and so he insisted that he take the blame for it." As Dillon observed, "Ike was a man of principle and couldn't see the point in sending someone else out to take the blame."[74] Jean Edward Smith, one of Eisenhower's major biographers, argued that

Ike's acceptance of responsibility for the Powers flight "may have been the finest hour of his presidency. Rather than force Allen Dulles or Richard Bissell to walk the plank for reasons of state, Eisenhower acknowledged his culpability."[75]

In the final analysis, however, a lot of damage had occurred, for at least two reasons. First, the episode showed the degree to which Eisenhower had loosened his grip on foreign policy at a particularly critical moment. For his entire presidency, Eisenhower had given his Cabinet officers and members of the national security organization wide latitude in discharging their responsibilities without excessive interference while still keeping a firm hold on the final decision making. One can cite such examples as Ike's role in the armistice negotiations that led to the end of the Korean conflict in 1953, his handling of the two crises in the Formosa Straits in 1955 and 1958, the Suez crisis in 1956 and the intervention in Lebanon in 1958, the situation in Berlin in 1959, and even previous U-2 flights over the Soviet Union, to prove that particular point. But, as Andrew Goodpaster later observed, "In Washington, the U-2 no longer served American foreign policy. Instead, national policy was endangered for the sake of the U-2. Intelligence gathering had become important for its own sake."[76] With the U-2, as John Eisenhower later recalled, Ike "just gave in" to the pressure of those who wanted more overflights in the spring of 1960.[77]

Second, Eisenhower's acceptance of responsibility created a virtually impossible situation for Khrushchev in terms of saving face within the Politburo and within the Soviet military, as it involved his trust in Eisenhower. As Harrison Salisbury later observed, "[What] Khrushchev was trying to do was create a bond of confidence [between himself and Eisenhower], so they could engage in diplomatic discussions that were very important to Khrushchev. This was in Khrushchev's own self-interest, obviously. He had staked his career on this détente with the United States, and it was going to work or not on how he got along with Eisenhower, and he worked to get along with him and he did . . . but the shooting down of the U-2 was a weapon of enormous weight put in the hands of Khrushchev's opponents."[78]

Summing up the entire chain of events between May 1 and 11, Andrew Goodpaster observed that "the handling of that critical international situation—and it was critical—was about as clumsy as anything our government has ever done."⁷⁹ The fact remained that Khrushchev's speech on May 7, and Eisenhower's press conference on May 11, had set the two leaders on a collision course for the most dramatic face-to-face confrontation of the Cold War.

May 16–18: The Collapse

The four leaders—Dwight D. Eisenhower, Nikita S. Khrushchev, Harold Macmillan, and Charles de Gaulle—met in Paris in mid-May 1960, intending to discuss disarmament primarily, but also the future of divided Berlin. Eisenhower and Macmillan arrived in Paris on May 15; both men were apprehensive. Khrushchev left Moscow on May 14 and arrived in Paris in a defiant mood. Prior to the opening of the summit conference on May 16, the possible effect of the U-2 crisis on the summit had captured the attention of the press. On May 14, Secretary of State Herter, who had come to Paris ahead of Eisenhower, met with reporters and was asked if the United States intended to continue the overflights in the future. Herter gave an evasive response, saying only that the "United States had a responsibility for whatever we could to . . . cover the threat of surprise attack."⁸⁰ How did he account for Khrushchev's "theatrical behavior" in advance of the summit? Asked if he thought that Khrushchev's harder line may have been due to some pressure from the Soviet military, Herter responded that "I think that he may be [under such pressure]." Ambassador Tommy Thompson, who had arrived in Paris several days earlier, shared Herter's view and was extremely pessimistic about any positive outcome for the Summit.⁸¹

Any expectations about Khrushchev's intentions ended early on May 15 when he met with de Gaulle and Macmillan, submitting a list of demands that Eisenhower must accept before the Soviets would participate in the conference. In his meeting with Macmillan, the Soviet leader outlined the demands: Eisenhower must condemn the overflights, express regret (in the form of a public apology), discontinue the flights, and punish those responsible for them. Interestingly, Anatole Dobrynin, the future Soviet ambassador to the United States, was with Khrushchev's delegation in Paris and has written that Khrushchev "had no instructions [from the Politburo] to demand a personal apology from

Eisenhower. That happened because of Khrushchev's emotional attempt to bluff an apology out of Eisenhower by threatening to ruin the Summit."[82] For the second time, Khrushchev had hoped to use Macmillan as an intermediary with Eisenhower, but, in this case, the problem was not with the messenger but with the message. Prior to leaving for Paris, Eisenhower had discussed with Herter the possibility of meeting with Khrushchev in Paris, in advance of the first day's meeting, "say at 4 P.M.," at the American embassy to see if the two leaders "might clear things up" before the official opening of the conference. Herter objected, stating that such a meeting "would be a sign of weakness" and Ike never extended the invitation, essentially sending Khrushchev to Macmillan and de Gaulle as intermediaries rather than engaging Eisenhower directly.[83]

In the early evening on May 15, Eisenhower, Macmillan, de Gaulle, and their advisers met at the Élysée Palace to prepare for the formal opening of the summit conference on the next day. Macmillan and de Gaulle explained the nature of their individual meetings with Khrushchev. Macmillan interpreted Khrushchev's behavior as indicative of a leader who was concerned with domestic difficulties. Regardless of Khrushchev's attitude regarding espionage, Eisenhower said that "he was not going to be the only one at the conference to promise not to undertake something [that] everybody else was doing."[84]

Both Macmillan and de Gaulle addressed the possibility that Khrushchev was attempting to use the U-2 incident to force a discussion on the future of Germany. The French president even thought that he could visualize an agreement whereby the United States would promise not to overfly the Soviet Union while Khrushchev would agree not to negotiate a separate treaty with East Germany. The discussion then moved off in the direction of disarmament and Berlin. Clearly, the four leaders were uncertain as to what the discussions with Khrushchev might involve.[85]

Khrushchev's erratic behavior on May 15 troubled Herter, Gates, and John "Jack" Irwin, assistant secretary of defense for international security affairs. The presence of Marshal Rodion Malinovsky, the Soviet defense minister (known as the "Rocket Marshal") appeared ominous, as though Khrushchev was, in Macmillan's words, "on a very short leash with the Soviet military."[86] Malinovsky's presence in Paris, however, was another misreading of the situation by both sides. According to Sergei Khrushchev, Malinovsky was a longtime ally of Khrushchev in the Soviet Union's military bureaucracy, a man who had served in the Red Army during World War II and who was only in Paris because the Soviets had learned that Thomas Gates, the American secretary of defense, was going to be in the American delegation and the Soviets wanted to have an individual in Paris on a corresponding level.[87] The irony of that situation, of course, was that Gates was in the American delegation because the Americans had learned that Malinovsky was coming to Paris with Khrushchev.[88]

After attending the meeting with Eisenhower, Macmillan, and de Gaulle, Gates got a twinge of Pearl Harbor neurosis, remembering that, on December 7, 1941, the Japanese had struck the American fleet in Hawaii while their diplomats were negotiating with the Americans in Washington. Khrushchev's statements in Paris, and especially his previous threats to attack countries with U-2 bases, such as Norway, Turkey, Pakistan, and of course, Great Britain, troubled the SECDEF. Therefore, on the night of May 15, Gates contacted James H. Douglas, the DEPSECDEF, in Washington and instructed him to raise the communications alert level to the Pentagon's unified commands. Douglas contacted General Nathan Twining, the chairman of the Joint Chiefs of Staff, who was authorized to inform American forces around the world about the situation. This alert was intended primarily for communications purposes and did not mean any upgrading of American military preparedness. With Gates when he asked Douglas to proceed with the alert were Jack Irwin and Margaret Stroud, who moved from their rooms at the Ritz Hotel in Paris to the American embassy, where they remained in contact with the Pentagon throughout the night of May 15 and the early morning of May 16.[89] Before communicating with Douglas, Gates hastily cleared the alert with Herter and Eisenhower, although the initial decision to proceed with the alert began with him.[90]

In still another stroke of bad luck for the Americans on May 15–16, however, the alert ceased to remain a secret and news of it soon reached Paris. As Robert J. Watson has written, "In Washington, the JCS [Joint Chiefs of Staff] relayed Gates's order to the unified commands, some of whom went beyond the intent of the order by recalling off duty personnel. Thus the alert became a matter of public knowledge. Confusion resulted when officers on duty in the Pentagon could not explain to inquiring reporters the purpose of the order, thus contributing to the impression of administration ineptitude."[91]

Chapter 6

On May 16, Eisenhower, Macmillan, and their advisers ate breakfast at the American embassy. Macmillan, who had not slept well himself the night before, thought Eisenhower "looked depressed and uncertain," and "the Americans were in considerable disarray."[92] John Eisenhower, however, thought that a meeting of this type "brought out the best" in Ike, and "when he left [the embassy] for the first meeting of the Summit . . . he walked with amazing bounce."[93]

The opening meeting of the summit began at 11 A.M. and the American delegation, reflecting the tension, was not optimistic. Before the leaders convened, Herter sent a cable to Douglas Dillon in Washington. The cable read, "Mounting evidence suggest Soviets intend [to] wreck conference at opening session on U-2 issue. Please inform vice president."[94]

Shortly after the four leaders were seated, Charles de Gaulle, as moderator, convener, and host of the meeting, nodded to Eisenhower to make the opening statement. In retrospect, de Gaulle's action appeared to be a gesture of support for Ike by giving him the opportunity to speak first and thereby seize the rhetorical initiative against Khrushchev. In fact, prior to the opening of the first meeting, Eisenhower and de Gaulle had agreed on a procedure whereby Ike was to make the first statement. Eisenhower's opening statement included a reference to the discontinuance of the U-2 flights that, while certainly not the apology that Khrushchev sought, was at least a gesture of conciliation.[95] But Khrushchev immediately sprang to his feet and demanded the right to speak first. De Gaulle then glanced at Eisenhower, awaiting a response. Ike shrugged his shoulders and yielded the floor to Khrushchev.[96] In yielding the floor to Khrushchev, Eisenhower made a tactical mistake, although it was admittedly a mistake that by itself would not have enabled him to salvage the conference.

Why was Eisenhower's yielding of the floor to Khrushchev a mistake? First, Eisenhower failed to take advantage of de Gaulle's attempt to allow him to take the high ground in the meeting and also show that he and de Gaulle held the same positions on the matter of the U-2 flights. On May 15, de Gaulle had made it clear to Ike that he intended to support the United States if Khrushchev chose to go on the attack. "You obviously cannot apologize [to Khrushchev] and I will do everything I can to help you," de Gaulle told Eisenhower.[97] Before the summit conference began, the CIA sent Arthur Lundahl, its most respected photo-interpreter, and James Cunningham, representing Richard Bissell, to Paris to give de

Gaulle a briefing of the images that had been acquired by the U-2 flights. "Formidable, formidable," de Gaulle declared to Lundahl and Cunningham, upon viewing the images. On May 16, de Gaulle walked into the conference room at the Élysée Palace with Ike and whispered to him, "Now I see why Khrushchev is so mad."[98]

Second, Eisenhower's prepared remarks were not provocative nor in any way insulting to Khrushchev. Had Ike given his remarks first, they would have stood in stark contrast to those of Khrushchev, which certainly were provocative and disrespectful both to Eisenhower and to the United States. In his prepared remarks, Eisenhower noted that his "colleagues" (an interesting choice of words) Macmillan and de Gaulle had informed him of the nature of Khrushchev's demands and how those demands threatened the success of the summit conference. Eisenhower also reiterated his statements of May 9 and May 11 about "the distasteful necessity of espionage in a world where nations distrust each other's intentions. . . . As is well known, not only the United States but most other countries are constantly the targets of elaborate and persistent espionage of the Soviet Union."[99] Eisenhower then indicated that the United States was making no aggressive threats against the Soviet Union with its overflight program, other than that it will not "shirk its responsibility to safeguard against surprise attack."[100] Next he indicated that he had come "to Paris to seek agreements with the Soviet Union which would eliminate the necessity for all forms of espionage, including overflights" and the U-2 episode should not be a reason "to disrupt the conference."[101] Had Eisenhower taken the opportunity provided to him by de Gaulle to make that statement before Khrushchev's lengthy accusations, the tone in the meeting room might been considerably different. Had Eisenhower made the opening statement, it may very well have been Khrushchev, instead of Ike, who had been placed on the rhetorical defensive.

As it happened, Khrushchev took the floor after demanding it from de Gaulle. As described by Macmillan, "with a gesture reminiscent of Mr. Micawber . . . [Khrushchev] pulled a large wad of typewritten pages out of his pocket and began to speak. Khrushchev tried to pulverize Ike (as Micawber did Heep) by a mixture of vitriolic and offensive, and legal argument."[102]

Certainly, Khrushchev minced no words, making generous use of such adjectives as "provocative" and "treacherous" to describe the actions of the United States government. He also repeated his previous refrain that "a small frantic group in [the] Pentagon and in [its] militarist quarters [that] benefit from the armaments race, gaining huge profits" were responsible for the overflights.[103]

Khrushchev waited until near the end of his diatribe before withdrawing the offer for Eisenhower to visit the Soviet Union, scheduled for June 10. "The President of the USA was to make a return visit to our country on June 10. And we were prepared to accord a good welcome to the high guest," Khrushchev declared. "Unfortunately, as a result of provocative actions against the USSR there has now been created such conditions when we have been deprived of a possibility to receive the President with proper cordiality. . . . That is why at present the visit of the President of the USA to the Soviet Union should be postponed and agreements should be reached as to the time of the visit when the conditions for the visit would mature."[104]

Khrushchev's defiance must have struck Eisenhower with a grim sense of finality, especially after the Soviet leader withdrew the invitation to visit his country. Ike's plan to thaw the Cold War, begun in the summer of 1959 and carried through with Khrushchev's visit to the United States in September, the Western Summit in Paris in December, and the preparations by diplomats in both countries that were carried on literally up to the time of the summit, had largely come to naught. Khrushchev obviously had no intention of negotiating with Eisenhower and was prepared to postpone high-level discussions with the United States until a new presidential administration took office in January 1961.[105] No possibility existed for an agreement that limited nuclear testing, or for the future status of Berlin, and more important, Eisenhower would never again have the opportunity to visit the Soviet Union and witness for himself how his presence in Moscow might have succeeded in reducing world tensions.

For those attending the meeting, however, Khrushchev's histrionics were interpreted as mere theatrical gestures intended primarily for a domestic constituency. Thomas Gates, present during Khrushchev's outburst and certainly a member of "that frantic group of militarists in the Pentagon," described the scene as "true theater, great theater. Eisenhower managed to keep his legendary temper in check."[106] Likewise, Macmillan was aghast at Khrushchev's behavior. "Oh, it was terrible," he told interviewer Robert McKenzie in 1972. "It was insulting. Ike looked very uncomfortable."[107]

In their remarks following Khrushchev's tirade, both Macmillan and de Gaulle searched for a method of continuing the conference, mainly by proposing a reconsideration of the U-2 episode for a later time. Khrushchev continued to create rhetorical roadblocks. In his statement, Eisenhower referred to his Open Skies proposal and his intention to submit another such proposal to the United Nations for its consideration. Khrushchev wanted no part of any proposal that dealt with the concept of Open Skies. He said, "I heard it in Geneva in 1955. At that time, we declared categorically that we were opposed to it, and I can repeat it now. We will permit no one, but no one, to violate our sovereignty."[108]

As the discussion continued, Secretary Herter raised the matter of Khrushchev's withdrawal of the invitation to Eisenhower to visit the Soviet Union. "Please understand this . . . ," Khrushchev replied, "How can we invite as a dear guest the leader of a country which has committed an aggressive act against us? No visit would be possible under present circumstances. How could our people welcome him? Even my small grandson would ask his grandpa: 'How could we welcome [as] an honored guest one who represents a country that sends planes to overfly and which we shot down with a rocket?'"[109]

Several weeks later, in a conversation with Ambassador Tommy Thompson in Moscow, Khrushchev described the predicament that the U-2 crisis had created for him when it came to keeping his invitation to Eisenhower to visit the Soviet Union. "If someone comes to visit you and you catch him redhanded throwing a dead cat over your fence, you could not respect yourself if you received him as an honored guest," Khrushchev told Thompson.[110]

When Khrushchev finished with his attacks on Eisenhower, President de Gaulle came to Ike's defense. Vernon Walters, one of Eisenhower's interpreters, recalled the direct manner in which de Gaulle confronted Khrushchev. "The day after the U-2 was shot down," de Gaulle told Khrushchev, "I sent my ambassador to you to ask you whether there would be any point in having this conference. You knew everything then that you knew now. And yet you have imposed conditions that the President of the United States cannot possibly accept, and you know it. And in so doing you have brought General Eisenhower here from the United

States for nothing; you have brought the British prime minister here for nothing; and you have put me to grave personal inconvenience."[111]

The meeting on May 16 and, in effect, the Paris summit conference ended at 2:00 P.M. Khrushchev stood up from the table and strode from the room, accompanied by his delegation. The collapse of the meeting on May 16 dealt a withering blow to any optimistic beliefs in the efficacy of summitry. After Khrushchev's departure, Eisenhower, Macmillan, and de Gaulle met to talk briefly in adjacent room. Macmillan and de Gaulle offered Ike their support. Firmly, de Gaulle told the president, "Whatever happens, we are with you to the end." Eisenhower tried to blow off some steam. "I'm just fed up," he muttered, furious at Khrushchev's deliberate attempt to humiliate him. More angry still was Chip Bohlen, who had listened to Khrushchev's tirade against Eisenhower and recognized it as a profane, obscene series of insults, delivered in Khrushchev's earthy, peasant idiom. Since Bohlen spoke fluent Russian, he recognized that Khrushchev's interpreters had deliberately "sanitized" many of the premier's remarks, making them less offensive in translation.[112]

Thus, Nikita Khrushchev scuttled the Paris summit conference on May 16 and his behavior on May 17 and May 18 demonstrated that he intended to keep it scuttled. Later, on May 16, he resisted Macmillan's efforts to mediate the differences between himself and Eisenhower, unless Eisenhower offered an apology. On May 17, the summit conference reconvened at 10:00 A.M., but Khrushchev failed to come to the meeting, nor would he attend another meeting proposed for 3:00 P.M., unless he first received an apology from Ike. That apology was out of the question, of course. At 11 A.M. on May 17, Secretary Herter met with Maurice Couve de Murville, the French foreign secretary, and Selwyn Lloyd, the British foreign secretary, to assess the damage from May 16. Lloyd, perhaps echoing Macmillan's frustrations, asked Herter why Eisenhower could not have apologized and thereby "removed this as an obstacle to the Summit meeting." Herter told Lloyd bluntly that Eisenhower refused to "say he was sorry for the good reason that he was not."[113]

Khrushchev spent part of May 17, accompanied by Marshal Malinovsky and Andrei Gromyko, the Soviet Union's foreign minister, walking the streets of Paris and then driving out to visit the battlefield of the Marne, where Malinovsky had fought as a 16-year-old in World War I. En route to their destination, the Russian party was stopped by a downed tree in the road. Khrushchev left his car, took an axe from one of the workers on the site, cut off part of the tree, and joined the effort to clear the road.[114] Throughout the day on May 17, Khrushchev continued to refuse efforts by the other three leaders to resume the conference unless he received his apology from Eisenhower. In fact, by the end of the day on May 17, Khrushchev had given up hope for receiving his apology and began making plans for his departure from Paris.[115]

On May 18, at a final press conference, Khrushchev took the occasion once again to criticize Eisenhower and the United States. The press conference began with a group of West Germans standing outside the conference room and directing their boos at Khrushchev. Hearing the commotion, Khrushchev went on the counteroffensive, telling the reporters that "[West German] Chancellor [Konrad] Adenauer has some of his riff-raff that escaped the beating at Stalingrad and it is they that are indulging in this booing, they that at that time we did not send three meters under ground."[116] Then a reporter from Bridgeport, Connecticut, asked him if, even considering the controversy over the U-2 flights, it might still be better to hold the summit conference now rather than wait six or eight months, as he had proposed. Khrushchev responded that the United States was acting "like an aggressor" and, "like a cat that had stolen" the family's cream, should be "[taken] by the scruff of the neck and [given] a good shaking" as a consequence of the overflights.[117] He then continued in that menacing tone, referring to the U-2 episode as "what happened [when] someone tried to poke his nose into our affairs and we punched his nose so that now he certainly knows where the border is. If he comes again, he will receive another blow as will the bases from which he takes off and where he intends to land."[118]

Throughout the news conference Khrushchev had blamed the U-2 flights on "reactionary forces in the Pentagon," and then he took a question from a reporter with the West Berlin station Berlin Radio about the role played by Secretary of Defense Thomas Gates in the crisis. The question was stated, "It follows from American press reports that the American delegate Gates has from here declared an emergency alarm to the American forces. How do you evaluate that act?" Khrushchev appeared to be unaware of the circumstances of the alert, as well as unfamiliar with Gates. "I have heard nothing of that report yet, but I certainly have no reason to disbelieve what the correspondent said. If this is really so it can be qualified as nothing short of a provocation designed to trick the Americans and impose more taxes on them. Perhaps also it can be explained by ordinary cowardice. Sometimes a coward is more dangerous than a provocation-monger. A provocation-monger is trying to provoke war while a coward can unleash war out of pure cowardice. I don't know this Gates. It's not for me to judge him. Let the American people themselves see what sort of a person he is."[119]

While Khrushchev may have reserved his judgment about Thomas Gates, the Soviet propagandists at *Tass* wasted no time broadcasting their profile of him on a radio program on May 21. According to *Tass*, Gates was one "of a number of millionaires in the Eisenhower Administration." Gates was also an investor "in a number of large corporations, including those closely linked with the arms race. It is not surprising," said *Tass*, "that Gates makes every use of his position to expand the arms race."[120]

On May 19, Eisenhower, Khrushchev, and Macmillan left Paris, with the summit in shreds. Khrushchev went to East Germany before returning to Moscow. Eisenhower visited Portugal before returning to the United States on May 20. An exhausted Eisenhower returned to a hero's welcome but also with the realization that he had lost an opportunity to thaw the Cold War. Descending the steps from Air Force One at Andrews Air Force base, Ike noticed Mamie "with tears in her eyes."[121]

Gates did not return to Washington until May 22. By then, the administration's critics had begun to speak out on the U-2 crisis. The first to offer such criticism was Adlai Stevenson, Eisenhower's opponent in 1952 and 1956 and considered a presidential aspirant again in 1960. In a speech in Chicago on May 19, Stevenson admitted that Khrushchev had wrecked the summit but that the administration handed him "the crowbar and sledgehammer" for that purpose.[122] Stevenson then went on to recite the mistakes committed by the administration: approving the flight so close to the summit conference, giving a false cover story, finally having Eisenhower admit responsibility, and so forth. He also mentioned the alert called by Gates "at the height of tension last Sunday night."[123]

When Gates returned to the United States, reporters quickly asked him for his version of the alert and, more importantly, did he believe that it was a provocative act? For his part, Gates continued to believe that the alert was a responsible act, later telling the Senate Foreign Relations Committee that "I stated when I got off the airplane and was asked the question by the press on my return, I said it was incredible to me that anybody would question it."[124]

Privately, however, Gates was feeling the pressure, especially with the implication that calling the communications alert was partly to blame for the collapse of the summit conference. As Walter Lippman wrote in his syndicated column, "Today and Tomorrow," on May 19, "On Sunday night Mr. Macmillan and General de Gaulle were still struggling to find a way out of the affair of the spy plane. Yet this was the time chosen by the Secretary of Defense to stage a worldwide readiness alert which, though not the last stage before actual war, is one of the preliminary steps leading up to it. Why Sunday of all days? This blunder was not the work of a colonel on a Turkish battlefield. This was the work of the Secretary of Defense and of the President. The timing of the exercise was just a shade worse than sending off the U-2 on a perilous mission two weeks before the Summit. The timing of the so-called alert makes no sense whatever. For if the alert was concerned with a possible surprise attack, when in the name of common sense could there [have been] less of a danger of a surprise attack on the Western world than when Mr. K. was in Paris? Unhappily, too, Secretary Gates's exercise was just about as incompetently administered at the top as was the affair of the spy plane."[125]

So, when Gates arrived home on the evening of May 22, he was, as he later told the author, "pretty disturbed at life in general." Sitting in his living room, however, and waiting for his arrival, was Gates's friend and neighbor, Arthur Krock, a respected columnist for the *New York Times* and the author of the widely syndicated column "In the Nation." As Gates recalled, "In spite of his role as a commentator, and later as an author, [Arthur Krock] never really got over the fact that he was basically a damn good reporter." And Gates was about to give Arthur Krock a scoop. "Sit down, Tom, and tell me all about it," Krock said.[126] So Gates told Krock what had happened to him in Paris, in meticulous detail.

Arthur Krock had his scoop. The result was a column in "In the Nation" on May 24, "An Act of Prudence in the Right Place," in which Krock defended Gates and his judgment. Krock began by noting the five points of criticism raised by Adlai Stevenson in his speech of May 18: the poor timing of the flight, the intervention of Macmillan and de Gaulle with Khrushchev, the unfortunate timing of the alert on May 15, the poor coordination between the Pentagon and the unified commands about the nature of the alert, and, since the alert was called from Paris, the concern as to whether the United States was facing a surprise attack by the Soviet Union.[127]

After recounting the criticisms, Krock came to the defense of Gates. "The actual circumstances in which the order was issued greatly weaken this argument and support the view that the alert was an act of prudence in the Secretary's plain line of duty," he wrote.[128] Without mentioning Gates, of course, Krock wrote that the Americans knew by early Sunday evening, May 15, that Khrushchev had made impossible demands that would lead inevitably to the failure of the conference, and that the interventions of Macmillan and de Gaulle were going to prove futile. To summarize, Krock concluded that the "vigilance" demonstrated by Gates "should be reassuring to the American people."[129]

Krock's column silenced the critics of Thomas Gates—at least for the moment. As Gates later recalled, the column "saved my neck, you might say. It was extraordinarily helpful to me; after it was written, everything quieted down."[130] Nor did he wait long to express his gratitude to Krock. On May 25, he wrote Krock, "I am indebted to you for putting things in proper perspective and saying them in your remarkable way. . . . I thought you covered all the points well, and I am sure your article will be of great personal help to me, as well as permitting a fuller understanding on the part of the great body of American people who read your column."[131] Also, recognizing a good source when he had one, Krock responded to Gates on May 26, writing that "I appreciate your generous estimate of the factual presentation I attempted to make in my account of the background of the alert order from Paris."[132]

Nevertheless, was Gates guilty of hasty judgment leading to a careless provocation of the international environment at a critical time? Judging from his response to the West German reporter at his news conference on May 18, Khrushchev did not appear to know that such an alert had been called, even though he took advantage of the situation by attempting to link Gates to the American arms industry. So, Khrushchev did not express any unusual negative reaction to an event that he had been hearing about for the first time. Based on Khrushchev's comments at the news conference on May 18, therefore, the action by Gates had no effect on the outcome of the conference, at least from the perspective of the Soviet delegation.

And what about Eisenhower? In an interview with the author, Andrew Goodpaster observed that, in Eisenhower's mind, the alert "was a good cautionary thing which [he] was always willing to support. Here was a man, Khrushchev, who was acting very irrationally . . . Eisenhower always wanted to be sure of basic readiness in a situation like that."[133] As far as Gates being criticized for the alert, then? "Not by Eisenhower," Goodpaster said emphatically. "No, not one bit."[134]

Another perspective on the episode was offered by Jack Irwin, who was in Paris with Gates when the alert was called. Recalling the event, Irwin stated that "I think you have to judge it on the circumstances of the moment rather than [with] leisurely hindsight, and I think that in all those cases where there is any potential danger, or even a very remote possible danger—the Russian forces are generally in a more alert position than [those of the] United States—and therefore I think it's only prudent to take a precautionary step such as increasing an alert if there's any remote possibility of something happening. And those that criticize it, I think it would be better to suffer the criticism of someone [who] says you shouldn't have done something much later [than] someone saying you did too little."[135]

So the 1960 Four Power summit came to naught, with the major casualty of the collapse being the revocation by Khrushchev of Eisenhower's visit to the Soviet Union in June. Several observers— Thomas Gates, Robert Murphy, and, later, Vladimir Toumanoff in the American embassy in Moscow—were convinced that Khrushchev's primary motivation in scuttling the summit was to use it as an excuse to deprive Eisenhower of his second visit to Russia. For example, Gates was asked that question directly when he testified about the U-2 crisis before the Senate Foreign Relations Committee in early June 1960. Senator Frank Lausche (D-Ohio) asked Gates, "Now, then have you given any thought as to why [Khrushchev] revoked the invitation to the President to come to the Soviet land?" Gates responded, "Well, we again speculate but in my opinion the last thing [Khrushchev] wanted was for the President to travel around his country and be acclaimed and received by the population of Russia." Lausche continued, "Do you think he got flashes in his mind about the acclaim that [Vice President Richard] Nixon got in Poland, and in other places?" Gates replied, "He probably did."[136] Again Lausche continued his questioning, "And do you think he kind of thought there would be demonstrations for the President of the United States unparalleled anywhere?" Gates replied, "I believe there would have been." Lausche concluded, "That is my honest conviction, that he did not dare have the President meet the Ukrainian people and the normal Russian people, excluding the Communists, in that trip to the Soviet [Union] and that is why the invitation was revoked."[137]

Years later, in his memoirs, Robert Murphy gave essentially the same response to the reason Khrushchev chose not to negotiate in Paris. As Murphy wrote in *Diplomat among Warriors,* "The immediate and most conspicuous result of the President's statement [to accept responsibility for the U-2 flight] was that Khrushchev refused to attend the Summit Conference and on May 17, 1960, that international meeting was called off. . . . What was important was that Khrushchev also utilized the U-2 flight as an excuse to revoke the invitation to Eisenhower to visit the Soviet Union. The President's tour could have made a tremendously favorable impression on the Soviet people. Communist leaders feared it."[138] Since Murphy had been one of the first senior officials in the Eisenhower administration to propose a visit by Ike to the Soviet Union, he was understandably dismayed by the results of the U-2 crisis, even going so far as to blame Eisenhower for allowing it to happen.[139]

How did Eisenhower view the possible connection between Khrushchev's behavior in Paris and the withdrawal of the invitation? He was not willing to rule out a connection, at least not completely. At a meeting of Eisenhower's Cabinet on May 26, 1960, the minutes reveal that Eisenhower "commented that some of his colleagues [Gates and Murphy, to name two] were of the opinion that the Russians were not so much concerned by the U-2 as they were of the prospect of his visit to Russia, so they seized upon the U-2 as a means of getting out of it."[140] Then Ike expressed the view that such an intention helped to explain why Khrushchev demanded to speak first at the opening meeting on May 16. In his opening statement, Khrushchev outlined the reasons for the withdrawal of Ike's invitation, essentially arguing that the Soviet people would have treated Eisenhower impolitely because of his authorization of the U-2 flights. Had Ike gone first in the meeting and made his reasonable opening remarks, the impact of Khrushchev's speech may have been considerably less dramatic.

In the aftermath of the U-2 crisis, the collapse of the summit conference, and the revocation of Ike's invitation to visit the Soviet Union, the atmosphere in Moscow turned harsh and ugly. As Vladimir Toumanoff recalled, "[T]he President took personal responsibility for the flight. The summit in Paris was aborted and Eisenhower's visit to the Soviet Union was canceled. The Soviet public understood the message, contact with Americans was once again taboo, and broken off. I think the extreme Soviet reaction to the U-2 was prompted, in part, by their fear of a public welcome for Ike so massive as to generate a spontaneous and general public escape from their control. The population, massed in welcome, might realize that opposition to the regime was common, and act on it, as happened later in Eastern Europe. Whether that fear was accurate or not none can say. But atomization of society, and ruthless suppression of opposition, especially when grouped, was a key component of Soviet rule."[141]

Hans Tuch experienced the same negative sentiment in Moscow after the collapse of the summit. It "dropped American-Soviet relations to the bottom," Tuch recalled, while also adding that "the Soviets definitely capitalized on the U-2 for propaganda purposes" but "the reaction of the Soviet people [to the crisis] was hard to tell." The staff of the American embassy treated the collapse of the summit as a "natural consequence of events. We took it in stride."[142]

In conclusion, the comments made by Gates, Murphy, Toumanoff, and Tuch raise an interesting question: how *would* Eisenhower have been received in the Soviet Union, even in the aftermath of the U-2 crisis? Tommy Thompson let Khrushchev know that, that in his opinion, Eisenhower would have been warmly welcomed by the Russian people. Both Khrushchev and the members of the Soviet hierarchy may have recalled the spontaneous outpouring of affection for Eisenhower in 1945 and may have viewed another such demonstration as a threat to their leadership. It might have happened in that fashion, even though the Soviet people understood that Eisenhower had actively authorized an extensive surveillance program over their country. It was a risk that Khrushchev and the Soviet leadership were apparently not prepared to take.

And thus everything collapsed. On May 16 in Washington, Douglas Dillon, acting as secretary of state while Christian Herter was in Paris, sent the following cable to the American embassy in Moscow: "Assume on basis [of] developments that should now proceed to cancel arrangements made in connection [with] President's trip to Soviet Union. For example, Copenhagen has made hotel reservations for May 23 for

Chapter 6

advance technical flight party. Should we also proceed to cancel hotel reservations [in] Moscow?"[143] Eisenhower's trip to the Soviet Union was officially canceled.

In Moscow, Vladimir Toumanoff had a different problem as it affected the cancellation of Eisenhower's visit. As he recalled, "In the garage at the [American] embassy was a large motor boat, intended as Ike's gift to Khrushchev. It was one of the first motor boats which was water-jet propelled rather than propeller driven. It had to be sent back to America."[144] Ambassador Tommy Thompson tried to save the boat, however, wishing to make it available for use by the American embassy's naval attaché in Moscow. But the sight of an American cruising down the Moskva River in a new boat that had once been identified as a gift to Khrushchev was more of a diplomatic risk than the Americans were prepared to consider, given the highly charged international environment that existed at the time.[145] The boat went back to the United States and never became the gesture of goodwill between the United States and the Soviet Union that Douglas Dillon and the State Department had originally contemplated.

Chapter 7

Eisenhower in the Soviet Union
Moscow, Leningrad, and Kiev, June 10–15, 1960

The Soviet Union's capture of Francis Gary Powers on May 1, 1960, altered the course of Soviet-American relations for the remainder of Dwight D. Eisenhower's presidency. It was left to future events to determine the impact of Powers's capture on plans for the upcoming summit conference on May 16 as well as the effect it might have on Eisenhower's proposed visit to the Soviet Union in June. For his part, of course, Eisenhower publicly stated that he did not expect the U-2 controversy to have a negative effect on his visit. As mentioned previously, Eisenhower told the White House reporter Lawrence Burd on May 11 that he still "expected to go" to Russia.[1]

At the working level in Moscow, both at the American embassy and at the Soviet Union's Ministry of Foreign Affairs (MFA), plans proceeded for Eisenhower's visit almost as though the international situation had not changed. On May 5, Hans Tuch sent a letter to M. A. Kharlamov, chief of the press section of the MFA, in which he listed the correspondents, photographers, cameramen, and technicians who were "accredited as members of the President's Press Party." Tuch sent Kharlamov four lists that contained various personnel: news media personnel who were covering the president's entire journey, from the Soviet Union to Japan, to South Korea, and then returning to the United States; news media personnel who planned to enter the Soviet Union in advance of Eisenhower's arrival on June 10; technicians for American radio, television, and photographic services who planned to enter the Soviet Union prior to Eisenhower's arrival and who planned to travel to places on Eisenhower's itinerary to prepare for coverage of the visit; and personnel who would be traveling on Soviet press planes within the Soviet Union. [2]

Then, on May 7, ironically the day that Khrushchev gave his explosive speech to the Supreme Soviet acknowledging that the Soviets held Powers in custody, the American embassy and the MFA gave final approval to Eisenhower's itinerary. Interestingly, the itinerary contains a typewritten entry showing that Leonid Brezhnev was to replace Kliment Voroshilov in greeting Eisenhower at the airport and in terms of an appointment later in the day.[3]

Then, on May 14, Edward Freers of the State Department sent a letter to S. V. Kaftanov, chair of the State Committee for Radio Broadcasting and Television, confirming the arrangements for Eisenhower's speeches and addresses, in particular where they would originate in the Soviet Union—Moscow, Leningrad, or Kiev. These arrangements also included the transmission of Eisenhower's speeches back to the United States. Freers's letter of May 14 and Hans Tuch's letter of May 5 confirmed the obvious: the coverage of Eisenhower's visit to the Soviet Union by the American and international press, with the cooperation of the Soviet authorities, was going to be unprecedented in its size and scope.[4]

Around the same time, Hans Tuch sent a short memorandum to James Hagerty that delineated "Points of Agreement" between the American embassy and the MFA regarding the accommodations for the visiting press. These included accommodations for a total of four hundred correspondents in Moscow and three hundred on a tour of the country. More important, the Soviets intended to honor American Express Traveler's checks and traveler's checks from the First National City Bank, which could be used "everywhere."[5] The difference between the experiences of the press who were to cover the Eisenhower visit, by contrast with that of Vice President Richard Nixon in July 1959, was going to be considerable. As Tuch's memo showed, the Soviets had agreed with virtually every one of the stipulations that Hagerty had mentioned to them.

Elsewhere in Moscow, life went on in anticipation of Eisenhower's upcoming visit. On May 16, Roberta Peters, the famous American opera performer, gave a recital that thrilled her Soviet audience, leaving

Moscow, Leningrad, and Kiev

it "cheering and applauding for encore after encore." After her performance, Peters contacted the American embassy to ask for assistance in extending her stay in the Soviet Union until Eisenhower arrived in June. Peters had a previous engagement in the United States from which she wished to withdraw and wanted the embassy's help to cancel the engagement.[6]

On May 16, however, Khrushchev walked out of the negotiations in Paris and canceled Eisenhower's visit. Questions as to how the Soviet people would have responded to Eisenhower, and what Eisenhower would have said to the Soviet leadership and the Russian people, will never be known. It now appears, however, that journalist Robert J. Donovan, who covered the White House for the *New York Herald Tribune*, wanted to explore an idea with James Hagerty about how the world might learn about the comments that Eisenhower would have made in Russia had he taken the trip. So Donovan began discussing the possibility of publishing the drafts of the speeches that Eisenhower was scheduled to give while in the Soviet Union. Donovan, it will be remembered, was the author of *Eisenhower: The Inside Story of the First Term* and a journalist who had been granted special access within the administration to write an account that, not surprisingly, was a sympathetic treatment of Eisenhower's presidential leadership.[7]

After the failure of the summit, Donovan set out to obtain approvals within the administration to release the texts of the speeches that Eisenhower was to have given. For this "project," as Donovan described it, he needed the assistance of James Hagerty, who apparently was not totally sold on the idea but also not willing to discount it, either. On June 7, 1960, Hagerty received a message from Donovan which read as follows:

> Thought you would like report I had with [Christian] Herter. I found he was laboring under misunderstanding that we were interested only in summit material. He did oppose releasing summit text. However, he was wholly open-minded on question (which is of primary importance to us) of our using speech drafts planned for Soviet Union so that we could report on what the president would have told the Russian people. Herter said he would review the speech drafts personally and discuss the matter with the president.

Even with the project this far advanced, however, I feel at great disadvantage because of your absence. My concern is that the White House may not be fully aware about the merits and purpose of this undertaking. Would respectfully raise the question, therefore, whether you feel any further communication by you would be desirable in light of new development. Many thanks. Donovan.[8]

After this message, the trail goes cold. It is not clear as to whether Herter ever discussed the idea of a public release of the speech drafts with Eisenhower or whether they discussed the relative advantages and disadvantages of taking such a step. It is also not clear as to Hagerty's views about Donovan's message. Hagerty's only action in this direction appeared to be a suggestion to Eisenhower that it might be advisable to publish his opening statement of May 16 at the Paris summit. At the Cabinet meeting on May 26, Eisenhower "remarked on Mr. Hagerty's belief that there would be some merit in publishing the President's originally planned opening statement which carried the date of May 11th. Mr. [Livingston] Merchant [assistant secretary of state for European affairs] said that Mr. Herter was considering this and that there might be some merit in doing so after consultation with Messrs. Macmillan and de Gaulle. The President said that he was not urging this be done but it might be a way of setting forth some solid views on the way to make progress toward a reduction in tensions."[9] Regardless, the drafts of the speeches that Eisenhower was scheduled to give have never been published—until now.

By examining the details of the events on Eisenhower's itinerary, along with the content of the drafts of the speeches that he was scheduled to give, it is possible to reconstruct a documentary record of how Eisenhower's visit to the Soviet Union might have unfolded. What is impossible to ascertain, of course, is how the people of the Soviet Union would have responded to Eisenhower or whether the trip would have resulted in any meaningful agreements.

As for the drafts of Eisenhower's speeches, specialists in Soviet-American relations at the State Department prepared three different sets of remarks that Eisenhower was to give: remarks upon arrival and departure from the airports in the cities that Eisenhower visited; toasts and official comments at formal receptions, luncheons, and dinners; and the prepared remarks for speeches that Eisenhower was to give while visiting Moscow, Leningrad, Kiev, and Irkutsk. The individuals chosen to draft the speeches and statements were John A. Armitage, Harry G. Barnes, Jr., Richard T. Davies, and Heyward Isham. Each of these men was currently involved in Soviet-American diplomacy at the State Department in Washington and had previously served in the American embassy in Moscow. All of the men were on the State Department's list to accompany Eisenhower to Moscow.[10] On some of the drafts, the identity of the author is revealed. On other drafts, there is no record of authorship.

All of the drafts, however, have some common themes, many of which were reflected in Ambassador Llewellyn Thompson's cable to Secretary Herter on March 15, 1960. (See chapter five, above.) One such theme was Eisenhower's expression of common purpose with the Russian people, first in the war against Nazi Germany and then in the pursuit of peace after the war. The second theme was that the United States and the Soviet Union shared in the responsibility for the Cold War that followed World War II. Ike did not seek to absolve the United States from its part in the deterioration of Soviet-American relations after World War II, but neither did he avoid making direct, pointed criticisms of the behavior of the Soviet Union where he thought such criticism was appropriate. Third, he chose to talk about the benefits of a future world in which the United States and the Soviet Union competed in the economic realm but cooperated in the cause of peace. He spoke of the value of exchanges in the area of culture and education, as exemplified by the Lacy-Zaroubin Agreement. The tenor of these comments shows an Eisenhower who is candid but conciliatory, friendly but not familiar, and a person with a heartfelt, genuine desire for peace.

At this point, it is important to remember that the various drafts of the statements and speeches that Eisenhower was to give in the Soviet Union were written in mid-April, almost two months before his scheduled arrival in Moscow. It is reasonable to assume that the speeches would have undergone numerous revisions before Eisenhower gave them, especially if the Paris summit had produced satisfactory results. But it is also clear that Eisenhower had read many of the drafts and made suggestions for revisions in them. The drafts that have survived, therefore, provide the best glimpse into the prospective nature of Eisenhower's remarks when he was visiting the Soviet Union.

Chapter 7

On to Moscow

The final itinerary for Eisenhower's visit to the Soviet Union was completed by representatives from the White House, the State Department, the American embassy in Moscow, and the Soviet Ministry of Foreign Affairs on May 7, 1960. Representatives from both countries had agreed on a tentative itinerary back in March and the final version resembled the earlier plan with only a few modifications.[11] The final itinerary called for Eisenhower and the presidential party to leave Andrews Air Force Base in Maryland on Thursday, June 9; arrive in the Soviet Union on Friday, June 10; conduct official business in the Soviet Union between June 10 and 18; and then depart from the Soviet Union for Japan on June 19.[12] After visiting Japan, Eisenhower was scheduled to visit South Korea before flying to Honolulu and then back to the United States.

The entire Far Eastern trip could only be described as a great demonstration of stamina and endurance, not only for Dwight D. Eisenhower, then nearing his 70th birthday, but also for the members of the presidential party. For Eisenhower's critics in the United States who often complained that Ike was a president who was disengaged from the physical demands of the presidency, the itinerary of the Far Eastern trip served to demonstrate how Ike was fully capable of handling the rigors of extensive travel.

The presidential party consisted of two groups of people, conveniently divided into Group I and Group II. Group I consisted of Eisenhower and the First Lady, Mamie Eisenhower; Ike's son, Major John Eisenhower, and his wife Barbara; Secretary of State Christian Herter and his wife, Mary; Charles "Chip" Bohlen, former American ambassador to the Soviet Union who was then serving as special assistant for Soviet affairs to Secretary Herter, and his wife, Avis; General Andrew J. Goodpaster, Eisenhower's staff secretary and perhaps his closest adviser; Dr. George Kistiakowsky, the president's assistant for science and technology; James Rowley, the special agent in charge of Eisenhower's Secret Service detail; and Gerald Behn, another Secret Service agent. Also traveling with Group I was Alexander Akalovsky, Eisenhower's Russian interpreter, and his wife, Maria. The pilot of Air Force One was Colonel William Draper.

Some discussion is in order about the composition of Group I. First, as mentioned previously, Mamie Eisenhower had an aversion to flying, caused primarily by her affliction with Miniere's Syndrome, a disorder of the inner ear that caused her to become dizzy and nauseous. For that reason, she only rarely accompanied Eisenhower on his travels outside of the United States. Obviously it was an indication of the importance that Eisenhower attached to the visit to the Soviet Union that Mamie agreed to participate in the trip, just as Khrushchev had been accompanied by his wife, Nina Petrovna, when he visited the United States. Even so, Mamie Eisenhower's travel schedule inside the Soviet Union was going to be limited and she did not intend to accompany her husband when he traveled outside of Moscow.

Second, Eisenhower included Dr. George Kistiakowsky, his adviser on science and technology, on the trip. Kistiakowsky had been extensively involved, for the previous year, on the nuclear test-ban issue and, more specifically, on how an inspection and verification system could be established to monitor each country's adherence to the terms of a possible test-ban agreement.[13] When Eisenhower, Macmillan, de Gaulle, and Khrushchev met in Paris on May 16 for what turned out to be the abortive summit conference, Kistiakowsky was not included in the American delegation, even though disarmament was considered to be the primary item on the conference's agenda. The inclusion of Kistiakowsky in Group I, prior to the collapse of the summit conference in Paris, may have indicated that, had the four leaders made some progress on the issue of disarmament in Paris, Eisenhower would have planned to pursue the subject further in a bilateral meeting with Khrushchev while he was in Russia.

The membership of Group II of the presidential party primarily included members of the White House staff. These individuals included Thomas Stephens, Eisenhower's appointments secretary; James Hagerty, the press secretary, and Mary Caffrey, Hagerty's secretary; Andrew Berding, the assistant secretary of state for public affairs; Dr. Howard Snyder, Eisenhower's personal physician and Captain Olive Marsh, a nurse to assist him; Alice Boyle, the secretary to General Goodpaster; Polly Yates, the secretary to John Eisenhower; Dr. Kevin McCann, Eisenhower's primary speechwriter; Ann Whitman, Eisenhower's personal secretary; Sergeant John Moaney, Ike's valet; and Rose Woods, the personal assistant to Mamie Eisenhower. Also included were some additional Secret Service agents and security officers.[14]

Chapter 7

Had the presidential party been underway on June 9, it would have been obvious that its members had embarked on a grueling and even exhausting journey. On June 9, the party intended to travel to Goose Bay, Labrador, for a brief stop. From there, they were to fly to Copenhagen, Denmark, arriving at 8:30 A.M. on June 10, given the time change. Just an hour later, at 9:40 A.M., Air Force One was to be airborne and headed for a two-hour-and-twenty- minute flight to Moscow. Given the time change once again, the scheduled arrival of the presidential party was 2:00 P.M.

Eisenhower's itinerary of travel and meetings in the Soviet Union in 1960 bore a slight resemblance to the itinerary he had followed in 1945 on his first visit. On that occasion, Eisenhower flew to Moscow from Berlin, in the company of Marshal Georgi Zhukov and several of his military staff, including John Eisenhower, and then after two days in Moscow, he traveled to Leningrad prior to returning to his command in Germany. In 1960, Eisenhower was scheduled to spend three days in Moscow, June 10–12, then visit Leningrad on June 13, then visit Kiev on June 14, return to Moscow for two days on June 15–16, fly to Irkutsk in Siberia for two days on June 17–18, and finally leave for Japan on June 19. Ike's visit to Siberia came as a special request; he wished to see that particular region of Russia and it was also convenient for departure to his next destination of Japan.[15]

The daily schedule of activities and events for most of the presidential party was so highly planned as to be exhausting. When Eisenhower landed in Moscow at 2 P.M. on June 10, he was to be greeted at the airport by Premier Khrushchev. Then Eisenhower would review the honor guard assembled to welcome him, along with Colonel Draper and Alex Akalovsky. The official welcoming ceremony was scheduled to last from 2:00 to 2:45.

At the welcoming ceremony, Eisenhower was prepared to give the following remarks, drafted by John A. (Jack) Armitage, an experienced Foreign Service officer who had served in the American embassy in Moscow between 1951 and 1952.[16]

> Chairman Voroshilov, Chairman Khrushchev, friends:
> Thank you, Mr. Chairman, for your generous words of welcome.[17] And thank you, kind people, for your cordial and heartwarming reception. You have confirmed, in a most unmistakable way, the reputation for the friendliness of your peoples.

Moscow, Leningrad, and Kiev

I am very glad to be the first President of the United States to visit your country in a time of peace—and it is in the interest of making peace more secure in the world that I have come.[18]

My visit has three aims.

I have come to return the official visit which Chairman Khrushchev so kindly paid our country. It seems fitting to me that I should be here at the invitation of the Chairman of your Council of Ministers. He has played a leading role in promoting broader exchanges of artists, technicians, students, political figures and just plain people between our two countries—And we firmly believe that both our countries stand to gain in mutual understanding from the continuation and expansion of this exchange of people and ideas.[19]

I also look forward to see something of your broad land—and especially of its people. The last [time] I was in Moscow we and our allies had just emerged victorious in a terrible and costly war.[20] In the course of the almost exactly fifteen years since then you have wrought many changes in this country. Your impressive stadiums in Luzhniki and new apartment buildings in the area of the [Moscow] University were visible from the airplane as we came in.[21] I want to see more of how you have developed—your works of construction, your scientific and artistic achievements. I wish that my official duties allowed me more time so that I could see all parts of the Soviet Union. As it is I hope to greet the citizens of Leningrad on the 13th [of June], to see Kiev on the 14th [of June] and to be in Irkutsk on the 17th [of June].

Most of the time we shall spend here in Moscow where I hope to have occasion to talk freely and frankly with Chairman Khrushchev and other Soviet leaders. We shall not be negotiating the issues that divide us.[22] However, in the less formal atmosphere of my visit, the opportunity exists for an exchange of points of view which may improve mutual understanding of the problems confronting us.

Building the basis for a genuine and lasting peace and freedom and security for all is a task for all nations—all people. Because of their strength and influence our two countries bear a special responsibility. Our statesmen will be judged in history by the measure of their efforts toward mutual understanding, toward a stable

Chapter 7

world order accommodating peaceful change, toward tolerance of diverse outlooks and toward respect for the rights and views of others. These are the bases for a world peace. These are the ends toward which my visit to you is dedicated.

I am very glad to be here.[23]

After the conclusion of the opening ceremony, President and Mrs. Eisenhower and the members of the presidential party were to travel by motorcade for the seventeen-mile ride to the Kremlin. Once the party reached Red Square, the itinerary specified different directions for their accommodations. Ike and Mamie, John and Barbara, Dr. Snyder, Andrew Goodpaster, John Moaney, and Rose Woods were to go to the Kremlin, where they were to stay in apartments reserved for them. Secretary of State Herter and his wife, Mary, were to go to Spaso House, the residence of Llewelyn Thompson, the American ambassador, and his wife, Jane. The remaining members of the presidential party were given accommodations at the Ukraine Hotel along the Moscow River in the middle of the city.

Eisenhower's schedule for June 10 called for him to rest in the Kremlin apartment until 4:50 P.M., when he was scheduled to pay a courtesy call on Leonid I. Brezhnev, the chairman of the Presidium of the Supreme Soviet. The meeting with Brezhnev, harmless though it appeared, nevertheless had its own intrigue. When the State Department prepared Eisenhower's preliminary itinerary in March, Kliment I. Voroshilov was the chairman of the Presidium, not Brezhnev. But Voroshilov committed a serious diplomatic indiscretion some weeks earlier when he suggested to the newly appointed Iranian ambassador to the Soviet Union that his government should remove the shah, Mohammad Reza Pahlavi, from power. News of this serious diplomatic blunder quickly reached Khrushchev and he promptly removed Voroshilov from his position on May 7, replacing him with Brezhnev.[24] In that fashion, Khrushchev gave Brezhnev a significant increase in his status and responsibilities, the result of Voroshilov's exercise of poor judgment. So, accompanied by Thompson, Bohlen, John Eisenhower, and Alex Akalovsky, Eisenhower was to call on Brezhnev, with the appointment to finish by 5:30 P.M.

Next, Eisenhower and the same group of advisers were to leave Brezhnev's office to meet with Khrushchev. Here one may speculate that, at this meeting, Eisenhower would inform Khrushchev of the gifts that had been delivered to the American embassy and that would be given to Khrushchev, members of his family, and selected members of the Soviet hierarchy. The State Department had recommended gifts for Khrushchev; his wife; his children and grandchildren; Andrei Gromyko, the foreign minister; Vasily Kuznetsov, the deputy foreign minister; and Anatoly Dobrynin; the head of the American section of the MFA.[25] Khrushchev received the best gift, a watercraft that was water-jet propelled, instead of propeller-driven. The boat was being kept in a garage at the American embassy. Khrushchev loved to take his boats, stored at his luxurious dacha outside of Moscow, for cruises down the Moskva River, and he had taken Vice President Nixon on just such a cruise when Nixon visited the Soviet Union in July 1959.[26] One can envision the sight of Khrushchev beaming in anticipation when Eisenhower showed him a picture of his new watercraft.

Following the brief meeting with Khrushchev, Eisenhower was to return to his apartment for an hour of rest prior to the formal dinner that was to be held in his honor that evening. The attendees at the formal dinner were the members of Group I of the presidential party, in addition to Tommy and Jane Thompson, and Richard M. Davis, the first secretary in the American embassy below Thompson. The dinner was scheduled to last from 8:00 to 10:00 P.M., after which Eisenhower was to return to his apartment in the Kremlin at 11:15, presumably to enjoy the first comfortable night's sleep since he left the United States for the Soviet Union.

At the formal dinner, Eisenhower was prepared to offer the following toast:

Chairman Voroshilov, Chairman Khrushchev, Ladies and Gentlemen,

This is the second time that I have been in the Soviet Union. Both on my first visit and today I have been moved by the warm welcome received.

I am glad I could come to the Soviet Union again. Mr. Khrushchev and I had useful talks last fall at Camp David and I was impressed at the time by his frankness and the breadth of his knowledge about world affairs. I am looking forward to another free exchange of views with him now.

Chapter 7

When I was here fifteen years ago we were allies and partners in a victorious coalition against common enemies. Since then there have been years of disputes and disagreements. Still, over the century and a half since diplomatic relations were established between our two countries, there has always been an underlying feeling of friendship between our two peoples, and they have never fought against the other.[27]

There are few unsettled questions between our countries as such. What causes our difficulties is rather the fact that we have found no common ground for solutions to many international issues. These are not easy problems on which to reconcile our varying points of view. They are difficult and vital questions because they involve differing convictions. They will not be solved easily or quickly but at least we must both try.

Mr. Khrushchev and I talked a lot at Camp David about the need for peace and for peaceful solutions to problems. As Mr. Khrushchev remarked, we are two strong countries and if we quarrel the whole world will suffer.

We need to build on the friendship which already exists between our two peoples. To do this we must talk with one another, but talking, though important, is not enough. We must try to understand each other and yet even understanding is not enough. We must both respect each other's real interests and acknowledge the responsibility each of us bears.

As I see it, Mr. Khrushchev's visit to the United States and my visit to the Soviet Union are important, therefore, because they help both our countries to appreciate better the real motives, interests and responsibilities of one another.

We share a common responsibility to strive for a world of peace and prosperity.

It is in the hope that our efforts will succeed that I raise my glass to Chairman Voroshilov, Chairman Khrushchev and to the peoples of the Soviet Union.[28]

Eisenhower's busy schedule was to resume on Saturday, June 11. After breakfast, he was to tour the Pushkin State Museum of Fine Arts, accompanied by the Thompsons, John and Barbara Eisenhower, Alex and

Maria Akalovsky, and James Hagerty. By that point in Ike's visit, we may assume that the American and international press was well into its coverage and that quite possibly thousands of Muscovites were beginning to assemble in the streets to get a glimpse of the American president. We may also assume that, by this time, Hagerty and his small staff, as well as the staff of the American embassy, were becoming overwhelmed by the requests of the reporters who were covering the visit.

After visiting the Pushkin Gallery, the itinerary called for Eisenhower's return to the Kremlin at 9:30 A.M. for a brief rest before his first official meeting with Nikita Khrushchev, scheduled to last from 10 A.M. to 12 noon. Accompanying Eisenhower to the meeting were Secretary Herter, Ambassador Thompson, Chip Bohlen, Andrew Goodpaster, James Hagerty, and Alex Akalovsky. Dr. Snyder was also to accompany the president but was not included in the meeting. With Khrushchev were Andrei Gromyko, Vasily Kuznetsov, Anatoly Dobrynin, Anastas Mikoyan, and Victor Sukodrev, Khrushchev's interpreter. Since the itinerary does not specify any formal agenda or discussion topics, we may only speculate as to the nature of these talks. It may be fair to assume, though, that Ike and Khrushchev continued their discussions about a nuclear test ban that had begun a month earlier in Paris. Since Harold Macmillan, Charles de Gaulle, and especially Konrad Adenauer were not with Eisenhower in Russia, however, we may also assume that Ike most likely was not inclined to raise the future status of Berlin as a topic for discussion.

After the first meeting with Khrushchev, Eisenhower was to return to his apartment for a private luncheon and, quite logically, further discussions with his advisers about the nature of the meeting with Khrushchev. These discussions would form some of the early preparations for subsequent negotiations with the Soviet leader.

On the afternoon of June 11, Eisenhower was to visit the Exhibition of Soviet Economic Achievements, accompanied by John and Barbara Eisenhower, Tommy Thompson, Dr. Howard Snyder, and the Akalovskys. The exhibition was a massive complex of buildings, largely completed during the Stalinist era, that celebrated Soviet achievements in agriculture, industry, and science. While visiting the United States in 1959, Khrushchev had toured one of IBM's factories in San Jose, California. Eisenhower's visit to the Exhibition of Soviet Economic

Chapter 7

Achievements may have been scheduled as a response to Khrushchev's tour of IBM.[29]

At 3:50 P.M., Eisenhower and his group were to leave the exhibition and drive to Spaso House, where the president was to rest until 5 P.M. Then, between 5:00 and 6:30 P.M., Eisenhower was to host a diplomatic reception for Soviet officials and guests. By 7:00 P.M., Ike was to be on the move once again, this time to the Bolshoi Theater to attend a performance of *Swan Lake* by the Bolshoi Ballet. Accompanying him to the performance were Mamie, John and Barbara, and the Thompsons. Other members of the presidential party, both from Group I and Group II, also attended the performance but were seated in different parts of the theater. At 11:00 P.M., with the performance concluded, Eisenhower and the other members of the presidential party were to return to their overnight accommodations. The schedule that was outlined for Eisenhower's first two days in Moscow was obviously physically demanding and taxing.

On Sunday, June 12, accompanied by the Thompsons, John and Barbara Eisenhower, Dr. Howard Snyder, James Hagerty, and the Akalovskys, Eisenhower was to leave the Kremlin for a short ride to the Central Baptist Church of Moscow, located at Maly Tryokhsvyatitelsky Street, not far from Red Square. Ike and his party were scheduled to attend the first hour of a two-hour worship service.

Moscow's Central Baptist Church had an interesting history. It had been started two hundred years earlier and, according to one account, President Franklin D. Roosevelt made the opening of the church a condition of American assistance to the Soviet Union after it had been attacked by Germany in 1941. Stalin allowed the church to remain open, the only such Protestant church allowed to do so.[30]

Interestingly, Ike would not have been the first member of the Eisenhower administration to worship at Moscow's Central Baptist Church. That distinction belonged to Ezra Taft Benson, Eisenhower's secretary of agriculture, who worshipped at the church while he was on a tour of eastern Europe and the Soviet Union in October 1959. A devout Mormon, Benson wished to attend worship services while he was in the Soviet Union but, not surprisingly, his Russian hosts and guides steered him away from such events. Finally, on the night of October 1, 1959, Benson and his party, somewhat surprisingly, were taken to the Central Baptist

Church. Services at the church were held on Tuesday evenings, Thursday evenings, and Sunday evenings. When Benson and his group arrived at the church, they found that it was packed with more than 1,000 worshipers. Some worshipers were even standing outside the church, trying to hear the words of the service inside.

When Secretary Benson and the Americans entered the church, completely unannounced, the worshipers were immediately astonished to see a group of Americans attending the service with them. As Benson recounted, "Every face in the old sanctuary gasped incredulously as our obviously American group was led down the aisle. They grabbed for our hands as we proceeded to our pews which were gladly vacated for our unexpected visits. They gripped our hands like frightened children."[31]

The service began with the congregants enthusiastically singing a hymn. Then the minister asked Benson to come to the pulpit and address the worshippers. Benson, by now overwhelmed with the intensity of the greeting and the emotional nature of the singing, agreed and went to the front of the church. Speaking through an interpreter, Benson told the worshipers, "It was very kind of you to ask me to greet you. I bring you greetings from millions and millions of church people in America and around the world. Our heavenly father is not far away. He can be very close to us. God lives, and I know that He lives. He is our father. Jesus Christ, the redeemer of the world, watches over the earth. He will direct all things. Be unafraid, keep His commandments, pray for peace, and all will be well."[32]

As Benson spoke, hundreds of worshippers responded, saying "ja, ja, ja" ("yes," yes," "yes"). Women in the church took out white handkerchiefs, waving them in Benson's direction when he returned to his seat in the pew. Then the congregation began singing one of Benson's favorite hymns, *God Be with You till We Meet Again*. When Benson and the Americans got up and started to leave the church, the congregants continued to wave their white handkerchiefs in his direction. Many worshipers wept openly.[33] Benson even left an impression on one of his Russian interpreters, a "young girl," in Benson's words, who told him, on the ride back to the airport, "I felt like crying."[34]

When Eisenhower was scheduled to visit the Central Baptist Church, he would come with gifts to present to the rector (senior minister) of the church on the occasion of his visit. These gifts would include copies of the King James Version of the Bible, the Revised Standard Version, and some hymnals that contained selections of the best-loved hymns sung in American churches. By that point in his life, Eisenhower was used to participating in the worship services that he attended. For example, when Prime Minister Harold Macmillan visited the United States in March 1959, Ike took him to the Gettysburg Presbyterian Church, the church that Eisenhower regularly attended on the weekends that he spent in nearby Camp David. Reverend James MacAskill, the pastor, asked Eisenhower to read the Scripture lesson at the service on March 22, 1959, that he attended with Macmillan.[35]

Eisenhower had even sought out Khrushchev to attend worship services with him when Khrushchev visited the United States in 1959. In making the invitation, Eisenhower was apparently acting on the knowledge that "Khrushchev had been very active as a youth in the Orthodox Church and won prizes for his church work."[36] Khrushchev declined Eisenhower's invitation to accompany him to worship services, however.

Given the outpouring of enthusiasm that the worshippers of the Central Baptist Church gave to Secretary Benson, one can only imagine how the worshippers would have greeted Eisenhower. It would have been a monumental, historic scene within this avowedly atheistic country, still then engaged in a persecution of Christians, as the president of the United States and his associates took their seats in the pew of the Central Baptist Church and worshipped along with the Russian congregation.

After leaving the church service, Eisenhower's itinerary called for a return to the Kremlin, after which he was to go on a one-hour driving tour of Moscow with his Russian hosts. The rest of the day was to be spent at Khrushchev's dacha at Gorky II outside of Moscow. Scheduled to travel to the dacha were Ike and Mamie, Tommy and Jane Thompson, John and Barbara Eisenhower, Chip and Avis Bohlen, Andrew Goodpaster, James Hagerty, Dr. Howard Snyder, and the Akalovskys. Eisenhower and the presidential party were scheduled to spend the afternoon with Khrushchev, Nina Petrovna, and Khrushchev's children.

In Khrushchev's mind, the visit by Eisenhower and his party to the dacha may have been planned to resemble Eisenhower's invitation to visit his farm at Gettysburg in a relaxed setting during his visit to the United States in 1959. Sergei Khrushchev recounted that what his father had in mind was a visit to the dacha, "show [Eisenhower] some crops," and take a boat cruise down the Moskva River.[37] By that time, Khrushchev would have been in possession of his new American watercraft and he would have enjoyed the experience of cruising in the Moskva River in his new American boat. A boat ride for Ike would have been in keeping with Khrushchev's hospitality shown the previous year for Vice President Nixon.

However, in the itinerary, one also finds the words that "following the luncheon [at the dacha], the president and N. S. Khrushchev will have a talk"—a talk that was scheduled to last from 2:00 to 5:00 P.M. Was this "talk," therefore, similar to the negotiations at Camp David that occurred between Ike and Khrushchev in which they reached an agreement on the subject of the removal of Khrushchev's ultimatum on Berlin and the scheduling of a summit conference?[38] The fact that three hours had been reserved for the talk, and that Ike was going to be accompanied by Thompson, Bohlen, and Goodpaster, appeared to suggest that this meeting with Khrushchev may have had a purpose beyond its purely social aspects, perhaps even to hold follow-up discussions relating to a possible nuclear test-ban agreement. If there was finally going to be a breakthrough on this issue, was it going to occur at Khrushchev's dacha?

The Visits to Leningrad and Kiev

After three days in Moscow, Dwight Eisenhower was scheduled to spend June 13 and June 14 in Leningrad and Kiev, respectively. In August 1945, Ike had visited Leningrad but not Kiev. He would be anxious to see Leningrad once again to witness how the city had changed since its bitter experiences in World War II as well as to see Kiev for the first time.

The entire presidential party, except for Mamie Eisenhower, who remained in Moscow and moved her accommodation from the apartment in the Kremlin to Spaso House, was to depart Moscow at 9:30 A.M. on Monday, June 13, for the one-hour flight to Leningrad. Once in Leningrad, Ike and his party were to participate in the official welcoming ceremony and greet the city's mayor and leading officials. Eisenhower's remarks, prepared for delivery upon arrival in Leningrad, were drafted by Harry G. Barnes, Jr., an experienced Foreign Service officer who was serving in the American embassy in Moscow as the publications procurement officer when Hans Tuch arrived in 1959. Tuch and Barnes often

Chapter 7

"helped each other out," as Tuch later recalled. Tuch was occasionally overwhelmed by his duties as the embassy's first press and cultural attaché and Barnes was able to assist him with the intricacies of diplomatic service in Moscow. Barnes was assigned the responsibility of acquiring relevant books about the Soviet Union, written in Russian, and seeing that those volumes were available to American diplomats throughout the embassies. Tuch was often able to help Barnes in carrying out that responsibility.[39] Eisenhower's remarks for the arrival in Leningrad went as follows:

> Mr. Chairman, Citizens of Leningrad, fifteen years ago I made my first visit to the Soviet Union. Before leaving your country I wanted to come to Leningrad and fortunately was able to do so briefly. During the war, we had followed the siege of Leningrad and had watched with great admiration the magnificent defense of your city.
>
> I know that Leningrad from its own experience knows the horrors of war. I know, therefore, that Leningrad shares the hopes of millions of Americans and of people everywhere that the pattern of the past need not be repeated—that another catastrophe need not come.
>
> There has been no war in our land for a century.[40] But do not think that we know nothing of the evils of war. I myself know them and in the last twenty years the tragedy of war has been felt in every town and village in America.
>
> Peace that is only an armed truce is not enough. We must strive for a dynamic peace that promises a worthy future for every human being. I can tell you that the American people will never slacken in this search for a just and lasting peace.
>
> Unfortunately my schedule gives me little time with you but I do hope to visit one of your factories and talk with some of the workers there, as well as to renew my acquaintance with your historic and beautiful city.
>
> It is good to come to Leningrad again. Thank you for your welcome.[41]

From the airport, Eisenhower and the Americans were to be driven to a massive industrial complex, the Electrosila ("Electric Power" in

Russian) Association for the Building of Electrical Machines. At Electrosila, there were two factories that managed electrical power, one apparatus factory, and an institute for scientific research. The Germans had bombed the factory complex extensively during World War II but "work did not stop for a single day," the Russians boasted.[42] Eisenhower's tour of Electrosila would be brief, lasting only thirty minutes, after which the presidential party was to travel to the center of Leningrad, where they would reach their overnight accommodation. After a private luncheon at the guesthouse reserved for him, Ike was scheduled for a meeting with a group of seven American students who were studying in Leningrad as part of an educational exchange with the Soviet Union. Then, between 3:00 and 5:30 P.M., Ike and the Americans were to go sightseeing. First, they would visit the Hermitage, Russia's enormous, magnificent gallery of art. The visit to the Hermitage would last from 3:00 to 4:00 P.M., hardly enough time to appreciate the vast treasures of art on display in the Hermitage's five-building complex.[43]

After the Hermitage, Ike and the presidential party were to take a forty-five-minute drive to the Peterhof, the ornate, magisterial palace built by Peter the Great in the early eighteenth century, and sometimes referred to as the "Russian Versailles."[44] Eisenhower would have marveled at what he saw both of the Hermitage and the Peterhof. In August 1945, both structures suffered extensive damage at the hands of the Germans and had since been rebuilt to magnificent proportions. Eisenhower admired the people of Leningrad and would have been pleased to see the rebuilding and restoration of this magnificent Russian city.

With the sightseeing concluded, Eisenhower was scheduled to return to his guesthouse in Leningrad at 6:30 P.M. His day was hardly even close to being finished, however. After a short rest, Ike was to go to Leningrad's Radio-Television Studio and then, between 7:30 and 8:15, he was to deliver an address to the Russian people. The address marked the first occasion that any American president had spoken directly to the Russian people via radio and television. Eisenhower was prepared to give the following remarks:

> When in 1945 I was in Russia, my stay necessarily had to be short. Nevertheless, I then insisted that I could not return to my post of duty in Berlin until I paid homage to the valiant defenders

Chapter 7

of Leningrad against Nazi outrage. After fifteen years' absence, I return here more firmly convinced than ever that this city is a world landmark, an enduring monument to the noblest of human traits—superb heroism and intellectual greatness.[45]

Through many months, the men and women and children of Leningrad withstood siege guns and bombers and swarming armies; hunger and disease and violent death. The whole world watched them through winter months and summer months and winter months again. They wrote for mankind to read, even centuries from now, an epic of courage and sacrifice and unfaltering faith.

In the passage of years, the stones of your city may wear away; the physical image of Leningrad may alter. But wherever men honor the brave and the resolute, never will the memory of the evil siege and the glorious triumph be forgotten.

So today, foremost in my thoughts—even as fifteen years ago this summer—is a salute from the heart to the greatness of Leningrad—to the epic its people wrote in the annals of heroism.

Not by an iota have the years diminished my respect and admiration for the heroes of Leningrad. Quite the contrary. But I must assert as strongly as I can that many of the hopes I then nourished have faded; many of the fears I then tried to brush away have been realized.

Only a few months before my visit here in that year of Russia's and America's mutual triumph, I wrote to the Allied troops who served me this sentence in an Order of the Day: "Let us have no part in the profitless quarrels in which other men will inevitably engage as to what country, what service, won the European war."

Worse than profitless quarrels have come to pass. Suspicion and rancor and fear, voiced often in the harshest words of threat, too often mark the relations of peoples once tightly joined in a common cause and by a common victory. All of us here are at fault that there have been such tragic crimes against friendship.

But our fault will be the most tragic of all crimes, if we shrug our shoulders and say, "This sort of thing has always happened," if we fail—you and I, all of us—to act positively that suspicion and rancor and fear be banished.

Moscow, Leningrad, and Kiev

When I was a boy, we put blinders on horses so they would not shy in fright of a scarecrow, a shadow, a rabbit. But today we human beings put blinders on ourselves, not to avoid the sight of frightful things, but to ignore a central fact of human existence.

I mean that mankind too often blinds itself to the common lot, to the common purposes, to the common aspirations of humanity everywhere. I mean that all of us too much live in ignorance of our neighbors; or, when we take off our blinders, view them through the contortionist spectacles of propaganda.

And we will continue that way—forever fearful, forever suspicious—until we convince ourselves that the only way to peace is through the mutual[ly] open society. Then, at long last, seeing our human neighbors as they really are, we shall come to realize that we need no more fear them than the horse the rabbit.

So I come to this home of heroes with a feeling of inescapable duty upon me to understand better your achievements, your concerns, your beliefs and your hopes—the great and good you share with all our country.

To reach such understanding is a compelling duty on all Americans; on myself and on my 181 million fellow citizens. To ignore is as senseless as to read only the odd-number pages in a book.

And what applies to Americans should apply to Russians, too. What is sauce for the goose is sauce for the gander.

Your warm welcome assures me that we can find ways to understand each other. I hope that you will come to my country by the tens of thousands, as Americans have come here, to see and examine our way of life in America.

If you travel over America in our jets you will see all America. Our country is not as large as yours. It is crossed and criss-crossed by commercial air lanes. At forty thousand feet on a clear day, nothing can be hidden from a citizen or from a visitor who wants to look—hundreds of miles of countryside lie exposed on either side of the plane.[46] And we don't prohibit cameras or binoculars. Were we to do that, my desk would be buried under complaints of outraged camera fans; the manufacturers of film and optical wares would give me no rest.

Chapter 7

But most important of all, we would hope you could see the vigor with which our Republic grows and changes. So seeing you would understand, I think, that our way of life is not destined to wither and to be buried in the limbo of history's failures. You would understand, I think, that there is no single inevitable system that will envelop the earth.

And my first compelling duty is matched by another—to assure, to persuade, to convince you that above all else the American people want in this world and in their lives peace with all nations; a peace strong in mutual understanding; a peace warm with friendship; a peace enjoyed in freedom—freedom from war and its threat; freedom from propaganda and its hate; freedom from manmade curtains and walls of every sort that make nations ignorant, suspicious, fearful of each other.

My purpose is not one of debate; but as we welcomed Premier Khrushchev in our nation to describe to us the ideals, procedures, and forms of the Soviet system, I shall, without criticism of that system, try to explain the aspirations, principles and methods on which we operate.

To no more fitting place can I come for the discharge of this duty. Peter [the Great], who founded this city, thought of it as [the] "Window on the West."[47]

Today, I ask you and all Russia to look through your windows across eight thousand miles of land and water to my homeland. As you look, I ask that you forget for the moment this or that incident whose nearness in time magnifies and distorts its significance. I ask you to remember more than seventeen long decades of friendly, cooperative, profitable relations between our two people.

Remember an American naval hero who became a Russian admiral.[48]

Remember a Russian fleet entering our largest port to hearten and encourage the American Republic in a dark hour when its survival was at stake.[49]

Remember, as we Americans proudly remember, the Russian discovery and settlement of the fiftieth state in our Union, Alaska; and how in the most peaceful and friendly of international transactions Russia added half a million square miles to American territory.[50]

Remember the tens upon tens of thousands of Russians who, before your Revolution, found in our ports gateways to freedom from the oppression of tyrants—and a warm, friendly welcome from America. [51]

Remember the hundreds of wartime ships, full-laden with arms and food, sailing to Russia from many ports. Remember they sailed so that you, who had spent your blood and your treasure in a righteous war, might gain new strength to reach Torgau on the Elbe where Russians and Americans embraced—comrades in arms; partners in victory. [52]

As you look and as you recall those years, I ask that you try better to understand that we Americans seek of you only your cooperation in establishing a peace in which you and we, and every other people, can develop our destinies in freedom.

As I attempt the discharge of these two duties: to convince you of America's decent purposes; to learn and better to understand your way, I have in my mind the words of a distinguished Russian who counseled the American people in an address in Chicago more than sixty years ago. He was Prince Serge Wolkonsky [Sergei Mikhailovich Volkonsky]. Permit me to read a paragraph from his talk.

"When you want to learn what a nation is, what a nation is capable of, when you want to know her ideas, her aspirations, her character, when you want to know a Nation's soul,—do not study her from the reports of the daily papers or the cheap pamphlets which are written for one occasion and the fame of which lasts but a month or two. Learn a nation from the precious contributions she has given to the eternal treasures of humanity; learn her from what she did for universal science, universal art; learn to know the nation from her beacons, from those men she is proud of, and first of all—let politics alone."[53]

So spoke Serge Wolkonsky. We Americans strive to heed his counsel—even the last pungent warning.

Our belief in your right to your form of government, and in the similar right of the American people and every other people, stems from our conviction that each individual has the right to choose his own destiny in freedom. This is the essence of our American heritage.

Chapter 7

Our traditions go beyond the oceans which border our country. They have their origins in every country—Russia is certainly one—in which men of courage have challenged authoritarian institutions and have worked to win rights that could not be violated by their rulers. We had then and have today the good fortune to be a haven for men who were too free for their homelands.[54]

We have retained our links with the past without revolutionary disruption. But we have changed vastly. We are changing now. We must always change—since progress creates new problems and our society is far from perfect.[55]

If the American system is described simply as "Capitalism," its whole essence is missed. We hold to the freedom of an individual to apply his talents and means to fulfilling the needs of his community—and to profit from this effort, if he can meet his neighbors' needs better or more cheaply than his competitor. At the same time, we engage in voluntary co-operatives in the fields of agricultural sales, housing, medicine, and social works. We assign Government an economic role—when Government can do for the people what they themselves cannot do so well or do at all.

Choosing what works best in each situation is characteristic of Americans. They will study and test any worthy proposal; continuously try new ways and change old patterns in a most worthy purpose—to assure the pursuit of happiness by the individual in freedom and dignity, under a framework of law legislated by freely elected representatives responsive to the will of the majority.

The system which provides us with the best opportunity towards the realization of our ideals may not suit you. That is for you to decide. Yours does not suit us. We do not believe that our system any more than yours is the inevitable solution for the other peoples of the world. They must—as we are doing—seek their own way, taking what they wish from the experience of others.

Our concern is that it be genuinely their way—that it be the product of their choice, of their heritages, and of their growth, not of interference by other powers.

We work for a world in which diverse development will be guaranteed. We do not seek a world divided in co-existing camps locked in a struggle for supremacy. We hope and work for a single world community which recognizes and respects a code of international law governing the relations between diverse peoples.

Briefly, plainly, candidly, I have tried to tell you of the American system and purpose as I see them. So complex a way of life, so varied by its expressions, comprising the lives of many millions of people and so many ventures in human affairs cannot be compressed into a talk of fifteen minutes—or fifteen hours, for that matter. But I hope that I may have aroused in you an interest to learn more about us, more often to look through this "Window on the West" to America where, even as here, a just and enduring peace among all nations is the great human goal.

If you give me that response, I shall be in your debt all my life.

Following the speech, Eisenhower was to travel to the Leningrad Soviet (city hall) for an official dinner with the leaders of the city. Finally, at 11:00 P.M., Eisenhower and the members of the presidential party would arrive back at the guesthouse and the conclusion to what had been an active, eventful day.

By 8:20 the following morning, June 14, Eisenhower and the presidential party were to be up and moving again. At 9:20, there would be a brief departure ceremony for Ike at the Leningrad Civil Airport. By 10 A.M., the presidential party would be in the air for a ninety-minute flight to Kiev in Ukraine. At 11:30, the Americans were to land at Boryspil Airport, where, in a thirty-minute welcoming ceremony, they would be greeted by the mayor of Kiev and other city officials. At the welcoming ceremony, Eisenhower was scheduled to give the following remarks:

Thank you for your welcome to my party and myself. As you know, my visit to the Soviet Union can only be a brief one. I am very pleased that in that short time I have been able to come to the Ukraine and Kiev.

Both the Ukraine and Kiev are known to us in America. A number of my fellow citizens are of Ukrainian descent and perhaps some of you have relatives living in America. The Ukrainians who came to the United States brought with them cultural and spiritual values which have contributed much to the heritage of our country.

Chapter 7

We have heard, too, of the "Golden Gate" of Kiev and of the city's great tradition as a center of culture that dates back more than a thousand years ago.[56] We know, too, your difficult days: the famine years in the 20s when the American people tried to be of help, as well as the years of World War II when so much of Kiev was destroyed.

I can understand how, from your own experience, you strongly desire to live in a peaceful world. Believe me, the United States is aware of the great responsibility it and the other nations bear to work toward a world of peace, freedom, and prosperity.

I assure you from the bottom of my heart that we will continue to strive for these goals. Permit me to thank you for your fine welcome by saying thank you. (Sacrdetchno Dyakouyu).

From the airport, Eisenhower and the presidential party were to travel by motorcade to the official guesthouse, arriving at 1:00 P.M. At a private lunch, Eisenhower would be prepared to give the following toast:

Mr. Chairman, Ladies and Gentlemen, someone has told me there is an expression that goes something like this: "Talking will get you to Kiev." I am not sure if my tongue has gotten me here; but as I said at the airport, I am very pleased to visit Kiev and the Ukraine.

It is true, of course, that I have done a lot of talking since I came to the Soviet Union. I have tried to talk to as many people of the Soviet Union as I could. I have wanted to tell them about America and about our hopes for a better future for all people everywhere.

One thing I would say to everyone—if we work for peace and prosperity for all, we must learn to respect the rights and convictions of each other. We all wish to live a better life. In so doing we must let others live a better life of their own choosing.[57]

After some rest, the party was to be on the move again at 2:45 P.M. Visiting the Tomb of the Unknown Soldier (commemorating Russian soldiers who were lost or missing from World War I), Eisenhower was scheduled to lay a wreath and speak with the chairman of the Ukrainian Supreme Soviet and the chairman of the Ukrainian Council of Ministers. The wreath-laying ceremony would have brought back vivid memories of World War II to Eisenhower. By 4:45, Eisenhower would have returned to the guesthouse.

By 7:10, Eisenhower was scheduled for the major event of his visit to Kiev, a radio-television address to the people of Ukraine. Once again, Eisenhower was the first American president to speak to the people of Ukraine via radio and television. At the studio, Eisenhower was prepared to give the following speech:

> It is a great pleasure for me to be able to come here to the capital of the Ukraine, to this renowned and beautiful city. Our airmen, in particular, remember the Ukraine in World War II as a friendly haven at the end of their long, dark missions over Hitler's Europe. They also remember the warmth and welcome of Ukrainian hearts.[58]
>
> As an old soldier, I remember both the warmth of our comradeship in those years and the tragedy of the war. The world has suffered enough, and I know that we share the conviction that war should never again scourge the earth. Terrible as the last war was, another world conflict would not leave standing either your cities or ours. It would not spare civilian or soldier, farmer or factory worker, communist or non-communist. There would be no profit for any man, only destruction, ruin, and chaos.
>
> Looking back, I remember how we hoped to build the post-war world through our common, friendly efforts. It has been an aching disappointment to me that we have not realized the full measure of our hopes in the intervening years. Suspicion and distrust have crowded back the friendly confidence of our wartime partnership. On both sides, there have been mistakes, as well as opportunities lost, and opportunities wrongly taken.
>
> I have been told that today there are some of you who doubt the devotion of the American government to peace. This is difficult for me to understand, as I know my own abhorrence of war and the single-minded desire for peace of the men who work with me in the government of my country. Nevertheless, Americans who have visited you tell me, and I have learned from your press, that the peaceful intentions of America are not so clear to you as they are to us. Vice President Richard Nixon has told me that the question

about our policy which was most often asked him as he visited your factories was: "Why do you Americans surround us with bases and military blocs if you desire peace?"[59]

This question deserves a straightforward answer. It also requires me to speak frankly to you, which is as it should be. Understanding will not come through pretending that our differences do not exist. Chairman Khrushchev set a good example when he visited us in America, as a plain-speaking man who relied on his candor to turn away offense.

It is true that there are American troops and installations abroad, as there are also Soviet troops and installations abroad, most notably in the Eastern part of Germany, in Poland, and in Hungary. There is a difference, of course, in that some American forces are in countries close to Soviet borders, while there are no Soviet forces in Mexico or Canada or other countries near the United States.

To explain this difference, perhaps we should recall how the last great war started. Hitler's aggression had its roots in the occupation of the Rhineland, in the seizure of Austria, and in the bloodless conquest of the Czechoslovak borderlands. All of these territories were adjacent to or part of Germany, and they were far from America and even relatively distant from you. Yet both we and you were threatened, and international peace was ultimately destroyed as the result of these acts. I have taken this example to show from that tragic era of history, about which you and we see eye to eye, that geography and distance do not determine right and wrong in international affairs. War begins where the trouble is.

We cannot draw a line midway between your borders and ours and say that each side's political concern must stop on his side of that line. Smaller states also have a right to security and freedom, whether they be close to you or close to us.

The hard fact is that some countries close to your borders do feel threatened by the expansive world movement which has its center in your country. I realize that some of you may think such an expansion would be a very good thing, but I ask you to recognize that most of us in the world do not think so. We do not want your system for reasons we think are good ones, just as we have no wish to impose our system on you. As I explained in Leningrad last night, we Americans see values in our own society, for ourselves, which we are determined to preserve. Other countries also see values in their ways of life and government. Our view is that each society should be free to develop its own institutions in its own way.

Unfortunately, smaller states on the periphery of Communist power have felt this freedom endangered. They have been disturbed by the developments in East Europe and the Far East since 1945 which have formed a disquieting pattern. A single kind of regime seems to have developed in places where Soviet military power was present after the past war. In our view, the right of self-determination was denied the peoples of Eastern Europe. Moreover, fears in many countries were increased by the events in Korea in 1950. They have not been dissipated by more recent events in Hungary and in Tibet.[60]

We are reproached in your press for participating in military blocs and having bases, but these developments came after many of the events I have mentioned. Between 1945 and 1947 we reduced our armed forces by ten and a half million men, leaving only one and a half million soldiers, sailors, and airmen under arms. NATO was not organized until 1949 and CENTO and SEATO were formed six years later.[61] We did not begin to increase our forces until after the Korean War had broken out, and our bases have not been used for an assault on anyone or to impose our political system on other peoples.

I have spoken bluntly, but I do not know how these things can be said blandly. I know that not everyone will look at these things the way we do, but I must tell you our point of view with honesty and forthrightness. Realities must be recognized to be changed. I am here in your country for the same reason that I trust your Chairman came to my country, which is to change our relationship for the better. To do this, we must know the hard and unpalatable facts as well as the easy and sweet-tasting ones.

Today our countries are deeply divided on the questions of Berlin and of German unity. As you know, we had all hoped at the end of the war that the four wartime allies would be able to work together to help the German people construct a peaceful and democratic country. Unfortunately, such cooperative relationships were not achieved, and the unhappy result has been the division of Germany along the borders of the occupation zones established by four-power wartime agreements. You may remember that American troops voluntarily withdrew from large areas of Germany which they had captured from the German forces in accordance with the terms of these agreements, thus permitting the Soviet forces to enter them. For its part, the Soviet Union agreed to govern the whole of Germany as one economic unit, to administer the whole of Berlin together with its wartime allies, and to guarantee free Western access to the city.[62]

However, as time went on, the division of Germany became deeper and created more difficulties for ourselves and for the German people. This division was also reflected locally in Berlin. I do not wish to oversimplify the present proposals of the Soviet government, but they do not provide a cure for this situation. Indeed, they would make it permanent.

History shows that the continued arbitrary division of a single people by force is abnormal, unnatural, and potentially dangerous. The German population has shown that it has learned from its wartime experience. Its view of Germany's role in the world is fundamentally changed.[63] This is a good and healthy development. But it appears unrealistic to believe that the German people will ever cease to desire the unity of their own country. There are ways of providing security and stability in Central Europe. We are prepared to enter into the most grave and binding undertakings for the protection of European security against any possible threat arising out of German unification. We have again and again made concrete proposals to this end. Such a solution would be a better way to secure the peace than by the continued frustration of the German people's legitimate desire for self-determination.

In Berlin itself we have been asked by the Soviet Government to accept a new arrangement which does not apply to the whole of the city but only to the Western part, as well as the unilateral abrogation of the Soviet Union's firm obligation to guarantee access to the city. The way to settle the Berlin problem is not to attempt to make permanent the division of the city, but to unify Germany with appropriate political and security safeguards.[64] I do not expect you to agree with me on this problem now, but I would like to suggest that you think over what I have said in the future and to consider whether our Western viewpoint may not be a constructive one.

In explaining our American point of view on the great issues that confront us, I must also speak about the arms race, the so-called "position of strength" policy, and disarmament. In this respect, I must confess my perplexity in being told that the balance of military power is shifting in favor of the Soviet Union while my country is wickedly aggravating the race in arms. It takes two to make a race, and it is strange for the fellow who claims he is drawing ahead to ask his competitor why he runs so hard. It is also difficult to understand how a nation can say it is disarming unilaterally and yet assert that it is afterwards even stronger in military might. It is deeply disturbing to us in America to be told that the means by which peace is being strengthened is through this alleged shift in military power. To us this looks like a "position of strength" policy.

We are accused of having pursued such a policy ourselves. But please remember that in the years after the Second World War, we were alone in the possession of atomic weapons, yet we did not use this monopoly to force our ideas or our system on other nations. In 1946 we proposed full international control of atomic energy.[65] Unfortunately, our two countries could not agree on adequate control of this awesome weapon, and the tragedy of our disagreement has been acted out through the ensuing years before the eyes of a saddened world.

Let me explain why the principle of inspection and control in disarmament has remained fundamental to our position. First, we remember the spectacle of uncontrolled and unpoliced disarmament prior to the Second World War. German, Italian, and Japanese militarism spread like a cancer under just those conditions.

Even though we might have nothing to fear from each other, the world has many countries who sooner or later will be able to build and test atomic weapons, with no help from either of us. The disarmament negotiations in which our countries are engaged will set the pattern for these countries, too. We cannot ignore the possibility that in the future there may appear somewhere on this earth a country selfish enough to take advantage of his neighbor's trust.[66]

Chapter 7

Let us recognize the frailty of men, whether they be everyday citizens or the leaders of states. The opportunity for evasion is a temptation. Conversely, the knowledge that infractions will be known is an encouragement and support for responsible leadership. This is true both within the councils of a particular government and in the broader councils of the international community. Disarmament without control breeds suspicion, evasion, and distrust. It sows the seeds of war. For our part, we are ready to have our country fully inspected under any system that can be truly relied upon to detect evasions. We are convinced that only through adequate control can our nations build the mutual trust and confidence so necessary to international disarmament.

I should also like to tell you my country's attitude toward complete and general disarmament. The people and the Government of America desire nothing more fervently than the opportunity to lay down the vicious, wasteful burden of arms. Most of us Americans remember the days before the last war when we had only 250,000 men in uniform in our country. We are strongly in favor of general disarmament, properly controlled. Moreover, we believe concrete steps toward this goal should be undertaken immediately.

We couple our desire for general disarmament with the need for international security forces, which you have already agreed on in principle in the Charter of the United Nations. However, the problem is still more fundamental. Hand in hand with disarmament must come a universally accepted rule of law and a firm means of assuring that no nation, however powerful, can block the enforcement of that law. I realize that this last principle is a stumbling block, as the Soviet Union is reluctant to place its security in hands which it considers unsympathetic to its form of government. Nevertheless, I fervently hope that we shall be able to reconcile the legitimate concerns of each nation with the need for an international order that can preserve the peace. This would be a far better way to secure the peace than through alliances or bases.

In these past few minutes, I have talked very frankly with you. It is in the cause of friendship that I speak openly when we are face to face. You would not think me an upright, grateful guest if my words here were sugar-sweet, while my words at home, when I return, were of a different taste. We must find our way back to confident friendship through honest, open talk leading to constructive self-examination on both sides.

I believe that we have already taken steps along this happier road. During the past two or three years there have been many encouraging developments in our relations. The simple fact that we are seeing and talking with each other is an auspicious thing. Fruitful contacts between your Chairman and myself have resulted from his visit to my country, from our common labors in Paris during May, and already from my visit to you.[67] Just as important, Soviet and American engineers, scientists, doctors, writers, lawyers, dancers, actors, students and countless others have visited back and forth. Our recent national exhibitions and other exchanges help open new ventures toward understanding and improved relations.[68]

We have also agreed to explore the opportunities for joint projects in the peaceful uses of atomic energy. We have agreed to pursue joint efforts in the United Nations in the peaceful uses of outer space. If the promise of our opportunity is realized, we can move forward toward the harnessing of science and technology to man's benefit instead of his destruction.

There are other fields in which cooperative efforts are moving forward, and our future possibilities expanding. We have agreed on mutual programs in medicine, and it is our hope that Soviet and American scientists and doctors, working together, can contribute to the final conquest of cancer, polio and other dread diseases. Our two countries, with other interested powers, have been able to make a treaty for the peaceful development of Antarctica in cooperation and friendship. Soon after I return home from this trip, representatives of our two countries will be sitting down together in Washington to negotiate a civil air agreement, which will establish regular flights of American and Soviet planes for the first time.[69]

Our countries are blessedly free of the ancient enmities that mar the relations of so many states. We have a valuable heritage of good relations going back almost two centuries. We had ideological differences with Imperial Russia, which you will understand, but that did not prevent our historic friendship. Neither did ideological differences in a more recent time prevent our cooperation and alliance during the past war. We must show that we can do in peace what we were able to do in war.

Let us do more than coexist.[70] Peace is not a condition where you seek to defeat your partner, albeit short of war. We should not be struggling over peace; we should be building it together. Peace is more than an armed truce. Your task and our task is not to vanquish the other point of view, but to understand it. Only from being able in our understanding, to stand in each other's shoes and see how the world looks to the other will we be able to find a true accommodation.

Through understanding we must build respect. Like a man, a nation which is truly confident feels no need to sound belligerent. I hope we can put behind us the point of view that interprets each success of our own country as an ideological arrow aimed at our neighbor. I also hope the future will not find us regarding our neighbor's discomfitures as the cause for rejoicing. We look at the world through different eyes but that does not mean that the perspective of the other must be an evil one. The ultimate objective of peace is not struggle, but concord. Let us find a way to live together on this earth in respect, in friendship and in concord.

Following the speech, as with the evening before in Leningrad, Eisenhower and the presidential party were to be the guests of honor at a formal dinner, followed by a thirty-minute musical concert at the Mariinsky Palace. The concert was given by the Mariinsky Opera. The following morning, Eisenhower and the presidential party were to depart Kiev for their return to Moscow and to continue the second half of their visit to the Soviet Union.

In conclusion, we may assume that Eisenhower's first five days in the Soviet Union served to focus the world's attention on his visit. In particular, three events—his prospective visit to the Central Baptist Church on the morning of Sunday, June 12; his prospective motor tour of Moscow on June 12; and his speech at Kiev on June 14—merit some closer examination in terms of their potential impact on the purposes of Eisenhower's visit. The events on the morning of June 12 would have occurred at a time when the people of Moscow would have been fully aware of Eisenhower's presence in the city. If the response of the people of Moscow to Eisenhower's visit to the Soviet Union in August 1945 was an indicator of how he may have been received in June 1960, we may assume that massive crowds would have gathered in anticipation of an opportunity to see the president of the United States in person.

What might have happened when Eisenhower visited the Central Baptist Church? In the first place, unlike Secretary Benson's visit, Eisenhower would have not come unannounced to the church services. The crowds around the church, awaiting Eisenhower's arrival, would have been massive, perhaps stretching for blocks in the nearby vicinity. Then, when Eisenhower and his presidential party entered the church, one could expect that the worshippers would have pressed in to touch the president, as they had with Secretary Benson. Moreover, Benson had been given the opportunity to speak to the congregants in 1959; it is therefore highly likely that the rector of the church would have given the same opportunity to Eisenhower. We know that, at a minimum, Eisenhower would have been granted the opportunity to present the gifts of the American Bibles and the American hymnals to the rector.

But then, the question arises: what would Ike have said to the worshippers, beyond extending greetings from the American people? Would he have mentioned the principles of religious freedom, freedom of worship, and religious pluralism, as they were practiced in the United States? If so, this could only be taken by the worshippers, and by the Soviet authorities as well, as a rebuke of the Soviet regime's attitude toward religious observances in its country. Would the white handkerchiefs have come out as Eisenhower spoke, as they had for Benson? If so, would the waving of these white handkerchiefs have been seen as a symbol of protest against the Soviet regime? Would the waving of white handkerchiefs have persisted throughout the remainder of Eisenhower's public appearances in the Soviet Union, and be taken as further symbols of protest? We may also assume that the members of the American and international press would have been able to attend the service at the Central Baptist Church and photograph Eisenhower and the members of the presidential party worshiping in the church, and even of Eisenhower presenting his gifts to the rector. How would people in the rest of the Soviet bloc—such as Poland, Czechoslovakia, and Hungary—have responded to the sight of a president of the United States worshiping in a church in

Chapter 7

Moscow? Eisenhower's visit to the Central Baptist Church in Moscow, at the height of the Cold War, had the potential to alter the direction of Soviet-American relations.

The same might be said of Eisenhower's driving tour of Moscow, presumably with Khrushchev riding along, that was to follow after Ike left the Central Baptist Church. Once again, thoughts return to the spontaneous reception from the crowds in Moscow that Ike received in August 1945, when he was discovered walking on the streets before the National Sports Parade. We may assume that massive crowds would have lined the streets of Moscow as Eisenhower rode by and his limousine made its way around the streets of the city. Would the crowds have been such as to slow Eisenhower's motorcade to a crawl, as had happened when Eisenhower visited London, Paris, Bonn, and New Delhi? What would have been the international impact of a picture of Eisenhower, sitting on top of the back seat of the limo, arms upraised in his familiar pose, smiling enthusiastically at the crowds? The potential impact would have been enormous, certainly as a gesture on Eisenhower's part for improved relations between the United States and the Soviet Union.

A third important event that would have occurred in Eisenhower's first five days in the Soviet Union involves a section of his speech in Kiev. It is important to emphasize that, at this point, Eisenhower's public statements in the Soviet Union had not been provocative, but, in this speech, he raised a warning, and this warning involved the potential for the proliferation of nuclear weapons beyond those countries that currently possessed them, and of the necessity of a system of control that prevented their spread. To quote from the speech,

> Let me explain why the principle of inspection and control in disarmament has remained fundamental to our position. First, we remember the spectacle of controlled and unpoliced disarmament prior to the Second World War. German, Italian, and Japanese militarism spread like a cancer under just those conditions. Even though we might have nothing to fear from each other, the world has many countries who sooner or later will be able to build and test atomic weapons, with no help from either of us. The disarmament negotiations in which our countries are engaged will set the pattern for these countries, too. We cannot ignore the possibility

that in the future there may appear somewhere on this earth a country selfish enough to take advantage of his neighbor's trust.[71]

Historian David Nichols and journalist Evan Thomas, to name two, have written about Eisenhower's fear of nuclear weapons and a possible nuclear war that involved the United States and the Soviet Union.[72] However, in his speech at Kiev, Eisenhower raised another troublesome concern: that the advance of science might enable other, more reckless, countries to acquire nuclear weapons and plunge the world into a frightening military catastrophe. Had Eisenhower given this speech at Kiev in 1960, the country on his mind was obviously the People's Republic of China, which was then involved in its own massive effort to produce an atomic weapon. Given Ike's concerns and goals, though, it is even more of a tragedy that the U-2 crisis prevented him and Khrushchev from having serious discussions about a nuclear test ban and thereby begin a process of moving the world away from a proliferation of these weapons.

On June 15, Eisenhower and the presidential party would have returned to Moscow. Ahead of him were two more days of meetings with Soviet leaders, as well as a pleasant meeting at Moscow University and the opportunity to visit with some American students who were then studying in Russia. He was also scheduled to give perhaps the most important speech of his career, a nationwide address to the people of the Soviet Union from a studio in Moscow. Then, he was scheduled to depart Moscow for Irkutsk in Siberia, where he could expect a two-day sojourn of rest and relaxation before leaving for Japan on June 19. Like the first half of his visit, the second phase of Ike's visit to the Soviet Union promised to have its share of headlines.

Chapter 8

Eisenhower in the Soviet Union
Moscow and Irkutsk, June 15–19, 1960

President Dwight D. Eisenhower and the presidential party were scheduled for departure from Kiev at 9:50 A.M. on June 15, thereby ending the first half of Ike's visit to the Soviet Union. The itinerary called for him to arrive at Moscow later that morning, and then continue on to a full slate of activities for the second half of his visit. On June 15, the major events on the itinerary were a visit to Moscow University and speeches both to faculty and students, followed by a brief meeting with the American students who were studying in Moscow at that time. Then, on the evening of June 15, Eisenhower was to host the president's dinner at the American embassy for Premier Nikita Khrushchev and other high-ranking guests from the Soviet government. On June 16, Eisenhower was scheduled for his final meeting with Khrushchev and, then, in the evening, to give his long-awaited speech to the Russian people, carried on a live broadcast throughout the Soviet Union and also transmitted back to the United States.

Eisenhower's itinerary called for him to leave Moscow on June 17 and then spend the better part of two days in Irkutsk, in Siberia. He was to visit the beautiful Lake Baikal and meet with local political leaders. It was in Irkutsk that Eisenhower would have discovered the lengths to which Khrushchev had gone to impress him with his hospitality. He would have discovered the magnificent guest residence, known as the "Eisenhower Dacha," overlooking Lake Baikal, that Khrushchev had built for him. He would have been driven along the forty-four-mile paved road, the "Eisenhower Highway," leading to the guesthouse. And Ike would have played golf on the four-hole course that Khrushchev had built especially for him. This golf course, which we shall refer to as the Eisenhower Links, was most likely the only course in the Soviet Union at the time and Ike would have been given time to indulge his passion for the game before he left the Soviet Union. It is entirely possible that the Soviet Union had never rolled out a welcome mat for any visiting head of state as it did for Eisenhower. In Irkutsk, Eisenhower would have had a veritable resort at his disposal.

The Final Days in Moscow

Following the flight from Kiev, Eisenhower was to arrive in Moscow at 11:10 A.M. on June 15. Following a short ceremony of greeting at Vnukovo Airport, Eisenhower and the presidential party were to drive to Spaso House for a short rest and then a private lunch between 1:00 and 2:00 P.M. Accompanied by Ambassador Llewellyn Thompson, John Eisenhower, Chip Bohlen, Dr. Howard Snyder, and Alex Akalovsky, Eisenhower was then to visit Moscow University. While at the university, Eisenhower was to be introduced by the rector, who would award him an honorary doctoral degree, which Ike would accept with pleasure. He was also scheduled to give two short speeches at the university, one to the faculty and one to the students. His remarks to the faculty were as follows:

> Mr. Rector, Members of the Faculty of Moscow University,
> For several reasons it is a real pleasure for me to visit Moscow University. As some of you know, I was once President of one of our great Universities, Columbia University, and so I have a little experience in the challenge and opportunities which higher education presents.[1]
> I have been glad, too, that under our Cultural Exchange Program, students from both countries are studying at Columbia and Moscow Universities and that arrangements have been made for exchanges of professors between your University and Columbia.
> I cannot overestimate the importance of the role played by our Universities in the task of developing mutual understanding

and confidence which are primary requisites for a peaceful world. In your University and in ours we are training young men and women who will soon be the leaders of our countries. The Universities have the great responsibility of giving their students the widest possible acquaintance with the whole world, both through their own personal experience and through their studies. No one country has a monopoly on knowledge or on truth. It is for these reasons that I especially value the exchange of students, professors and publications between our Universities. I hope these exchanges will grow.

In his speech to the students at Moscow University, Eisenhower's prepared remarks were the following:

Students of Moscow University,

As I was just saying to the Rector and to some of the members of the faculty, I am no stranger to a university. I was President of Columbia University in New York for several years and although other duties have kept me busy since then, I have never lost my interest in university education. Our approaches to higher education may differ from yours in some respects, but we certainly agree on its great importance. It seems to me that it is particularly important to train our students to think critically about the past, the present, and the future, not to be afraid of new ideas but not reject old ideas just because they are old.

I wish there were time for me to tell you more about our universities and colleges where over 3 million young men and women are studying.[2] Every year more and more students are receiving a higher education and these are not only the wealthy as is sometimes thought. The programs of study at these institutions are characterized by considerable diversity, which we believe gives each university an opportunity to pursue most effectively the goals of education in the light of the needs of its students.

In recent years more and more American university students have been traveling and studying abroad trying to learn about the life and experience of other countries. I am glad that there are now some American students in your University and that some students from here have come to our universities. I hope that still more of you will come to America to study or just to visit. I can assure you of a warm welcome.

After the speech, Eisenhower planned to spend some time talking to the twenty American students, and their wives, who were studying at Moscow University at that time.

After the visit to the students and faculty at Moscow University, Eisenhower was to return to Spaso House. The other remaining major event on the itinerary for June 15 was a black-tie dinner, hosted by the president and held at Spaso House for the presidential party, Khrushchev, and other high-ranking Soviet leaders. The dinner was scheduled to begin at 8:00 and last well into the later hours of the evening. At the dinner, Eisenhower was prepared to offer the following toast:

Chairman Voroshilov, Chairman Khrushchev, Ladies and Gentlemen,

My visit to the Soviet Union is already half over. I have had a chance to become reacquainted with Moscow and Leningrad and for the first time to see the Ukraine and Kiev.

I have been impressed again by the people of the Soviet Union and by their accomplishments as they strive to build a better life. It is easier for me to understand why Mr. Khrushchev has so often remarked with pride about the people of the Soviet Union in science and in industry.

I am glad to be able to welcome you to the American Embassy tonight. May I take this opportunity to say a word about how vital I consider the work of our Embassies. They have the important day-to-day job of promoting better understanding between our two countries and their efforts have already contributed much.

I had useful talks a few days ago with Mr. Khrushchev and we will be talking again tomorrow. I have noticed that he is fond of quoting proverbs, as I gather most Russians are. I hope you will not mind if I quote one as well. I understand that you have in Russia a saying that goes something like this:

"Without some work you can't pull even a little fish out of a pond."

Chapter 8

We also have [a] saying, "If at first you don't succeed, then try, try again."

I think that both these sayings apply to our situation in the world today. We are struggling with many problems and it takes and will take a lot of work and patience to make even a little progress.

So I want to propose a toast to our efforts. May they be marked by patience and hard work!! And may they be successful!![3]

Eisenhower's last full day in Moscow was Thursday, June 16, 1960, and it potentially was the most historic. The day was to begin at 9:00 when Eisenhower toured the Manesh Gallery, where he viewed a special collection of paintings on American subjects by Russian artists.[4] After the viewing, Eisenhower, accompanied by Herter, Thompson, Bohlen, Goodpaster, Hagerty, Dr. Howard Snyder, and Akalovsky, was to go to the Kremlin for the final meeting with Khrushchev. The meeting was scheduled to last from 10 A.M. to 12 noon. We may speculate that if there were talks between Eisenhower and Khrushchev that yielded a breakthrough on a nuclear test ban, the announcement about the agreement would have occurred at this meeting. Following the final meeting with Khrushchev, regardless of the outcome, Eisenhower was scheduled to spend the afternoon resting at Spaso House.

Ike had one major event remaining on June 16 and that was his long-awaited speech from Moscow, scheduled to begin at 8:00 P.M. from the television studio in Moscow. That speech was to be broadcast, without interruption, throughout the Soviet Union. First, however, Eisenhower was scheduled to attend a reception given for him by Nikita Khrushchev between 5:30 and 7:30 P.M. Then it was off to the television studio, where Ike was to speak to the Russian people for sixty minutes. Once again, he was to be the first American president to speak to the Russian people from Moscow via television, although Vice President Richard Nixon previously had given a televised address to the Russian people on August 1, 1959, during his visit to the Soviet Union.[5] In the speech, Eisenhower was to mention three principles: "live and let live," "grow and let grow," and "learn and let learn," which Ike proposed as the basic elements of a new era of cooperation between the United States and the Soviet Union. Richard T. Davies, an experienced Foreign Service officer who worked in the American embassy in Moscow in 1951–1952, drafted the remarks.⁶ Eisenhower's lengthy televised address was to proceed as follows:

I. Introduction

It is a great pleasure for me to be able to speak to you tonight from Moscow.

First of all, I wish to extend the warmest of greetings and good wishes from the people of my country to the peoples of the Soviet Union.

I have just come back from a journey to Leningrad and Kiev. The people of Leningrad and Kiev impressed me, as the people of Moscow had done when I was here earlier, by their deep devotion to peace.

I am an old soldier and I have seen a great deal of war and bloodshed. I do not speak lightly when I tell you that we in America know how terrible was the suffering of the peoples of the Soviet Union, of the Polish people, of the people of Czechoslovakia, of Yugoslavia, and of all the other nations in both Western and Eastern Europe who passed through the fire of the Second World War.

For, in war, it is not states that suffer, it is not governments, it is not economic systems, or ideologies. It is people, families and individuals, communities large or small. And the violent subtraction from the family, from the village, from the city, from the commonwealth of mankind, of even one human life diminishes the whole. Each of us is the poorer for the untimely death of his brother man, who, if he had had lived, might in his lifetime have contributed to the enrichment of the lives of his fellowmen.

Tomorrow, I leave for a brief visit to Irkutsk, in your Far East. I have heard a lot about Siberia. Vice President Nixon told me of the heartwarming welcome he received in Novosibirsk and of the impression of great vitality made upon him by what he saw and heard on the banks of the Ob.⁷ He said Siberia reminded him of the pioneer spirit and enterprise of our Far West. Like our Vice President, I come from America's West. It is hard for me to think of Siberia as "East." Somehow, I shall feel I am going "back West" when I travel to Irkutsk.

II. The Double Revolution

This is a revolutionary age we are living in.

We Americans think we know something about revolution. Our forefathers were inhabitants of what we should nowadays call a backward colonial area. 184 years ago, three weeks from next Monday, on July 4, 1776, they proclaimed their independence of foreign rule. The banner they raised was inscribed with the following words: "We hold these truths to be self-evident, that all men are created equal; that they are endowed by their Creator with certain inalienable Rights, that among these are Life, Liberty, and the pursuit of Happiness. That to secure these rights, Governments are instituted among Men, deriving their just powers from the consent of the governed."

Our American Revolution was the first successful colonial revolution. It was the first in a series of revolutions which established liberty, justice, and equality as the ideals of men.

Our Revolution coincided with the beginnings of a great process of change, which is still going on in the world. We can call that process the double revolution, for it is two revolutions combined in one: the industrial-scientific revolution and the democratic revolution.

A. *The Industrial-Scientific Revolution*

The first of these, the industrial-scientific revolution, has spread until in our time it embraces the whole world.

Industrialization means that back-breaking manual labor can be replaced more and more by work done by machines. It means that man can increasingly provide abundantly more for his material needs and simultaneously increase the amount of time available for education, recreations, and other activities which fulfill his spiritual needs.

At the same time, science has made discoveries about the world and about the universe which no one could have conceived of at the beginning of this century. These discoveries have resulted in enormously increasing our ability to make nature serve us. Journeys that only fifty years ago took weeks are now accomplished in hours. Man now speaks to man by radio around the globe. He shoots his rockets into space and their findings are sent back to him over millions of miles. And the fact that I am able to speak to you tonight while you, sitting in your clubhouses, not only hear, but also see, me, is yet another striking innovation produced by the scientific revolution.

The greatest single achievement of the scientific revolution so far has been the discovery and mastering of nuclear energy. Like so many earlier scientific and technological advances, this one was brought to pass in the forcing-bed of war. But its true promise for mankind lies not in its use in bombs or rocket-heads. It lies rather in the application of nuclear energy to peaceful uses.

Great inventions and discoveries do not by themselves determine the course of human history. Men do that, through the use they make of their inventions.

Thus it is that nuclear energy, which offers so many hopeful possibilities for man's future, also represents a terrible menace. The force that can level mountains and create new harbors for man's peaceful purposes can also level cities and poison the seas, if it is used malevolently.

That is the main reason why I am making this visit to you. The American and Soviet peoples have in their keeping great weapons of destruction. They must ensure that these are never used in a war which would mean a terrible disaster for all mankind, a war in which no one could win, which everyone would lose. To make sure that this never happens, our two peoples must so understand each other that peace is made secure.

B. *The Democratic Revolution*

The changes wrought by technology and science have been accompanied by far-reaching changes in the social and political habits of men everywhere.

For our part, we Americans have always believed in change. The United States as we know it today is a child of revolutions. Born on the era of successful upheavals, it has stood the test of time as a way of life, capable of offering its people an unparalleled standard of living, personal security, and individual freedom. In a sense the growth of America has reflected the course of the two great

Chapter 8

revolutions of our age: the industrial-scientific revolution and the democratic revolution. It was the industrial-scientific revolution of the eighteenth and nineteenth centuries which made possible the growth and prosperity of our country, and it is the democratic tradition nurtured by our Founding Fathers, the belief in certain basic individual rights and the obligations of government to guarantee them, which is America's most precious heritage today. In our view, no one knows better what is best for the people than the people themselves. Our government is set up to give concrete expression to this belief.

But the democratic revolution has not been restricted to one people, or a few nations. The goals of personal security, individual liberty under law, and the responsibility of government to the people, have spread to the whole world.

One major aspect of the democratic revolution has been the increasing demand for self-determination, for the right of each people to determine its own destiny.

Let me say here that America unreservedly supports that right. I was consequently happy to read in Chairman Khrushchev's speech of March 5 that the Soviet government also supports it.[8] We regard free elections, in which the people have a real choice, as the only practical way in which self-determination can be realized. We support the application of this right in Eastern Germany and in Eastern Europe. Of course, there is an important proviso attached to the exercise of self-determination. No nation that chooses one or another form of governmental system should subsequently be permitted to threaten its neighbor or to threaten the peace of the world. Self-determination cannot be a cloak for aggressive intentions. For our part, we are ready to fulfill all of our obligations under the United Nations Charter to insure that self-determination should result in good neighborliness, and not in enmity.

Exercising their right of self-determination, peoples under colonial rule have moved, over the past fifteen years, into independence and out of foreign tutelage.[9] Many of these peoples took their inspiration from the example of our own American Revolution. Since the end of the war, 21 countries with 720 million people have achieved independence. The roll is already a long one, and new names will soon be added to it. The banners of freedom grow ever more numerous as each year passes.

Once the new nations have won their political revolutions and have achieved independence, their industrial revolution begins in earnest. Other less developed countries, which long ago won political independence, are now also awakening and beginning their economic revolutions.

The rising expectations of the world's less developed peoples are challenges to us who live in advanced industrial societies.

We Americans know that our own economic growth was greatly furthered by assistance from abroad. We remember the technical advances which came to us from foreign countries: the principal of the steam engine; the Bessemer process for making steel, from England; the open-hearth method, from Germany; the Diesel engine, and many, many others.

And, remembering how much we owe to others for the wellbeing and prosperity we enjoy today, we can well understand the feelings of the peoples of the new nations as they look to us for help in fulfilling their aspirations.

But the goals of the awakening less-developed nations are not only economic. As they succeed in accomplishing their economic plans and as literacy and education spread, they also come increasingly to realize that personal security and the opportunity to enjoy a better life depend upon constructing and maintaining governments which are responsive to the will of the people.

Here again, we believe, the American experience can be of use to those peoples which wish to call upon it. The American approach is based on the belief that, if society is to provide a more secure and fruitful life for its individual members, it must serve their hopes and ambitions. It must not be regarded as something outside of, and above, the human beings who compose it, something with separate goals of its own, to which its members must subordinate the fulfillment of their own goals.

Translated onto the international scene, the precepts and goals which we Americans pursue domestically also guide and motivate our relations with other peoples. Peace to us is not only an economic and political necessity, but the very essence of our spiritual and religious heritage and the very guarantee for the realization of our national goals. Because of this conviction, we welcome every opportunity to discuss outstanding issues with your leaders and leaders of other countries, and we leave no stone unturned to arrive at a meeting of minds on the problems facing us.

III. The "Two Camps"

Now, I have spoken about the great double revolution of our time: the industrial-scientific revolution and the democratic revolution, which are going on in various combinations and at various rates throughout our world. The challenge of these revolutions lies in the necessity of finding peaceful methods to help them succeed. They must not become the source of new strife and new dangers to the peace. They must be accomplished in such a way that they benefit mankind. They must lead to the building of a better world.

It would be difficult enough to solve the enormous problems of this age of revolution if all the peoples of this world were agreed upon the method to be pursued in solving them. The tragedy is that there is no agreement.

When the Second World War ended, the peoples resolved to establish an organization by means of which they could maintain the peace and cooperate to solve international problems. The Preamble to the Charter of the United Nations expresses these intentions. It says:

"We, the peoples of the United Nations Determined to save succeeding generations from the scourge of war, and To reaffirm faith in fundamental human rights, in the dignity and worth of the human person, in the equal right of men and women and of nations large and small and . . . to promote social progress and better standards of life in larger freedom, and to insure . . . that armed forces shall not be used, save in the common interest . . . have resolved to combine our efforts to accomplish these aims."[10]

Fifteen years ago, we started out with high hopes.

Today, we stand divided. Hope has been weakened. Fears have grown.

The peoples expect that the great problems which confront them will be solved, peacefully and constructively, so that all mankind may know a better future.

You, on your side, and we, on ours, are declared to be members of different "camps." These "camps," we are told, represent different ideologies, different philosophies, different solutions to the problems of future development. These ideologies, we are told, must contend until one triumphs over the other. Then, we are told the victorious ideology will form the basis upon which the world's future will be organized, the pattern to which all political, social, and economic systems must conform.

Now, we welcome competition, with you and any other people on earth. We rejoice when we see other nations progressing and prospering. Your rising standard of living, like our own and those of other prospering nations, can only bring good. More and better food, more spacious and comfortable housing, finer clothes and shoes, automobiles, refrigerators, washing-machines, more leisure, more education, more culture—all these things add up to a better and richer life for those who create them. Even more important, they mean a still better life for our children and their children.

And let me assure you that we shall not be standing still during our competition. We are fully confident of our ability to run this race successfully. So we shall call to you over our shoulder, "Come on, run harder if you want to catch us."[11]

Mr. Khrushchev says, "Eat bread and salt, but tell the truth." And, in truth, I must tell you that we wonder why any of you should feel it is necessary for anyone to suffer as a result of this competition. We wonder what Mr. Khrushchev means when he tells us, as he did last year when he came to America, that your success in this competition will result in our defeat. We are puzzled when leaders of the Soviet Government insist that, as a result of your success, our grandchildren will live under Communism.

Imagine how we feel when we read in your [news]papers that, while Communism may triumph peacefully in some countries, in others, force may be necessary to win the victory and bring a Communist government to power.

In Kiev, I spoke about the defensive measures we had been forced to take when we saw, following the War, that Communist governments sprang up only in those countries where Soviet military power was present or near at hand. And we read in the letter sent by the Central Committee of the Soviet Communist Party to the Central Committee of the Communist Party of Yugoslavia that Communism had not come to power in France and Italy only because the Soviet Union was not a position to help the French and Italian Communists.[12]

So, we ask ourselves, "Is this part of the competition?" If it is, we cannot call such a competition good.

We say frankly that the words, "two camps," "struggle for Communism," "the fight for peace," and so forth, sound too warlike for us. If Communism means building a better and richer life for the Soviet people, we can only applaud it. If "the fight for peace" means sincerely joining with all peoples who want peace, you will find us fighting for it by your side.

But, if these words really mean that Communism must be spread by force or the threat of force, by subversion or by other conspiratorial means, to peoples who do not want it, then we must say that we cannot and will not accept that.

We are happy to compete in providing the people with ever better conditions of life and work. Should that not be our aim? Is it not far better than contending so that this or that ideology may be extended to some people far away, who do not want it?

And, while we are contending, will the problems that press in upon us today wait? Can we afford to stand and argue with each other while time urges us forward? Must we waste ourselves in barren wrangling, while a new world struggles to be born?

IV. The American Approach

We, in my country do not think so. That is why, following the end of the War, we offered to help all the war-torn countries of Europe in their efforts at reconstruction.[13] That is why we entered upon a great program of economic and technical assistance to countries which wish to make progress. That is why we support the many international organizations which are engaged in programs of economic and technical assistance: the United Nations, the World Health Organization, the Food and Agriculture Organization, the International Finance Corporation, the International Bank for Reconstruction and Development, the International Development

Association, the International Atomic Energy Agency, and many others.

We regard the solution of the grave problems posed by the revolutionary age in which we live as a task for all mankind. If they are to be solved, all men must work together in the common cause—the cause for a better tomorrow.

What is needed to enable them to do so?

There are a few simple principles, it seems to me, the implementation of which would enable us all to cooperate in winning the struggle for a better future.

First of all, every nation, large or small, has a right to determine freely for itself the political, economic, and social institutions under which it wishes to live. No nation has a right to attempt, by whatever means, to impose its system upon any other. Every nation must refrain from aggression, whether it be by armed force or conspiracy.

We must recognize that different environments, different histories, different resources, different systems of belief, all combine to produce different approaches among the nations to the solution of the problems that confront them. A system that is good for the American people may not be good for the Soviet peoples, and vice versa. Neither the American nor the Soviet system may be right for other nations.

So we Americans see tomorrow's world as one in which a number of different systems will continue to exist side by side. In my country, we say, "Live and let live." I think that is a good motto for a world of free nations, each solving its problems in accordance with what it believes to be the best way for itself.

"Live and let live"—that is the first principle which must be the basis for tomorrow's world.

But agreement upon this first principle alone is not enough.

We must agree to cooperate with each other and with all the other nations of the world to find just and truthful solutions to our common problems.

I spoke earlier of the help the United States had received from abroad during its progress from a backward agricultural nation to its present status as an advanced industrial nation. I mentioned that today the United States believes it must help the less developed nations in their efforts to progress. Other advanced countries have joined in this effort.

So the pre-conditions exist for the implementation of the second principle. I call it, "Grow and help grow."

Thirdly, we must say, "Learn and help learn."

Wherever one looks in the world, one finds, at one age or [an]other, great minds at work, creating not just for themselves, not just for their own people, but for all mankind. The great law-givers of ancient Egypt; the great philosophers of Greece; the great civilizers of Rome; Confucius, Lao-tse, Asoka; Justinian, Shakespeare; Racine, Goethe, and many more. Franklin, Lincoln, Emerson, Edison, Poe, Walt Whitman, Mark Twain, in our country. Mendeleyev, Pushkin, Tolstoy, Dostoyevsky, Turgenev, Chaikovsky, Mussorgsky, A. S. Popov, Gogol, Chekhov, Pavlov, Prokofiev, in yours.[14] They did not labor for a narrow section of humanity; their work has enriched the lives of us all.

So, in a world governed by the principle "Learn and help learn," the experiences, the labor, the genius of everyone, whether he be Russian or American, Indian or Englishman, Chinese or Arab, black or white, would be shared for the common weal.

Let me say here that I am particularly pleased to note the success of our Soviet-American exchange agreement.[15] We in America have enjoyed your great Bolshoi dancers, the Moiseyev and Beryozka troupes, the Georgian State Dance Ensemble.[16] You have seen and heard our Philadelphia and New York Philharmonic Orchestras, our "Porgy and Bess," our "My Fair Lady." We saw your Soviet Exhibition in New York, and you saw our Exhibition in Moscow. Last year, some 10,000 American tourists visited the Soviet Union, while 206 Soviet tourists visited the United States. We hope many more of you will come to see us. When you do, you will see how our system works and why we like it. You will see, too, that it is not likely to disappear soon.

I know that Chairman Khrushchev agrees with me when I say that our Soviet-American exchange agreement is a good beginning towards applying the principle of "Learn and help learn" in the relations between our peoples.

But we need to go farther. We, and all the other nations of the world, need to learn about each other, to exchange our ideas freely, to profit by each other's successes and to be warned by each other's failures, to read each other's newspapers and books, to discuss our hopes and our fears frankly—even to argue with each other, if that is necessary. Such arguments need do no harm if they are conducted, not in bad blood, not in a spirit of dogmatism and sectarianism, but in the spirit of our three principles: "Live and let live," "Grow and help grow," and "Learn and help learn."

Now, if we could agree on these principles, and adopt them as our own, wholeheartedly and without reserve, what could we accomplish?

First of all, we could make a great contribution towards securing the peace by continuous progress toward disarmament. As a result of disarmament, we would save that portion of our national wealth that now goes into the manufacture of weapons and the maintenance of armies. That would mean that we could all have a fuller and richer life. We could devote part of the savings that would accrue from disarmament to the solution of the problems of the double revolutions of our time.[17] We could help the less developed nations grow in a direction which would benefit us all. We could envisage as our final goal a world free of international strife and unencumbered with weapons of horrible destructive power. We could have the peace for which all the world's peoples so desperately long.

Secondly, we could develop a stable international order, in which potential aggressors would not dare to break the peace. We could outlaw war. For this, we would need an international peace force, which would serve no one government, but the interests of all peoples who want peace.

Thirdly, we could ensure that international disputes would be settled peacefully in accordance with international law. We could develop a body of law on the basis of which international courts would mete out justice to the nations, so that recourse to force would become obsolete. There would then be no reason for any nation, large or small, to fear that it would seek in vain the justice of its peers—its brother peoples.

But these goals cannot be won simply by talking about them.

Chapter 8

Nor can they be realized merely by signing a treaty in which they are solemnly inscribed. They must first be fostered by an understanding of each other's ways of life and ways of thinking. They must be nourished by a readiness to hear each other's point of view and to respect it. They must be cultivated through development of trust. They must be brought to fruition through active cooperation.

A great choice stands before us. We offer the hand of friendship and constructive cooperation to any nation which wishes to work for a better future for itself and the world, without attempting to impose his ideas upon those who do not want them. What happens within the borders of a country is the business of the people of that country. But we shall oppose international conspiracy with all the strength at our command.

I and my assistants have had good talks with Chairman Voroshilov, Chairman Khrushchev, and their aides. We want to go forward and succeed in the work that we have so well begun.

For our part, we Americans will strive to do this in accordance with the precept of Abraham Lincoln:

"To do all which may achieve and cherish a just and lasting peace . . . with all nations."

You and we fought side by side during the War. Can we not now cooperate constructively and harmoniously to assure the peace?

Thank you for your kind attention, friends. Good night!

Following the address, Eisenhower was to return to Spaso House for a private supper on his last night in Moscow. On Friday, June 17, Eisenhower and the presidential party were scheduled to drive from Spaso House to the Vnukovo Airport for their departure from Moscow and their flight to the city of Irkutsk in Siberia. Before leaving Moscow, Eisenhower would be prepared to give closing remarks, drafted by Heyward Isham. Isham had served in the American embassy in Moscow from 1955 to 1957 as the chief of the consular section and political office under Ambassador Chip Bohlen. In 1960, he was the special assistant to Bohlen.[18] Eisenhower's closing remarks were to read as follows:

My visit to this great country nears its close. Through the hospitality of your government, I shall sleep tonight on the edge of Lake

Moscow and Irkutsk

Baikal and tomorrow I shall visit Irkutsk, the last stop on a trip that has been all too brief for my liking.[19]

But now I must bid farewell to the many friends I have made during my visits to Moscow, Leningrad, and Kiev. The words you have spoken and the expressions I have seen on your faces have their own story of hard work, hope for a better future, and anxiety lest a new conflagration engulf us all. My visits to your factories, collective farms, universities, and scientific research institutes have confirmed reports I had already received of the enormous feat of reconstruction that has been achieved. I have noticed slogans in the factories and collective farms urging great effort to catch up and surpass the United States in per capita production. We welcome this competition, for honest competition is the mainspring of our own free enterprise system and we regard you as worthy rivals in this peaceful economic race from which our two peoples will be the primary beneficiaries.

I know from the questions that have been put to me how deeply you fear the recurrence of war. You are impressed just as we are with the disastrous price of nuclear war and the terrifying consequences of human miscalculation in the missile age.

We have no higher purpose than to continue our efforts to establish peace with justice. That is the reason I have come here to visit you. That is the reason we welcomed the visits last year of Mr. Khrushchev, Mr. Kozlov, and Mr. Mikoyan.[20] That is why we have persevered in the negotiations on a nuclear test ban and on a disarmament agreement, both safeguarded by workable controls. That is why we favor the cultural exchange agreements that have already been reached between us and would like to see their further development.

On all these points we proceed from a positive estimate that our mutual national interests are being best served by this kind of development in our relations. We do not feel that in supporting further steps along this path of constructive cooperation we are being forced to do so by some combination of forces beyond our control. On the contrary, the more orderly and normal state of our relations today corresponds to our desires immediately after the end of hostilities in 1945. Fortunately, we now seem have reached a point in our national destinies where, for a combination of military, political, and economic reasons, the prospects for improved relations are greater than at any previous time in the past fifteen years.

To this end, that our two peoples may continue to learn more of each other's real aspirations and achievements, free of malicious distortion, I shall continue my efforts to the utmost of my ability. I know that my successor as President, from whatever Party he may come, will assume his duties with an equal sense of dedication and responsibility.

Mr. Khrushchev, I have greatly enjoyed our frank talks with you, President Voroshilov, and your colleagues. I think that this second of our meetings on each other's soil has been as mutually profitable as the one we had last year at Camp David. It is now our job to carry forward in our day-to-day policy decisions the general agreements that we have reached as they affect relations between the Soviet Union and the United States. Goodbye and thank you.

On to Irkutsk

The flight to Irkutsk would take two and one half hours, but with a five-hour time change Ike and the presidential party would be landing in Irkutsk at 8:15 P.M. After a short welcoming ceremony at the airport, Eisenhower and the presidential party were to make a brief drive to their accommodations for the evening. Upon arrival in Irkutsk, Eisenhower was prepared to give the following statement:

> I am delighted to be able to visit Siberia at last and particularly Lake Baikal and the historic city of Irkutsk. I have been looking forward to this moment for a long time. The name of Lake Baikal is renowned in your literature, poetry, and song. I have known, of course, what an enormous and richly endowed country yours is. But until our flight from Moscow today, I think I had no adequate idea of its real grandeur. The flight path of our jet aircraft provided us an unforgettable panorama: the majestic Volga, with all its historic meaning for the advance of Russian civilizations and its great potential for further contributions to Soviet economic growth;

the Urals, a legendary storehouse of natural resources upon which modern industrial complexes are based; the broad steppes of Kazakhstan where cultivation in recent years has provided new supplies of grain for the nation; and the great hydroelectric station at Bratsk which will provide energy and light for your future economic and cultural development.[21] Americans have a particular appreciation for the rugged qualities that you Siberians have displayed in conquering this enormous wilderness and turning its resources to the good of mankind. I look forward to making the closer acquaintance of some of the citizens of Irkutsk tomorrow. In the meantime, thank you for this welcome and good night.

Reading from Eisenhower's proposed itinerary for this portion of his journey, it is not clear whether Khrushchev planned to meet Ike in Irkutsk and continue to serve as his host. Considering what Khrushchev had planned as accommodations for Eisenhower in the region around Irkutsk, however, it is entirely possible that Khrushchev planned to remain with the presidential party until Ike's departure from Russia. On the other hand, by Eisenhower's scheduled farewell remarks in Moscow on June 17, it appeared that Khrushchev was planning to remain in Moscow while Eisenhower traveled to Siberia.

On Saturday, June 18, Eisenhower and the presidential party were scheduled to drive for forty-four miles on a paved highway from Irkutsk to Lake Baikal, a body of water that Eisenhower had wished to see for many years. Upon reaching Lake Baikal, the plan was for Ike to stay at a beautiful guesthouse built by Khrushchev expressly for Eisenhower's visit. Even at that time, the guesthouse was known as the Eisenhower Dacha and the paved road leading to it was the "Eisenhower Highway."[22]

There was also another feature. In the city of Irkutsk, Khrushchev had constructed a four-hole golf course for Eisenhower. As the picture comes into closer focus, it appears that Khrushchev had constructed virtually an entire resort for Ike: the guesthouse, known as the Eisenhower Dacha; the paved highway, the Eisenhower Highway; and the Eisenhower Links golf course.[23] Prior to Ike's visit and to no avail, Khrushchev had attempted to learn to play golf so that he could play a round with Eisenhower. If Ike were to play golf in Siberia, his playing partners would have to have been Americans.[24] As Sergei Khrushchev later told the author, the lavish amenities at Irkutsk and at Lake Baikal were designed by Khrushchev to approximate Camp David, where Khrushchev had been Eisenhower's guest and where they conducted their negotiations in September 1959.[25]

On June 17, Eisenhower and the presidential party had no further events scheduled. However, the next day, Saturday, June 18, would have been a full one. First, Eisenhower was to leave Irkutsk at 9:30 and arrive at Lake Baikal at 10:30. Then, he was to take a leisurely boat ride around Lake Baikal (no fishing, though), a distance of thirty-seven miles. Then, it was back to Irkutsk for some so-called "free time" that Eisenhower could quite possibly have used to play golf, perhaps with John Eisenhower, James Hagerty, and Dr. Howard Snyder as his partners. After the round (rounds?) of golf, Eisenhower and the presidential party were scheduled for a rest period before attending the final official dinner in the president's honor. The dinner at Irkutsk was scheduled to last from 8 P.M. to 11 P.M., a longer time than most of the dinners planned for Ike. At the dinner, Eisenhower was prepared to make the following remarks:

> I wish to thank my new Siberian friends for the splendid welcome you have given me today. In America, the expression "frontier hospitality" is justly applied to the effort on the part of the host to make his guests feel truly at home.[26] Irkutsk of course, is no longer the frontier settlement and frontier outpost it was in the seventeenth century. On the contrary, it has become an important administrative center with a population close to four hundred thousand people. Nevertheless, I think your welcome today belongs in the finest traditions of frontier hospitality.
>
> As you know, our own pioneers, as they advanced across the entire continent from the original settlements along the Eastern seaboard, played a cardinal role in shaping American institutions and forming [the] American national character. The development of local self-government, beginning at the county level; the preference for devising individual solutions of problems; the determination to bring education and science along with the material benefits of civilization; the faith in a code of conduct based on biblical precepts—these developments in our governmental system and our national character all have their origins in our experience with the

Moscow and Irkutsk

wilderness. Some American historians think that every significant development in our civic affairs can ultimately be traced to the influence of this vast area of unsettled land.[27] Opinions may differ on this score, but there is no question that America today is to a very great degree the product of this migration.

Of course, the essence of the frontier psychology is composed of diverse elements: curiosity to seek the unknown and the untried; impatience with conventional limits placed upon man's capacities; willingness to trade comfort for hard work and new kinds of achievement; ingenuity in overcoming all kinds of obstacles. All these qualities are, of course, essential for man in the twentieth century when new kinds of frontiers are constantly opening before us.

Soviet scientists have themselves been in the forefront of exploring outer space and we admire their achievements. In this field, of course, there should be no sense of national ownership or exclusive rights of disposition over invaluable data that the man-made satellites send back to earth.[28] We have made available to Soviet and other world scientists the information produced by our eight satellites still circling in orbit and we have been pleased at the reciprocity already achieved with Soviet satellites in this regard.

Returning to achievements that are closer at hand, I was enormously impressed this morning to see your Irkutsk hydro-electric plant which harnesses the waters of the Angara [River] to man's use. It took determination, fortitude, and boldness of vision to bring this great project to conclusion. The importance of these qualities is clear to us from [our] own experience in building the dams in the rugged country of our Pacific Northwest.

Gentlemen, my visit is almost over. It has been a landmark in our relations. I consider my talks with Mr. Khrushchev to have been of considerable importance for the future, but have a common proverb, "One swallow does not make a summer." We should not delude ourselves that the accumulation of misunderstanding and suspicion of past years can be dissipated by one series of conversations or by one joint communique. There is much work ahead of us to carry forward the good beginning that has been made.

From many questions that Soviet citizens have put to me, I can judge for myself how persistent and fundamental are certain

Chapter 8

misconceptions of American life and the objectives of our government. In trying to answer briefly the questions that were put to me, I found myself coming back again and again to certain basic truths about our country and its people. In these talks I spoke of the inability of any US government to initiate hostilities in the absence of attack because of [our] constitutional system of checks and balances. I have mentioned post-war developments in Eastern Europe and Asia which convinced leaders of both our political parties that strong defensive alliances were essential for our national security. I have also reminded my questioners that the hatred of war among all our people is no less deep or genuine because our suffering from the war was not so great in magnitude as that of others.

So I urge that we look upon each other with glances not of suspicion, envy, and fear, but with rational temperate interest and respect for each other's point of view. On the basis of such reciprocal understanding of one another's true motivations we shall be able to bring to fruition the encouraging prospects of better relations between our two countries.

After dinner, Eisenhower and the presidential party returned to their accommodations for their final night in the Soviet Union.

Eisenhower's final day in the Soviet Union was scheduled for Saturday, June 19, 1960. The day was to begin at 8:30 with the drive to the airport at Irkutsk. After a brief departure ceremony, Air Force One would lift off for the five-hour flight to Khabarovsk in the far eastern region of the Soviet Union. After a brief welcoming ceremony in Khabarovsk, Eisenhower would be airborne at 3:50 for his flight to Tokyo. He was scheduled to arrive in Tokyo at 5:00 P.M.

After their visit to Japan, Eisenhower and the presidential party were scheduled to stop in South Korea before flying on to Honolulu and then back to Washington. The journey that had been planned for Eisenhower would have been arduous, but the hope was that the president would have succeeded in opening the door to a new era in relations between the United States and the Soviet Union.

In retrospect, it appears that Eisenhower's nine-day visit to the Soviet Union in June 1960 was to bear some resemblance to Khrushchev's visit to the United States in September 1959. Both leaders spent, or were to spend, considerable time in each other's capitals, Moscow and Washington, in conference with each other and their respective advisers. Both leaders also would have traveled extensively throughout each other's countries: Khrushchev on his cross-country train ride to California and Eisenhower on his visits to Leningrad, Kiev, and Irkutsk. Both leaders would have visited the cultural attractions of the host countries. In their respective travels, both leaders were to be given the opportunity to meet individual citizens from all walks of life. And, of course, the international news media would have covered the activities of each leader's trip from the beginning to the end. Eisenhower's visit, in particular, given the amount of press coverage, would have been a spectacle not witnessed before in the era of the Cold War.

And what of Eisenhower's final televised address in the Soviet Union on June 16?

What would have been the impact of that speech which, as of its drafting in April, still lacked a title? Would it have ranked up there with Eisenhower's other memorable speeches: the Cross of Iron speech in 1953, the Open Skies speech in 1955, and the warning against the power of the military-industrial complex in his farewell address in 1961? Certainly the potential existed for the speech to have a great impact, especially given Ike's emphasis on the three principles of "live and let live," "grow and let grow," and "learn and let learn."

Assuming that the U-2 crisis had not occurred, we may speculate that Eisenhower also would have received unprecedented welcomes in Tokyo and Seoul as the Far Eastern trip continued. Ike would have returned to Washington triumphantly. Within a month of his return, the Democrats and Republicans would be putting the finishing touches on their national conventions and the presidential campaign would have entered a new and more urgent period. Under those circumstances, the political climate could not have been more favorable for Richard Nixon as Eisenhower's heir apparent and successor to the presidency. And Eisenhower would have ended his presidency with perhaps a breakthrough in foreign policy, taking much of the tension out of the international environment.

Conclusion
"The Stupid U-2 Mess"

In the aftermath of the U-2 crisis, the collapse of the Paris summit, and the cancellation of his trip to the Soviet Union, Dwight D. Eisenhower attempted to carry out his presidential duties as before, without revealing publicly or even in conference with his advisers the extent of his disappointment about the end of his hopes for thawing the Cold War. With six months left in his presidency, Eisenhower faced the sobering reality that he was essentially keeping the political house in order until a new administration took office on January 20, 1961.

For Eisenhower, the residual disappointment caused by the failure in Paris was a new emotional experience for a man who was unaccustomed to defeat, especially on the big things. Throughout his life, Eisenhower had encountered moments of great triumph, whether it was planning and executing Operation Overlord, taking the surrender of Nazi Germany, working out an armistice to end the Korean War, facing down Nikita Khrushchev over Berlin, or winning two presidential elections by landslides. The disappointment caused by the U-2 incident left Eisenhower with an emptiness that went beyond mere resignation. As Evan Thomas has written, after the debacle in Paris, Eisenhower "bravely masked his discouragement, but his inner circle could not miss his symptoms."[1]

Two individuals who were closer to Eisenhower than most people, James Hagerty, his press secretary, and Barbara Eisenhower-Foltz, his daughter-in-law, also sensed Ike's disappointment and discussed the subject in oral history interviews that were conducted several years after the administration left office. Both Hagerty and Eisenhower-Foltz identified Khrushchev's cancellation of Ike's visit to the Soviet Union, and not the collapse of the Paris summit, as Eisenhower's major source of disappointment. As Hagerty told an interviewer, "One of the greatest disappointments was that [Eisenhower] did not go to Russia. Mr. Eisenhower would have an hour on Moscow television and would have half an hour on television when he visited Leningrad and half an hour when he visited Kiev, with the understanding that all those programs would be filmed and/or played on all television stations that day or the next day throughout the Soviet Union. And what he was going to do there was what he did in many other places, just talk informally, some from prepared text, some from notes, about peace. And working together as people of two nations. I can't help but feel that it would have contributed somewhat" to a lessening of tensions between the United States and the Soviet Union. Then Hagerty added, "Now this is why I say that one of the great regrets of Mr. Eisenhower was that he wasn't able to go there. And I am quite sure in my own mind that he would have been welcomed by the people of Russia."[2]

Barbara Eisenhower-Foltz also sensed the president's disappointment, as well as her own, about the cancellation of the trip to Moscow, since she and her husband John Eisenhower were scheduled to accompany Ike on his Far Eastern trip in 1960. When asked by interviewer John Wickman, "What do you think [Eisenhower's] greatest disappointment was when he was in the White House? Were you aware of anything that deeply affected him?," Eisenhower-Foltz answered immediately, "I think the U-2 incident was a disappointment. [It meant] that we weren't going to be able to go to Russia and I think that he felt like he was developing a really good relationship with Khrushchev and that something constructive might have come out of the whole thing. It would have been a help and then it went 'poof,' and it seems to me, I can't tell exactly when it struck me how well he handled disappointment. That was the way it was. I was so taken. I mean he just said, 'That's the way it is.' Adjusted to it."[3]

In terms of any of Eisenhower's revelations to individuals in the administration about his regrets, the only substantive, published recollection came from George Kistiakowsky who, in his diary, recalled a conversation with Eisenhower about the U-2 crisis several weeks after the collapse of the Paris summit.[4] As Kistiakowsky recalled the conversation,

Ike "spoke with much feeling how he had concentrated his efforts the last few years on ending the cold war, how he felt that he was making big progress and how the stupid U-2 mess had ruined all his efforts . . . [Eisenhower] saw nothing worthwhile to do until the end of his presidency."[5]

Making Big Progress

Upon reflection, Eisenhower was correct in his comment to Kistiakowsky that he was "making big progress," if not toward ending the Cold War, at least to removing some of the tension from the international environment. In the summer of 1959, Ike had set in motion the four elements of his strategy: a successful visit by Khrushchev to the United States in the autumn of 1959, the passage of the FY 1961 defense budget, the preparation and eventual implementation of a Four Power summit in the spring of 1960 that was to deal with the issue of a nuclear test ban, and finally, his own long-awaited trip to the Soviet Union in June 1960. The first two elements of the strategy had occurred or were about to occur. The third element in the strategy had been planned and was on the verge of happening when Francis Gary Powers was captured by the Soviet Union on May 1. As for Ike's trip to the Soviet Union, due to the efforts of the diplomats in the State Department, the Soviet Union's Ministry of Foreign Affairs, the American embassy in Moscow, and the Soviet embassy in Washington, the plans were virtually in place for Ike's arrival at the time of the U-2 mishap. Both sides had agreed on an itinerary for Ike's time in the Soviet Union, the president's speeches and other public remarks were being drafted, and accommodations were in order for the visiting press from the United States and other countries.

In addition, we now know that Khrushchev had gone to great lengths to welcome Eisenhower and the presidential party, ranging from his agreement to allow Eisenhower to fly east across the Soviet Union (where Air Force One's cameras could take photographs of the vast Russian landscape and its utility stations, railroads, and even suspected military bases), to allowing Eisenhower and the presidential party to bring Bibles and American hymnals into the Soviet Union for distribution to Russian Christians, to the lavish resort that Khrushchev had built for him in the

Conclusion

region of Irkutsk and Lake Baikal. Just as Eisenhower held out hope for positive results to come from Khrushchev's visit to the United States in 1959, so also did Khrushchev have great expectations for Eisenhower's visit to the Soviet Union in 1960.

But the "stupid U-2 mess" intervened and "ruined all of [Ike's] efforts." Certainly the "stupid U-2 mess" ruined the third and fourth elements of Eisenhower's strategy. Negotiations at the Paris summit, which never happened, did not produce a nuclear test-ban agreement. Eisenhower never had the opportunity to test out his personal magnetism for a second time in the Soviet Union. The international political climate went from hopeful to hostile in a matter of weeks. As Peter Boyle has written, following the U-2 crisis, "the Cold War reverted to freeze."[6] Khrushchev became more assertive, even adventurous, in such "hot spots" as the Congo and in Cuba throughout the summer of 1960.

Probably worse from Eisenhower's perspective, the U-2 incident helped to reignite the "missile gap" as a political issue in the 1960 presidential campaign as well as a clamor, in both political parties, for more defense spending on the magnitude of an additional $3 billion annually.[7] And, one might argue convincingly, anxiety about potentially sizable increases in military spending by Ike's presidential successor, whoever he turned out to be, was one reason he had launched his peace offensive late in 1959. The "stupid U-2 mess" essentially ruined Ike's desire for a continuation of his policy of restraint on defense spending.

Thus, the question needs to be asked: with so much riding on the success of his strategy, why did Eisenhower permit himself to agree to such a dangerous flight so close to the Paris summit, and thereby jeopardize the diplomatic initiative he had nurtured so carefully for the previous seven months? At least three reasons come to mind. First, Eisenhower had little reason to believe that Powers's flight would not be successful, based on the nearly flawless record of the U-2 program up to that point. By April 1960, U-2 pilots had flown 38 successful missions over Soviet bloc countries, 13 over China and Tibet, and 239 over non-bloc countries, including many over the Middle East during the Suez crisis in 1956 and the crisis in Lebanon in 1958.[8] Except for some technical mishaps, none of the U-2 missions had resulted either in failure or in any controversial international incidents. The U-2 flight on April 9 appeared to be an indicator of the Soviet Union's inability to challenge a mission in progress.

Conclusion

Other than the unusual set of circumstances that led to frequent postponements in Powers's date of departure, no compelling reason existed not to believe that Powers would bring back information on the Soviet missile complex at Plesetsk that would show convincingly that the Soviets were not strengthening their military posture.

Eisenhower spoke to that exact point at a breakfast with congressional leaders at the White House on May 26, 1960. Asked by Senate Majority Leader Lyndon B. Johnson why the U-2 flights "weren't stopped before the Summit Meeting," Eisenhower replied that "previous flights had been successful" and that Powers's flight was necessary "to take advantage of the weather to get the needed information that would not be available later on."[9]

Second, Eisenhower remained convinced by Allen Dulles and Richard Bissell that, in the event of an accident during one of its missions, neither the pilot nor the aircraft would survive and the administration would never have to respond to any charges or accusations that involved espionage. Eisenhower himself confirmed that understanding when he covered the subject in his memoirs.[10] Nevertheless, we also know of the fury that erupted in the administration once it became known that Powers had survived the attack. John Eisenhower, for example, in an interview with historian Stephen E. Ambrose, expressed his outrage that the CIA had given Powers a parachute.[11] That Powers managed to survive the attack on his U-2, and the Soviet Union was able to acquire parts of the aircraft, including the incriminating film that Powers used in his cameras, was even more damaging to the administration.[12] The fact the Soviets had captured Powers, when Ike had been told of the virtual impossibility of such an occurrence, may help to explain the president's profanity-laced tantrum at the Gettysburg Country Club on May 7 when he learned about Powers's survival.[13] At that point, Eisenhower realized that he faced a totally unpredictable set of embarrassing circumstances and that he had, in effect, lost control of events.

Third, Eisenhower's agreement to authorize the mission revealed the extent of his ongoing concern about American vulnerability to a surprise attack by the Soviet Union on the United States, using intercontinental ballistic missiles. It was one thing for Ike to applaud Khrushchev's efforts to improve relations with the United States, even to the point of sizably reducing the manpower levels of the Red Army. It was another matter to underestimate the overall military strength of the Soviet Union. As Dino Brugioni explained, Operation Grand Slam on May 1 was designed to fly over the entire complex of military bases, test centers, and industrial facilities that comprised the Soviet Union's strategic arsenal. Should the Powers flight have succeeded, Eisenhower would have gone to Paris armed with the most accurate knowledge of the Soviet Union's military forces. Should a nuclear test-ban agreement have been negotiated, Eisenhower would have been confident that America's strategic capability relative to that of the Soviet Union had not been compromised. It also helps to explain why, at his press conference on May 11, Eisenhower spoke so forcefully when he stated that "no one wants another Pearl Harbor" as the justification for espionage, even the kind of espionage that violated another country's air space.[14]

The Hostages: Francis Gary Powers, Freeman Bruce Olmstead, and John R. McKone

Throughout the duration of the U-2 crisis, and after, few questions were asked about the future of Francis Gary Powers once he was convicted of espionage on August 17 and sentenced to ten years in captivity.[15] In the aftermath of the incident Powers's status was unclear, except that he was a Soviet prisoner. Had Eisenhower and Khrushchev been able, miraculously, to resolve their differences in Paris so the summit could have proceeded and Eisenhower's trip to the Soviet Union had gone off as scheduled, how would Powers's situation as a hostage and captive been affected? It is not possible to believe that the subject of his status would not have come up in Khrushchev's discussions with Eisenhower, and it is equally unlikely that Eisenhower would have left the Soviet Union without an agreement about his eventual release.

Once Francis Gary Powers was taken into custody in the Soviet Union, however, he became a pawn in the power rivalry between the United States and the Soviet Union. As we know, the United States and the Soviet Union arranged a prisoner exchange of Powers and Rudolf Abel, a Russian spy, on February 10, 1962, thereby ending what Powers believed was certain to be a lengthy captivity in the Soviet Union.[16] But would Powers's situation have come up as a subject for discussion

Conclusion

between Eisenhower and Khrushchev, either in Paris or in Moscow, had the two men engaged in substantive negotiations in 1960? Recognizing how Eisenhower valued loyalty and responsibility, one must speculate that Ike would have raised the matter of Powers and his release with Khrushchev. If Ike did not fire Allen Dulles for the U-2 mishap, neither was he likely to allow, with no objection, a lengthy captivity for Powers in a Soviet prison. After all, Ike had already told Khrushchev in Paris that U-2 flights over the Soviet Union had been canceled and, therefore, the Soviets had no reason for concern about this particular form of American espionage. Could the Americans and the Soviets, working through their respective embassies, have negotiated some sort of face-saving agreement that would have resulted in Powers's release?

Given Khrushchev's weakened position within the Soviet leadership at the time, however, discussions about the status of Francis Gary Powers would have been a subject that Khrushchev may have wanted to avoid in any future negotiations with Eisenhower. Cancellation of Ike's visit to the Soviet Union took that subject off the table and doomed Powers to what appeared to be a prolonged incarceration, unless other circumstances intervened to improve relations between the two countries.

Then, on July 1, 1960, a potentially more damaging incident occurred that resulted in two more American airmen being taken captive by the Soviet Union. On July 1, an American RB-47 reconnaissance airplane departed from Brice Norton Royal Air Force Base in England on a mission to fly across a northern route of the Soviet Union to gather electronic intercepts of Soviet communications. The members of the RB-47's six-man crew were Major Willard Palm, the flight commander; Captain Freeman Bruce Olmstead, the pilot; Captain John R. McKone, the navigator; and three reconnaissance officers: Major Eugene Posa, Captain Dean Phillips, and Captain Oscar Goforth, who operated the electronic surveillance equipment in the former bomb bay of the aircraft.[17]

The planned route of the flight took the RB-47 northeast over the international waters of the Arctic Ocean, where the plane turned east and into the Barents Sea and traveled about fifty miles from the Kola Peninsula, staying in international waters. The RB-47 quickly attracted the attention of Soviet radar, and a ground station sent pilot Vasiliy Polyakov to fly his MiG-19 aircraft to intercept and "escort" the American airplane. After pursuing the RB-47 in international waters, Polyakov wiggled the wings of his MiG to signal the RB-47 to land. The Americans ignored the signal and the Soviet Union's ground navigator ordered Polyakov to attack and destroy the RB-47. Polyakov opened fire and, after two attacks, the RB-47 burst into flames. Palm gave the order for the crew to eject from the burning aircraft. Palm, Olmstead, and McKone managed to escape and parachuted into the freezing waters of the Barents Sea. Palm was apparently lifeless when he hit the water, but Olmstead and McKone quickly resorted to their survival equipment. Posa, Phillips, and Goforth were unable to free themselves and were incinerated in the burning aircraft.

The Soviet attack on the American RB-47, in international waters, was a naked act of aggression by the Soviet Union and potentially a much more serious matter than the U-2 episode. After all, Powers had not been killed by the Russians and, in the RB-47 situation, four American airmen lost their lives. Polyakov's subsequent explanation for the order for the shoot-down was that it was "a combination of Soviet internal pressure to protect its territory and his belief that the RB-47 was headed for [reconnaissance over] a secret naval base."[18]

McKone later expressed his belief that the attack was related to the "favorable publicity" around the world that the Soviets received from their attack on Powers and the humiliation that the United States received from the U-2 crisis. As McKone told an interviewer, "I think the reason we were shot down is that [the Soviets] had a successful shoot-down of the U-2, and here is a sitting duck, an RB-47, flying at thirty thousand feet, four hundred and twenty five miles an hour true air speed, chucks (sic) let's go out and shoot one of them down."[19] McKone also told his interviewer that, on the same day, July 1, some RB-47 aircraft had taken off from their bases in Yukota, Japan on reconnaissance missions and were ordered to return to base because they saw several Soviet interceptors taking off from bases in the Eastern part of the Soviet Union to track them.[20]

It was possible, of course, that other factors also played a role in the Soviet attack on the RB-47. After the collapse of the Paris summit, relations between the United States and the Soviet Union turned downright nasty. American Air Force planes began to buzz Soviet merchant ships on the high seas, behavior that, in Ambassador Tommy Thompson's view, drove the Soviet military "literally wild" with anger. As Jenny Thompson and Sherry Thompson have written, the attack on the RB-47 may have been in retaliation by the Soviets for the American buzzing of their merchant ships.[21]

Regardless, after landing in the Barents Sea, Olmstead and McKone managed to inflate their small life rafts and stay afloat in the freezing waters. After six hours at sea, Olmstead and McKone were rescued by a Soviet fishing trawler and handed over to military authorities, who took them to Moscow and imprisoned them in the infamous Lubyanka prison, where they awaited an uncertain future as captured spies.

Interestingly the United States air force and navy, with cooperation from the Soviet Union, began an immediate search for the missing RB-47. But in the immediate aftermath of the incident, neither government made any public mention of what had transpired. Then, on July 11, Khrushchev broke the silence and announced that the Soviets had captured Olmstead and McKone and intended to put them on trial as spies. It looked like the U-2 crisis all over again. At Lubyanka, the two airmen were placed in solitary confinement and, once in prison, neither Olmstead nor McKone knew about the whereabouts of the other.

Both men were treated harshly by their captors and endured extensive daily interrogations for the next two months. The worst aspect of their treatment was the virtual starvation diet that the Soviets inflicted on them. Their meals were restricted to five hundred calories per day, consisting of two tablespoons of rice and a cup of coffee for breakfast; a couple of tablespoons of macaroni, a piece of black bread with no butter, and a cup of tea for lunch; and a bowl of borsch and a cup of coffee for dinner. Despite these meager rations, both airmen needed to be careful about what they ate. As McKone explained, with the rice, "you'd got (sic) to take your table spoon, which was the only utensil we had to eat with, and take all the sticks and stones and pieces of glass, aluminum, and everything else you found in it, put that in one pile and then you had the rice in another pile, and then you'd have a cup of black coffee, and that would be breakfast."[22] In their first two months of captivity, McKone lost sixty pounds and Olmstead estimated that he lost "about seventy pounds."[23]

Following Khrushchev's disclosure of the whereabouts of the pilots, the administration began concerted efforts to obtain the release of Olmstead and McKone, arguing that they were in international waters when they were attacked. Henry Cabot Lodge took up their plight between

July 23 and 26 in the United Nations. The State Department began sending diplomatic notes to the Soviet Union's Ministry of Foreign Affairs every two weeks, asking for their release. Neither of these approaches resulted in any action by the Soviet government.[24]

On September 8, 1960, Ambassador Llewelyn Thompson met with Khrushchev to discuss the detention of Olmstead and McKone. Thompson wanted both men released, "impressing [upon Khrushchev] personally the seriousness [of] my government [about] their continued detention."[25] Khrushchev was uncooperative and compared the RB-47 flights to those of the U-2. Thompson disagreed, of course, and pointed out that the RB-47 was in international waters when attacked, while Powers was clearly in Soviet airspace when his plane was brought down. Khrushchev replied dismissively, "This was our [American] opinion" and then he launched into a lengthy diatribe about how the United States was consistently, and arrogantly, overflying the sovereign territory of countries around the world. The United States, Khrushchev said, "had taken upon itself [the] right to fly planes over other countries."[26] He again justified his cancellation of Eisenhower's visit to the Soviet Union on the basis of the U-2 flight, saying "if this incident had not happened [the] President would have had [a] wonderful and hospitable reception in [the] Soviet Union."[27] Gary Powers and his U-2 were still obviously stuck in Khrushchev's craw.

This unpleasant meeting on September 8 ended with Khrushchev's refusal to rule out the possibility that Olmstead and McKone, like Powers, might be placed on trial for espionage. Equally firmly, Thompson cautioned Khrushchev against taking such a step and continued to insist on their release.[28] For the next two months, Tommy Thompson made "a permanent track in the snow between the [American] embassy and the Soviet Foreign Office," attempting to secure the release of Olmstead and McKone.[29.]

While Khrushchev did not place Olmstead and McKone on trial, neither was there any movement on negotiations leading to their release in the last three months of 1960. The American presidential election came and went, as did the Thanksgiving holidays. On December 19, 1960, *Life* magazine published a lengthy article about the plight of Olmstead and McKone in the Soviet Union and Americans responded with letters and gifts to the American embassy in Moscow for delivery to the two captured fliers.[30] Otherwise, 1960 ended with Powers in captivity in the Vladimir prison 150 miles east of Moscow, and Olmstead and McKone imprisoned at Lubyanka. They were hostages of the nasty international environment caused by the "stupid U-2 mess."

A Setback for Nixon

The "stupid U-2 mess" obviously had tremendously negative political consequences for Eisenhower, Khrushchev, and Harold Macmillan, the three leaders who had hoped that summitry would lead to an early détente in the Cold War. Eisenhower lost his place in history as the president who changed the tenor and direction of the Cold War. Khrushchev witnessed a diminution of his authority in the Kremlin as a consequence of the U-2 crisis. "From the time Gary Powers was shot down in a U-2 over the Soviet Union, I was no longer in full control. Decision-making powers were weakened after the U-2 crisis," Khrushchev later wrote. "It scared the Kremlin militarists. My own ascendancy was over."[31] Harold Macmillan saw his vision of a series of summits, held periodically in the capital cities of the four powers, dashed in the wreckage of Powers's U-2 and the refusal of Khrushchev to negotiate in Paris. The collapse of the Paris summit was a "disappointment amounting almost to despair—so much attempted, so little achieved," Macmillan later said.[32] Future summit meetings were destined to be bilateral events that involved only the United States and the Soviet Union. To Macmillan's great regret, the U-2 fiasco had cost the British their seat at the "top table."

The big loser from the U-2 mess, in a political sense, was Richard Nixon. Although Nixon sought to pursue a political strategy somewhat independent of Eisenhower in the 1960 presidential campaign, he knew how important it was to be associated with the successful aspects of Eisenhower's foreign policy, especially with regard to his record of "keeping the peace" in the 1950s.

Had Eisenhower succeeded in his trip to the Soviet Union, it would have been the perfect bookend to Nixon's trip to the Soviet Union in 1959. Nixon would have been in the politically advantageous position of Eisenhower's heir apparent, pursuing a policy of negotiation with the Soviet Union from the standpoint of strength, and not weakness. Instead,

Eisenhower's failure to visit the Soviet Union, along with the collapse of the Paris summit, definitely worked to Nixon's political disadvantage. Khrushchev's attempt to humiliate Eisenhower in Paris, when combined with the renewal of political rhetoric about the missile gap and Soviet achievements in the race for outer space, led to anxieties about America's position of world leadership, a so-called "loss of prestige," which the administration's critics raised repeatedly throughout the campaign.

In the fourth presidential debate on October 21, 1960, for example, John F. Kennedy asked, "Is, as Mr. Nixon said, our prestige at an alltime high, as he said a week ago, and that of the Communists, at an alltime low? I don't believe it is. I don't believe that our relative strength is increasing, and I say that not as a Democratic standard-bearer, but as a citizen of the United States who is concerned about the United States." Kennedy then offered a critique of American foreign policy in Latin America, Africa, Asia, and the Middle East, concluding that the United States had lost influence to the Soviets in each of those areas. Then, he included a reference to the "missile gap": "I think we're going to have to do better. Mr. Nixon talks about our being the strongest country in the world. I think we are today, but we were far stronger relative to the Communists 5 years ago, and what is of great concern is that the balance of power is in danger of moving with them. They made a breakthrough in missiles, and by 1961, 2, and 3, they will be outnumbering us in missiles. I'm not as confident as he is that we will be the strongest military power in 1963."[33]

The question of whether to respond to the criticism of leading Democrats, such as John F. Kennedy, about the missile gap had been on the administration's mind since early in 1960. At a meeting with Eisenhower on February 4, 1960, Thomas Gates asked Ike whether, "as the period of the [presidential] campaign approaches, Defense officials should speak in support of specific candidates."[34] Eisenhower advised Gates to use his judgment but, since the secretary of defense was "not running for office himself," Ike had no objection if Gates was "a Republican and act[ed] like one."[35] The president encouraged Gates to speak before "any body of Americans . . . to give a proper account of his stewardship."[36]

Throughout 1960, Gates avoided any association with political candidates or making any public comments about the presidential campaign. He did, however, follow Eisenhower's advice and defended the administration's defense program in his press conferences and in the few speeches he gave, such as at the annual convention of the Associated Press in New York on April 26. (See chapter five, above.) Gates gave his most vigorous defense of the administration's defense program in a speech to the United States Postmasters convention in Miami, Florida, on October 25, four days after Kennedy's remarks in the fourth presidential debate. In that speech, Gates assailed the views of the administration's critics and forcefully asserted that the Eisenhower administration's approach to national security had given the United States eight years of peace. "Some time ago, Winston Churchill proclaimed that the he did not intend to preside over the dissolution of the British Empire," Gates told the postmasters. "I would like to paraphrase that statement: those of us charged with the responsibility of our national defense effort do not intend to preside over the dissolution of our nation's strength. We have, I believe, every right to deeply resent the implications now current that we have been dissipating that strength. We have, I believe, every reason to assert that we have and are building that strength. I would resign my position as Secretary of Defense this moment if I had any reason to believe that our national policies were building a second-rate defense. Our strength today is deterring the Soviets. For eight years, it has deterred them. It can deter them in the future and it will, if we back our physical strength with moral strength and resolution undismayed by vague and confounded doubts. The cries of American weakness are not heard in the Soviet Union. The Soviet leadership damns us not for our weakness but for our strength."[37]

Despite the strong words of Thomas Gates, however, the reemergence of the missile gap issue, helped along by the renewed anxieties created by the U-2 crisis, definitely worked to Kennedy's advantage. In Joseph Alsop's reckoning, "President Kennedy would probably not have won the 1960 election without the 'missile gap' issue to aid him."[38] By the middle of the 1960 presidential campaign, the after-effects of the U-2 mess were turning into a nightmare for Richard Nixon and the Republicans. As John Farrell, one of Nixon's biographers wrote, "The U-2 was a setback for Nixon. It gave credence to Kennedy's clamor for change."[39]

The aftermath of the U-2 crisis also led to perhaps the most serious mistake Nixon made in his campaign against John F. Kennedy, the selection of Henry Cabot Lodge as his vice presidential running mate. Nixon was forced to recognize that the U-2 crisis had once again introduced the

Conclusion

vulnerability of the Republican Party on national defense and foreign policy. To compensate for this vulnerability, and also under pressure applied by Eisenhower, Nixon chose Lodge, who had served effectively as the American ambassador to the United Nations as well as Khrushchev's host during his visit to the United States. Lodge's diplomatic experience may have been commendable but, in the realm of political calculation, he was the worst choice that Nixon could have made for a running mate. Lodge had already been defeated in 1952 by John F. Kennedy for his Senate seat in Massachusetts and clearly was unable even to hold his own state for the Republican ticket. Moreover, from the standpoint of energy and political savvy, Lodge was a poor, lackluster, even disinterested candidate.

Leading up to the Republican National Convention in Chicago in July 1960, Nixon had considered several possible running mates: Lodge; two Cabinet members (Secretary of Labor James Mitchell and Secretary of the Interior Fred Seaton); Senator Thruston Morton (Kentucky); Congressmen Walter Judd (Minnesota); and Gerald Ford (Michigan). By the time the convention opened, Mitchell and Seaton had removed themselves from Nixon's consideration. Nixon should have selected Ford, especially since Kennedy's selection of Lyndon B. Johnson as his running mate virtually assured that the Southern states that had voted for Eisenhower in 1952 and 1956, most prominently Texas, were poised to tilt back to the Democrats in 1960. Among other reasons, Ford could have carried the Republican message in the Midwestern states of Ohio, Michigan, Illinois, Indiana, Iowa, Wisconsin, and Minnesota.

There were a host of reasons why Ford made sense for Nixon. First, he and Nixon were contemporaries, both forty-seven, and representative of the next generation of Republican leadership after Eisenhower left the scene. Second, both Nixon and Ford were political moderates who held similar views on domestic policy and foreign policy. Third, Ford's personal history was a powerful political statement by itself, especially in the Midwest. A graduate of the University of Michigan and Yale Law School, Ford had been an All-American football player at Michigan in the 1930s. He was also a decorated combat veteran, with nine bronze stars, from his service in the navy in the Pacific during World War II. His distinguished service would have contrasted sharply with Johnson's limited naval experience in World War II and even with Kennedy's acknowledged heroism with PT 109.

Conclusion

Fourth and most important, Ford was an experienced legislator with eleven years in Congress as well as being a proven vote-getter. Ford was the ranking Republican member on the House subcommittee on Defense Appropriations and had participated in all of the congressional debates about defense policy throughout the 1950s. He was the perfect candidate to challenge the Democrats if (when?) they raised the issue of the missile gap.[40] In the summer of 1960, Ford expressed a willingness to be considered Nixon's running mate and a Gerald R. Ford for Vice President Committee was established in his home town of Grand Rapids. Paul Goebel, a former mayor of Grand Rapids and, like Ford, a former football star at Michigan, was the nominal director of the committee. The committee was poised to go to Chicago and rally the delegates behind Ford as vice president. The committee even wrote its own song, to be sung to the melody of Louis Elbel's *The Victors,* the famous Michigan fight song. The song's words were:

> FORD, HE'S OUR CANDIDATE
> FORD, IN EACH SINGLE STATE,
> PLEASE VOTE FOR JERRY FORD,
> THE MAN WHO IS THE BEST.
> FORD, WITH DICK NIXON LEADING,
> FORD, FOR YOUR VOTE WE'RE PLEADING
> PLEASE VOTE FOR JERRY FORD,
> A WINNER AND OUR BEST.[41]

At the Republican National Convention, however, Nixon quickly dismissed Ford and the other prospective candidates in favor of Lodge. Nixon later explained that Ford would have been "more useful to him in Congress" than as vice president, a strange comment given that Ford was not even a member of the Republican leadership in the House at the time.[42] So while Lyndon Johnson was locking up the South for Kennedy, the Republicans went without a strong campaigner in the Midwest.[43] Nixon managed to carry Ohio, Indiana, Iowa, and Wisconsin comfortably but, by the narrowest of margins, he lost Illinois (27 electoral votes), by .2%, Michigan (20 electoral votes), by 2.1%, Minnesota (11 electoral votes), by 1.4%, and Missouri (13 electoral votes), by .6%. Could a strong campaign by Ford in the Midwest have counter-balanced Johnson's effort for Kennedy in the South, and thereby swung the election to Nixon? The odds may have been against such a result, but it appears undeniable that Ford would have given Nixon a better chance with Midwestern voters against Kennedy than Lodge. If Ford could have helped Nixon carry Illinois, Minnesota, and Missouri, Nixon would have won 270 electoral votes and the presidency.

In addition, Nixon had another determined political opponent in 1960, Nikita Khrushchev. Convinced that Nixon had used the celebrated "kitchen debate" in July 1959 to promote himself at Khrushchev's expense, the Soviet leader kept his unflattering opinion of the vice president from that point forward. To Khrushchev, Nixon was a supporter of Joseph McCarthy, bad enough as that was, but he was also heavily influenced by the foreign policy views of John Foster Dulles, a person thoroughly despised by Khrushchev.[44] In Soviet circles, Khrushchev began referring to Nixon as a "shopkeeper," a derisive term that Khrushchev first used when Nixon mentioned that Frank Nixon, his father, had run a grocery store in California. "All shopkeepers are thieves!" Khrushchev told Nixon in Moscow.[45] By scuttling the Paris summit and canceling Eisenhower's trip to the Soviet Union, Khrushchev was essentially handing himself a political twofer: he was striking back at Eisenhower while creating the circumstances whereby Nixon could not politically exploit Eisenhower's popularity.

Then, in July, Khrushchev received another political gift to use against Nixon with the capture of Olmstead and McKone. As mentioned previously, despite repeated diplomatic efforts by the administration, the Soviets refused to release the two American airmen. Nixon wanted to secure their release, and that of Powers, before the election, and he quietly sent Henry Cabot Lodge to visit Khrushchev in Moscow to negotiate the return of the three Americans to the United States. Nixon hoped that Lodge could use his prior relationship with Khrushchev to secure their freedom. Lodge failed. Khrushchev refused to surrender the airmen but neither did he place them on trial for espionage. According to Sergei Khrushchev, his father intended to wait "until after the election" to release Olmstead and McKone, but not Powers.[46]

Khrushchev obviously watched the American presidential election very closely. In his meeting with Ambassador Thompson on September 8, he stated that "there was no possibility of resolving our problems during [the] rest of [the] current administration."⁴⁷ As for the presidential candidates, Khrushchev "frankly had not been charmed by Nixon . . . [and] knew very little of Kennedy."⁴⁸ But, Thompson reported, Khrushchev said "he had no desire to interfere" in the American elections and would "stay out of them," certainly a false statement.⁴⁹

John F. Kennedy defeated Richard Nixon for the presidency on November 4, 1960. According to Sergei Khrushchev, his father was "overjoyed" by Kennedy's victory and began thinking of plans to give Kennedy an "inauguration present."⁵⁰ With Kennedy's election, and Nixon headed into what Khrushchev hoped was political oblivion, the Soviet premier moved quickly in an attempt to repair the strained relations with the United States. For his "inauguration present" to Kennedy, Khrushchev chose to end the captivity of Olmstead and McKone, especially because the publication of the article in *Life* magazine in December had turned world opinion in favor of the two Americans.

On January 21, 1961, Tommy Thompson notified Washington that Khrushchev intended to release Olmstead and McKone according to terms that "meet [the] wishes of [the] American side."⁵¹ Then Thompson received word from Washington that the administration wished to have the airmen released by the time of President Kennedy's first press conference on January 25. On January 24, therefore, the Soviet captors told Olmstead and McKone to dress and, riding in an ambulance, the two airmen were taken clandestinely to the American embassy. The two airmen remained out of sight at the embassy for the entire day until the early evening, when they were driven to the airport in Moscow for a flight to Amsterdam aboard KLM, the Dutch national airline. The KLM flight was the first flight out of the Soviet Union to the West. From Amsterdam, they were to board a flight to the United States.

Shortly after the agreement was reached for the release of the airmen, Ambassador Thompson told Hans Tuch that he wanted to speak with him in his office. "Tom, I want you to take the two airmen to the airport," Thompson told Tuch. "You can't allow anyone to speak to them until the announcement of their release is made in Washington. Once the plane takes off, I want you to call me so that I can notify Washington."⁵² So Tuch got a car from the embassy and drove Olmstead and McKone to the airport. Once at the airport, a problem quickly presented itself in the form of a reporter for a British newspaper, who recognized

Tuch. "Who are those guys?" the reporter asked Tuch, apparently expecting to be introduced. "Just a couple of men from the Embassy," Tuch replied, while hurrying Olmstead and McKone in the direction of the KLM gate.[53] Once the KLM flight left the airport, Tuch called Thompson to inform him that the pilots were in the air and on their way to Amsterdam. At his press conference on January 25, Kennedy announced the release of Olmstead and McKone. On January 26, the president welcomed the two returning airmen and their families to Washington and hosted them with a reception at the White House.[54]

As for Khrushchev, when he met JFK in June 1961 for their summit meeting in Vienna, he joked with the new president and told him that "we had cast the deciding ballot in his election." Kennedy asked the Soviet leader what he meant by "cast[ing] the deciding ballot." Khrushchev told him that "by waiting to release the RB-47 pilots until after the election we kept Nixon from being able to claim that he could deal with the Russians," thereby giving Kennedy "at least half a million votes" for his margin of victory.[55] Khrushchev's behavior was an example of at least indirect meddling in an American presidential election.

"The damnedest show you ever saw"

Neither John F. Kennedy's defeat of Richard Nixon in 1960, nor Governor Edmund P. "Pat" Brown's defeat of Nixon in the 1962 California gubernatorial election, ended Nixon's political career nor his presidential aspirations. After spending most of the 1960s out of the national political limelight, Nixon reemerged on the national scene in 1966 to campaign extensively for Republican candidates in the off-year elections. Nixon's role in the GOP's success in those elections propelled him to front-runner status and to the party's eventual presidential nomination in 1968. In another historically close election, Nixon defeated Hubert Humphrey, Lyndon Johnson's vice president, and won the prize that had eluded him in 1960.

Once in office, Nixon's thoughts never strayed far from the presidential election in 1972. Given his own background and interests, Nixon planned to build his reelection campaign around his achievements in foreign policy. In the summer of 1971, Nixon announced that he planned

Conclusion

to visit the People's Republic of China in 1972, certainly a bold move designed to re-shape the international political landscape. Shortly after the announcement of the trip to China, Nixon announced that he also intended to visit the Soviet Union in 1972. China was to come first, in February. The Soviet Union was to come second, in May. Both of these visits would enable Nixon to receive the best possible publicity for his diplomatic efforts prior to the election in November.

On May 20, 1972, Richard Nixon descended the steps of Air Force One to meet Soviet Premier Leonid Brezhnev, who came to power after Khrushchev was deposed in 1964. Nixon was the first president since Franklin D. Roosevelt to visit the Soviet Union, a distinction that Eisenhower had sought for himself in 1959–1960. It was Nixon's second visit to the Soviet Union. Nixon had succeeded in visiting the Soviet Union where Eisenhower had failed. Eisenhower passed away on March 28, 1969, just two months into Nixon's presidency. We may assume, however, that Ike, had he been alive at the time, would have approved of Nixon's effort to begin a substantive dialogue with the leaders of the Soviet Union. Nixon came to the Soviet Union to complete an arms control treaty, provisions of which were far different than those that Eisenhower had intended to negotiate with Khrushchev in 1960.

Thinking about a possible visit to the Soviet Union in 1972, Nixon laughed and said, "An American president walking the streets of Moscow. Wouldn't that be the damnedest show that you ever saw?"[56] In some respects, it was the damnedest show as Richard Nixon, once an arch-enemy of the Kremlin for two decades, was welcomed into the Soviet Union to negotiate with its leadership. In 1960, had Dwight D. Eisenhower managed to visit the Soviet Union, that trip also would have been the "damnedest show that you ever saw."

Notes

Abbreviations

AWF   Ann Whitman File
COHP   Columbia Oral History Project
DDE   Dwight D. Eisenhower
EL   Eisenhower Library
FRUS   Foreign Relations of the United States
IS   International Series
OSS   Office of the Staff Secretary
PP   Papers as President
WHO   White House Office

Preface

1. Oral history interview with Robert J. Donovan, Oral History Archives at Columbia, Rare Book and Manuscript Library, Columbia University in the City of New York, 36-37.

2. Thomas S. Gates, interview with the author, April 29, 1982. Audiotape in possession of the author.

Introduction

1. For Eisenhower's account of his visit to the Soviet Union in August 1945, see his *Crusade in Europe* (Garden City, NY: Doubleday, 1948), 457–78.

2. The President's News Conference of August 3, 1959, in *Public Papers of the Presidents of the United States: Dwight D. Eisenhower, 1959* (Washington, DC: Government Printing Office, 1960), 560 (hereinafter cited as *Public Papers, Eisenhower, 1959*).

3. E. Bruce Geelhoed and Anthony O. Edmonds, *Eisenhower, Macmillan, and Allied Unity, 1957–1961* (Basingstoke, UK: Palgrave Macmillan, 2003), 92.

Notes to Introduction

4. The prospect of Eisenhower and Khrushchev continuing their negotiations on the issue of a nuclear test-ban treaty after the Paris summit and during Eisenhower's visit to the Soviet Union was mentioned to the author by Sergei Khrushchev, son of Nikita Khrushchev, in an interview on April 5, 2011. The transcript of the interview is in the author's possession.

5. Geelhoed and Edmonds, *Eisenhower, Macmillan, and Allied Unity*, 1.

6. Oral history interview with Harrison Salisbury (1972), p. 15, Oral History Archives at Columbia, Rare Book and Manuscript Library, Columbia University in the City of New York (hereinafter cited as Harrison Salisbury oral history, COHP).

7. William I. Hitchcock, *The Age of Eisenhower: America and the World in the 1950s* (New York: Simon and Schuster, 2018), xii. In his masterful biography of Eisenhower, Hitchcock argues that the "age of Eisenhower" began shortly after the end of World War II, in 1946, and continued until the beginning of John F. Kennedy's presidency, in 1961.

8. Clint Hill with Lisa McCubbin, *Five Presidents: My Extraordinary Journey with Eisenhower, Kennedy, Johnson, Nixon, and Ford* (New York: Gallery Books, 2016), 3–76. See also Hitchcock, *Age of Eisenhower*, 409.

9. Thomas S. Gates, interview with the author, January 20, 1982. Audiotape in author's possession.

10. Monte Reel, *A Brotherhood of Spies: The U-2 and the CIA's Secret War* (New York: Doubleday, 2018), 193.

11. Sergei Khrushchev, interview with the author, op. cit. On the matter of Eisenhower's decision to allow the Red Army to conquer Berlin, see Stephen E. Ambrose, *Eisenhower and Berlin, 1945: The Decision to Halt at the Elbe* (New York: W. W. Norton, 1967), 94–96.

12. Oral history of Milton S. Eisenhower (1975), pp. 45–46, Dwight D. Eisenhower Library.

13. "Master List," telegram, Washington to Moscow, Tokyo, Seoul, regarding accredited correspondents for President Eisenhower's visit, May 3, 1960, in Dwight D. Eisenhower Library, Papers as President, Ann Whitman File, International Series, International Meetings and Trips, Far Eastern Trip (withdrawn), Box 50 (hereinafter cited as EL, PP, AWF-IS, Far Eastern Trip).

14. Richard Nixon, *Six Crises* (Garden City, NY: Doubleday, 1962), 302–03; Richard Nixon, RN: *The Memoirs of Richard Nixon* (New York: Warner Books, 1978), 1:262–63; Jonathan Aitken, *Nixon: A Life* (New York: Regnery, 1993), 263–65.

15. Stephen E. Ambrose, *Ike's Spies: Eisenhower and the Intelligence Establishment* (Garden City, NY: Doubleday, 1981), 278.

16. The President's News Conference of May 11, 1960, *Public Papers of the Presidents of the United States. Dwight D. Eisenhower. 1960–61* (Washington, DC: Government Printing Office, 1961), 403 (hereinafter cited as *Public Papers, Eisenhower, 1960–61*).

17. William Taubman, *Khrushchev: The Man and His Era* (New York: W. W. Norton, 2003), 458–59; Aleksandr Fursenko and Timothy Naftali, *Khrushchev's Cold War: Portrait of an American Adversary* (New York: W. W. Norton, 2006), 281–82.

18. Few subjects in the Eisenhower presidency have received more attention from historians, political scientists, journalists, and memoirists than the U-2 crisis. For specific works on the subject, see Charles C. Alexander, *Holding the Line: The Eisenhower*

Notes to Chapter 1

Era, 1952–1961 (Bloomington, IN: Indiana University Press, 1975), 263–68; Ambrose, *Ike's Spies*, 279–92; Ambrose, *Eisenhower. Vol. II. The President* (New York: Simon and Schuster, 1984), 571–80; Michael Beschloss, *May Day: Eisenhower, Khrushchev, and the U-2 Affair* (New York: Harper and Row, 1986); Peter G. Boyle, *Eisenhower* (New York: Pearson Longman, 2005), 136–40; Dwight D. Eisenhower, *Waging Peace: The White House Years, A Personal Account 1956–1961* (Garden City, NY: Doubleday, 1965), 550–557; John S. D. Eisenhower, *Strictly Personal* (Garden City, NY: Doubleday, 1974), 270–79; Geelhoed and Edmonds, *Eisenhower, Macmillan and Allied Unity*, 105–31; Irvin F. Gellman, *The President and the Apprentice* (New Haven, CT: Yale University Press, 2015), 540–42; Hitchcock, *Age of Eisenhower*, 456–74; Peter Lyon, *Eisenhower: Portrait of the Hero* (Boston, MA: Little Brown, 1974), 808–15; Jim Newton, *Eisenhower: The White House Years* (Garden City, NY: Doubleday, 2011), 312–18; Herbert S. Parmet, *Eisenhower and the American Crusades* (New York: Macmillan, 1972), 555–59; Curtis Peebles, *Shadow Flights: America's Secret Air War against the Soviet Union* (Novato, CA: Presidio, 2000); Reel, *Brotherhood of Spies, 200;* Jean Edward Smith, *Eisenhower in War and Peace* (New York: Random House, 2012), 751–55; Evan Thomas, *Ike's Bluff: President Eisenhower's Secret Battle to Save the World* (New York: Little, Brown, 2012), 365–93; Jenny Thompson and Sherry Thompson, *The Kremlinologist: Llewellyn E. Thompson, America's Man in Cold War Moscow* (Baltimore, MD: Johns Hopkins University Press, 2017), 208–25; Robert J. Watson, *Into the Missile Age, 1956–1960* (Washington, DC: Historical Office of the Secretary of Defense, 1997), 718–24; and David Wise and Thomas Ross, *The U-2 Affair* (New York: Random House, 1962). See also Fursenko and Naftali, *Khrushchev's Cold War*, 262–91; Sergei Khrushchev, *Nikita Khrushchev and the Creation of a Superpower* (University Park, PA: Pennsylvania State University Press, 2001), 380–94 (hereinafter cited as *Nikita Khrushchev*); and Taubman, *Khrushchev*, 454–68.

19. Robert A. Divine, *Eisenhower and the Cold War* (New York: Oxford University Press, 1981), 151–52.

20. Telegram, [Christian] Herter to [Llewellyn] Thompson, March 22, 1960, in EL, PP, AWF-IS, International Meetings and Trips, Box 50, contains the preliminary itinerary for Eisenhower's trip to the Soviet Union. The final itinerary may be found in "Itinerary of the President's Visit to the U.S.S.R., May 7, 1960," in EL, PP, AWF-IS, Far Eastern Trip.

21. George B. Kistiakowsky, *A Scientist at the White House: The Private Diary of President Eisenhower's Special Assistant for Science and Technology* (Cambridge, MA: Harvard University Press, 1976), 332–33.

22. David Reynolds, *Summits: Six Meetings That Shaped the Twentieth Century* (New York: Basic Books, 2007), 5.

23. On that point, see the provocative chapter by George Feifer, "If the U-2 Hadn't Flown," in Robert Cowley, ed., *What-Ifs of American History* (New York: G. P. Putnam's Sons, 2003), especially 248–49.

Chapter 1

1. Eisenhower, *Crusade in Europe*, 457–78.
2. Norman Gelb, *Ike and Monty* (New York: Morrow, 1994), 30–31.

3. David Kennedy, *Freedom from Fear: The American People in Depression and War, 1929–1945* (New York: Oxford University Press, 1999), 688.

4. Gelb, *Ike and Monty*, 88.

5. When *Time* magazine published its commemorative issue for the fiftieth anniversary of D-Day, 6 June 1994, the magazine cover carried a picture of Eisenhower with the caption, "The Man Who Beat Hitler." See Bruce W. Nelan, "Ike's Invasion," *Time*, vol. 143, No. 23 (6 June 1994), 36–49. See also Steve Neal, *Harry and Ike: The Partnership That Remade the Postwar World* (New York: Scribner, 2001), 37. William Hitchcock discussed the upward trajectory of Eisenhower's military career in *Age of Eisenhower*, 3–24.

6. See Geoffrey Roberts, *Stalin's General: A Life of Georgi Zhukov* (New York: Random House, 2012), 67–233, for Zhukov's wartime exploits against the Germans. An especially valuable explanation of Zhukov's role in the defeat of Nazi Germany may be found in Alistair Horne, *Hubris: The Tragedy of War in the Twentieth Century* (New York: HarperCollins, 2016), 147–240.

7. Harrison Salisbury oral history, COHP, 4–6.

8. Eisenhower, *Crusade in Europe*, 459–60.

9. Stephen E. Ambrose, *Eisenhower: Soldier and President* (New York: Simon and Schuster, 1990), 217. See also Robert D. Murphy, *Diplomat among Warriors* (Garden City, NY: Doubleday, 1964), 257–63.

10. No author, "Eisenhower Flies to Moscow Fete," *New York Times*, August 12, 1945.

11. Eisenhower, *Crusade in Europe*, 459–60; John R. Deane, *The Strange Alliance: The Story of Our Efforts at Wartime Cooperation with Russia* (New York: Viking, 1946), 213. John S. D. Eisenhower also gives an account of his visit to Russia with his father in his book, *Strictly Personal*, 100–110.

12. Eisenhower, *Crusade in Europe*, 460.

13. Ibid., 459–60.

14. Ibid.

15. Deane, *Strange Alliance*, 213–14.

16. Ibid., 215.

17. Ibid.

18. Eisenhower, *Crusade in Europe*, 460–61; Deane, *Strange Alliance*, 215. See also Brooks Atkinson, "Eisenhower and Stalin Review Parade of 40,000 in Red Square," *New York Times*, August 13, 1945.

19. Eisenhower, *Crusade in Europe*, 460–61.

20. Ibid.

21. Deane, *Strange Alliance*, 215–16.

22. W. Averell Harriman and Elie Abel, *Special Envoy to Churchill and Stalin, 1941–1946* (New York: Random House, 1975), 502.

23. Brooks Atkinson, "Eisenhower Hails Russian Amity," *New York Times*, August 14, 1945.

24. Eisenhower, *Crusade in Europe*, 462.

25. Atkinson, "Eisenhower Hails Russian Amity," *New York Times*, August 14, 1945.

26. Harriman and Abel, *Special Envoy*, 501–02.

27. Deane, *Strange Alliance*, 217.

28. Eisenhower, *Crusade in Europe*, 464–65; Deane, *Strange Alliance*, 217–18; Atkinson, "Eisenhower Hails Russian Amity," *New York Times*, August 14, 1945.
29. Deane, *Strange Alliance*, 217–18.
30. Ibid.
31. Ibid.
32. No author, "Eisenhower Praises U.S. Press Freedom," *New York Times*, August 15, 1945.
33. Ibid.
34. Ibid.
35. Eisenhower, *Crusade in Europe*, 465.
36. Horne, *Hubris*, 9–126.
37. Anna Reid, *Leningrad: The Epic Siege of World War II, 1941–1944* (New York: Walker Books, 2012) 1–2.
38. Harrison Salisbury, *900 Days: The Siege of Leningrad* (New York: Da Capo Press, 2013), 516. In *Crusade in Europe*, 466, Eisenhower placed the number of civilian casualties at 350,000 in Leningrad during World War II.
39. Eisenhower, *Crusade in Europe*, 466.
40. Ibid., 466–67; John Eisenhower, *Strictly Personal*, 109–10.
41. Harriman and Ebel, *Special Envoy*, 503; Roberts, *Zhukov*, 239.
42. Harriman and Ebel, *Special Envoy*, 502–03.
43. Harrison Salisbury oral history, COHP, 7–8.
44. Harriman and Ebel, *Special Envoy*, 502–03.
45. Harrison Salisbury oral history, COHP, 6–7.
46. Deane, *Strange Alliance*, 220.
47. Harriman and Ebel, *Special Envoy*, 501–02.
48. Deane, *Strange Alliance*, 220.
49. Harriman and Ebel, *Special Envoy*, 501–02.
50. Eisenhower, *Crusade in Europe*, 469.
51. Thomas, *Ike's Bluff*, 176; Sergei Khrushchev, interview with the author.
52. Emmett John Hughes, *The Ordeal of Power: A Political Memoir of the Eisenhower Years* (New York: Atheneum, 1963), 107.
53. Andrew Goodpaster, quoted in Bret Baier, with Catherine Whitney, *Three Days in January: Dwight Eisenhower's Final Mission* (New York: Morrow, 2017), 179.
54. John Eisenhower, *Strictly Personal*, 102.
55. Ibid., 104.
56. Ibid., 111–12.

Chapter 2

1. Hughes, *The Ordeal of Power*, 65–66. For a profile of James Hagerty and his role as Eisenhower's press secretary, see Robert H. Ferrell, ed., *The Diary of James C. Hagerty: Eisenhower in Mid-Course, 1954–1955* (Bloomington, IN: Indiana University Press, 1983), xi–xvi.
2. The President's News Conference of August 3, 1959, *Public Papers, Eisenhower, 1959*, 560–63.
3. Ibid.

4. Ibid. When Eisenhower read the statement, he pronounced Khrushchev's first name as "Nikito," instead of "Nikita." As a result of his illness early in November 1957, Ike occasionally had difficulty pronouncing certain words when he spoke. Such may have been the case in this particular instance. The statement can be viewed on the internet at http//www.youtube.com, "Eisenhower, Khrushchev, New Diplomacy, 1959/8/3."

5. The President's News Conference of August 3, 1959, *Public Papers, Eisenhower, 1959*, 561–62.

6. Ibid., 562–63.

7. Ibid., 563.

8. Ibid., 564.

9. Sergei Khrushchev, *Nikita Khrushchev*, 319–20.

10. Robert S. Jordan, *An Unsung Soldier: The Life of General Andrew J. Goodpaster* (Annapolis, MD: Naval Institute Press, 2013), 66–67; Andrew Goodpaster, interview with the author, February 22, 1983. Transcript in author's possession.

11. Sergei N. Khrushchev, interview with the author.

12. David M. Glantz and Jonathan M. House, *When Titans Clashed: How the Red Army Stopped Hitler* (Lawrence, KS: University Press of Kansas, 1995), 41–42.

13. David E. Murphy, *What Stalin Knew: The Enigma of Barbarossa* (New Haven, CT: Yale University Press, 2005), 162–163.

14. George Feifer, "If the U-2 Hadn't Flown," in Cowley, ed., *What Ifs of American History*, 230.

15. Text of Lacy-Zaroubin Agreement, January 27, 1958, https://librariesandcoldwarculturalexchange.wordpress.com.

16. Ibid.; Thompson and Thompson, *Kremlinologist*, 161–62. For a full account of Cliburn's tour of the Soviet Union in 1958, and specifically of his interactions with the Thompson sisters, see Stuart Isakoff, *When the World Stopped to Listen: Van Cliburn's Cold War Triumph and Its Aftermath* (New York: Alfred A. Knopf, 2017), 167–69, 170–71, 174–75.

17. Text of Lacy-Zaroubin Agreement, op. cit. Followers of international track and field competition, like the author, will undoubtedly remember the track meets that were held each summer, alternating between the United States and the Soviet Union, between American and Russian athletes. The first of these meets was held in July 1958.

18. Thompson and Thompson, *Kremlinologist*, 207.

19. Hans N. Tuch, *Arias, Cabellas, and Foreign Affairs: A Public Diplomat's Quasi-Musical Memoir* (Washington, DC: New Academic Publishing, 2008), 51–83.

20. Ibid., 77–78. Hans Tuch also discussed the Nixon visit to the American Exhibition in a telephone interview with the author, August 19, 2015. Audiotape in author's possession.

21. Message from the president to be read by the Honorable Richard M. Nixon at the opening of the American National Exhibition, Moscow, July 25, 1959, EL, PP, AWF-IS, Far Eastern Trip. Richard Nixon also gave a speech on the opening of the American exhibition in the Soviet Union. See Stephen E. Ambrose, *Vol. I. Nixon: The Education of a Politician, 1913–1962* (New York: Simon and Schuster, 1987), 525–26.

22. Henry Kissinger, *Diplomacy* (New York: Simon and Schuster, 1994), 569–71; Geelhoed and Edmonds, *Eisenhower, Macmillan, and Allied Unity*, 63–64; Sergei Khrushchev, *Nikita Khrushchev*, 302–10.

23. John Lewis Gaddis, *The Cold War: A New History* (New York: W. W. Norton, 2005), 113.

24. Ibid.

25. Campbell Craig, *Destroying the Village: Eisenhower and Thermonuclear War* (New York: Columbia University Press, 1998), 90–92.

26. Alistair Horne, *Macmillan. Vol. II, 1957–1986* (London: Macmillan, 1989), 121–22.

27. Geelhoed and Edmonds, *Eisenhower, Macmillan, and Allied Unity*, 64–65.

28. Harold Macmillan, *Pointing the Way, 1959 to 1961* (London: Macmillan, 1972), 102–03. See also Richard Aldous, "A Family Affair: The Art of Personal Diplomacy," in Richard Aldous and Sabine Lee, eds., *Harold Macmillan and Britain's World Role* (London: Macmillan, 1995), 18.

29. Kissinger, *Diplomacy*, 508.

30. Harold Macmillan, *Riding the Storm, 1956 to 1959*. (London: Macmillan, 1971), 490; Richard Aldous and Sabine Lee, "Staying in the Game: Harold Macmillan and Britain's World Role," in Aldous and Lee, eds., *Harold Macmillan and Britain's World Role*, 158. I am also indebted to Alexander Macmillan, Lord Stockton, a grandson of Harold Macmillan, for his thoughts on Nellie Macmillan's views on American isolationism and how those views influenced Harold Macmillan's understanding of American foreign policy. Alexander Macmillan, interview with the author, May 8, 1987.

31. Eisenhower to Macmillan, April 3, 1958, and Macmillan to Eisenhower, April 10, 1958, in E. Bruce Geelhoed and Anthony O. Edmonds, eds., *The Macmillan-Eisenhower Correspondence, 1957–1969* (Basingstoke, UK: Palgrave Macmillan, 2005), 138–39.

32. Macmillan, *Riding the Storm*, 493.

33. Geelhoed and Edmonds, *Eisenhower, Macmillan, and Allied Unity*, 64–65.

34. Ibid., 65.

35. Ibid., 71.

36. Ibid., 65.

37. Ibid., 68.

38. For a thorough discussion of Macmillan's visit to the Soviet Union and its outcome, see Kitty Newman, *Macmillan, Khrushchev, and the Berlin Crisis of 1958–1960* (London: Routledge, 2007), 63–82.

39. Geelhoed and Edmonds, *Eisenhower, Macmillan and Allied Unity*, 65–66.

40. Townsend Hoopes, *The Devil and John Foster Dulles* (Boston, MA: Little, Brown, 1974), 475–76.

41. Andrew Goodpaster, interview with the author, June 13, 1996.

42. Kissinger, *Diplomacy*, 631–32.

43. The President's Press Conference of August 3, 1959, *Public Papers, Eisenhower, 1959*, 564.

44. Eisenhower, *Waging Peace*, 405–7.

45. The President's Press Conference of August 3, 1959, *Public Papers, Eisenhower, 1959*, 563.

46. Ibid.

47. Murphy's memoir, *Diplomat among Warriors*, explores the relationship between Murphy and Eisenhower, but also between Murphy and Harold Macmillan and between Murphy and Charles de Gaulle. Another helpful source is "Robert Murphy and the Middle East Crisis of 1956," in H. W. Brands, *Cold Warriors: Eisenhower's Generation and American Foreign Policy* (New York: Columbia University Press, 1988), 99–100. Brands's account of Murphy's importance to Ike does not, unfortunately, mention Murphy's role in the overture to Khrushchev in 1959.

48. Harrison Salisbury oral history, COHP, 6.

49. Eisenhower, *Waging Peace*, 405–7.

50. Andrew Goodpaster, interviews with the author, February 22, 1983, July 13, 1996.

51. Eisenhower, *Waging Peace*, 405–07.

52. Ibid. See also John Eisenhower, *Strictly Personal*, 236–37; Ambrose, *Eisenhower, II*, 434–35; Parmet, *Eisenhower and the American Crusades*, 547–48; Smith, *Eisenhower in War and Peace*, 746–47; Fursenko and Naftali, *Khrushchev's Cold War*, 216–27.

53. Andrew Goodpaster, interviews with the author, February 26, 1983, July 13, 1996.

54. Eisenhower, *Waging Peace*, 407. For a helpful chronology of the issuance of the two invitations, see Thompson and Thompson, *Kremlinologist*, 176.

55. Craig, *Destroying the Village*, 104–05.

56. Geelhoed and Edmonds, *Eisenhower, Macmillan, and Allied Unity*, 75–76.

57. Craig, *Destroying the Village*, 104–5. See also Thomas, *Ike's Bluff*, 333–34.

58. Taubman, *Khrushchev*, 416; Newton, *Eisenhower*, 296.

59. Murphy, *Diplomat among Warriors*, 438.

60. Ibid. In his interview with the author, Sergei Khrushchev confirmed the popular admiration and affection that Eisenhower enjoyed with the Soviet people, prior to the U-2 incident of May, 1960, as a result of his cooperation with the Russians in World War II.

61. Murphy, *Diplomat among Warriors*, 438.

62. John S. D. Eisenhower, interview with the author, February 22, 1982. See also Geelhoed and Edmonds, *Eisenhower, Macmillan, and Allied* Unity, 22. For a concise treatment of *Sputnik's* effect on the American psyche, see Hitchcock, *Age of Eisenhower*, 376–99.

63. In his superb book, *Eisenhower's Sputnik Moment: The Race for Space and World Prestige* (Ithaca, NY: Cornell University Press, 2013), 244, Yanek Mieczkowski established the link between the launch of *Sputnik* and the emergence of the "missile gap" as a political issue in the late 1950s and in the presidential campaign of 1960. This link can also be found in Douglas Brinkley, *American Moonshot: John F. Kennedy and the Great Space Race* (New York: HarperCollins, 2019), 166-67. See also Greg Grandin, *In Kissinger's Shadow: The Long Reach of America's Most Controversial Statesman* (New York: Picador, 2015), 25–32.

64. Boyle, *Eisenhower*, 136.

65. In his acceptance speech for the 1968 Republican presidential nomination, Richard Nixon used the language of moving from "an era of confrontation" with the Communist world to "an era of negotiation." See Nixon, *Six Crises* (New York:

Doubleday, 1968), ix; Theodore H. White, *The Making of the President: 1968* (New York: Atheneum, 1969), 255.

66. Eisenhower, quoted in Thomas, *Ike's Bluff*, 314.

67. Andrew J. Goodpaster, "Cold War Overflights: The View from the White House," in R. Cargill Hall, ed., *Early Cold War Overflights, 1950–1956* (Washington, DC: National Reconnaissance Office, 2003), 40.

Chapter 3

1. Eisenhower, *Waging Peace*, 412. For a challenge to the overall effectiveness of personal diplomacy in general, and meetings of heads of state specifically, see Keith Eubank, *The Summit Conferences, 1919–1960* (Norman, OK: University of Oklahoma Press, 1966).

2. Ambrose, *Eisenhower, II*, 537; Eisenhower, *Waging Peace*, 415. See also Alexander, *Holding the Line*, 250–51, for a discussion of Eisenhower's meeting with his Allied counterparts.

3. Harold Macmillan, *Riding the Storm, 1956–1961* (London: Macmillan, 1971), 747.

4. Andrew Goodpaster, interviews.

5. Geelhoed and Edmonds, *Eisenhower, Macmillan, and Allied Unity*, 84–85.

6. Harold Evans, *Downing Street Diary: The Macmillan Years, 1957–1963* (London: Hodder & Stoughton, 1981), 43.

7. Alexander Macmillan, interview with the author, May 8, 1987. Audiotape in the author's possession. See also Geelhoed and Edmonds, *Eisenhower, Macmillan, and Allied Unity*, 87–89.

8. Script of televised broadcast with Prime Minister, August 31, 1959, Dwight D. Eisenhower Library, Papers as President, Ann Whitman File, International Series, Box 25A, Macmillan, 7/1/59/—12/31/59, folder 6 (hereinafter cited as EL, PP, Ann Whitman File, International Series).

9. Eisenhower, *Waging Peace*, 423; Macmillan, *Riding the Storm*, 749; Geelhoed and Edmonds, *Eisenhower, Macmillan, and Allied Unity*, 87; Newman, *Macmillan, Khrushchev, and the Berlin Crisis*, 122–23.

10. Ambrose, *Eisenhower, II*, 541.

11. Robert Blake, *The Conservative Party from Peel to Thatcher* (London: Fontana Press, 1985), 24, 41.

12. Eisenhower to Macmillan, 9 October 1959, EL, PP, Ann Whitman Files, International Series, Box 25A, "Macmillan, 7/1/59–12/31/59," folder 5; Geelhoed and Edmonds, *Eisenhower, Macmillan, and Allied Unity*, 89–90.

13. Thomas S. Gates, interview with the author, January 20, 1982. Ambrose, Eisenhower, II, 538–41; Alexander, *Holding the Line*, 250; Hitchcock, *Age of Eisenhower*, 422–24.

14. John Hay Whitney to Secretary of State, September 8, 1959, 2–3, in Dwight D. Eisenhower Library, Papers as President, Ann Whitman File, International Meetings and Trips Series, Box 3, "London: August 27–September 3, 1959" (hereinafter cited as EL, PP, Ann Whitman File, International Meetings and Trips series).

15. Memorandum, September 14, 1959, in Dwight D. Eisenhower Library, Papers as President, James C. Hagerty Papers, Far Eastern Trip, 1953—1961, Box 33 (hereinafter cited as EL, PP, James C. Hagerty Papers, Far Eastern Trip). Accounts of Khrushchev's visit to the United States are found in numerous sources. For two, see Sergei Khrushchev, *Nikita Khrushchev*, 319–48, and Peter Carlson, *K Blows Top: A Cold War Comic Interlude, Starring Nikita Khrushchev, America's Most Unlikely Tourist* (New York: Public Affairs, 2009), 70–71, for the episode described in the text.

16. Carlson, *K Blows Top*, and *Cold War Roadshow*, The American Experience, PBS Home Video, DVD released December 23, 2014.

17. Eisenhower's statement about his hopes and expectations for the Khrushchev visit has been documented in a number of sources. For example, see Ambrose, *Eisenhower, II*, 536, and David Eisenhower, *Going Home to Glory: A Memoir of Life with Dwight D. Eisenhower, 1961 to 1969* (New York: Simon and Schuster, 2010), 12. See also http//www.youtube.com, "Universal Newsreel Vol. 32, Release 65–72, Eisenhower Comment on Khrushchev Visit (1959)," for the televised footage of Ike's comment.

18. Carlson, *K Blows Top*, 168–71.

19. Reel, *Brotherhood of Spies*, 159–60.

20. Ibid.

21. Thomas J. Watson Jr., with Peter Petre, *Father, Son & Co.: My Life at IBM and Beyond* (New York: Bantam, 1990), 326.

22. Ibid., 328–30.

23. Ibid., 328; "Khrushchev Visits IBM: A Strange Tale of Silicon Valley History," https://www.fastcompany.com/3037598/khrushchev-visits-ibm-a-strange-tale-of-silicon-valley-history.

24. Carlson, *K Blows Top*, 195.

25. Ibid., 196; Watson, *Father, Son & Co.*, 330.

26. Watson, *Father, Son & Co.*, 328–29.

27. Goodpaster, quoted in Thomas, *Ike's Bluff*, 332–33.

28. Oral history of General Vernon Walters (1970), p. 43, Dwight D. Eisenhower Library (hereinafter cited as Walters oral history).

29. Harrison Salisbury oral history, COHP, 38–41.

30. John N. Irwin, interview with the author, October 6, 1981. Transcript in author's possession. Carlson also reported on this conversation between Eisenhower and Khrushchev in *K Blows Top*, 233.

31. Goodpaster, "Cold War Overflights: A View from the White House," in Hall, ed., *Early Cold War Overflights*, 44.

32. Memorandum, President Eisenhower's Talks with Chairman Khrushchev at Camp David, September 30, 1959, EL, PP, AWF-IS, Macmillan, 7/1/59–12/31/59, folder 5, 4. See also Geelhoed and Edmonds, *Eisenhower, Macmillan, and Allied Unity*, 92.

33. Carlson, *K Blows Top*, 241.

34. Fursenko and Naftali, *Khrushchev's Cold War*, 241–42.

35. Eisenhower to Khrushchev, November 2, 1959, in Louis Galambos and Daun van Ee, eds. *The Papers of Dwight David Eisenhower. The Presidency: Keeping the Peace. Vol. XX.* (Baltimore, MD: Johns Hopkins University Press, 2001), 1718–19 (hereinafter cited as Galambos and Van Ee, *Papers of DDE*).

36. Ibid., Eisenhower to Khrushchev, November 28, 1959, 1757.
37. Ibid.
38. Ibid., Eisenhower to Khrushchev, December 3, 1959.
39. Draft Statement for Ambassador Lodge, Dwight D. Eisenhower Library, Ann Whitman File, Dulles-Herter Series, Box 13, Herter, Christian, Box 13, May, 1960 (2). This statement was drafted for Ambassador Henry Cabot Lodge when he was to appear before the United Nations in May, 1960, to defend the use of the U-2 surveillance program against attacks made by the Soviet Union that the U-2 flights had an aggressive, hostile intent.
40. Memorandum of Discussion at the 444th Meeting of the National Security Council, May 9, 1960, *FRUS, 1958–1960, X*, Doc. 149, 516–17, https://history.state.gov/historicaldocuments/frus1958-60v10p1/d149 (hereinafter cited as *FRUS, 58–60, X*).
41. Ibid. See also Jerald F. Terhorst and Captain Ralph Albertazzi, *The Flying White House: The Story of Air Force One* (New York: Coward, McCann, and Geoghegan, 1979), 196–98. See also Beschloss, *May Day*, 228–29.
42. Terhorst and Albertazzie, *The Flying White House*, 196–98.
43. Ibid.
44. Ibid.
45. Chronology of Heads of Government, Paris, December 18, 1959. Record of Meeting at the Elysee, December 19, 1959, 5. Dwight D. Eisenhower Library, Papers as President, White House Office: Office of the Staff Secretary, International Meetings and Trips, Box 10 (hereinafter cited as EL, PP, WHO/OSS, International Meetings and Trips). See also Geelhoed and Edmonds, *Eisenhower, Macmillan, and Allied Unity*, 93–95. Regarding the lack of attention given by scholars to the Western summit in December 1959, it should be noted that Charles C. Alexander, Stephen E. Ambrose, Peter Boyle, Jim Newton, Herbert S. Parmet, Jean Edward Smith, and Evan Thomas give the conference hardly any discussion. In *Waging Peace*, however, Eisenhower writes about the Western summit, 508–09.
46. Record of Meeting at the Elysee, December 19, 1959, EL, PP, WHO/OSS, International Meetings and Trips, 10–11.
47. Ibid., 11.
48. Ibid.
49. Ibid.
50. Ibid., 9.
51. Ibid. See also Telegram, American Embassy to SecState, Washington, December 21, 1959, EL, PP, WHO/OSS, International Meetings and Trips, 2.
52. Eisenhower, *Waging Peace*, 582.
53. Chronology of Meeting of Heads of Government, December 18, 1959, EL, PP, WHO/OSS, 10.
54. Ibid.
55. Macmillan, *Pointing the Way*, 103. See also Newman, *Macmillan, Khrushchev, and the Berlin Crisis*, 136–38.
56. Chronology of Meeting of Heads of State, December 18, 1959, EL, PP, WHO/OSS, International Meetings and Trips, 2.
57. Ibid., 3. See also American Embassy to SecState, December 21, 1959, in Galambos and Van Ee, *Papers of DDE*, XX.

Notes to Chapter 4

58. Eisenhower to Khrushchev, December 29, 1959, in Galambos and Van Ee, *Papers of DDE*, XX, 1779.
59. Eisenhower to Khrushchev, January 12, 1960, in Galambos and Van Ee, *Papers of DDE*, XX, 1790–91.
60. Eisenhower to Khrushchev, January 21, 1960, in Galambos and Van Ee, *Papers of DDE*, XX, 1806–07.
61. Ibid.
62. Eisenhower, *Waging Peace*, 444.
63. Eisenhower to Khrushchev, December 3, 1959, in Galambos and Van Ee, *Papers of DDE*, XX, 1766.
64. Ibid.
65. Hitchcock, *Age of Eisenhower*, 421.
66. Sergei Khrushchev, *Nikita Khrushchev*, 353–54.

Chapter 4

1. Telegram from the Embassy in the Soviet Union to the Department of State, February 9, 1960. 4 P.M. *Foreign Relations of the United States, 1958–1960, Vol. X*, Doc. 146, 507–09.
2. Memorandum, John A. Calhoun, Department of State, to Brig. Gen. A. J. Goodpaster, The White House, March 9, 1960, Dwight D. Eisenhower Library, Papers as President, Ann Whitman File, DDE Diary Series, Box 47, Staff Notes, February 1960 (1, 2) (hereinafter cited as EL, PP, Ann Whitman File, DDE Diary Series, Staff Notes). Also, Mikhail Menshikov, occasionally referred to by the Washington press corps as "Smiling Mike," succeeded Georgy Zaroubin as the Soviet ambassador to the United States in January 1958, and served in that office until January, 1962. See John Eisenhower, *Strictly Personal*, 255–56, 258, and Carlson, *K Blows Top*, 61–64.
3. Memorandum, Calhoun to Goodpaster, March 9, 1960, op. cit.
4. Ibid.
5. Ibid.
6. No author, "Cold War: I Like Him," *Time*, August 30, 1962.
7. Oral history of Hans N. Tuch (1989), p. 6, Association for Diplomatic Studies and Training, Foreign Affairs Oral History Project, Arlington, VA, copyright 1998.
8. Oral history of Hans N. Tuch (1988), pp. 7–8, The Association for Diplomatic Studies and Training, Foreign Affairs Oral History Project, Information Series, Arlington, VA, copyright 1998.
9. Thompson and Thompson, *Kremlinologist*, 155.
10. "Cold War: I Like Him," *Time*, op. cit., "Llewellyn E. Thompson (1957–1962, 1967–1969)," https://en.wikipedia.org/wiki/Llewellyn_Thompson. See also Llewellyn E. Thompson, Jr., (1904-1972), https://history.state.gov/departmenthistory/people/thompson-llewellyn-e for a profile of Thompson. The information in the profile was supplied by the Office of the Historian, Department of State. See also oral history of Vladimir I. Toumanoff (1999), p. 90, The Association for Diplomatic Studies and Training. Foreign Affairs Oral History Project, Arlington, VA, copyright 1999 (hereinafter cited as Vladimir Toumanoff oral history).
11. Thompson and Thompson, *Kremlinologist*, 154.

12. Vladimir Toumanoff oral history, 75. 80.
13. Telegram, Herter to Thompson, March 14, 1960, EL, PP, AWF-IS, Far Eastern Trip, 2; Telegram, Thompson to Herter, March 15, 1960, EL, PP, AWF-IS, Far Eastern Trip, 2.
14. Thompson to Herter, March 15, 1960, EL, PP, AWF-IS, Far Eastern Trip, 2.
15. Ibid.
16. Ibid., 3.
17. Ibid.
18. Elmer W. Lower to James C. Hagerty, March 30, 1960, 1–4, EL, PP, James C. Hagerty Papers, Far Eastern Trip. Ray Scherer was a television correspondent for NBC News.
19. Bob Pierpoint to James Hagerty, April 4, 1960, EL, PP, James C. Hagerty Papers, Far Eastern Trip.
20. John Scali to James Hagerty, April 4, 1960, EL, PP, James C. Hagerty Papers, Far Eastern Trip. In an interview with the author on October 26, 2017, Hans Tuch reinforced many of the problems that Scali explained to Hagerty. Covering the Nixon trip, according to Tuch, was "a nightmare" for the reporters.
21. Scali to Hagerty, April 4, 1960. EL, PP, James C. Hagerty Papers, Far Eastern Trip.
22. Ibid.
23. Ibid.
24. Ibid.
25. Ibid.
26. Telegram, Thompson to Herter, March 22, 1960, EL, PP, AWF-IS, Far Eastern Trip.
27. Kliment Voroshilov was the chairman of the Presidium of the Supreme Soviet at this time and, therefore, technically the head of state in the Soviet Union. Khrushchev removed Voroshilov from office, replacing him with Leonid Brezhnev, a decision that later had consequences for Khrushchev's leadership of the Soviet Union, as we now know. See Sergei Khrushchev, *Nikita Khrushchev*, 385.
28. The Hermitage is, next to the Louvre in Paris, the most distinguished art museum in the world. Built in the mid-eighteenth century, it was the home for Russia's ruling family during the Tsarist era. Its collections include some of the magnificent works of art and sculpture in the world. See https://www.hermitagemuseum.org.
29. Telegram, Thompson to Herter, March 22, 1960; EL, PP, AWF-IS, Far Eastern Trip.
30. Telegram, Herter to Thompson, March 23, 1960, EL, PP, AWF-IS, Far Eastern Trip.
31. Ibid.
32. Newton, *Eisenhower*, 93–94. On September 26, 2016, the author put the question of Mamie Eisenhower's aversion to flying to Susan Eisenhower, one of her granddaughters. Ms. Eisenhower provided a lengthy explanation as to how Miniere's ailment negatively affected her grandmother's capacity to travel comfortably by air. Susan Eisenhower was lecturing that evening at the Hamilton campus of Miami University of Ohio.
33. Telegram, Thompson to Herter, March 23, 1960, EL, PP, AWF-IS, Far Eastern Trip.

34. Telegram, Herter to Thompson, March 14, 1960, EL, PP, James C. Hagerty Papers, Far Eastern Trip.
35. Telegram, Thompson to Herter, March 17, 1960, EL, PP, AWF-IS, Far Eastern Trip.
36. Ibid.; Telegram, Herter to Thompson, March 31, 1960.
37. Ibid.; Telegram, Thompson to Herter, April 2, 1960.
38. Letter, Hans N. Tuch to V. I. Avilov, April 18, 1960, EL, PP, James C. Hagerty Papers, Far Eastern Trip.
39. Ibid., letter, Hans N. Tuch to James Hagerty, April 19, 1960.
40. Ibid., letter, Hans N. Tuch to James Hagerty, no date.
41. Ibid., letter, Hans N. Tuch to M. A. Kharlamov, Chief, Press Section, Ministry of Foreign Affairs, Moscow, May 5, 1960, EL, PP, James C. Hagerty Papers, Far Eastern Trip. Also, C. Douglas Dillon to Thompson, May 3, 1960.
42. Ibid.
43. Memorandum for the President, Subject: Gifts for Presentation during the Visit to the USSR, May 13, 1960, EL, PP, AWF-IS, Far Eastern Trip.
44. For a discussion of Khrushchev's marriages, his children, and grandchildren, see Sergei Khrushchev, *Nikita Khrushchev*, 9–11, 12, 14.
45. Gifts for presentation, EL, PP, AWF-IS, Far Eastern Trip, op. cit.
46. Ibid.
47. Ibid.
48. Ibid.
49. Ibid.
50. Ibid. One wonders what the effect on religious life in the Soviet Union might have become if President Eisenhower, and members of his party, had been photographed while worshiping on Sunday morning at Moscow's Central Baptist Church.
51. Fursenko and Naftali, *Khrushchev's Cold War*, 263.
52. Vladimir Toumanoff oral history, 79.
53. Sergei Khrushchev, *Nikita Khrushchev*, 352–53.
54. Ibid.
55. Harrison Salisbury oral history, COHP, 45–47. In his memoir, *In Confidence: Moscow's Ambassador to Six Cold War Presidents* (New York: Random House, 1995), 42, Anatoly Dobrynin refers to the dacha as the "Eisenhower Cottage."
56. Milton S. Eisenhower oral history, Eisenhower Library, 46–47.
57. Harrison Salisbury oral history, COHP, 46.
58. C. L. Sulzberger, *The Last of the Giants* (New York: Macmillan, 1970), 672–73.
59. Harrison Salisbury oral history, COHP, 46.
60. Hans N. Tuch, telephone interview with the author, August 14, 2015.
61. Vladimir Toumanoff oral history, 61.
62. Ibid.
63. Ibid.

Chapter 5

1. Specifically, these agreements included the Truman-Attlee agreement of 1950, enabling the United States to base long-range bombers in Britain, and Eisenhower's

agreement with Macmillan in 1957 to station intermediate-range Thor missiles in Britain. See Geelhoed and Edmonds, *Eisenhower, Macmillan, and Allied Unity*, 27–28.

2. Robert B. Anderson, interview with the author, October 6, 1981.

3. Thomas, *Ike's Bluff*, 308–14; Watson, *Into the Missile Age*, 307. Virtually every historian of the Eisenhower presidency, or biographer of Eisenhower, has written on various aspects of the missile gap controversy. For purposes of clarity, I will rely on the accounts of Thomas, Watson, and Reel. More detailed studies, to name several in the order of their publication, are Edgar Bottome, *The Missile Gap* (Fairfield, CT: Fairleigh Dickinson Press, 1971); John Prados, *The Soviet Estimate: U.S. Intelligence Analysis and Russian Military Strength* (New York: The Dial Press, 1982); Fred Kaplan, *The Wizards of Armageddon* (Stanford, CA: Stanford University Press, 1991); and Peter Roman, *President Eisenhower and the Missile Gap* (Ithaca, NY: Cornell University Press, 1999). The quotation from Brugioni may be found in Dino A. Brugioni, *Eyes in the Sky: Eisenhower, the CIA, and Cold War Aerial Espionage* (Annapolis, MD: Naval Institute Press, 2010), 356. Eisenhower's quotation may be found in Eisenhower, *Waging Peace*, 389–390. For an explanation of the "bomber gap" controversy of 1960, see E. Bruce Geelhoed, *Charles E. Wilson and Controversy at the Pentagon, 1953 to 1957* (Detroit, MI: Wayne State University Press, 1979), 121–34, and especially, Richard Leighton, *Strategy, Money, and the New Look, 1953–1956* (Washington, DC: Historical Office of the Secretary of Defense, 2001), 370–98.

4. William Bragg Ewald, Jr. *Eisenhower the President: Crucial Days, 1951–1960* (Englewood Cliffs, NJ: Prentice-Hall, 1981), 243–44.

5. Goodpaster, "Cold War Overflights," in Hall, ed., *Overflights*, 38–39. See also Louis Galambos, *Eisenhower: Becoming the Leader of the Free World* (Baltimore: Johns Hopkins University Press, 2018), 204.

6. Goodpaster, "Cold War Overflights," 40.

7. Ibid.

8. Thomas, *Ike's Bluff*, 175–76; Goodpaster described Khrushchev's behavior at the Geneva summit in an interview with the author, February 26, 1983. Transcript in the author's possession.

9. Goodpaster, "Cold War Overflights," in Hall, ed., *Overflights*, 37, 40.

10. James J. Killian, *Sputnik, Scientists, and Eisenhower* (Cambridge, MA: The MIT Press, 1978), 69–93; Hitchcock, *Age of Eisenhower*, 69–73.

11. Reel, *Brotherhood of Spies*, 29–30.

12. Beschloss, *May Day*, 5.

13. Richard Bissell, *Reflections of a Cold Warrior* (New Haven, CT: Yale University Press, 1995), 111–12.

14. Thomas S. Gates, interview with the author, May 7, 1982. Transcript in author's possession.

15. Beschloss, *Mayday*, 81–94; Bissell, *Reflections of a Cold Warrior*, 115–16.

16. Macmillan to Eisenhower, March 23, 1957, EL, PP, AWF-IS, Box 22, "Harold Macmillan," folder 2.

17. Eisenhower to Macmillan, March 23, 1957, EL, PP, AWF-IS, Box 22, "Harold Macmillan," folder 6.

18. Beschloss, *May Day*, 103–04; Bissell, *Reflections of a Cold Warrior*, 116–17.

19. Ambrose, *Ike's Spies*, 277.
20. Oral history with Thomas S. Gates, (1967, 1972), p. 33, Oral History Archive at Columbia, Rare Book and Manuscript Library. Columbia University in the City of New York (hereinafter cited as oral history of Thomas S. Gates, COHP). See also Reel, *Brotherhood of Spies*, 154.
21. Brugioni, *Eyes in the Sky*, 340–41.
22. Max Frankel, "Khrushchev Says Soviet Will Cut Forces A Third, Sees 'Fantastic' Weapon," *New York Times*, January 15, 1960.
23. Fursenko and Naftali, *Khrushchev's Cold War*, 252–53. Gates's comment about a "damn good" test can be found in "Red Rocket Shot Nearly 7800 Miles," *Washington Post*, January 22, 1960.
24. Thompson to Herter, January 18, 1960, in *Foreign Relations of the United States, 1958–60*, Volume X, Part 1, Doc. 141, https://history.state.gov/historicaldocuments/frus1958-60v10p1/d141.
25. Fursenko and Naftali, *Khrushchev's Cold War*, 256–58. Lodge's conversation with Khrushchev is documented in Telegram from the Embassy in the Soviet Union to the Department of State, February 9, 1960. Eyes Only Secretary from Lodge. *FRUS*, 1958–1960, X, Doc. 146, 507–09, https://history.state.gov/historicaldocuments/frus1958-60v10p1/d146.
26. Watson, *Into the Missile Age*, 315–16; Prados, *Soviet Estimate*, 87–88.
27. Thompson and Thompson, *The Kremlinologist*, 203–4.
28. Fursenko and Naftali, *Khrushchev's Cold War*, 251–52.
29. Thomas S. Gates, interview with the author, April 19, 1982.
30. Thomas, *Ike's Bluff*, 364.
31. John Wadleigh, "Thomas Sovereign Gates," in Paolo Coletta, ed., *American Secretaries of the Navy. Vol. II, 1913–1972*. (Annapolis, MD: Naval Institute Press, 1980), 890; Thomas Gates oral history, COHP, 13; Watson, *Into the Missile Age*, 323–48; Dwight D. Eisenhower, *Waging Peace*, 254; and C. W. Borklund, *Men of the Pentagon* (New York: Praeger, 1968), 184–205. See also Watson, *Into the Missile Age*, 346–48.
32. Thomas S. Gates, interview with the author, January 13, 1982. A parallel account of this episode may be found in Thomas Gates oral history, COHP, 14.
33. Interview with the author, Thomas S. Gates, January 13, 1982.
34. Jack Raymond, "Sailor for the Top Job," *New York Times Magazine*, November 29, 1959, 123. See also Thomas S. Gates, interview with the author, January 13, 1982.
35. Interview with the author, Thomas S. Gates, January 13, 1982.
36. Margaret Stroud, interview with the author, October 8, 1982.
37. Ibid.
38. Watson, *Into the Missile Age*, 346–48.
39. The circumstances surrounding the appointment of Thomas S. Gates as SECDEF remain somewhat unclear. In her interview with the author, Margaret Stroud expressed the belief that Gates understood that he would become SECDEF once Neil McElroy resigned. Although Gates denied that Eisenhower had ever made a commitment to him to become SECDEF after McElroy's resignation, many political observers in Washington believed as Stroud did about the subject. For example, the journalist Arthur Krock believed that Gordon Gray, Eisenhower's

national security adviser, was in line for both DEPSECDEF and SECDEF, but Eisenhower eventually decided not to appoint Gray because of the "commitment to Gates." Krock maintained that Gray had confirmed this information in an off-the-record conversation with him. See Krock, "Confidential Memorandum, 7 December 1959," in Arthur Krock Papers, Seeley G. Mudd Library, Princeton University. Gates believed that Eisenhower offered him the position while at the Augusta National Golf Club in November 1959 and maintained that he had no expectations to succeed McElroy when he accepted the DEPSECDEF position. Thomas S. Gates, interview, April 29, 1982. Gates's calendar shows a meeting with Eisenhower at the Augusta National Golf Club on November 22. See Thomas S. Gates Papers, Van Pelt Library, University of Pennsylvania, Box 15, Diaries and Appointment Books. In an interview with the author on February 26, 1983, Andrew Goodpaster said that he also believed that Eisenhower told Gates of his impending appointment as SECDEF while at Augusta.

40. Interview, Thomas S. Gates, April 29, 1982. Milton Eisenhower was Eisenhower's youngest brother, who was serving at the time as the president of Johns Hopkins University in Baltimore. Jones, Slater, Woodruff, and Robinson belonged to what historians have called Eisenhower's "Gang," a group of wealthy businessmen who were personal advisers and confidants to the president. See Hitchcock, *Age of Eisenhower*, 41–45, 286–87, for profiles of these men. Alfred M. Gruenther was a protégé of Dwight D. Eisenhower who served with Ike during World War II and then when Eisenhower was NATO commander between 1950 and 1952. He was Eisenhower's favorite partner at bridge and became a close adviser to Ike throughout much of Eisenhower's second term. See http://arlingtoncemetery.net/gruenthe.htm.

41. The President's News Conference of January 13, 1960, *Public Papers of the President. Dwight D. Eisenhower. 1960–61* (Washington, DC: Government Printing Office, 1961), 25–26 (hereinafter cited as *Public Papers, Eisenhower 1960–61*).

42. Ibid., 28–29.

43. Watson, *Into the Missile Age*, 348–49.

44. U.S. Congress. House. 86th Congress, 2d Session. Department of Defense Appropriations 1961. *Hearings* before a Subcommittee of the Committee on Appropriations (Washington, DC: Government Printing Office, 1960), 7 (hereinafter referred to as the House Subcommittee on Defense Appropriations, 1960). See also *Statements and Addresses of Thomas S. Gates, Jr., II* (Washington, DC: Government Printing Office, 1960), 70. In his interview with the author, Robert B. Anderson made the same point as did Gates about comparisons between the military strength of the United States and that of the Soviet Union. "You really can't compare American and Soviet forces," Anderson said. "[For one thing], the Soviets need a large standing Army because they have enemies on all sides, particularly China."

45. *Hearings* before the House Subcommittee on Defense Appropriations, 1960, 26. See also *Statements and Addresses of Thomas S. Gates, Jr.*, II, 89.

46. Ibid., 132–33. For a discussion of the DEW line, see also Watson, *Into the Missile Age*, 404–5.

47. Watson, *Into the Missile Age*, 349–50.

48. Minutes of Press Conference Held by the Hon. Thomas S. Gates, Jr., January 21, 1960, in *Statements and Addresses of Thomas S. Gates, Jr., II*, 255–56.

Notes to Chapter 5

49. "U.S Is Eaves-dropping on Russian Missiles," *Washington Daily News*, January 20, 1960.

50. Beverly Smith, "On the Hottest Spot in the Pentagon," *Saturday Evening Post*, May 28, 1960, 113. See also Watson, *Into the Missile Age*, 356.

51. Memorandum for the Record, by Thomas S. Gates, Jr., 16, January 1960 in Thomas S. Gates Collection, Van Pelt Library, University of Pennsylvania., Thomas S. Gates, Secretary of Defense, 1959-60, Box 12, Memoranda.

52. Russell Porter, "S.A.C. Chief Urges Defense Speed-Up," *New York Times*, January 20, 1960. See also Edward Kolodziej, *The Uncommon Defense and Congress, 1945–1963* (Columbus, OH: Ohio State University Press, 1966), 314–15.

53. "Secretary Gates Answers Questions on National Defense," *Department of State Bulletin*, Vol. XLII, No. 1085 (April 11, 1960), 557–59.

54. Thomas S. Gates, interview with the author, April 19, 1982.

55. Thomas Gates oral history, COHP, 50–51.

56. Thomas, *Ike's Bluff*, 308–14; Watson, *Into the Missile Age*, 305–08; Reel, *Brotherhood of Spies*, 153–54.; Brinkley, *American Moonshot*, 166–67.

57. Thomas, *Ike's Bluff*, 308–14.

58. Joseph Alsop, "Matter of Fact," *New York Herald Tribune*, January 26, 1960, January 27, 1960.

59. Alsop, "Matter of Fact," *New York Herald Tribune*, January 28, 1960, January 29, 1960, January 30, 1960. Early in 1961, Alsop admitted in his columns that the missile gap had never existed, referring to new information obtained by the United States later in 1960 from satellite photography, not from U-2 flights. See Joseph W. Alsop with Adam Platt, *"I've Seen the Best of It"" Memoirs* (New York: W. W. Norton, 1992), 414–15.

60. Eisenhower, quoted in Thomas, *Ike's Bluff*, 309.

61. Thomas S. Gates, interview with the author, April 19, 1982.

62. Fursenko and Naftali, *Khrushchev's Cold War*, 254. Douglas Brinkley also covers Kennedy's exploit of the missile gap in its early stages in *American Moonshot*, 119–20, 165–67.

63. Calendar for January 1960, Diaries and Appointment Books, Box 15, Thomas S. Gates Collection, Van Pelt Library, University of Pennsylvania.

64. Memorandum of Conference with the President, February 2, 1960, Dwight D. Eisenhower Library, Papers as President, Ann Whitman File, DDE Diary Series, Box 47, Staff Notes (2). Andrew Goodpaster was the note-taker for the meeting. His memo is addressed February 4, 1960.

65. Ibid.

66. Ibid.

67. The President's News Conference of January 26, 1960, *Public Papers, Eisenhower, 1960–61*, 126–27.

68. The President's News Conference of February 3, 1960, *Public Papers, Eisenhower, 1960–61*, 144–45.

69. Ibid.

70. Ibid.

71. Interview on television with Senator Prescott Bush of Connecticut, Washington, D.C., January 28, 1960, 3, *Statements and Addresses of Thomas S. Gates, Jr., II*.

72. James D. Hittle, interview with the author, October 27, 1982.

73. U.S. Congress. Senate. 86th Congress, 2d Session. Department of Defense Appropriations. *Hearings* before the Subcommittee on Appropriations. February 1, 1960. (Washington, DC: Government Printing Office, 1960), 41–42. See also *Statements and Addresses of Thomas S. Gates, Jr, II*, 372–73.

74. The President's News Conference of February 11, 1960, *Public Papers, Eisenhower, 1960–61*, 198.

75. Ibid.

76. Radio and Television Address to the American People on the Eve of South American Trip. February 21, 1960, *Public Papers, Eisenhower, 1960–61*, 203–5.

77. Ibid.

78. James D. Hittle, interview with the author.

79. Investigation of the Preparedness Program. *Fifteenth Report of the Preparedness Investigating Subcommittee of the Committee on Armed Services*. United States Senate. 86th Congress. 1st Session. The Closing of the Overhaul and Repair Department, Naval Air Station, Corpus Christi, Tex. (Washington, DC: Government Printing Office, 1959), 11.

80. Noel Gayler, interview with the author, October 26, 1982. Transcript in the author's possession.

81. Ibid. See also Letter, Lyndon B. Johnson to Thomas S. Gates, February 10, 1959, in *Fifteenth Report of the Preparedness Subcommittee*, 1959, 14. Gates also recounted the meeting with Johnson, Rayburn, George Mahon, and Ken Belieu in an interview with the author, October 5, 1981.

82. Ibid.; also, Thomas Gates oral history, COHP, 29–30. Also, Gates's calendar for 1960 shows appointments with Johnson in his office on January 15 and March 7. The closing of the work at Corpus Christi remained a point of contention between Gates and Johnson for many years. After leaving the Pentagon, Gates was visiting Washington on one occasion when Johnson was the president of the United States. Learning of Gates's presence in Washington, LBJ contacted him and asked him to come over to the White House. "Have you closed any naval bases recently?" Johnson asked, humorously this time. Gates also recalled that LBJ was not the only member of the preparedness subcommittee who was angry when not consulted on navy business. "Margaret Chase Smith (R-Maine) was murder on those things, too," Gates remembered. "She was absolutely furious when she wasn't consulted about any navy work done anywhere in the country. She was tough when she didn't get the business." Thomas Gates, interview with the author, October 5, 1981.

83. Thomas Gates oral history, COHP, 32–33. The nature of the meeting between Eisenhower and Gates to discuss the hearings of the preparedness subcommittee on March 16 needs to be handled with a certain measure of caution since the meeting does not appear on the calendars either of Eisenhower or Gates for that particular day, March 15. The calendars of each man were scrupulously maintained and documented. Gates's calendar does not show any meeting with Eisenhower on March 15 but does show one on March 8 from 3:15 to 4:00. Gates's calendar also shows a meeting with Lyndon Johnson for 5:30 on March 7, perhaps one of the LBJ/Sam Rayburn/John McCormack discussions of defense policy. Information about Gates's calendar of appointments may be found in the Thomas Sovereign Gates, Jr. Collection, University Archives, Van Pelt Library, the University of Pennsylvania, Box 15. Gates recalls that his meeting with Ike took place in the family residence of

the White House, not in the Oval Office. As for Eisenhower, the only meeting at the Mansion that is recorded with Gates, off the record, is for March 18, two days after the March 16 hearings. Also attending that meeting, however, were members of the Republican leadership in the House and Senate. "Appointments Cards," Dwight D. Eisenhower Library.

84. Interview with the author, Thomas S. Gates, October 5, 1981.

85. James D. Hittle, interview with the author.

86. U.S. Congress. Senate. 86th Congress. 2d Session. Missiles, Space, and Other Defense Matters. *Hearings* Before the Preparedness Investigating Committee of the Committee on Armed Services in Conjunction with the Committee on Aeronautical and Space Sciences. (Washington, DC: Government Printing Office, 1960), 461–62. See also *Statements and Addresses of Thomas S. Gates, III*, 444–45.

87. Ibid., 463–64.

88. Ibid., 485–86.

89. For a comprehensive account of the revisions in the FY 1961 defense budget and their effect on individual defense programs and weapons systems, see Watson, *Into the Missile Age*, 358–59.

90. Ibid. A full reading of the testimony given by Gates before the House Subcommittee on Defense Appropriations may be found in U.S. Congress. House. 86th Congress. 2d Session. Modification of Defense Budget. *Hearings* before The Subcommittee on Appropriations (Washington, DC: Government Printing Office, 1960), 311–17.

91. The President's News Conference of March 30, 1960, *Public Papers, Eisenhower, 1960–61*, 319–25.

92. Text of Address by Secretary of Defense Thomas S. Gates, Jr., before the Annual Meeting of the Associated Press. New York, New York. April 25, 1960, *New York Times*, April 26, 1960, 26; see also *Statements and Addresses by Thomas S. Gates, Jr., III*, 12–14.

93. Watson, *Into the Missile Age*, 358–60.

94. Once passed by Congress, the defense budget contained approximately $600 million more in additional spending than the administration requested. These sums occurred as a result of increases in the House bill, and increases in the Senate bill, that were added in conference committee. The administration, Gates in particular, chose not to challenge the relatively modest increases passed by Congress. See Watson, *Into the Missile Age*, 358–59.

95. Gates quoted in Ewald, *Eisenhower the President*, 29.

96. Dwight D. Eisenhower to Thomas S. Gates, April 6, 1960, Box 2, Thomas Sovereign Gates Collection, University Archives, Van Pelt Library, University of Pennsylvania.

97. Reel, *Brotherhood of Spies*, 47.

Chapter 6

1. The President's News Conference of April 27, 1960, *Public Papers, Eisenhower, 1960–61*, 364–65.

2. Ibid., 365.

3. For reading on the U-2 crisis, see Ambrose, *Eisenhower, II*, 571–80; and *Ike's Spies*, 279–90; Beschloss, *May Day;* Boyle, *Eisenhower*, 136–40; Brinkley, *American Moonshot*, 197–98; Eisenhower, *Waging Peace*, 550–57; Fursenko and Naftali, *Khrushchev's Cold War*, 263–91; Galambos, *Eisenhower*, 204, 206; Hitchcock, *Age of Eisenhower*, 462–69; Lyon, *Eisenhower: Portrait of the Hero*, 808–815; Newton, *Eisenhower*, 312–18; Parmet, *Eisenhower and the American Crusades*, 555–59; Reel, *Brotherhood of Spies*, 173–97; Smith, *Eisenhower in War and Peace*, 551–55; Thomas, *Ike's Bluff*, 365–93, Thompson and Thompson, *The Kremlinologist*, 202–21; Watson, *Into the Missile Age*, 718–24; and Wise and Ross, *The U-2 Affair*. I also wish to add that Anthony Edmonds and I gave extensive coverage to the U-2 crisis in our book, *Eisenhower, Macmillan and Allied Unity, 1957–1961*, 97–130, and I relied heavily on that research for many of the conclusions in this chapter. In addition, I covered the U-2 crisis and the collapse of the Paris summit in my article, "Dwight D. Eisenhower, the Spy Plane, and the Summit: A Quarter Century Retrospective," *Presidential Studies Quarterly*, XVII, 1 (Winter, 1987), 95–106.

4. Thomas, *Ike's Bluff*, 336–37.

5. Memorandum of Discussion at the 444th Meeting of the National Security Council, May 9, 1960, *FRUS, 1958–1960*, X, Doc. 149, 516–17, https://history.state.gov/historicaldocuments/frus1958-60v10p1/d149; The President's News Conference of May 11, 1960, *Public Papers, Eisenhower, 1960–61*, 403.

6. C. Douglas Dillon, interview with the author, October 21, 1981.

7. Khrushchev, quoted in Harrison Salisbury, *A Journey for Our Times* (New York: Harper and Row, 1983), 489–90; see also Beschloss, *May Day*, 256–57.

8. Charles E. Bohlen, *Witness to History, 1929–1969* (New York: W. W. Norton, 1991), 466.

9. Thompson and Thompson, *The Kremlinologist*, 187; Feifer, "If the U-2 Hadn't Flown," Cowley, ed., *What Ifs of American History*, 236.

10. Memorandum for the Record, February 8, 1960, written by A. J. Goodpaster, Dwight D. Eisenhower Library, Online documents, U-2 Crisis, https://www.eisenhowerlibrary.gov/research/online-documents/u-2-spy-plane-incident. See also https://www.independent.co.uk/news/uk/home-news/revealed-the-rafs-secret-cold-war-heroes-1285189.html.

11. John Eisenhower, quoted in Thomas, *Ike's Bluff*, 369–70; also Boyle, *Eisenhower*, 138.

12. Brugioni, *Eyes in the Sky*, 341–44; Paul Lashmar, "Revealed: The RAF's Secret Cold War Heroes," https://www.independent.co.uk/news/uk/home-news/revealed-the-rafs-secret-cold-war-heroes-1285189.html.

13. Telegram from the Embassy in the Soviet Union to the Department of State, February 9, 1960, op. cit.

14. Osgood Caruthers, "Khrushchev Back Home, Urges Pre-Summit Calm," *New York Times*, March 6, 1960.

15. Bissell, *Reflections of a Cold Warrior*, 122–23; Ambrose, *Eisenhower II*, 567; Geelhoed and Edmonds, *Eisenhower, Macmillan, and Allied Unity*, 104–05.

16. Peebles, *Shadow Flights*, 256–57.

17. Thompson and Thompson, *The Kremlinologist*, 211.

18. Sergei Khrushchev, *Nikita Khrushchev*, 367–69; Geelhoed and Edmonds, *Eisenhower, Macmillan, and Allied Unity*, 106.

Notes to Chapter 6

19. Thompson to Herter, March 31, 1960, EL, PP, AWF-IS, Far Eastern Trip.

20. Memorandum for the Record, April 25, 1960, prepared by A. J. Goodpaster. Eisenhower Library online, https://www.eisenhowerlibrary.gov/research/online-documents/u-2-spy-plane-incident. A useful account of the roles played by Allen Dulles and Richard Bissell may be found in Peter Grose, *Gentleman Spy: The Life of Allen Dulles* (Boston, MA: Houghton Mifflin, 1994), 479–90.

21. Prados, *Soviet Estimate*, 96–98. See also Brugioni, *Eyes in the Sky*, 345–46, for a precise listing of the targets that Powers was supposed to photograph; also Peebles, *Shadow Flights*, 260–61, and Reel, *Brotherhood of Spies*, 167–81.

22. Feifer, "If the U-2 Hadn't Flown," in Cowley, ed., *What Ifs of American History*, 234, 256.

23. Gregory W. Pedlow and Donald E. Welzenbach, *The Central Intelligence Agency and Overhead Reconnaissance: The U-2 and OXCART Programs, 1954–1974* (New York: Skyhorse Publishing, 2016), 174–75.

24. Prados, *Soviet Estimate*, 98.

25. Powers, Francis Gary, with Curt Gentry, *Operation Overflight: A Memoir of the U-2 Incident* (New York: Tower Publications, 1970), 78.

26. Ibid., 78; Reel, *Brotherhood of Spies*, 178–79.

27. Ibid., 89; interview with the author, Thomas S. Gates, May 14, 1982; oral history of Douglas Dillon (1987), pp. 26–28, Association for Diplomatic Studies and Training, Foreign Affairs Oral History Program, Arlington, VA, copyright 1999. Dillon's oral history transcript does not have its pages numbered. I numbered the pages by hand and this reference was on "my" pages 26–27. Dillon was one of those who believed that Powers should have committed suicide with the poison pin. Dillon stated that "we didn't assume [that Powers would use the pin] but we knew that he was supposed to." Dillon oral history, 28. See also Hill with McCubbin, *Five Presidents*, 66.

28. Bissell, *Reflections of a Cold Warrior*, 127, 129.

29. C. Douglas Dillon, interview with the author.

30. Bohlen, *Witness to History*, 466; Sergei Khrushchev, *Nikita Khrushchev*, 374.

31. Robert Rhodamer, "Recollections," in Hall, ed. *Cold War Overflights*, 31.

32. Sergei Khrushchev, *Nikita Khrushchev*, 374–75; Fursenko and Naftali, *Khrushchev's Cold War*, 265–66, Reel, *Brotherhood of Spies*, 179, 186.

33. Sergei Khrushchev, *Nikita Khrushchev*, 376–77.

34. Hans N. Tuch, interview with the author, August 14, 2015. See also Fursenko and Naftali, *Khrushchev's Cold War*, 206.

35. Douglas Dillon oral history, Association for Diplomatic Studies and Training, 26–27.

36. Jordan, *Goodpaster*, 110. John Eisenhower believed that the CIA had betrayed his father by giving Powers a parachute to use in the event of an emergency. See Ambrose, *Ike's Spies*, 279.

37. John Eisenhower, *Strictly Personal*, 270–71.

38. Fursenko and Naftali, *Khrushchev's Cold War*, 267; Bohlen, *Witness to History*, 463–64; Reel, *Brotherhood of Spies*, 8, 9, 86.

39. Beschloss, *May Day*, 45.

40. Thomas S. Gates, interviews with the author, May 7, May 14, 1982. Gates maintained that Allen Dulles knew of Khrushchev's speech prior to his arrival at

the Rock. In *Brotherhood of Spies*, 8, 9, Monte Reel maintains that Dulles learned of the content of Khrushchev's speech once he arrived at the Rock.

41. Vladimir Toumanoff oral history, p. 89. See also Thompson and Thompson, *The Kremlinologist*, 211–12.

42. Geelhoed, "Dwight D. Eisenhower, the Spy Plane, and the Summit," *Presidential Studies Quarterly*, 98.

43. Editorial Note, *FRUS, 1958–1960*, X, Doc. 147, 511–12, https://history.state.gov/historicaldocuments/frus1958-60v10p1/d147; Bohlen, *Witness to History*, 465; Douglas Dillon oral history, Association for Diplomatic Studies and Training, 27.

44. Thomas S. Gates, interviews with the author, May 7, May 14, 1982.

45. Wise and Ross, *The U-2 Affair*, 49.

46. Thomas S. Gates, interview with the author, May 14, 1982.

47. Editorial Note, *FRUS, 1958–1960*, X, Doc. 147, 511–12, https://history.state.gov/historicaldocuments/frus1958-60v10p1/d147; as Anatoly Dobrynin reported in his memoir, *In Confidence*, Khrushchev severely disciplined Malik for his indiscretion but, following an intervention by Andrei Gromyko several weeks later, Malik was reinstated. Dobrynin, *In Confidence*, 39–40.

48. Sergei Khrushchev, *Nikita Khrushchev*, 382. See also Beschloss, *May Day*, 55–57. In his account, Beschloss indicates that Ambassador Thompson heard Malik's statement, directly, rather than from Rolf Solman, Sweden's ambassador to the Soviet Union, as some accounts have it.

49. Oral history interview with Hans N. Tuch (1988), 6, 7, The Association for Diplomatic Studies and Training, Foreign Affairs Oral History Project. See also Tuch, *Arias*, 82; Thompson and Thompson, *The Kremlinologist*, 212–14, Tuch, interview with the author.

50. Sergei Khrushchev, *Nikita Khrushchev*, 381. The text of the release for May 5, 1960, may be found in "National Aeronautics and Space Administration, Press Release on Missing U.S. Plane," May 5, 1960, EL, Online Documents, U-2 Crisis, see https://www.eisenhowerlibrary.gov/research/online-documents/u-2-spy-plane-incident.

51. Hill with McCubbins, *Five Presidents*, 66–67.

52. Thomas S. Gates, interview with the author, May 14, 1982. See also Ambrose, *Ike's Spies*, 285.

53. Ambrose, *Eisenhower*, II, 574.

54. Ibid., 574–75; Watson, *Into the Missile Age*, 721.

55. Memorandum for the Record, by Thomas S. Gates, Jr., 9 May 1960, Box 12. Thomas S. Gates, Jr. as Secretary of Defense, 1959–60, Thomas S. Gates, Jr. Collection, Van Pelt Library, University of Pennsylvania.

56. Horne, *Macmillan*, II, 226; Macmillan, *Pointing the Way*, 196.

57. Horne, *Macmillan*, II, 226, 228; Macmillan, *Pointing the Way*, 205.

58. Ibid. See also Murphy, *Diplomat among Warriors*, 441.

59. Telegram from the Embassy in the Soviet Union to the Department of State, *FRUS, 1958–1960, X*, Doc. 150, 519–20, https://history.state.gov/historicaldocuments/frus1958-60v10p1/d150. See also Khrushchev, quoted in Beschloss, *May Day*, 256–57; Salisbury, *Journey for Our Times*, 489–90.

60. Macmillan, *Pointing the Way*, 200–201.

61. Sergei Khrushchev, *Nikita Khrushchev*, 380.

62. The President's News Conference of May 11, 1960, *Public Papers, Eisenhower, 1960–61*, 403–4.

63. Ibid. Eisenhower had used the words "No one wants another Pearl Harbor" on November 3, 1959, to justify intelligence gathering when he appeared at the cornerstone-laying ceremony for the new headquarters of the CIA in Langley, Virginia. See Brugioni, *Eyes in the Sky*, 341.

64. The President's News Conference of May 11, 1960, *Public Papers, Eisenhower, 1960–61*, 403–4.

65. Ibid.
66. Ibid.
67. Ibid.
68. Ibid.

69. Oral history with C. Douglas Dillon (1972), pp. 56–58. Oral History Archives at Columbia Rare Book and Manuscript Library. Columbia University in the City of New York (hereinafter cited as Douglas Dillon oral history, COHP).

70. Oral history with James C. Hagerty (1982), p. 61, Oral History Archives at Columbia, Rare Book & Manuscript Library. Columbia University in The City of New York (hereinafter cited as James Hagerty oral history, COHP). Eisenhower also used the same words of "strapping an American plane to his back" in a meeting with congressional leaders on May 26, 1960, after the summit collapsed. See Reel, *Brotherhood of Spies*, 197, and Beschloss, *May Day*, 309.

71. Douglas Dillon oral history, Association for Diplomatic Studies and Training, 26.

72. Oral history interview with General Dwight D. Eisenhower (1964), 44–46, John Foster Dulles Oral History Collection, Public Policy Papers, Department of Rare Book and Special Collections, Princeton University Library. See also Eisenhower, *Waging Peace*, 550–53.

73. Max Frankel, *Times of My Life* (New York: Random House, 1999), 184–85.

74. Douglas Dillon oral history, COHP, 55. Dillon made the same comments with the author on October 21, 1981. "Ike was a man of principle and couldn't see the point in sending someone else out to take the blame."

75. Smith, *Eisenhower*, 753–55.
76. Jordan, *An Unsung Soldier*, 109.
77. Thomas, *Ike's Bluff*, 369–70.
78. Harrison Salisbury oral history, COHP, 41, 45.
79. Goodpaster, "Cold War Overflights," in Hall, ed., *Cold War Overflights*, 44.
80. State Department Cable, Paris to Washington, 14 May 1960, Dwight D. Eisenhower Library, Papers as President, White House Office: Office of the Staff Secretary, International Trips and Meetings, "Summit, etc.," Box 11, folder 2, 1–2.
81. Ibid., 8–9.
82. Macmillan, *Pointing the Way*, 202–03, Horne, *Macmillan, II*, 227. There are differences of interpretation as to Khrushchev's demands for a public apology from Eisenhower. In his memoirs, *In Confidence*, Anatoly Dobrynin expressed the view that Khrushchev added the public apology from Eisenhower as a condition for negotiations without approval by the Politburo. See Dobrynin, *In Confidence*, 42. Khrushchev's biographer William Taubman is of the view that the Politburo expected an apology from Eisenhower as a condition for negotiations and Khrushchev

was not authorized to negotiate without such an apology. See Taubman, *Khrushchev*, 460. Fursenko and Naftali tend to support Dobrynin's position. See Fursenko and Naftali, *Khrushchev's Cold War*, 282.

83. Sergei Khrushchev, *Nikita Khrushchev*, 386–87. In Paris, the American journalist C. L. Sulzberger recorded a conversation with Yuri Zhukov from the Soviet embassy that Khrushchev "cannot understand" why Eisenhower refused to see him prior to the opening of the summit conference; Sulzberger, *The Last of the Giants*, 669.

84. State Department Cable, Tripartite Heads of Government Meeting, Paris, May 16, 1960, EL, PP, WHO:OSS, International Trips and Meetings, Box 11, folder 4, 1–2.

85. Ibid., 9.

86. Thomas S. Gates, interview with the author, May 7, 1982. See also Macmillan, *Pointing the Way*, 204; Horne, *Macmillan, II*, 207.

87. Memorandum for the Record by Ambassador Llewelyn Thompson, May 16, 1960, EL, PP, WHO:OSS, International Trips and Meetings, "U-2" (2 [May 16–21]. Also, Sergei Khrushchev, interview with the author.

88. Thomas S. Gates, interview with the author, May 14, 1982.

89. Ibid. See also John N. Irwin, interview with the author; Margaret Stroud, interview with the author. In testimony later given to the Senate Foreign Relations Committee, Gates mentioned that the surprise attack at Pearl Harbor in 1941 figured into his thinking about calling for the alert in Paris. Asked by Senator Alexander Wiley (R-Wisconsin), "You had in mind what the condition of the country was at the time of Pearl Harbor, how we were asleep?" Gates replied, "I certainly did." See Events Incident to the Summit Conference, *Hearings*, Committee on Foreign Relations, U.S. Congress, 86th Congress, 2nd sess. (Washington, DC: Government Printing Office, 1960), 132.

90. Ibid., 394. See also Interview with Senator Leverett Saltonstall, June 26, 1960, in *Statements and Addresses of Thomas S. Gates, Jr., III*, 5–6; Beschloss, *May Day*, 282–84, and Watson, *Into the Missile Age*, 722–23. Eisenhower acknowledged his support of Gates's action in a conversation during a meeting of the National Security Council on May 24, 1960. See Memorandum of Discussion at the 445th Meeting of the National Security Council, May 24, 1960, *FRUS, 1958–1960, X*, Doc. 155, 524, https://history.state.gov/historicaldocuments/frus1958-60v10p1/d155.

91. Watson, *Into the Missile Age*, 723; Wise and Ross, *The U-2 Affair*, 146–47.

92. Macmillan, *Pointing the Way*, 204–05.

93. John Eisenhower, *Strictly Personal*, 223–24.

94. State Department Cable, American Embassy Paris to SecState, Washington, 16 May 1960, in EL, PP, WHO:OSS, "U-2," Box 11, folder 2.

95. Minutes of the Cabinet meeting, May 26, 1960, *FRUS, 1958–1960, IX*, Doc. 194, 515–16, https://history.state.gov/historicaldocuments/frus1958-60v10p1/d194.

96. Thomas, *Ike's Bluff*, 381; Fursenko and Naftali, *Khrushchev's Cold War*, 284–85; Beschloss, *May Day*, 284–85.

97. Charles de Gaulle, quoted in Brugioni, *Eyes in the Sky*, 352.

98. Ibid., 352.

99. Statement by President Eisenhower, May 16, 1960, in EL, PP, WHO:OSS, Box 11, "U-2" (2) [May 16–21].

100. Ibid.

Notes to Chapter 6

101. Ibid.

102. Macmillan, *Pointing the Way*, 205; Horne, *Macmillan, II*, 208.

103. Statement by N. S. Khrushchev, Chairman of the USSR Council of Ministers to President Charles de Gaulle of France, Prime Minister Harold Macmillan of Great Britain, and President Eisenhower of the USA, 16 May 1960, in EL, PP, WHO:OSS, International Trips and Meetings, Box 11, Folder 4.

104. Ibid., 16.

105. There was discussion in Paris at the time of the summit that Khrushchev deliberately overplayed the U-2 controversy because, according to Yvan Koudriastsev, the counselor for economic affairs in the Soviet embassy, "the Soviets want to wait until there is a new administration in the United States before taking up the important problems which were to have been discussed at the Summit." Memorandum of Conversation, "Summit Meeting," 18 May 1960, American Embassy, Paris, EL, PP, WHO:OSS, Box 11, International Trips and Meetings, U-2, II [May 16–21].

106. Thomas S. Gates, interview with the author, May 14, 1982.

107. Harold Macmillan, interview with Robert McKenzie, British Broadcasting Corporation, regarding his book *Pointing the Way*, 1972, Conservative Central Office (CCO) Papers, 20/8/6, 14, Bodleian Library, Oxford, UK.

108. Official Transcript, Meeting of Heads of Government, Paris, 16 May 1960, EL, PP, WHO:OSS, Box 11, "International Trips and Meetings," "U-2" [May16–21], Box 11, folder 1.

109. Ibid., 11.

110. Telegram from the Embassy in the Soviet Union to the Department of State Moscow, September 9, 1960, 9 p.m., *FRUS, 1958–60:* X, Doc. 165, https://history.state.gov/historicaldocuments/frus1958-60v10p1/d165.

111. Vernon Walters oral history, 91.

112. Thomas S. Gates, interviews with the author, May 7, 1982, May 14, 1982. See also John Eisenhower, *Strictly Personal*, 274–75.

113. Telegram from the Delegation at the Summit Conference to the Department of State, Paris, May 17, 1960, *FRUS, 1958–1960,* IX, Doc. 176, 460–61, https://history.state.gov/historicaldocuments/frus1958-60v10p1/d176.

114. Fursenko and Naftali, *Khrushchev's Cold War*, 288–89.

115. Wise and Ross, *The U-2 Affair*, 161, 164. Fursenko and Naftali, *Khrushchev's Cold War*, 288–89.

116. "Transcript of the Questions and Answers at Khrushchev's News Conference," *New York Times*, May 19, 1960, 8, 9, 10. Khrushchev's reference to the Battle of Stalingrad was made in view of his experience as an officer in the Red Army who participated in that campaign in World War II.

117. Ibid.

118. Ibid.

119. Ibid.

120. "Eisenhower Millionaire Threatens Peace," *Tass*, May 21, 1960, reported in the *New York Times*, May 21, 1960.

121. Beschloss, *May Day*, 304.

122. Donald Janson, "Stevenson Holds U.S. To Blame, Too," *New York Times*, May 20, 1960. See also Lyon, *Portrait of the Hero*, 813, for criticism of Gates's action

in calling the alert as an example of overreaction to the situation in Paris. Lyon referred to Gates's action as "further foolishness."

123. Ibid.

124. Events Incident to the Summit Conference, *Hearings*, Senate Foreign Relations Committee, 135.

125. Walter Lippman, "Today and Tomorrow," *Washington Post*, May 19, 1960.

126. Thomas S. Gates, interview with the author, April 19, 1982. There were several occasions when Gates told the author about his encounter with Arthur Krock in May 1960. On one occasion, Gates recalled that Krock said to him, "Sit down, Tom," and on another, he said, "Sit down, pal." I have chosen to use the first version.

127. Arthur Krock, "An Act of 'Prudence' in the Right Place," in "In the Nation," *New York Times*, May 24, 1960.

128. Ibid.

129. Ibid.

130. Thomas S. Gates, interview with the author, April 19, 1982.

131. Thomas S. Gates to Arthur Krock, May 25, 1960, in Arthur Krock Papers, Seeley G. Mudd Library, Princeton University, Princeton, New Jersey.

132. Krock to Gates, May 27, 1960, Krock Papers, Seeley G. Mudd Library, Princeton University.

133. Andrew Goodpaster, interview with the author, February 26, 1983.

134. Ibid. In fact, when Eisenhower gave his televised report to the nation on May 25, 1960, to discuss the collapse of the Paris summit, he specifically mentioned his support and approval of Gates's measure. Radio and Television Report to the American People on the Events in Paris, *Public Papers, Eisenhower, 1960–61*, 438–39.

135. John N. Irwin II, interview with the author, October 6, 1981.

136. Events Incident to the Summit Conference, *Hearings*, Senate Foreign Relations Committee, 161. Richard Nixon visited Poland in August 1959 on the return from his trip to Russia. See Ambrose, *Nixon, I*, 532.

137. Events Incident to the Summit Conference, *Hearings*, Senate Foreign Relations Committee, 161.

138. Murphy, *Diplomat among Warriors*, 440–41.

139. Ibid.

140. Minutes of the Cabinet Meeting, May 26, 1960, *FRUS, 1958–1960*, IX, Doc. 195, 515–16.

141. Vladimir Toumanoff oral history, 90.

142. Hans N. Tuch, telephone interview with the author, August 14, 2015.

143. Dillon to Amembassy PARIS TO SEC, May 16, 1960, EL, PP, AWF-IS, International Meetings and Trips, Far Eastern Trip.

144. Vladimir Toumanoff oral history, 90.

145. Sulzberger, *The Last of the Giants*, 672–73.

Chapter 7

1. The President's News Conference of May 11, 1960, *Public Papers, Eisenhower, 1960–61*, 405.

Notes to Chapter 7

2. Hans N. Tuch to M. A. Kharlamov, May 5, 1960, in EL, James Hagerty Papers, Far Eastern Trip.

3. President Eisenhower's Itinerary, May 7, 1960, EL, PP, AWF-IS, Far Eastern Trip. See also President Eisenhower's Itinerary, March 22, 1960. Kliment Voroshilov had been demoted by Khrushchev in the Soviet hierarchy on May 7, 1960, following a diplomatic indiscretion that involved the Iranian ambassador to the Soviet Union. Khrushchev chose Leonid Brezhnev to replace Voroshilov and it was, therefore, highly likely that the future leader of the Soviet Union would have been standing on the tarmac to welcome Eisenhower to the Soviet Union on June 10, 1960. See Sergei Khrushchev, *Nikita Khrushchev*, 385.

4. Edward Freers to S. V. Kaftanov, May 14, 1960, EL, PP, James Hagerty Papers, Far Eastern Trip.

5. Hans N. Tuch to James Hagerty, n.d., EL, PP, James C. Hagerty Papers, Far Eastern Trip.

6. Moscow (Thompson) to Secretary of State, May 16, 1960, EL, PP, AWF-IS, Far Eastern Trip, Box 50. Roberta Peters was apparently scheduled to perform at the annual meeting of the Westinghouse Corporation in Atlantic City in June 1960, around the time of Eisenhower's scheduled visit to the Soviet Union. "For patriotic considerations," she wanted the State Department and the White House to intervene with Westinghouse to cancel her engagement. Westinghouse was not inclined to cooperate, however.

7. Robert J. Donovan, *Eisenhower: The Inside Story of the First Term* (New York: Harper, 1956).

8. Robert J. Donovan to James C. Hagerty, June 7, 1960, James C. Hagerty Papers, Far Eastern Trip. This message was delivered to Hagerty through Betty Allen, a member of his staff. Following the receipt of this message, there is no indication that Secretary of State Herter followed up with President Eisenhower about Donovan's request. There appears to be no memorandum of conversation, or telephone message, between the two men, either in Eisenhower's files or those of Herter.

9. Minutes of Cabinet Meeting, May 26, 1960.

10. *Tentative List of State Department Personnel for the President's Trip to the USSR (approved by the Secretary)*, April 10, 1960, EL, PP, James C. Hagerty Papers, Far Eastern Trip. On the list, Heyward Isham is identified as a staff assistant to Mr. [Charles] Bohlen. John A. Armitage, Harry G. Barnes, Jr., and Richard T. Davies are representing the State Department's Office of Soviet Union Affairs.

11. President Eisenhower's Itinerary, May 7, 1960, op. cit.

12. Ibid.

13. Kistiakowsky, *A Scientist at the White House*, 208–40.

14. President Eisenhower's Itinerary, May 7, 1960, op. cit.

15. Ibid.

16. "Armitage, John Austin," in *The Biographic Register of the Department of State, 1963*. I am indebted to Tiffany A. Cabrera, Ph.D., in the Office of the Historian of the Department of State for providing the information about Armitage, Harry G. Barnes, Richard T. Davies, and Heyward Isham. See also *Tentative List of State Department Personnel for the President's Trip to the USSR (approved by the Secretary)*, April 10, 1960, EL, PP, James C. Hagerty Papers, Far Eastern Trip.

17. Arrival Remarks at Moscow—June 10, EL, PP, AWF-IS, Far Eastern Trip.

18. Franklin D. Roosevelt was the first American president to visit the Soviet Union, his visit occurring on February 4–11, 1945, at Yalta in the Crimea. With World War II in Europe nearing its completion, Roosevelt, Churchill, and Stalin met to discuss the issues confronting each country in the postwar era. For a worthy sample of the scholarship about Roosevelt and the Yalta Conference, see Reynolds, *Summits*, 103–61, and James MacGregor Burns, *Roosevelt: The Soldier of Freedom* (New York: Harcourt, Brace, Jovanovich, 1970), 564–80.

19. Arrival Remarks at Moscow, June 10, op. cit. Eisenhower's reference to "promoting broader exchanges" is a direct mention of the value that Ike placed on the American-Soviet interactions made possible by the Lacy-Zaroubin Agreement.

20. As mentioned previously in this book, Eisenhower visited the Soviet Union in August 1945, near the end of World War II. See Eisenhower, *Crusade in Europe*, 457–71.

21. Arrival Remarks at Moscow, June 10, op. cit. The Luzhniki Stadium opened in 1956 and was known as the Central Lenin Stadium between 1956 and 1992. It was the Soviet Union's largest athletic complex and hosted a large number of national and international sporting events, including track and field and soccer. The complex was also the site of the 1980 Summer Olympics, boycotted by the United States because of the Soviet Union's invasion of Afghanistan. See https://theculturetrip.com/europe/russia/articles/everything-you-need-to-know-about-luzhniki-stadium/.

22. Ibid. At this point the draft of the remarks, the writer inserted the words "here some reference to the [Paris] Summit meeting and any arrangement for the future made there." The insertion of that language appeared to show that the Americans at least entertained the idea that talks between Eisenhower and Khrushchev may have carried over from Paris during Ike's visit to the Soviet Union.

23. Arrival Remarks at Moscow—June 10, op. cit. As mentioned previously, the author of Eisenhower's welcoming statement on June 10 was John A. Armitage, with the date of Armitage's draft being April 15, 1960. The citation reads EUR:SOV:JAArmitage, 4-15-60.

24. Khrushchev replaced Voroshilov with Brezhnev as the chairman of the Presidium of the Supreme Soviet on May 7, 1960. Sergei Khrushchev, *Nikita Khrushchev*, 385.

25. Memorandum, Subject: Gifts, op cit. These gifts, also mentioned in chapter four, above, were suggested by C. Douglas Dillon, the undersecretary of state, to Eisenhower on May 13, 1960.

26. Nixon, *Six Crises*, 283–84.

27. Toast at Kremlin Dinner—June 10, EL, PP, AWF-IS, Far Eastern Trip. Eisenhower's comments about the date of the establishment of diplomatic relations between the United States and the Soviet Union may have startled many Soviets in the audience that evening. While Russia accepted its first U.S. Consul in 1803, indicating a formal establishment of recognition and diplomatic relations, those relations were severed during the Bolshevik Revolution in 1917. It was not until November 1933 that the United States formally recognized the Soviet Union. See "Highlights in the History of U.S. Relations with Russia, 1780–June 2006." https://2009-2017.state.gov/p/eur/ci/rs/200years/c30272.htm.

28. The draft of these remarks makes no mention of an author.

Notes to Chapter 7

29. The Exhibition of Soviet Economic Achievements was the site of a trade show emphasizing science and technology. Begun during the Stalinist era in 1935, the exhibition initially focused on Soviet achievements in agriculture. By the time of Khrushchev's leadership, the focus of the exhibition had turned to Soviet achievements in technology. See https://en.wikipedia.org/wiki/VDNKh_(Russia).

30. This account of the history of the Central Baptist Church of Moscow is found in Brian Stiller, "Russia—Rich in History," https://www.worldea.org/news/4320/russia-%E2%80%93-rich-in-history-by-brian-stiller. In future years, the American evangelist Billy Graham visited the Central Baptist Church during his trips to the Soviet Union. In 1959, he visited the church as a tourist. In 1982 and 1984, he preached at worship services in the church. In 1988 and 1992, Graham preached again in Moscow, but he doesn't mention any visits to the Central Baptist Church on those occasions. See Billy Graham, *Just as I Am: The Autobiography of Billy Graham* (HarperSanFrancisco: Zondervan, 1997), 500, 503–04, 518–19, 546–56.

31. Ezra Taft Benson wrote extensively about his religious encounter in Russia in his memoir, *Cross Fire: The Eight Years with Eisenhower* (Garden City: Doubleday, 1962), 485–88.

32. Ibid.

33. Ibid.

34. Ibid.

35. Harold Macmillan, *Riding the Storm* (London: Macmillan, 1971), 433–34. Eisenhower's relationship with Rev. James MacAskill, the pastor of the Gettysburg Presbyterian Church, is explained in David Eisenhower, *Going Home to Glory*, 105–06. See also Alan Sears and Craig Osten, with Ryan Cole, *The Soul of an American President: The Untold Story of Dwight D. Eisenhower's Faith* (Grand Rapids, MI: Baker Books, 2019), 162–90.

36. Telegram from the American Embassy in the Soviet Union to the Department of State, February 9, 1960; Minutes of Cabinet Meeting, May 26, 1960.

37. Sergei Khrushchev, *Nikita Khrushchev*, 387.

38. President Eisenhower's Itinerary, May 7, 1960, op. cit.

39. Hans N. Tuch, telephone interview with the author, October 26, 2017. See also the obituary for Harry G. Barnes, Jr., in the *New York Times*, August 17, 2012. Harry G. Barnes, Jr., had a distinguished career as a diplomat. In addition to his service in the American embassy in Moscow, he served as the American ambassador to Romania, India, and Chile. In Chile, Barnes associated himself with the forces opposed to General Augusto Pinochet and the movement for free elections in that country. In Hans Tuch's opinion, Barnes "was the best Foreign Service officer I ever knew."

40. Eisenhower's reference to "no war for a century" refers to the American Civil War, 1861–1865.

41. Arrival Remarks at Leningrad—June 13, EL, PP, AWF-IS, Far Eastern Trip, Box 50. These remarks were drafted by Harry G. Barnes, Jr., and dated 4-15-60.

42. References to the Elektrosila Complex may be found at pure.iiasa.ac.at/id/eprint/2932/1/WP-87-120.pdf.

43. For additional information on The Hermitage, see Geraldine Norman, *Dynastic Rule: Mikhail Piotrovsky and the Hermitage* (London: Unicorn, 2016).

44. For additional information on the Peterhof Palace, see T. Burkova, *Peterhof: The Palace and the Fountains* (St. Petersburg: Peterhof State Museum, 2007).

45. Draft for Leningrad, EL, PP, AWF-IS, Far Eastern Trip, Box 50. The draft has no author but a date of May 12, 1960, is given. In his copy of the draft, Ike crossed out the words "intellectual greatness" and inserted the words "intellectual progress" in their place.

46. Ibid. Eisenhower inserted the words "hundreds of miles" into the text. It is also worth pondering here that Eisenhower was inviting his Russian audience to come to America and fly over the country, almost in the fashion of "Open Skies." Also, Eisenhower must have been aware that the Soviets had used commercial airliners as tools of espionage throughout the 1950s. For example, after the Paris summit collapsed, Ambassador Henry Cabot Lodge noted that the Soviets had "taken advantage of our free and open society to collect extensive aerial photographs of the United States" in a speech before the Security Council of the United Nations. Dwight D. Eisenhower Library, Ann Whitman File, International Series, Dulles Herter-Series, Box 13, Confidential: Draft Statement for Ambassador Lodge.

47. Ibid. Peter the Great, the leader of Russia between 1696 and 1725, originally named the city St. Petersburg in 1703, which it remained until 1914, when it was renamed Petrograd. Following the Bolshevik Revolution and the death of Vladimir Lenin in 1924, the Communist regime renamed the city Leningrad. After the collapse of the Soviet Union, the city returned to its original name, St. Petersburg, in 1991.

48. The reference here is to John Paul Jones, the father of the American navy. After Jones served in the American Revolution, he accepted an invitation from the Russian Czarina Catherine the Great to lead the Russian navy in 1787–1788. For references to Jones's naval experience in Russia, see Evan Thomas, *John Paul Jones: Sailor, Hero, Father of the American Navy* (New York: Simon and Schuster, 2003), 267–99.

49. Eisenhower's reference to the specific episode where the Russian navy came to the help of the United States may be somewhat unclear, but it probably deals with the period of the American Civil War. The most obvious reference is to the Russian Baltic Fleet, which sailed into New York on September 24, 1863, following the Union victory over the Confederacy at Gettysburg in July 1863. Some have argued that the presence of the Russian fleet was meant to be a show of support for the Union in view of the fact that both the English and French had flirted with support for the Confederacy and appeared to welcome a Confederate victory at Gettysburg. See Webster G. Tarpley, "U.S. Civil War: The US-Russia Alliance that Saved the Union," https://www.voltairenet.org/article169488.html. See also C. Douglas Kroll, *"Friends in Peace and War": the Russian Navy's Landmark Visit to Civil War San Francisco* (Dulles, VA: Potomac Books, 2007). Others have argued that the presence of the Russian fleet in New York was a mere coincidence in view of the fact that the Russians, at the time, feared a general European war over Poland and wanted to place their fleet in a neutral port and away from the more powerful British and French navies, who would be their enemies if such a war should break out. According to this view, it was, therefore, a myth that the Russians were sailing to the United States as a show of force against the British and the French. See Thomas A. Bailey, *A Diplomatic History of the American People* (New York: Appleton-Century-Crofts, 1964), 363.

Notes to Chapter 7

50. For the details of the American purchase of Alaska from Russia in 1867, see Bailey, *Diplomatic History of the American People*, 363–71.

51. According to immigration historian Roger Daniels, there were 1,597,306 Russians who immigrated to the United States between 1901 and 1910. See Daniels, *Coming to America: A History of Immigration and Ethnicity in American Life* (New York: Perennial, 2002), 188.

52. Draft of Leningrad, op. cit. Eisenhower added the word "wartime" to the text of the speech and deleted the word "treasure" from the draft. The meeting of American and Soviet troops at Torgau is covered in Ambrose, *Eisenhower and Berlin*, 83n.

53. Ibid. Serge Wolkonsky (1860–1937) was an influential Russian theatrical teacher and theatre critic. Wolkonsky married Mary Walker Fearn, the daughter of the American diplomat J. Walker Fearn. Wolkonsky's work took him, at various times, to France and the United States, in addition to his theatrical career in the Soviet Union. See https://en.wikipedia.org/wiki/Serge_Wolkonsky.

54. Ibid. This sentence reads awkwardly. Eisenhower had made some comments in the margin of the draft that indicated that he wanted a revision of this section of the speech. The marks and comments were illegible, however.

55. Ibid. In the third section of this paragraph of the draft, Eisenhower crossed out the word "problems" and inserted the word "situations."

56. Arrival Statement at Kiev—June 14, EL, PP, AWF-IS, Far Eastern Trip, Box 50. The Golden Gates of Kiev is a reference to the historic monument originally constructed in the eleventh century as a fortification for the city from its enemies. See http://www.encyclopediaofukraine.com/display.asp?linkpath=pages%5CG%5CO%5CGoldenGate.htm. The draft of this statement listed no author.

57. Toast at Kiev Luncheon—June 14, EL, PP, AWF-IS, Far Eastern Trip. The draft does not list an author.

58. President's Speech—Kiev—June 14, EL, PP, AWF-IS, Far Eastern Trip. The reference here is to the assistance provided to American pilots who used bases in Ukraine on their various combat missions over Germany. John Deane covered that particular episode in his book *The Strange Alliance*, 114–25.

59. Ibid. We may assume that Nixon made these observations when he reported to Eisenhower after his visit to the Soviet Union in July 1959, although Nixon was never quoted publicly according to the description made by Eisenhower of these remarks. See Ambrose, *Nixon: The Education of a Politician*, 533–34. Nixon does not discuss any conversations he may have had with Eisenhower about his talks with Khrushchev either in *Six Crises* or in his memoirs, *RN: The Memoirs of Richard Nixon*. Irvin F. Gellman does mention a conversation that occurred when Nixon briefed Eisenhower about the trip, as well as Nixon's advice to Ike about his forthcoming trip to Moscow. Nixon said that Ike should make the trip brief, avoid Siberia, and spend two or three days in Moscow. It does not appear that Ike followed Nixon's advice. See Gellman, *The President and the Apprentice*, 534.

60. President's Speech—Kiev—June 14, op. cit. Ike made reference here to the overwhelming negative reaction throughout the world to the Soviet suppression of the revolt in Hungary in October 1956. See David Nichols, *Eisenhower, 1956: The President's Year of Crisis* (New York: Simon and Schuster, 2011), 238–41. For a brief reference to the suppression of a revolt in Tibet in 1959 by the People's Republic of

China, see Steven Kinzer, *The Brothers: John Foster Dulles, Allen Dulles, and Their Secret World War* (New York: Henry Holt, 2013), 277. Nevertheless, Ike's remarks, if ever given, would have struck the Soviet leadership as hollow and hypocritical. It was the Eisenhower administration, after all, that throughout the 1950s had undermined popularly elected governments in such countries as Iran and Guatemala when it viewed those governments as inimical to American interests. See, for example, Ambrose, *Ike's Spies*, and Kinzer, *The Brothers*.

61. The North Atlantic Treaty Organization came into existence on April 4, 1949. Its original members were the United States, Great Britain, Canada, France, Italy, Belgium, The Netherlands, Luxembourg, Norway, Denmark, Iceland, and Portugal. NATO's purpose was to deter the prospect of Soviet expansionism in western Europe after World War II. See Bailey, *Diplomatic History of the American People*, 808–09. The Southeast Asia Treaty Organization (SEATO) was established in September 1954. Its original members were the United States, Great Britain, France, Australia, New Zealand, the Philippines, Thailand, and Pakistan. Its purpose was to deter expansion by the People's Republic of China (PRC) in Asia, especially if it was directed against the Republic of China (ROC) on Taiwan. See Bailey, *Diplomatic History of the American People*, 832–33. The Central Treaty Organization (CENTO) came into existence on April 19, 1959, and included Turkey, Iran, Pakistan, and Britain. The purpose of the alliance was to deter Soviet expansion into the Middle East. Although the United States was not an original member of CENTO, the Eisenhower administration had negotiated separate agreements with Turkey, Iran, and Pakistan, offering military support. See Bailey, *Diplomatic History of the American People*, 851.

62. President's Speech—Kiev—June 14, op. cit. Eisenhower underlined the words "govern the whole" and put a question mark in the right margin of the draft, indicating some question about the accuracy of the sentence.

63. Ibid. On this point, Eisenhower could only have been referring to the Federal Republic of Germany, or West Germany, and not the German Democratic Republic, or East Germany, which was then under strict Communist rule.

64. Given the problems that the Soviets and the East German government were facing with refugees leaving East Berlin and fleeing to the West through the "escape hatch" of West Berlin, Eisenhower's words would hardly have been satisfactory to the Soviet government. By August 1961, the Soviets had constructed the Berlin Wall in an attempt to "make permanent the division of the city." See Gaddis, *The Cold War: A New History*, 112–14.

65. On this point, see Herbert Feis, *From Trust to Terror: The Onset of the Cold War, 1945–1950* (New York: Norton, 1970), 140–43.

66. For a discussion of these disarmament negotiations as they existed at the time, see Robert A. Divine, *Blowing on the Wind: The Nuclear Test-Ban Debate, 1954–1960.* (New York: Oxford University Press, 1978).

67. President's Speech—Kiev—June 14, op. cit. There were, of course, no "common labors in Paris during May" between Eisenhower and Khrushchev, due to the collapse of the summit conference.

68. Ibid. In this passage, Eisenhower made another reference to the positive outcomes of the Lacy-Zaroubin agreement. Also, at this point in the draft of the speech, Eisenhower penciled in, in parentheses, "Paragraph on test ban, if it materializes, with strong, positive emphasis."

Notes to Chapter 8

69. Ibid. At this point, Eisenhower also inserted the words, "Add sentence on Law of the Sea Conference, if it ends well," into the draft of the speech.

70. Ibid. Eisenhower's reference here, presumably, is to Khrushchev's advocacy of "peaceful coexistence" between the United States and the Soviet Union. For a description of the term itself, see Feifer, "If the U-2 Hadn't Flown," in Cowley, ed., *What Ifs*, 234.

71. President's Speech—Kiev—June 14, op. cit.

72. Nichols, *Eisenhower 1956*, 286; Thomas, *Ike's Bluff*, 98–108.

Chapter 8

1. Remarks to Faculty at Moscow University—June 16, EL PP, AWF-IS, Far Eastern Trip, Box 50. Eisenhower's itinerary called for him to speak at Moscow University on June 15, 1960, not June 16, as the draft indicates. There was no record of the author of the draft. For a study of Eisenhower's presidency at Columbia University in 1948–1950, see Travis Beal Jacobs, *Eisenhower at Columbia* (New Brunswick, NJ: Transaction Publishers, 2001).

2. Remarks to Students at Moscow University—June 16, EL, PP, AWF-IS, Far Eastern Trip. At this point in the draft, Eisenhower crossed out the words, "3 million," and inserted the words, "nearly four million." No author of the draft is recorded.

3. Toast at President's Dinner—June 15, EL, PP, AWF-IS, Far Eastern Trip. No author of the draft is given.

4. The Manesh Gallery was built between 1817 and 1825 and was designed by Agustin de Betancourt, the famous Spanish engineer. First used as an indoor riding academy for horsemanship, it later became an exhibit hall and, in the Khrushchev years, an art gallery. See https://en.wikipedia.org/wiki/Moscow_Manege.

5. Nixon's televised address to the Soviet people has been discussed by Nixon in his various writings as well as by his biographers. The biographer who gives the speech the most extensive account is Aitken, *Nixon*, 260–63.

6. Richard T. Davies was a career Foreign Service officer who later went on to several high-level posts, including ambassador to Poland from 1973 to 1978. In that capacity, he became well acquainted with Cardinal Karol Wojtyla, at the time the Roman Catholic Archbishop of Kraków. Cardinal Wojtyla later distinguished himself, of course, as Pope John Paul II. See Richard Davies obituaries, *New York Times*, April 3, 2005, and *Chicago Tribune*, April 6, 2005.

7. Moscow Speech, EL, PP, AWF-IS, Far Eastern Trip. The author of the draft, as mentioned previously, was Richard T. Davies. The explanatory note at the end of the draft reads EUR:SO V:Sov/P. RT Davies: fourth draft:4/19/60. Richard Nixon made only the briefest of mentions of his visit to Novosibirsk and Sverdlovsk in *Six Crises*, 296. See also Ambrose, *Nixon*, *I*, 529. Ambrose noted that Nixon did have the opportunity to meet many Soviet citizens during this encounter, as Eisenhower's speech indicates.

8. In his speech in Moscow on March 5, Khrushchev spoke about a dispute between Afghanistan and Pakistan over a territory on the border between the two countries. The area was known as Pushtunistan, and was then occupied by Pakistan.

The Soviet Union supported Afghanistan's claim to the territory, but Khrushchev advocated the holding of a plebiscite whereby the voters in Pushtunistan could act in their own self-determination. Eisenhower's speech spoke of each country's right of self-determination and the dispute between Afghanistan and Pakistan apparently was the example that he sought to highlight, although Eisenhower made no mention of Pushtunistan in his speech. See Caruthers, "Khrushchev Asks Pre-Summit Calm," *New York Times*, March 6, 1960.

9. Ike's reference to the previous fifteen years deals with successful independence movements in India, Indonesia, and Africa.

10. The full *Charter of the United Nations* may be found at https://www.un.org/en/charter-united-nations/index.html.

11. This language may have been a reference to Khrushchev's comment to Richard Nixon in Moscow during the vice president's trip to the Soviet Union in July 1959. During one of his spirited conversations with Nixon, Khrushchev stated that the Soviet Union expected to surpass the United States in terms of the living standards of its people and when it passed the United States, Khrushchev gestured, it would "wave bye-bye" to the Americans. See http//www.youtube.com, "Nixon vs. Khrushchev: The Kitchen Debate (1959)."

12. The Soviet Union's attempts to influence Communist parties in France and Italy is briefly discussed in John Lewis Gaddis, *George F. Kennan: An American Life* (New York: Penguin, 2011), 286–87. See also Walter La Feber, *America, Russia, and the Cold War, 1945–1966*. (New York: Wiley, 1967), 42.

13. Eisenhower's reference here is to the Marshall Plan for the economic reconstruction of Europe following World War II. See Gaddis, *The Cold War*, 32–33.

14. In this listing of the giants from Russian literature, science, music, and art, the author of the draft made sure to list the full name of A. S. Popov, the only individual in this listing so identified. This identification of A. S. Popov, instead of merely Popov, made sure that no mistake could be made to confuse him with Georgy M. Popov, who was the chief of the Communist Party's organization in Moscow in the early 1950s. Stalin suspected Georgy M. Popov of being involved in a plot against him and asked Khrushchev to investigate that possibility. Khrushchev knew that Popov was innocent of any such plotting but chose to have him transferred to a post far removed from Moscow where Stalin would not view him as a threat. Popov was apparently unaware of Stalin's suspicions and blamed Khrushchev for what he considered to be an embarrassing diminution of his status within the Communist Party as well as a permanent setback to his career. According to Sergei Khrushchev, Popov became a critic of Khrushchev from that point forward, not recognizing that Khrushchev had prevented Stalin from pursuing further investigations of him. See Sergei Khrushchev, *Nikita Khrushchev*, 28–29. The listing of the names of the Russian giants in literature, art, culture, and science is also somewhat unique in that virtually every one of the individuals mentioned lived during the Tsarist (Imperial) era, not the Communist era. See Nicholas V. Riasanovsky, *A History of Russia* (New York: Oxford University Press, 2000), 348–67, 435–52.

15. Ike's reference here is to the Lacy-Zaroubin agreement.

16. The Moiseyev and Beryozka dance troupes were two famous Soviet folk ensembles that performed around the world, including in the United States. See

Notes to Chapter 8

Anna Kisselgoff, "Dance Folk Ensemble: The Moiseyev Troupe," *New York Times*, September 15, 1986, and https://en.wikipedia.org/wiki/Beryozka_(Russian_dance_troupe).

17. Ike's reference here is to his famous speech, "A Chance for Peace," given on April 16, 1953, to the American Society of Newspaper Editors. The speech has also become known as the "Cross of Iron" speech. See, among others, Ambrose, *Eisenhower*, II, 94–95.

18. Heyward Isham was a career Foreign Service officer who compiled a distinguished record during the years of the Cold War. He served in the American embassy in Moscow under Ambassador Chip Bohlen during 1955–1957 and was scheduled to serve as Bohlen's assistant on Eisenhower's trip to the Soviet Union in 1960. Isham later belonged to the United States delegation to the Paris Peace Talks that involved ending the war in Vietnam. Speaking of Isham's work at the time, Secretary of State Henry A. Kissinger stated that Isham "made a tremendous contribution." He also served as Ambassador to Haiti during 1974–1977 and was involved in a number of humanitarian efforts designed to reduce hunger on that impoverished island. See Heyward Isham obituary, *New York Times*, June 23, 2009, and Heyward Isham, https://en.wikipedia.org/wiki/Heyward_Isham.

19. Departure Statement Moscow Enroute Irkutsk, EL, PP, AWF-IS, Far Eastern Trip. The notation for the remarks reads, "second draft, 4/18/60."

20. Khrushchev visited the United States in September 1959, and Kozlov visited the United States in July 1959. Mikoyan visited in January 1959. See Taubman, *Khrushchev*, 409–10. In Harrison Salisbury's view, Mikoyan was essentially "casing out" the United States for Khrushchev, in the event that Khrushchev might ever visit the United States. See Harrison Salisbury oral history, COHP, 32–34.

21. Arrival Statement at Irkutsk—June 17, EL, PP, AWF-IS, Far Eastern Trip. There is no record of the author of this statement. The cameras in the hold of Air Force One almost certainly would have photographed all of the sites that Eisenhower mentioned on the ride from Moscow to Irkutsk. See Terhorst and Albertazzi, *The Flying White House*, 196–98, and Beschloss, *May Day*, 228–29.

22. Harrison Salisbury oral history, COHP, 45–47.

23. Ibid. See also Hans N. Tuch, interviews with the author, August 14, 2015, August 19, 2015.

24. Harrison Salisbury oral history, COHP, 45–47.

25. Sergei Khrushchev, interview with the author, op. cit.

26. Irkutsk Speech, EL, PP, AWF-IS, Far Eastern Trip. There is no record of an author for the draft.

27. Ike's reference here is to the famous "Turner Thesis," first advanced by historian Frederick Jackson Turner in his essay "The Significance of the Frontier in America History," given at the annual meeting of the American Historical Association in Chicago in 1893. For a biography of Turner, see Ray Allen Billington, *Frederick Jackson Turner: Historian, Scholar, Teacher* (New York: Oxford University Press, 1973), especially pages 35–37. See also David S. Brown, *Beyond the Frontier: The Midwestern Voice in American Historical Writing* (Chicago: University of Chicago Press, 2009), 25–50.

28. The Eisenhower administration had promoted the peaceful, cooperative exploration of outer space through the efforts of scientists from sixty-seven nations

around the world in the International Geophysical Year, 1957–1958. See Mieczkowski, *Eisenhower's Sputnik Moment*, 35–37.

Conclusion

1. Thomas, *Ike's Bluff*, 384–85.
2. James C. Hagerty oral history, COHP, 56–60.
3. Oral history of Barbara Eisenhower-Foltz, (1982, 1983), pp. 130–33, Dwight D. Eisenhower Library.
4. Kistiakowsky, *Scientist at the White House*, 375.
5. Ibid.
6. Boyle, *Eisenhower*, 140.
7. John F. Kennedy, the Democratic Party's presidential nominee in 1960, spoke in numerous campaign speeches of the Soviet Union's potential leadership in missile production by 1963. See Robert Dallek, *An Unfinished Life: John F. Kennedy, 1917–1963*, 288–90. Richard Nixon, the Republican presidential candidate in 1960, under pressure from Nelson A. Rockefeller, the governor of New York, was also willing to consider a substantial increase in defense spending, if elected. See John A. Farrell, *Richard Nixon: The Life* (New York: Doubleday, 2017) 274, and Aitken, *Nixon*, 269–70.
8. Brugioni, *Eyes in the Sky*, 356.
9. Memorandum of Conversation, Bipartisan Leaders Breakfast, May 26, 1960, *FRUS, 1958–1960*, X, Doc. 154, 533, https://history.state.gov/historicaldocuments/frus1958-60v10p1/d154.
10. Eisenhower, *Waging Peace*, 546.
11. John Eisenhower, quoted in Ambrose, *Ike's Spies*, 279.
12. As Dino Brugioni explained, a Soviet scientist told Aaron Katz, an American scientist working for the RAND Corporation, at the Pugwash meeting of American and Soviet scientists in December 1960, that the film from Powers's U-2 produced "damn good pictures." Brugioni, *Eyes in the Sky*, 348.
13. Hill with McCubbin, *Five Presidents*, 67.
14. President's News Conference of May 11, 1960, *Public Papers, Eisenhower*, 1960–61.
15. Powers covered his trial, verdict, and sentencing in *Operation Overflight*, 157–60.
16. Ibid., 232–41. The story of the exchange of Powers and Abel was made into an Oscar-winning movie, *Bridge of Spies*, starring Tom Hanks and Mark Rylance, written by Steven Spielberg, produced by Touchstone Pictures, and released in October 2015.
17. A number of sources are available that cover the RB-47 flight and the fate of its crew members. For example, see "Interview with John McKone—30.8.1996," https://nsarchive2.gwu.edu/coldwar/interviews/episode-12/mckone1.html; "The Meaning of a Little Dog Toy," http://www.check-six.com/Crash_Sites/LittleDogToy_RB-57.htm; Emily Ludolph, "The Last Time the Russians Intervened in a U.S. Election https://narratively.com/the-last-time-the-russians-intervened-in-a-u-s-election/; "Freeman Bruce Olmstead," http://veterantributes.org/TributeDetail.php?recordID

=1249, and "John R. McKone," http://veterantributes.org/TributeDetail.php?record ID=1250. Powers refers to his knowledge of the RB-47 pilots and their capture by the Soviet Union in *Operation Overflight*, 204–05. See also Watson, *Into the Missile Age*, 725.

18. "Little Dog Toy."

19. Interview, John McKone, https://nsarchive2.gwu.edu/coldwar/interviews/episode-12/mckone2.html, op. cit.

20. Ibid.

21. Thompson and Thompson, *The Kremlinologist*, 224–25.

22. Interview, John McKone, https://nsarchive2.gwu.edu/coldwar/interviews/episode-12/mckone2.html, op. cit.

23. Ibid.

24. "Little Dog Toy." See also "July–September 1960: RB-47 Airplane Incident," *FRUS, 1958–1960*, X, Doc. 163, 549–51, https://history.state.gov/historicaldocuments/frus1958-60v10p1/d163.

25. Telegram from the Embassy in the Soviet Union to the Department of State, September 8, 1960, 2 P.M., *FRUS, 1958–1960*, X, Doc. 163, 549–51, https://history.state.gov/historicaldocuments/frus1958-60v10p1/d163.

26. Ibid.

27. Ibid.

28. Ibid.

29. Ludolph, "The Last Time the Russians Intervened in a US Election," https://narratively.com/the-last-time-the-russians-intervened-in-a-u-s-election/.

30. "U.S. Air Force's John McKone_50 years later," http://www.ssentinel.com/index.php/news/article/us_air_forces_john_mckone_50_years_later/.

31. Dr. A. McGehee Harvey, "A 1969 Conversation with Khrushchev: The Beginning of His Fall from Power," excerpted from "Playing for High Stakes," *Life*, vol. 69, no. 25 (18 December 1970), 48; Geelhoed, "The Spy Plane and the Summit," *Presidential Studies Quarterly*, op. cit., 104. See also Sergei Khrushchev, *Nikita Khrushchev, 730–36*; and Salisbury, *A Journey for Our Times*, 488–90. Salisbury recounts Khrushchev's interactions with Dr. Harvey but disagrees with the Soviet leader's analysis that it was the U-2 crisis that was the beginning of his loss of power. Salisbury believes that Khrushchev's problems began earlier in 1960 with his announced decision to reduce the size of the Red Army, resulting in the military's disaffection with his policies.

32. Harold Macmillan, interview with Robert McKenzie of the British Broadcasting Corporation about the publication of his book *Pointing the Way*, Bodleian Library, Oxford, UK, Conservative Party Archives, CCO/20/8/16, 14–15. See also Horne, *Macmillan*, II, 230.

33. "Face-to-Face, Nixon-Kennedy," Vice President Richard M. Nixon and Senator John F. Kennedy Fourth Joint Television-Radio Broadcast, October 21, 1960, https://www.jfklibrary.org/archives/other-resources/john-f-kennedy-speeches/4th-nixon-kennedy-debate-19601021. John T. Shaw covers Kennedy's use of the missile gap issue against Nixon in his *Rising Star, Setting Sun: Dwight D. Eisenhower, John F. Kennedy, and the Presidential Transition That Changed America* (New York: Pegasus Books, 2018), 226.

34. Memorandum of Conference with the President, February 4, 1960, Dwight D. Eisenhower Library, Ann Whitman File, DDE Diary Series, Box 47, Staff Notes (2).

35. Ibid.

36. Ibid.

37. Address by Secretary of Defense Thomas S. Gates before the Postmasters of America, 25 October 1960, Miami, Florida, *Statements and Addresses of Thomas S. Gates, Jr., III*. See also E. Bruce Geelhoed, "Thomas S. Gates and the Principles of National Security," unpublished paper presented at the University of Pennsylvania, September 19, 1984, Philadelphia, Pennsylvania. A summary of Gates's speech may be found in Mark Watson, "Gates Hits Defense Critics, Says 'We're First Rate,'" in the *Baltimore Sun*, October 26, 1960. See also Watson, *Into the Missile Age*, 770.

38. Alsop, *"I've Seen the Best of It,"* 414–15.

39. Farrell, *Nixon*, 274.

40. For an account of Gerald R. Ford's early life, including his military service and political career, see his autobiography, *A Time to Heal* (New York: Harper and Row/Reader's Digest, 1979), 1–72 and Scott Kaufman, *Ambition, Pragmatism, and Party: A Political Biography of Gerald R. Ford* (Lawrence, KS: University Press of Kansas, 2017), 1–76. For Lyndon Johnson's military service in World War II, see Robert A. Caro, *The Years of Lyndon Johnson. Vol. II. Means of Ascent* (New York: Knopf, 1990) 21–45. JFK's harrowing experience with PT 109 can be found in Dallek, *An Unfinished Life*, 95–100.

41. Allan Wisely, "More Than a Favorite Son: The Gerald Ford for Vice President Committee," Ball State University, unpublished, 2017; Kaufman, *Ambition, Pragmatism*, and Party, 74–75. In 1976, when Gerald Ford, then the president of the United States, secured the Republican Party's presidential nomination at its national convention in Kansas City, his campaign's band struck up *The Victors* in celebration.

42. Kaufman, *Ambition, Pragmatism, and Party*, 75.

43. Robert A. Caro, *The Years of Lyndon Johnson: The Passage of Power* (New York: Alfred A. Knopf, 2012), 155–56.

44. Fursenko and Naftali, *Khrushchev's Cold War*, 273; Taubman, *Khrushchev*, 484–85.

45. Farrell, *Nixon*, 271.

46. Sergei Khrushchev, *Nikita Khrushchev*, 425–26. See also Pierre Salinger, *With Kennedy* (Garden City, NY: Doubleday, 1966), 230. In his account, Salinger indicated that he accepted Khrushchev's contention that the RB-47 violated Soviet airspace and was not flying in international waters when shot down by Polyakov.

47. Telegram, American Embassy to State Department, September 8, 1960, op. cit.

48. Ibid.

49. Ibid.

50. Ludolph, "The Last Time the Russians Intervened in a U.S. Election"; Sergei Khruschev, *Nikita Khrushchev*, 426. See also Beschloss, *May Day*, 340–41.

51. Ibid.

Notes to Conclusion

52. Hans N. Tuch, interview with the author, October 26, 2017.
53. Ibid.
54. "Little Dog Toy." An excellent chronology of the diplomatic efforts to free Olmstead and McKone may be found in Taubman, *Khrushchev*, 485–87.
55. Nikita S. Khrushchev, *Khrushchev Remembers*, 458. See also Robert Dallek, *An Unfinished Life*, 406.
56. Farrell, *Nixon*, 489–90.

Bibliography

Manuscript Collections

Bodleian Library, Oxford University, Oxford, UK
    Conservative Party Central Office Papers
    Harold Macmillan Papers
Dwight D. Eisenhower Library, Abilene, Kansas
    Dulles-Herter Series
    James C. Hagerty Papers
    White House Office, Office of the Staff Secretary, International Trips and Meetings Series
    Ann C. Whitman File, Administration Series
    Ann C. Whitman File, DDE Diary Series
    Ann C. Whitman File, International Meetings Series
    Ann C. Whitman File, International Series
Public Papers of the Presidents of the United States, National Archives and Records Administration, Washington, DC.
    Dwight D. Eisenhower
    John F. Kennedy
Seeley G. Mudd Library, Princeton University, Princeton, New Jersey
    Arthur Krock Papers
Van Pelt Library, University of Pennsylvania, Philadelphia, Pennsylvania
    Thomas Sovereign Gates, Jr. Collection

Books and Other Secondary Sources

Aitken, Jonathan. *Nixon: A Life*. New York: Regnery, 1993.
Aldous, Richard, and Sabine Lee, eds., *Harold Macmillan and Britain's World Role*. London: Macmillan, 1995.
Alexander, Charles C. *Holding the Line: The Eisenhower Era, 1952–1961*. Bloomington: Indiana University Press, 1975.

Bibliography

Alsop, Joseph W., with Adam Platt. *"I've Seen the Best of It": Memoirs.* New York: W. W. Norton, 1992.
Ambrose, Stephen E. *Eisenhower and Berlin, 1945: The Decision to Halt at the Elbe.* New York: W. W. Norton, 1967.
———. *Eisenhower: Soldier and President.* New York: Simon and Schuster, 1990.
———. *Eisenhower: Vol. I. Soldier, General of the Army, President-Elect, 1890–1952.* New York: Simon and Schuster, 1983.
———. *Eisenhower: Vol. II. The President: 1953–1961.* New York: Simon and Schuster, 1984.
———. *Ike's Spies: Eisenhower and the Intelligence Establishment.* Garden City, NY: Doubleday, 1981.
———. *Nixon. Vol. I. The Education of a Politician, 1913–1962.* New York: Simon and Schuster, 1987.
———. *The Supreme Commander: The War Years of General Dwight D. Eisenhower.* Garden City, NY: Doubleday, 1970.
Baehler, David M., and Charles S. Sampson, eds. *Foreign Relations of the United States, 1958–1960,* Volume IX. Washington, DC: Government Printing Office, 1993.
Baier, Brett, with Catherine Whitney. *Three Days in January: Dwight Eisenhower's Final Mission.* New York: Morrow, 2017.
Bailey, Thomas. A. *A Diplomatic History of the American People.* New York: Appleton-Century-Crofts, 1964.
Benson, Ezra Taft. *Cross Fire: The Eight Years with Eisenhower.* Garden City, NY: Doubleday, 1962.
Beschloss, Michael. *Eisenhower: A Centenary History.* New York: Edward Burlingame, 1990.
———. *May Day: Eisenhower, Khrushchev, and the U-2 Affair.* New York: Harper & Row, 1986.
Bischoff, Gunter, and Stephen E. Ambrose, eds. *Eisenhower: A Centenary Assessment.* Baton Rouge: Louisiana State University Press, 1992.
Billington, Ray A. *Frederick Jackson Turner: Historian, Scholar, Teacher.* New York: Oxford University Press, 1973.
Bissell, Richard M., Jr. *Reflections of a Cold Warrior.* New Haven: Yale University Press, 1995.
Blake, Robert. *The Conservative Party from Peel to Thatcher.* London: Fontana Press, 1985.
Bohlen, Charles E. *Witness to History, 1929–1969.* New York: W. W. Norton, 1991.
Borklund, C. W. *Men of the Pentagon.* New York: Praeger, 1968.
Bottome, Edgar. *The Missile Gap.* Fairfield, CT: Fairleigh Dickinson Press, 1971.
Bowie, Robert B., and Richard H. Immerman. *Waging Peace: How Eisenhower Shaped an Enduring Cold War Strategy.* New York: Oxford University Press, 1990.
Boyle, Peter G. *Eisenhower.* New York: Pearson Longman, 2005.
Brands, H. W., Jr. *Cold Warriors: Eisenhower's Generation and American Foreign Policy.* New York: Columbia University Press, 1988.
Brinkley, Douglas. *American Moonshot: John F. Kennedy and the Great Space Race.* New York: HarperCollins, 2019.

Bibliography

Brown, David S. *Beyond the Frontier: The Midwestern Voice in American Historical Writing.* Chicago: University of Chicago Press, 2009.

Brugioni, Dino. *Eyes in the Sky: Eisenhower, the CIA, and Cold War Aerial Surveillance.* Annapolis, MD: Naval Institute Press, 2010.

Bundy, McGeorge. *Danger and Survival: Choices about the Bomb in the First 50 Years.* New York: Random House, 1988.

Burkova, T. *Peterhof: The Palace and the Fountains.* St. Petersburg: St. Petersburg State Museum, 2007.

Burns, James McGregor. *Roosevelt: The Soldier of Freedom.* New York: Harcourt, Brace, Jovanovich, 1970.

Carlson, Peter. *K Blows Top: A Cold War Comic Interlude, Starring Nikita Khrushchev, America's Most Unlikely Tourist.* New York: PublicAffairs, 2009.

Caro, Robert A. *The Years of Lyndon Johnson: The Passage of Power.* New York: Alfred A. Knopf, 2012.

———. *The Years of Lyndon Johnson. Vol. II. Means of Ascent.* New York: Alfred A. Knopf. 1990.

Collier, Peter, and David Horowitz. *The Rockefellers: An American Dynasty.* New York: Holt, Rinehart and Winston, 1976.

Craig, Campbell. *Destroying the Village: Eisenhower and Thermonuclear War.* New York: Columbia University Press, 1998.

Dallek, Robert. *An Unfinished Life: John F. Kennedy, 1917–1963.* New York: Little, Brown, 2003.

Daniels, Roger. *Coming to America: A History of Immigration and Ethnicity in American Life.* New York: Perennial, 2002.

Deane, John R. *The Strange Alliance: The Story of Our Efforts at Wartime Cooperation with Russia.* New York: Viking, 1946.

Dickson, Paul. *Sputnik: The Shock of the Century.* New York: Walker Books, 2001.

Divine, Robert A. *Blowing on the Wind: The Nuclear Test-Ban Debate, 1954–1960.* New York: Oxford University Press, 1978.

———. *Eisenhower and the Cold War.* New York: Oxford University Press, 1981.

Dobrynin, Anatoly. *In Confidence: Moscow's Ambassador to Six Cold War Presidents.* New York: Random House, 1995.

Donovan, Robert J. *Eisenhower: The Inside Story of the First Term.* New York: Harper, 1956.

Eisenhower, David. *Going Home to Glory: A Memoir of Life with Dwight D. Eisenhower, 1961 to 1969.* New York: Simon and Schuster, 2010.

Eisenhower, Dwight D. *Crusade in Europe.* Garden City, NY: Doubleday, 1948.

———. *Mandate for Change. White House Years, 1953–1956.* Garden City, NY: Doubleday, 1963.

———. *Waging Peace: The White House Years, A Personal Account 1956–1961.* Garden City, NY: Doubleday, 1965.

Eisenhower, John S. D. *Strictly Personal.* Garden City, NY: Doubleday, 1974.

Eubank, Keith. *The Summit Conferences, 1919–1960.* Norman: University of Oklahoma Press, 1966.

Evans, Harold. *Downing Street Diary: The Macmillan Years, 1957–1963.* London: Hodder and Stoughton, 1981.

Bibliography

Ewald, William Bragg, Jr. *Eisenhower the President: Crucial Days, 1951-1960*. Englewood Cliffs, NJ: Prentice-Hall, 1981.
Farrell, John A. *Richard Nixon: The Life*. New York: Doubleday, 2017.
Feis, Herbert. *From Trust to Terror: The Onset of the Cold War, 1945–1950*. New York: W. W. Norton, 1970.
Feifer, George. "If the U-2 Hadn't Flown?" In Robert Cowley, ed., *What Ifs of American History*. New York: G. P. Putnam's Sons, 2003.
Ferrell, Robert H., ed. *The Diary of James C. Hagerty: Eisenhower in Mid-Course, 1954–1955*. Bloomington: Indiana University Press, 1983.
———, ed. *The Eisenhower Diaries*. New York: W. W. Norton, 1981.
Ford, Gerald R. *A Time to Heal: The Autobiography of Gerald R. Ford*. New York: Harper and Row, Reader's Digest, 1979.
Frankel, Max. *Times of My Life*. New York: Random House, 1999.
Fursenko, Alexandr, and Timothy Naftali. *Khrushchev's Cold War: Portrait of an American Adversary*. New York: W. W. Norton, 2006.
Gaddis, John Lewis. *George F. Kennan: An American Life*. New York: Penguin, 2011.
———. *The Cold War: A New History*. New York: W. W. Norton, 2005.
Gates, Thomas S. *Statements and Addresses of Thomas S. Gates, Jr., II*. Washington, DC: Government Printing Office, 1960.
Galambos, Louis, and Daun van Ee, eds. *The Papers of Dwight David Eisenhower. Vol. XX. The Presidency: Keeping the Peace*. Baltimore: The Johns Hopkins University Press, 2001.
Geelhoed, E. Bruce. *Charles E. Wilson and Controversy at the Pentagon, 1953 to 1957*. Detroit: Wayne State University Press, 1979.
Geelhoed, E. Bruce. "The Spy Plane and the Summit: A Quarter-Century Retrospective." *Presidential Studies Quarterly* 17 (Winter 1987): 95–106.
Geelhoed, E. Bruce, "Thomas S. Gates and the Principles of National Security." Paper presented at the University of Pennsylvania, Philadelphia, Pennsylvania, September 19, 1984.
Geelhoed, E. Bruce, and Anthony O. Edmonds. *Eisenhower, Macmillan, and Allied Unity, 1957–1961*. Basingstoke, UK: Palgrave Macmillan, 2003.
———, eds. *The Macmillan-Eisenhower Correspondence, 1957–1969*. Basingstoke, UK: Palgrave Macmillan, 2005.
Gellman, Irvin F. *The President and the Apprentice: Eisenhower and Nixon, 1953–1961*. New Haven: Yale University Press, 2015.
Glantz, David M., and Jonathan M. House. *When Titans Clashed: How the Red Army Stopped Hitler*. Lawrence: University Press of Kansas, 1995.
Graham, Billy. *Just as I Am: The Autobiography of Billy Graham*. San Francisco: HarperCollins, 1997.
Grandin, Greg. *In Kissinger's Shadow: The Long Reach of America's Most Controversial Statesman*. New York: Picador, 2015.
Grose, Peter. *Gentleman Spy: The Life of Allen Dulles*. Boston: Houghton-Mifflin, 1994.
Hall, R. Cargill, ed. *Early Cold War Overflights, 1950–1956*. Washington, DC: National Reconnaissance Office, 2003.
Harriman, Averell, and Elie Abel. *Special Envoy to Churchill and Stalin, 1941–1946*. New York: Random House, 1975.

Bibliography

Hill, Clint, with Lisa McCubbin. *Five Presidents: My Extraordinary Journey with Eisenhower, Kennedy, Johnson, Nixon, and Ford.* New York: Gallery Books, 2016.
Hitchcock, William I. *The Age of Eisenhower: America and the World in the 1950s.* New York: Simon and Schuster, 2018.
Hoopes, Townsend. *The Devil and John Foster Dulles.* Boston: Little, Brown, 1974.
Horne, Alistair. *Harold Macmillan: Vol. I: 1894–1956.* London: Macmillan, 1988.
———. *Harold Macmillan: Vol. II: 1957–1986.* London: Macmillan, 1989.
———. *Hubris: The Tragedy of War in the Twentieth Century.* New York: Harper, 2015.
Hughes, Emmet John. *The Ordeal of Power: A Political Memoir of the Eisenhower Years.* New York: Atheneum, 1963.
Isakoff, Stuart. *When the World Stopped to Listen: Van Cliburn's Cold War Triumph and Its Aftermath.* New York: Alfred A. Knopf, 2017.
Jacobs, Travis Beal. *Eisenhower at Columbia.* New Brunswick, NJ: Transaction, 2001.
Jordan, Robert S. *An Unsung Soldier: The Life of General Andrew J. Goodpaster.* Annapolis, MD: Naval Institute Press, 2013.
Kaplan, Fred. *The Wizards of Armageddon.* Stanford, CA: Stanford University Press, 1991.
Kaufman, Scott. *Ambition, Pragmatism, and Party: A Political Biography of Gerald R. Ford.* Lawrence: University Press of Kansas, 2017
Kennedy, David M. *Freedom from Fear: The American People in Depression and War, 1929–1945.* New York: Oxford University Press, 1999.
Khrushchev, Nikita S. *Khrushchev Remembers.* Translated by Strobe Talbott. Introduction by Edward Crankshaw. Boston: Little, Brown, 1970.
Khrushchev, Sergei. *Nikita Khrushchev and the Creation of a Superpower.* University Park: Pennsylvania State University Press, 2001.
Killian, James J. *Sputnik, Scientists, and Eisenhower.* Cambridge, MA: MIT Press, 1978.
Kinnard, Douglas. *The Secretary of Defense.* Lexington: University Press of Kentucky, 1980.
Kinzer, Stephen. *The Brothers: John Foster Dulles, Allen Dulles, and Their Secret World War.* New York: Henry Holt, 2013.
Kissinger, Henry A. *Diplomacy.* New York: Simon and Schuster, 1994.
Kistiakowsky, George S. *Scientist at the White House: The Private Diary of President Eisenhower's Special Assistant for Science and Technology.* Cambridge, MA: Harvard University Press, 1976.
Kolodziej, Edward. *The Uncommon Defense and Congress, 1945–1963.* Columbus: The Ohio State University Press, 1966.
Kroll, C. Douglas. *"Friends in Peace and War": The Russian Navy's Landmark Visit to Civil War San Francisco.* Dulles, VA: Potomac Books, 2007.
La Feber, Walter. *America, Russia, and the Cold War, 1945–1966.* New York: Wiley, 1967.
Landa, Ronald D., James E. Miller, David S. Patterson, and Charles S. Sampson, eds. *Foreign Relations of the United States. 1958–1960. Volume VII.* Washington, DC: Government Printing Office, 1993.

Bibliography

———, eds. *Foreign Relations of the United States, 1958–1960. Volume X*. Washington, DC: Government Printing Office, 1993.
Leighton, Richard M. *Strategy, Money, and the New Look, 1953–1956. Vol. III. History of the Office of the Secretary of Defense*. Washington, DC: Historical Office of the Secretary of Defense, 2001.
Lyon, Peter. *Eisenhower: Portrait of the Hero*. Boston: Little, Brown, 1974.
Macmillan, Harold. *Riding the Storm, 1956 to 1959*. London: Macmillan, 1971.
———. *Pointing the Way, 1959 to 1961*. London: Macmillan, 1972.
Mieczkowski, Yanek. *Eisenhower's Sputnik Moment: The Race for Space and World Prestige*. Ithaca, NY: Cornell University Press, 2013.
Murphy, David E. *What Stalin Knew: The Enigma of Barbarossa*. New Haven: Yale University Press, 2005.
Murphy, Robert D. *Diplomat among Warriors*. Garden City, NY: Doubleday, 1964.
Neal, Steve. *Harry and Ike: The Partnership That Remade the Postwar World*. New York: Scribner, 2001.
Newman, Kitty. *Macmillan, Khrushchev, and the Berlin Crisis of 1958–1960*. London: Routledge, 2007.
Newton, Jim. *Eisenhower: The White House Years*. Garden City, NY: Doubleday, 2011.
Nichols, David. *Eisenhower, 1956: The President's Year of Crisis*. New York: Simon and Schuster, 2011.
Nixon, Richard M. *Six Crises*. Garden City, NY: Doubleday, 1962.
———. *RN: The Memoirs of Richard Nixon. Vol. I*. New York: Warner, 1978.
Norman, Geraldine. *Dynastic Rule: Mikhail Piotrovsky and the Hermitage*. London: Unicorn, 2016.
Ovendale, Ritchie. *Anglo-American Relations in the Twentieth Century*. New York: St. Martin's Press, 1998.
Pach, Chester J. and Elmo Richardson. *The Presidency of Dwight D. Eisenhower*. Lawrence: University Press of Kansas, 1991.
Parmet, Herbert S. *Eisenhower and the American Crusades*. New York: Macmillan, 1972.
———. *Richard M. Nixon: An American Enigma*. New York: Pearson, 2008.
Pedlow, Gregory W., and Donald E. Welzenbach. *The Central Intelligence Agency and Overhead Reconnaissance: The U-2 and OXCART Programs, 1954–1974*. New York: Skyhorse Publishing, 2016.
Peebles, Curtis. *Shadow Flights: America's Secret Air Wars against the Soviet Union*. Novato, CA: Presidio, 2000.
Perret, Geoffrey. *Eisenhower*. New York: Random House, 1999.
Powers, Francis Gary, with Curt Gentry. *Operation Overflight: A Memoir of the U-2 Incident*. New York: Tower, 1970.
Prados, John. *The Soviet Estimate: U.S. Intelligence Analysis and Russian Military Strength*. New York: Dial Press, 1982.
Reel, Monte. *A Brotherhood of Spies: The U-2 and the CIA's Secret War*. New York: Doubleday, 2018.
Reid, Anna. *Leningrad: The Epic Siege of World War II, 1941–1944*. New York: Walker Books, 2012.

Bibliography

Reynolds, David. *Summits: Six Meetings That Shaped the Twentieth Century.* New York: Basic Books, 2007.
Riasanovsky, Nicholas A. *A History of Russia.* New York: Oxford University Press, 2000.
Roberts, Geoffrey. *Stalin's General: A Life of Georgi Zhukov.* New York: Random House, 2012.
Rockefeller, David. *Memoirs.* New York: Random House, 2002.
Roman, Peter. *President Eisenhower and the Missile Gap.* Ithaca, NY: Cornell University Press, 1999.
Salinger, Pierre. *With Kennedy.* Garden City, NY: Doubleday, 1966.
Salisbury, Harrison. *A Journey for Our Times.* New York: Harper and Row, 1983.
———. *900 Days: The Siege of Leningrad.* New York: Da Capo Press, 2013.
Sears, Alan, and Craig Osten, with Ryan Cole. *The Soul of an American President: The Untold Story of Dwight D. Eisenhower's Faith.* Grand Rapids, MI: Baker Books, 2019.
Shaw, John T. *Rising Star, Setting Sun: Dwight D. Eisenhower, John F. Kennedy, and the Presidential Transition That Changed America.* New York: Pegasus Books, 2018.
Smith, Jean Edward. *Eisenhower in War and Peace.* New York: Random House, 2012.
Sulzberger, C. L. *The Last of the Giants.* New York: Macmillan, 1970.
Taubman, William. *Khrushchev: The Man and His Era.* New York: W. W. Norton, 2003.
Terhorst, Jerald F., and Col. Ralph Abertazzie. *The Flying White House: The Story of Air Force One.* New York: Coward, McCann & Geoghegan, 1979.
Thomas, Evan. *Ike's Bluff: President Eisenhower's Secret Battle to Save the World.* New York: Little, Brown, 2012.
———. *John Paul Jones: Sailor, Hero, Father of the American Navy.* New York: Simon and Schuster, 2003.
Thompson, Jenny, and Sherry Thompson. *The Kremlinologist: Llewellyn E. Thompson, America's Man in Cold War Moscow.* Baltimore: Johns Hopkins University Press, 2017.
Tuch, Hans N. *Arias, Cabellas, and Foreign Affairs: A Public Diplomat's Quasi-Musical Memoir.* Washington, DC: New Academic, 2008.
Wadleigh, John, "Thomas Sovereign Gates," in Paolo Coletta, ed. *American Secretaries of the Navy. Vol. II, 1913–1972.* Annapolis, MD: Naval Institute Press, 1980.
Watson, Robert J. *Into the Missile Age, 1956–1960. Vol. IV. History of the Office of the Secretary of Defense.* Washington, DC: Historical Office of the Secretary of Defense, 1997.
Watson, Thomas J., Jr. with Peter Petre. *Father, Son & Co.: My Life at IBM and Beyond.* New York: Bantam, 1990.
White, Theodore H. *The Making of the President, 1960.* New York: Atheneum, 1961.
———. *The Making of the President: 1968.* New York: Atheneum, 1969.
Wise, David, and Thomas Ross. *The U-2 Affair.* New York: Random House, 1962.
Wisely, Allen, "More Than a Favorite Son: The Gerald R. Ford for Vice President Committee." Unpublished manuscript, Ball State University, 2017.

Bibliography

Interviews and Oral Histories

By the Author
Robert B. Anderson
C. Douglas Dillon
James H. Douglas
John S. D. Eisenhower
Thomas S. Gates
Noel F. Gayler
Andrew J. Goodpaster
James D. Hittle
John N. Irwin II
Sergei N. Khrushchev
Alexander Macmillan, Earl of Stockton
Margaret Stroud
Hans N. Tuch

Association for Diplomatic Studies and Training Foreign Affairs Oral History Project
Alexander Akalovsky
C. Douglas Dillon
Vladimir I. Toumanoff
Hans N. Tuch

Columbia University Oral History Project
Joseph Alsop
Charles E. Bohlen
James V. Burke
C. Douglas Dillon
Robert J. Donovan
James H. Douglas
Thomas S. Gates, Jr.
James C. Hagerty
Robert D. Murphy
Harrison Salisbury

John Foster Dulles Oral History Collection
Arleigh A. Burke
Dwight D. Eisenhower
Livingston T. Merchant
Nathan F. Twining

Dwight D. Eisenhower Library
Milton S. Eisenhower
Barbara Eisenhower-Foltz
Vernon A. Walters

Index

Adenauer, Konrad, 3, 44, 48–49, 60, 173, 193
Adzubei, Aleksei (grandson of Nikita Khrushchev), 82–83
Adzubei, Ivan (grandson of Nikita Khrushchev), 83
Akalovsky, Alexander, 186, 190, 192–94, 196
Akalovsky, Maria, 186, 193
Allen, George, 158
Allied Control Council, 13, 41
Alsop, Joseph, 125–30, 142, 254, 278nn58–59
Ambrose, Stephen E., 41, 49, 246, 271n45, 294n7
Anderson, Robert B., 109–10, 135, 275n2, 277n44
Antonov, Alexei, 14–17, 24
AQUATONE, 113
Armitage, John A., 185, 188, 288n10, 288n16, 289n23
Arrowsmith, Marvin, 4
Asoka, 232
Atkinson, Brooks, 18
Atlas Missile, 109, 121, 127, 133, 137–38, 140
Avilov, V. I., 80–81

Ball, Ian, 5
Barnes, Harry G., Jr., 185, 197–98, 288n10, 288n16, 290n39, 290n41
Belair, Felix, 40, 42
Belieu, Kenneth, 134, 279n81
Belles, Joshua, 36
Benson, Ezra Taft, 194, 290n31
Berding, Andrew, 187
Bissell, Richard, 6, 112, 127, 144, 146–49, 151–52, 154, 158, 164, 168, 246
Bligh, Tim, 50
Bohlen, Avis, 196
Bohlen, Charles (Chip), 71, 145, 151, 172, 186, 190, 193, 197, 219, 222, 234, 288n10, 296n18
Bolshakov, Georgi, 53–54
Bolshoi Ballet Troupe, 31, 194, 232
Boyle, Peter G., 46, 245
Boyle, Alice, 187
Brandon, Henry, 5
Brezhnev, Leonid, 83, 182, 190, 260, 273n27, 288n3, 289n24
Brice Norton Air Force Base, U.K., 248
Brinkley, David, 5
Brinkley, Douglas, 268n63, 278n62
British General Election (1959), 49, 52
Brugioni, Dino, 110, 247
Bryuzov, Sergei, 153
Budyonny, Semyon, 20–21
Burd, Lawrence H., 162, 181
Bush, Prescott, 130, 141

Carlson, Peter, 54, 270n15
Carothers, Osgood, 5
Catroux, Georges, 14
CENTO (Central Treaty Organization), 209, 293n61
Central Baptist Church, Moscow, 194–95, 214–16, 274n50, 290n30
Chaikovsky, Peter, 232
Chancellor, John, 5
Chekhov, Anton, 232
Churchill, Winston, 5, 35–37, 254
Clay, Lucius, 15
Cliburn, Van, 32, 266n16
Cold War Roadshow (PBS), 53–54, 270n16
Collins, Norman, 51
Columbia University, 219, 220, 261n1, 262n6, 276n20, 284nn69–70, 294n1
Confucius, 232
Corwin, Eddie, 57
Craig, Campbell 42–43
Cronkite, Walter, 5
Cullen, Gav, 56
Cunningham, James, 168–69
Cutler, Robert, 127

Daly, John, 5
Davies, Richard T., 185, 222, 288n10, 288n16, 294nn6–7
Davis, Richard M., 191
Deane, John R., 15–20, 23–24
De Gaulle, Charles, 2, 3, 7, 35, 44, 48, 52–53, 60, 63–65, 117, 148, 165–69, 171–72, 175–76, 184, 187, 193, 268n47
DePauw University, 36
Dillon, Douglas, 40, 42, 68, 82, 145, 151–53, 155–57, 162–63, 168, 179–80, 284n74
Disneyland, 55
Dobrynin, Anatoly, 76, 83, 165, 191, 193
Donovan, Robert J., 5, 28, 183–84
Dostoyevsky, Fyodor, 232
Douglas, James H., 128, 167
Draper, William, 79, 186, 188

Drexel and Company, Philadelphia, 118
Dry, Leonard, 15
Dulles, Allen, 6–7, 61–62, 112, 117, 127–28, 144, 149, 154–55, 157, 159, 162–64, 246, 248, 282n40
Dulles, John Foster, 35–37, 39–40, 42, 49, 257

Eden, Anthony, 113
Edison, Thomas, 232
Ewald, William Bragg, 111, 141
Eisenhower, Barbara, 192–93, 196, 242–43
Eisenhower, Barbara Ann, 60
Eisenhower, David, 270n17
Eisenhower, Dwight D., 1, 3–4, 6, 8, 24–26, 29, 33, 68, 79, 81, 87, 143, 181, 186, 197, 218, 242, 260, 261n1, 262n4, 264n5, 266n4, 284n70, 287n134, 291n46, 292n52, 292n54, 293n63, 293n67, 293n68, 294n70, 295n11, 296n27; accepts responsibility for U-2 flights, 161–62; draft of proposed remarks in Irkutsk (1960), 238–40; draft of proposed speech in Kiev (1960), 207–14; draft of proposed speech in Leningrad (1960), 199–205; draft of proposed speech in Moscow (1960), 223–34; and Paris Summit (1960), 165–74; visit to Europe and the United Kingdom (1959), 49–54; visit to the Soviet Union, 1945, 11–22; at Western Summit (1959), 63–66
Eisenhower, John S. D., 21–22, 25, 42, 45, 146, 153, 164, 168, 186–88, 190, 238, 243, 246
Eisenhower, Mamie, 12, 78, 174, 186–87, 190, 194, 196–97, 273n32
Eisenhower, Mary Jean, 60
Eisenhower, Milton S., 4, 36, 90–91, 120, 277n40
Eisenhower, Susan, 60, 273n32
Eisenhower "Dacha," 77, 84–86, 191, 196–97, 218, 237

Index

Eisenhower "Highway," 84–86, 219, 237
Eisenhower "Links," 86, 219, 237
Electrosila Association for the Building of Electrical Machines, 198–99
Emerson, Ralph Waldo, 232
Ericson, Bob, 147–49, 151
Evans, Harold, 50
Evans, Rowland, 130
Exhibition of Soviet Economic Achievements, 193, 290n29

Falaleyeff, F. Y., 14
Farrell, John, 254
Feifer, George, 31
Folliard, Edward T., 121
Ford, Gerald R., 122, 255–56, 299nn40–41
Four Power Summit (Paris, 1960), 2, 6, 13, 44, 48, 109, 143, 148, 177, 244
Franke, William B., 118
Frankel, Max, 5, 163
Franklin, Benjamin, 232
Fursenko, Aleksandr, 42, 84, 128, 262n17

Gates, Millicent Anne, 118–19
Gates, Thomas, 3, 52–53, 87, 113–14, 116–17, 120, 127–28, 139, 161, 170, 173–74, 176, 253–54, 279nn82–83; at civil defense exercise (1960), 150–51, 154–57, 158–59; defense communications alert, 167, 175, 177; passage of FY 1961 defense budget, 121–29, 130–38, 141–42; U-2 crisis, 150–51
Gayler, Noel, 134–35
Geneva, Switzerland, as site for 1955 summit, 63–64
Georgian State Dance Ensemble, 232
Gettysburg Presbyterian Church, 196, 290n35
Glantz, David M., 30

Goethe, Johan, 232
Goforth, Oscar, 248–49
Gogol, Nikolai, 232
Goldberg, A. I., 5
Goodpaster, Andrew J., 24, 39–42, 46, 50, 57, 59, 111, 113–31, 133–42, 146, 149, 150–51, 153–59, 164, 166–67, 170, 173–79, 186–87, 190, 193, 196–97, 222, 253–56
Gray, Gordon, 155–57, 276n39
Griffith, James, 51
Gromyko, Andrei, 38, 83, 172, 191, 193, 283n47
Grover, Preston, 5
Gruenther, Alfred, 120, 277n40

Hagerty, James C., 3, 8, 26, 50, 53–54, 68, 84, 149, 156–58, 163, 182–, 187, 193–94, 196, 222, 238, 242–43, 265n1; advance party trip to the Soviet Union, 1960, 79–81; preparations for Eisenhower's trip to the Soviet Union, 73–76
Harlem Globetrotters, 31
Harriman, Kathleen, 15
Harriman, W. Averell, 14–18, 20, 22–24, 44
Hermitage, the, 46, 199
Herter, Christian, 37, 40, 51, 53, 68, 72, 78–80, 82, 145, 155, 157–59, 165–68, 171–72, 179, 183–86, 190, 193, 222
Herter, Mary, 186
Higgins, Marguerite, 5
Hill, Clint, 158
Hill, John, 36
Hiroshima, Japan, 11, 21
Hitchcock, William I., 2
Hitler, Adolf, 2, 12–13, 207–8
Hittle, James D., 131, 134, 136
Holiday on Ice figure skaters, 31
Hoopes, Townsend, 38
Hope, Bob, 31
Horne, Alistair, 13
Houghton, Amory, 64
House, Jonathan M., 30

311

Index

International Business Machines (IBM) Corporation, 55–57, 193–94
Irkutsk (Siberia), 66, 77–78, 85–86, 185, 188–89, 217–19, 223, 234–41, 245
Irwin, John N. (Jack), II, 59, 166–67, 177
Isham, Heyward, 185, 234

Johns Hopkins University, 36, 90, 277n40
Johnson, Clarence (Kelly), 112
Johnson, Lyndon B., 47, 124, 127, 133–35, 141, 246, 255–56, 259, 279, 299n40
Johnson, Stanley, 5
Jones, Pete, 120
Justinian, 232

Kalb, Marvin, 5
Kennedy, John F., 47, 106–7, 127, 253–55, 258–59, 297n7, 298n33
Kerr, Sir Clark, 14
Kharlamov, M. A., 53, 181, 274n41, 288n2
Khrushchev, Julia, 82–83
Khrushchev, Leonid, 82–83
Khrushchev, Nikita S., 1, 24, 27, 262n4, 294n8; at Paris Summit, 165–74; preparations for Eisenhower visit to the Soviet Union (1960), 84–86; speeches about downing of U-2, 155–56, 158–59; visit to the United States (1959), 53–66
Khrushchev, Nikita (grandson), 171
Khrushchev, Rada, 82–83, 124, 147, 153, 248
Khrushchev, Sergei N., 4, 24, 67, 82–85, 151, 158, 160, 166, 196, 237, 257–58
Khrushchev, Yelena, 82–83
Kiev, Ukraine, 5, 46, 66, 77–79, 149, 181–82, 188–89, 197, 205–7, 214, 216–19, 221, 223, 229, 235, 241, 243
Killian, James R., 112, 154
Kissinger, Henry A., 36, 39

Kistiakowsky, George B., 8, 186–87, 243–44
"Kitchen Cabinet," 33
Klein, Herbert, 32
KLM (Dutch Airline), 258–59
Knebel, Fletcher, 39
Koniev, Ivan, 16
Kozlov, Frol, 41–44, 235, 296n20
Krock, Arthur, 175–76
Kuznetsov, Vasily, 76, 83, 191, 193

Lacy, William S. B., 31
Lacy-Zaroubin Agreement (1958), 31–32, 46, 185
Lake Baikal, Siberia, 66, 77–78, 85–86, 218, 236–38, 245
Land, Edwin, 112, 154
Lao-Tse, 232
Lausche, Frank, 177
Leningrad, siege of, World War II, 198
Lincoln, Abraham, 232, 234
Lippman, Walter, 175
Lisagor, Peter, 5
Lodge, Henry Cabot, 55, 68, 115, 147, 250, 254, 257, 271n39, 291n46
Lower, Elmer, 73
Lubyanka prison, Moscow, 250
Lundahl, Arthur, 168–69

MacAskill, Rev. James, 196, 290n35
Macmillan, Alexander (Lord Stockton), 50–51, 267n30
Macmillan, Harold, 2, 35–36, 44, 46, 48, 60, 69, 93, 98, 113, 139, 146, 159, 162, 193, 196, 252; at Paris Summit, 1960, 165–74; visit to the Soviet Union (1959), 37–39
Macmillan, Helen Tarleton (Nellie) Bolles, 36
Mahendra Bir Bikram Shah Dev (king of Nepal), 64
Mahon, George, 122, 125, 134, 139, 141
Malinovsky, Rodion, 166–67, 172
Manesh Gallery, 222

Index

Mariinsky Opera, 214
Mariinsky Palace, 214
Marsh, Olive, 187
Marshall, George C., 12
McCann, Kevin, 187
McClendon, Sarah, 120
McCormack, John, 135, 279n83
McElroy, Neil, 116, 118–20, 129
McKenzie, Robert, 171
McKone, John R, 248–49, 250–52, 257–59
Mendeleyev, Dmitri, 232
Menshikov, Mikhail, 69, 272n2
Ministry of Foreign Affairs (MFA), Soviet Union, 20, 53, 71, 76, 86, 181, 186, 244, 251
"Missile Gap," 45, 47, 87, 88, 109–10, 117, 120–21, 126–33, 138–39, 144, 245, 253–57, 256
Moaney, John, 187, 190
Mohr, Charles, 5
Moiseyev and Beryozka dance troupes, 232
Molotov, Vyacheslav, 17
Moscow University, 83, 217–21
Murphy, Robert D., 40–44, 159, 177–78
Mussorgsky, Modest, 232

Naftali, Timothy, 42, 84, 128, 153
Nagasaki, Japan, 11, 21
National Sports Parade (Soviet Union), 14, 16–17, 22, 25, 216
NATO, 34, 209
Naval Air Station (NAS), Corpus Christi, Texas, 134
Newman, Kitty, 38
Newton, Jim, 43
New York Philharmonic Orchestra, 232
Nichols, David, 217
Nixon, Frank, 257
Nixon, Richard M., 4, 32, 252–58, 259–60, 268n65, 287n136
Nomonhan, Battle of, 12
Norris, John, 123

Olmstead, Freeman Bruce, 248–52, 257–59, 300n54
Operation Barbarossa, 30
Operation Grand Slam, 149, 247
Operation Square Deal, 147–49
Ormandy, Eugene, 31
Otten, Al, 75

Palm, Willard, 248, 249
Parmet, Herbert S., 41
Pauley, Edwin W., 14
Pavlov, Ivan, 232
Peebles, Curtis, 148
Peterhof, 199, 291n44
Peters, Roberta, 182, 288n6
Peter the Great, 199, 291n47
Petrovna, Nina, 53, 71, 82, 187, 196
Philadelphia Orchestra, 31
Phillips, Dean, 248–49
Pierpoint, Robert, 5, 73, 143
Ping-Sheung, Foo, 14
Pisoreva, Yefrosinya Ivanovna, 82–83
Poe, Edgar Allan, 232
Polaris, 109, 121, 126, 130, 133, 137–40
Polyakov, Vasily, 248
Polyansky, Dmitri, 69–70
Popov, A. S., 232, 295n14
Posa, Eugene, 248
Poulson, Norris, 55
Power, Thomas, 125
Powers, Francis Gary, 6, 104, 143, 145–46, 149–50, 162, 181, 244, 247–48
Prados, John, 150
President's Foreign Intelligence Advisory Board (PFIAB), 145–47
Project Lida Rose, 60, 62
Prokofiev, Sergei, 232
Pushkin, Alexander, 232
Pushkin State Museum of Fine Arts, 192–93

Queen Elizabeth II, 50, 52

Racine, Jean, 232
Rayburn, Sam, 134–35, 141
RB-47, attack on, 248–51, 259

Reel, Monte, 3, 142
Reilly, Patrick, 37
Reynolds, David, 9, 263n22
Reza Pahlavi, Mohammed, shah of Iran, 190
Rhodamer, Robert, 152
Roberts, Chalmers M., 5, 28, 129
Roberts, Charles, 5
Robinson, William, 120, 277n40
Rokossovsky, Konstantin, 16
Roosevelt, Franklin D., 5, 18, 23, 41, 43, 48, 194, 260
Rowley, James, 186
Russell, Richard B., 124

Salisbury, Harrison, 2, 5, 13, 21, 23, 41, 85, 164
Saltonstall, Leverett, 136, 141
SAM (surface-to-air missile), 150–51
Scali, John, 4, 73–75
Scherer, Ray, 5, 73, 273n18
Schorr, Daniel, 5
SEATO, 209, 255
Shakespeare, William, 232
Shutt, Charles, 132
Slater, Ellis "Slats," 120, 277n40
Smith, Jean Edward, 163, 271n45
Smith, Margaret Chase, 279n82
Smith, Merriman, 5, 129, 132–33
Snyder, Howard, 187, 193–94, 196, 219, 222, 238
Soviet National Exhibition (New York City, 1959), 32
Spaso House, Moscow, 15, 19, 71, 78, 157, 190, 194, 197, 219, 221, 222, 234
Sputnik, 45, 110, 114, 116
Stalin, Joseph, 1, 12, 14
Stalingrad, battle of, World War II, 13, 173, 286n116
St. Basil's Cathedral, Moscow, 19
Stephens, Thomas, 76, 79–80, 187
Stevenson, Adlai, 174–75
Strategic Air Command (SAC), 125–26
Strauss, Lewis, 67
Stroud, Margaret (Peggy), 119, 167
Stuart, Douglas, 5

Sukodrev, Victor, 193
Sunflower II, 11, 14
surface-to-air missile (SAM), 150–51
Symington, Stuart, 47, 124, 127, 131, 134–35, 137, 142

Taubman, William, 43
Thomas, Evan, 42, 127, 217, 242
Thompson, Jane, 191, 196
Thompson, Jenny, 32, 145, 148, 249
Thompson, Llewellyn E., Jr., 32, 101; downing of U-2, 1960, 156–57; preparations for Eisenhower's visit to Soviet Union, 1960, 76–79; works for release of RB-47 airmen, 251, 257–59
Thompson, Sherry, 32, 116, 145, 148, 249
Tolstoy, Leo, 232
Toumanoff, Vladimir, 71, 84, 86–87, 155, 177, 179–80
Truman, Harry S., 14, 17
Tuch, Hans N. (Tom), 32, 33, 68, 70, 80, 81, 86, 153, 157, 179, 181–82, 197–98, 258–59
Turgenev, Ivan, 232
Turner, Lana, 31
Turner, Frederick Jackson, 296n27
Twain, Mark, 232
Twining, Nathan F., 128, 146, 157–58, 167

U-2 crisis, 7, 10, 62, 145, 157–59, 161, 165, 171, 174, 177–79, 217, 241–43, 245, 247, 249–50, 252, 254

Vladimir prison, Soviet Union, 252
Volkov, Leon, 54
Voroshilov, Kliment, 83, 182, 273n27, 288n3

Walters, Vernon, 58, 171
Washington, George, 2
Watson, Robert J., 167
Watson, Thomas, Jr., 56

Weisl, Edwin, 136–37
Western Summit (Paris), 1959, 63–65, 148, 170
West Point, 11
Whitman, Ann, 8, 43, 187
Whitman, Walt, 232
Whitney, John Hay, 53
Wickman, John, 243

Wolkonsky, Prince Serge, 203, 292n53
Woodruff, Robert, 120, 277n40
Woods, Rose, 187

Yates, Polly, 187

Zaroubin, Georgy N., 31
Zhukov, Georgi, 11–16, 18–24, 188

www.ingramcontent.com/pod-product-compliance
Lightning Source LLC
Chambersburg PA
CBHW031641170426
43195CB00035B/250